SEVEN DAYS A WEEK

SEVEN DAYS A WEEK

Women and Domestic Service in Industrializing America

David M. Katzman

New York
OXFORD UNIVERSITY PRESS
1978

Copyright © 1978 by Oxford University Press, Inc.

Library of Congress Cataloging in Publication Data
Katzman, David M
Seven days a week.
Bibliography: p.
Includes index.
1. Servants—United States—History.   2. United
States—Social conditions—1865–1918.   3. Women—
United States—History.   I. Title.
HD6072.2.U5K37   331.7'61'640460973   77-13714
ISBN 0-19-502368-4

Printed in the United States of America

To Sharyn

PREFACE

THIS STUDY OF DOMESTIC SERVANTS IS AN OFFSHOOT OF A
larger study of black working-class occupations between the
Civil War and World War I. It began as an investigation of
black female wage earners, which then led to a study of black
servants, since a majority of black women workers were
domestics; finally it became a study of the occupation itself.

I was motivated not only by a belief in the centrality of
work in Western society but also by an assumption of the
underlying significance of economic factors in American society. The study of domestic servants has altered these as-
sumptions; the influences of status, race and ethnicity, and
sex are more salient features in household labor than are
economic factors.

I have been motivated also by a concern with contemporary American society, although the study ends with the early
1920s. The time period 1870–1920 was chosen because it was
the period of most rapid American industrialization and urbanization. Moreover, it was the key period in the transition
of service from a live-in to live-out occupation, and the last
twenty years saw the rise of the modern system of day work.
Thus the appearance of the contemporary pattern of the

black "cleaning woman" is covered as well. While providing little comfort to housewives of today, the book reflects my firm conviction that as long as the personalized mistress/servant relationship is retained, household labor will command low status, and unhappy mistresses and oppressed servants will persist.

Finally, this study is intended as an exercise in historical sociology; it is not meant to be a definitive history of women servants or black domestics during the period of rapid American industrialization. It is an attempt to communicate with historians and sociologists at the same time. For historians, I address myself to the study of work and occupations, a vital ingredient in the "new social history" that has been neglected or subsumed under the study of organized workers in labor history. For sociologists, I attempt to introduce historical elements too often absent from the sociology of work.

In Chapter 1, I have tried to let domestics speak for themselves. Previous historians have paid little attention to the words of servants; the statements of mistresses have dominated the literature. While the servants I quote were not a typical cross section—they were doubtless more articulate and outgoing than others—they should serve to awaken researchers to their presence.

Chapter 2 presents a statistical overview of domestic service. It shows the persistence of native-born servants in small towns and country districts, the domination by immigrants in large cities, and the presence of a black servant class in the South. As office and shop work opened to women, those who could left or did not enter service, and the proportion of servants who were native born declined. As the level and source of immigration changed after the turn of the century, the number of immigrant domestic servants fell as well. Blacks remained in service, and migration brought them to the urban areas of the North. Blacks brought with them a preference for live-out service or day work, which was most compatible with marriage, and live-in service began to fade away.

Chapter 3, "Household Work," is concerned with the tasks in household labor and the conditions of work and the environment.

Chapter 4 begins the discussion of the woman-to-woman relationship in domestic service. The woman's role, both as an employer and as an employee, set service apart from all other occupations. Indeed, the highly personalized relationship between the two was the one characteristic that most clearly defined household labor. Chapter 5 continues the discussion begun in Chapter 4, but within a racial and regional context—blacks and the South. Domestic service was inseparable from race and caste in the South. At the same time, the sexual tension between men of the household and servants appeared as an important theme.

Chapter 6 deals with the eternal servant problem. It explains why a perpetual shortage of servants existed, surveys the various attempts to reform household labor, and explains the failure of reform.

The conclusion, Chapter 7, attempts to place domestic service within the larger context of industrializing American society. Basically, household service was outside the major paths of modernization and industrialization, even though reformers attempted to modernize the household and the mistress/servant relationship. The presence of servants permitted traditionalism to dominate in the organization of the household; modernization, the "industrial revolution" in the home, accompanied the reduction in numbers of or the disappearance of servants.

The conclusions reached in this book—whether well founded or speculative, whether firm or tentative—stand only as hypotheses to be tested at the local level. Individual case studies—built on census, city directory, and vital statistics data—on domestic service and other occupations must be undertaken before more firm higher-order generalizations can be constructed. It is my hope that this work will stimulate such studies.

It is impossible to do justice to all my debts in the seven years I have been working on this study of black working-class occupations. So many individuals have provided help that I can barely indicate the extent of the kindness and time people have invested in this book and in my larger work.

This work has been supported financially by the Institute for Southern History, The Johns Hopkins University, Harvard University and the National Endowment for the Humanities, the Ford Foundation through a faculty research grant on the role of women in society, the American Council of Learned Societies, and the Research Fund of the University of Kansas. Without their assistance, this study would not have been possible. The work represents the author's views, which are not necessarily those of any of the funding agencies.

Many scholars have kindly shared their research with me, going beyond the ordinary requirements of scholarly pursuit. John Clark, Tom Cox, David Doyle, David Gerber, Tom Johnson, Michael M. Katzman, Peter Kolchin, Howard Rabinowitz, and William M. Tuttle, Jr., have all sent me sources and unpublished material from their own work.

Many more scholars have shared insights from their own research with me, and have listened to me talk about domestic servants through the years. The following people are in no way responsible for the outcome but have contributed greatly to the process of my work on servants by sharing their own research, critiquing my ideas or providing essential intellectual support: Deborah Dandridge, Larry Englemann, Norman Forer, Ronald Formisano, Basya Gale, Stephen Gale, Carol Golding, Gay Golding, Carl Graves, Herbert Gutman, Hugh Gough, Tamara Haraven, Ted Hershberg, Peter Knights, Leon Litwack, Kenneth Maxwell, Donald McCoy, John Modell, Phil Paludan, George Ritzer, Robert Rockaway, Elliott Rudwick, Charles Sidman, William Tuttle, Sam Warner, and Norman Yetman. The Women's Seminar of the University of Kansas critiqued some of my ideas, and Shirley Harkess and Janet Sharistanian have been especially generous critics of my work. Shirley Harkess edited my survey of contemporary domestic servants and helped me focus on major sociological patterns. The Fellows of the Institute of Southern History, The Johns Hopkins University, in 1971–1972 were very supportive, and Blaine Brownell, William Cooper, Peter Kolchin, and Phil Muller in particular aided me at the time and since.

John Clark and Regina Morantz have read parts of the manuscript, and their criticism has been essential in shaping the entire work. Without Regina Morantz's particular insight, this work would have been much poorer. Last, but not least, five people have provided constant encouragement and support throughout this project. Without their continued assistance, this book would not have been undertaken or completed. Aida and David Donald at The Johns Hopkins University in 1971–1972 and Frank Friedel at Harvard University in 1972–1973 did more than I could have asked in providing an environment for research and thought. At the same time, the ongoing support of Sidney Fine and August Meier has been equally critical. I am deeply in their debt.

Dublin, Ireland
April 1977.

CONTENTS

41950

LIST OF TABLES

SEVEN DAYS A WEEK

❧ I ❧

VOICES OF DOMESTICS

WHY DID WOMEN BECOME DOMESTIC SERVANTS? SOME OF those surveyed in 1889 and 1890 by Lucy Maynard Salmon of Vassar College linked their work with their low level of education:

"I went into housework because I was not educated enough for other work."
"I haven't education enough to do anything else."
"I would change my occupation if I knew enough to do anything else."[1]

Financial advantages were to some an important attraction:

"I choose housework in preference to any other [a Colorado domestic wrote] principally because for that I receive better pay. The average pay for store and factory girls is eight and nine dollars a week. After paying board and room rent, washing, etc., very little is left, and what is left must be spent for dress—nothing saved."
"My expenses are less than in any other kind of work."
"I can make more. I have put $100 in the savings bank in a year and a half."
"I began to live out when I was thirteen years old, and I am now twenty-seven. I have saved $1600 in that time. At first I had $.50 a week; now I have $3.00. One summer I earned $3.00 a day in the hop-picking season."[2]

Domestics responding to an investigation sponsored nearly three decades later by the Young Women's Christian Association agreed on the importance of monetary attractions: "The advantages are that she has room, board and washing free," a domestic wrote on a questionnaire, "and is less expensive than in any other position." Another servant replied, "Financially, we have our wages clear, as we have our board, room and laundry."[3]

Some felt that domestic work was healthier than other occupations open to women:

"We are not as closely confined as girls who work in stores, and are usually more healthy."

"There is no healthier work for women."

"You can have better-cooked food and a better room than most shop-girls."[4]

Still others felt that living within a home environment was an important attraction:

"I came to a strange city and chose housework, because it afforded me a home."

"I am well treated by the family I am with, feel at home and under their protection."

"Housework gives me a better home than I could make for myself in any other way."

"When I came to ——— and saw the looks of the girls in the large stores and the familiarity of the young men, I preferred to go into a respectable family where I could have a home."[5]

That it was traditionally woman's work could also make it comfortable and alluring:

"I choose housework as my regular employment for the simple reason that young women look forward to the time when they will have housework of their own to do. I consider that I or any one in domestic employment will make a better housekeeper than any young woman who works in a factory."

"My mother was a housekeeper and did most of her own work and taught me how to help her. When my father and mother died, and it became necessary for me to earn my own living, the question was, 'What can I do?' The answer was plain—housework."

"I like it best, was used to it at home, and it seems more natural-like."[6]

Whether they liked service or not, domestic servants who talked about their work were not often listened to between the Civil War and World War I. Servants were rarely consulted in discussions of the "servant problem" despite the voluminous late-nineteenth-century American literature that addressed this subject time and again in household guides, popular magazines, women's journals, and even state and federal reports. Those, such as Lucy Maynard Salmon, who surveyed the opinion of both employers and employees often buried the workers' statements in footnotes, where they seemed lost among the tabular results. The statistical data is important—and will be utilized in later chapters—but it conveys little of either the fabric of experiences or the texture of lives of the women themselves. This chapter provides a platform for the millions of anonymous servants, white and black, native and foreign-born, who worked as domestics between the Civil War and World War I; later chapters will discuss at length many of the themes presented here.

Domestics who wrote about themselves and their work were probably atypical. They represented a more self-consciously reflective and articulate group than most servants. The most extensive memoir by an American domestic, Lillian Pettengill's *Toilers of the Home*, was written by a college graduate who served two years in household labor. Upon graduation she failed to find employment as a journalist and entered domestic work after unsuccessfully looking into a number of other job openings. Most likely Pettengill, while working, looked upon service both as gainful employment and as participant-observer research. Inez A. Godman and others exchanged their mistress roles for servant ones and worked in other women's kitchens and parlors in order to understand and write from the servant's viewpoint. These women brought with them middle-class sensibilities which,

while precluding complete understanding of the realities ordinary servants faced daily and over time, shed brilliant light
upon the shadows which hid much of servants' lives.[7]

In an occupation in which illiteracy was widespread, those
women who wrote of their lives as domestics stood apart
from their fellow workers. The *Independent* and other journals
at the turn of the century published articles and brief autobiographies of domestic servants (though to what degree editors reshaped these articles is unknown). Lucy Maynard
Salmon also depended upon written responses to her printed
questionnaires, and her correspondents were atypical in their
willingness to participate in such surveys.[8]

Fortunately some investigators sought to find servants, talk
to them, and record their opinions. Helen Campbell, a journalist concerned about working women, reported lengthy interviews with servants in the 1880s. State labor bureaus sent
investigators into the field to gather servants' opinions.
Rarely did they publish lengthy statements of servants, however; in general more space was devoted to the opinions of
mistresses. Taken together, though, the brief statements of
servants reveal much about domestics and how they viewed
themselves and their work. Thus, it was not that material
couldn't be had on the servants' point of view; rather, most
observers of the day tended to pay no attention to the servants themselves.[9]

If they had listened, they would have discovered that not
all domestics were attracted by the work. Black women, for
instance, often did not have the alternatives to household
work that urban, native-born white women had. For black
women, domestic service was the most readily available
work. When Isabel Eaton investigated Negro domestic service in Philadelphia in 1896 and 1897, she asked servants,
"Have you ever tried to do other work?" A number replied,
"I never go any place I'm not sure of—I won't give them a
chance to refuse me." Eaton found two ex-teachers working
as domestics. They had lost their jobs, they felt, because of
prejudice in the school system. "The reason I don't try to

teach," said one, "is because I know I'd have trouble, and I can save as much this way."[10]

The disadvantages of domestic service, as perceived by servants and other working women, were numerous. Some domestics wrote to Lucy Maynard Salmon that household work was a dead end:

> "Housework soon unfits one for any other kind of work. I did not realize what I was doing until too late."
>
> "I should prefer to housework a clerkship in a store or a place like that of sewing-girl in a tailor-shop, because there would be a possibility of learning the trade and then going into business for myself, or at least rising to some responsible place under an employer."

Another common complaint was of the relative lack of freedom:

> "You are mistress of no time of your own; other occupations have well-defined hours, after which one can do as she pleases without asking any one."
>
> "Sunday in a private family is usually anything but a day of rest to the domestic, for on that day there are usually guests to dinner or tea or both, which means extra work."
>
> "I suppose the reason why more women choose other work is, they would rather work all day and be done with it, and have evenings for themselves."[11]

The 1915 YWCA Household Employment Commission report revealed the dislike many domestics felt toward their occupation. In cities across the country domestic servants responded no to the question "Do you think the [Young Women's Christian] Association ought to advise young girls to prepare for domestic service rather than business positions?" Some rejected the idea outright: "No, as long as conditions are not any better than they are now," wrote one servant. "I would not advise domestic service under the present conditions," responded another. "A young woman can have no pleasure, such as she wants and should have, in domestic service."[12]

Others gave conditional responses: "If she expects to work in the same town with her parents or home people, no," wrote one woman on the questionnaire. "If she is to earn her living away from her home town and be dependent on her own efforts, yes. However, if she has a training along any business line that pays well enough to support her easily and leave a small margin, let her follow up that line of work." "They should first be prepared for domestic service," another woman advised, "then if there is any possible chance for a business education, I think we should take advantage of it."

Finally, one domestic called for important guarantees for anyone entering service:

"I don't think a young woman should be advised to enter domestic service unless she could be very sure of a good home: first, without knowledge, she is not able to do the work of the home that requires skill, hence she does the hardest things, which is often beyond her strength, and is soon broken down. Besides, it is a very lonely life. . . . There is no place where one is more lonely than to be alone *with people*, and that is what working in a house means to so many, though not all."[13]

Why did women leave domestic service for other work? In 1911, federal investigators studying commercial laundries reported on why former servants were now working in laundries. A twenty-year-old German-American who had worked at housework for a year (from age fourteen to fifteen) maintained that "sweeping and scrubbing work was hard." Another German-American woman, age twenty-two, had done housework for five years, beginning at age thirteen. She reported that "lifting tubs and carrying slops, etc., [was] too heavy for her and provided pelvic troubles." A seventeen-year-old German-American who had also started as a thirteen-year-old domestic similarly found the work too hard. A twenty-six-year-old black woman began domestic service at age eleven and found "sweeping stairs and carrying slops was hard for her." After eighteen months in a commercial laundry, she thought "hand ironing not as hard work as general housework." A twenty-year-old Irish-American did not stay long with her first employer at age fifteen "because the mistress expected her to do more work than she was able." An Italian girl, sixteen years old, had worked as a domestic for three years and concluded that laundry work was not "as hard as domestic work." A twenty-four-year-old Danish woman began working at age eight after her father's death; she found "laundry work on flat mangle, which was [a] sitting occupation . . . easier for her." Similarly, an eighteen-year-old black woman who began work as a fourteen-year-old chambermaid testified that sweeping and turning mattresses was too hard for her.[14]

Other laundresses reported no differences in the physical demands of laundry work and their former tasks as domestic servants, or found such differences unimportant. They found household work unacceptable for other reasons. A recently widowed thirty-two-year-old black woman compared her experience as a domestic servant before she was married at age twenty-one with her four years work as a commercial laundress. She told her interviewers she "prefers laundry work because [she] has more time to herself, and receives better pay than domestic service." A twenty-two-year-old Irish immigrant thought "laundry work hard, but prefers it to domestic work as no harder, giving more time after work hours, and being better paid." Two German women, both twenty-two, had worked four years as domestics from ages fifteen to nineteen. One reported that she "does not think laundry work hard and has more time for other things than at domestic work," while the other said, "laundry work [is] much easier than domestic work because housework is never done."[15]

Two young Philadelphia women—one a shopgirl, the other a teacher—had tried domestic service and found certain aspects repulsive. The shopgirl told the president of the New Century Working Woman's Guild, who was investigating domestic service:

"I've tried it and I know now what I couldn't have known without trying it. Our world is a very narrow world, I know, but for all that it's all we've got, and we leave it behind when we go into service. A teacher or cashier, or anybody in a store, no matter if they have got common sense, don't want to associate with servants. Somehow you get a sort of smooch. Young men think and say, 'Oh, she can't be much if she hasn't got brains enough to make her living outside a kitchen.' You're just down, once for all, if you go into one."

The teacher disagreed: "There is no degradation at all," she responded to the shopgirl. She then went on to recount her own personal sense of degradation:

"What I minded, though, when I tried it, was being made to put on livery. I went as a nurse, because my health had broken down in teaching, and I loved the children dearly and they me. But when I asked not to put on the cap and apron, Mrs. L—— got very red and said, 'You must remember that if you take a servant's place you have to accept the limitations of a servant.' 'If you have no other thought of what I am to the children than that,' I said, 'I had better go,' and go I did."[16]

A dressmaker who found the sitting not sufficient exercise tried housework:

"My trouble was, no conscience as to hours, and I believe you'll find that is, at the bottom, one of the chief objections. My first employer was a smart, energetic woman, who had done her own work when she was first married and knew what it meant, or you'd think she might have known. But she had no more thought for me than if I had been a machine. She'd sit in her sitting-room on the second floor and ring for me twenty times a day to do little things, and she wanted me up till eleven to answer the bell, for she had a great deal of company. I had a good room and everything nice, and she gave me a great many things, but I'd have spared them all if only I could have had a little time to myself. I was all worn out, and at last I had to go. There was another reason. I had no place but the kitchen to see my friends. I was thirty years old and as well born and well educated as she, and it didn't seem right. . . . you couldn't make me try it again."

"My trouble was I hadn't any place that I could be alone a minute," a former cotton-mill worker confessed. She had left the mill to become a chambermaid in the home of one of the mill owners. "We were poor at home, and four of us worked in the mill, but I had a little room all my own. . . . In that splendid big house the servants' room was over the kitchen,—hot and close in summer, and cold in winter, and four beds in it. We five had to live there together, with only two bureaus and a bit of a closet, and one washstand for all. There was no chance to keep clean or your things in nice order, or anything by yourself, and I gave up." She left and found work with a small family. She felt the mistress in her new position was good and kind, but there was nothing pleasant and warm in the home. She found that service life wasn't for her: "It's hard to give up your whole life to somebody else's orders, and always feel as if you was looked at over a wall like; but so it is, and you won't get girls to try it, till somehow or other things are different."[17]

Even if the home and work were satisfactory, some women found their coworkers as reason to search for another position or leave domestic service. An American, a thirty-year-old fur sewer, recounted her experiences in domestic service to Helen Campbell:

"I got tired of always sitting, and took a place as chambermaid. The work was all right and the wages good, but I'll tell you what I couldn't stand. The cook and the waitress were just common, uneducated Irish, and I had to room with one and stand the personal habits of both, and the way they did at table took all my appetite. I couldn't eat, and began to run down; and at last I gave notice, and told the truth when I was asked why.

" 'If you take a servant's place,' the mistress replied, 'you can't expect to be one of the family.'

"I never asked it. All I ask is a chance at common decency.

" 'It will be difficult to find an easier place than this,' she said, and I knew it, but ease one way was hardness another, and she couldn't see that I had any right to complain. That's one trouble in the way. It's the mixing up of things, and mistresses don't think how they would feel in the same place."[18]

Rose Cohen, a young Jewish immigrant in the 1890s, later recalled her experience as a domestic servant. It had been three months since her father or mother had earned any money, and a family friend who "lived by doing all sorts of odd things, particularly by matchmaking and recommending girls to places of domestic service," came calling. She said that a good position was available.

My mother's face was white. "No!" she shook her head. She climbed up the stoop and went into the house.

I followed her and asked, "Why don't you let me go, mother? Out of the six dollars we could pay our share of the rent for a whole month and have a dollar over."

She turned away from me, leaned against the wall and cried, "Is this what I have come to America for, that my children should become servants."

Within a short time Mrs. Cohen had no choice but to let her daughter become a servant. "I did not mind going," Rose Cohen remembered. "It was not only that we were in dire need, I wanted to know how it felt to be a servant; also how the rich people lived. There was no doubt in my mind that the family where I was going would be rich. How else could they keep a servant." She was engaged for a period of two months, packed her few things in a newspaper, and went to work as a domestic and nurse. One day while working,

I remembered how I had wanted to know how it felt to be a servant and I laughed at myself. "I should not like to be a servant all the time," I thought. I looked out the window and gradually I began to reason it out. I realised that though in the shop too I had been driven, at least there I had not been alone. I had been a worker among other workers who looked upon me as an equal and a companion. The only inequality I had ever felt was that of age. The evening was mine and I was at home with my own people. Often I could forget the shop altogether for a time, while as a servant my home was a few hard chairs and two soiled quilts. My every hour was sold, night and day. I had to be constantly in the presence of people who looked down upon me as an inferior.

She feared that if she continued working as a servant she would become accustomed to it, and thus concluded: "I would rather work in a shop. A few days later I left. . . ."[19]

The stigma of inferiority was inescapable, and was a persistent irritant. One domestic recalled that her employer had entertained her Sunday school class, and one of the students came to help in the kitchen, where she found the maid.

"Miss M.," her mistress said to the student, "this is Kate."

"The maid, who never before had showed the slightest consciousness of occupying an inferior position, said, under her breath, " 'I am Miss, too.' "

Another servant told Frances Kellor, during the latter's 1902–1903 investigation of employment agencies in Boston, Chicago, New York, and Philadelphia,

"Of course when I am with a mistress and she knows me, I am glad to be called Mary, but why should every mistress do it before she even engages us, and why should it be done in such a way that the iceman and grocer's boy and every Tom, Dick, and Harry always calls us that? I am Mary to every guest in the house and every stranger who appears at the kitchen door; in fact, how can I respect myself when no one else shows me any!"[20]

It is not surprising then that servants disliked being called servants: "I fairly hate the word 'servant,' " one woman wrote to Lucy Maynard Salmon. Others voiced similar objections: "I don't like to be called a 'menial' "; "No woman likes to be called a 'hired girl' "; "American girls don't like the name 'servants' "; "I know many nice girls who would do housework, but they prefer doing almost anything else rather than be called 'servants' "; and, "I don't know why we should be called 'servants' any more than other people."[21]

The yearning to rid themselves of the badges of servitude were remembered long after leaving service. Sarah Clark, after years of household work, left service because of ill health and later opened a bakeshop.

"Well, Sarah, how do you like your work?" her former mistress asked in calling on her one day.

"I never thought of it before, but now that you speak," she replied, "I think the reason I like it so well is because everybody calls me 'Miss Clark.' "[22]

Mary E. Trueblood, an instructor at Mount Holyoke College, spoke with Massachusetts "working girls" and recorded their reasons for shunning domestic service to work in shops and factories. One former servant told her: "I did housework for four years before coming to the restaurant, but I must have independence." Another, who entered restaurant work after thirteen years as a servant, said, "I like this much better, for my time is my own and my room; if I wish to have my friends in and serve a cup of tea I can do it." A third revealed that she "tried housework, but came back to the mill; I will not be at everybody's beck and call."

Two women confessed that they enjoyed housework, but would not work at it again. "I prefer housework, but that takes me entirely away from home and takes more time," said one. "If conditions were right," said the other, "I would rather do housework than anything else, but I would not have a woman say '*my servant*,' referring to me."[23]

Working women who had never tried domestic service shared with former domestics a low opinion of household work. Many young women adamantly rejected domestic service. Edward A. Filene, the Boston merchant and reformer, recounted what happened when a woman came to his store with the mission of uplifting factory and store "girls" by placing them in good homes as servants and at the same time relieving the servant shortage. By chance, Filene and the recruiter spoke to three girls. The first girl declined a domestic position "with the explanation that she would not be a servant at any price; for if she were, her friends and schoolmates would look down upon her." Similarly, the two other women turned down the offer. The third salesgirl "emphasized the loss of social position in becoming a servant." She recalled her vaction the previous summer at a hotel, "where she had a good time." As a salesgirl she was accepted, but she declared that "no one there would have talked with her had she been a servant." Moreover, "none of the men with whom she associated . . . would marry a servant."[24]

Loneliness was a frequent complaint of domestics. A stationer's employee had tried a year at household work and found it unacceptable. She explained why to Helen Campbell:

"What I minded was the awful lonesomeness. I went for general housework, because I knew all about it, and there were only three in the family. I never minded being alone evenings in my own room, for I'm always reading or something, and I don't go out hardly at all, but then I always know I can, and that there is somebody to talk to if I like. But there, except to give orders, they had nothing to do with me. It got to feel sort of crushing at last. I cried myself sick, and at last I gave it up, though I don't mind the work at all. I know there are good places, but the two I tried happened to be about alike, and I shan't try again.

Even those who worked in homes with more than one servant complained of isolation. A domestic sent to an estate outside of Boston quickly returned to the city. "It was a big house in a big grounds and no one was home and the only other servant was so deaf she could not hear a thing and it seemed so dreary I knew I just couldn't stand it."[25] Another domestic told Lucy Maynard Salmon that

"Ladies wonder how their girls can complain of loneliness in a house full of people, but oh! it is the worst kind of loneliness. Their share is but the work of the house, they do not share in the pleasures and delights of a home. One must remember that there is a difference between a *house*, a place of shelter, and a *home*, a place where all your affections are centered. Real love exists between my employer and myself, yet at times I grow almost desperate from the sense of being cut off from those pleasures to which I had always been accustomed. I belong to the same church as my employer, yet have no share in the social life of the church."[26]

After working for ten weeks as a general houseworker and cook, Inez A. Godman concluded from her experiences that the isolation and loneliness was enforced by the employers. "I think generally mistresses are oversensitive about 'company,' " she wrote. "They like much of it themselves, but want the maid to have none. . . . During my ten weeks in a kitchen my father and mother dropped in twice for a few minutes in the evening and the lady was annoyed."[27]

One break in the isolation and loneliness was provided for in many homes by the weekly visits of women to wash and iron. In the Scharff household, Lillian Pettengill took tea with the laundresses on the days they came. "I came to attend these functions on Mondays and Tuesdays," she remembered, "more for the sake of the sisterhood than from any physical need for refreshment. My laundering friends, on the contrary, judging from my own earlier experience, must have found the institution a very practical and welcome help. To women at hard labour, unless after a heavier breakfast than they usually get, a cup of tea with bread and butter in the middle of the morning does not come amiss."[28]

The close watch which some employers kept on their servants could be just as oppressive as the enforced isolation. One domestic complained that "We are bossed eternally; they ask us where we are going, where we have been, and what we did, and who our friends are." Another woman wrote to the Kellor investigation: "Our employer feels, somehow, that she is our guardian and has the right to supervise all incomings and out goings, to question us about what we do in our leisure, and to be 'mistress' as well as employer. All this meddling is usually kindly meant, but none the less it reduces us from the status of a free employee to that of a vassal."[29]

Servants often had to face suspicion and distrust. Lillian Pettengill experienced this uneasiness on her first day in the Scharff household:

Her retreating footsteps seemed to drag heavy weights from off my breathing apparatus. I had never before been so openly and suspiciously watched, it made me nervous.

But Mrs. Scharff must have had trouble of another sort. None but an ostrich could have taken such a quick lunch and not known the pangs of indigestion. She went straight to her treasures as soon as she came into the room again. "Did you move the glasses I left on the bureau, while I was at lunch, Eliza?"

"No'm," I answered, and stooped as I spoke to replace a soap-dish and two bottles upon the now finished wash-stand.

"I wonder where they are," she said. "I left them here."

I put back two more bottles and a finger-bowl and said nothing.

"Have you seen them, Eliza?"

"No'm; I have not seen them," I answered evenly, and I put back another soap-dish and a match-receiver.

"I thought I left them here when I went to lunch," she said, peering about the floor.

"Then they are there now," I returned, starting across the room to help look for them.

"No, don't bother to come; I shall find them, I guess. Have you been over to this side of the room at all, Eliza?"

"No'm." I put back a box of matches, and the morning work in her room was done. Almost immediately the missing glasses were discovered on her desk, and I went down to my lunch wondering uncomfortably why she should trouble to inquire of my tongue if she could not trust my fingers.[30]

Later on, Pettengill learned that her employer left money around to test her honesty. While cleaning, she found ten cents, which she offered to Frieda, the cook in the Scharff household.

"*Nein.* It iss old voman's; she put to see if you find and take. Leaf it *auf* bureau. You *muss* nevair take even a cent you find anywhere in she room. She leaf it purpose." . . .

"Always brush under the mats, Eliza," had been her order. So, one morning in my first week, finding the rugs already suspiciously smooth and clean brushed, I lifted them, and side by side under one were two large black-headed pins lying heads together, like soldiers. I had also found pins lying in out-of-the-way corners.

"Oh, she try me, too, *mit* pins," said Frieda. "She take eight pins 'nd stick *zwei* in every corner; *und* I take out, sweep, and put back. 'Ah, Frieda,' she say to me, 'you no sweep in corners like I tell you. See, I find these eight pins, *zwei* in every corner.'

"Yes, I do sweep in corners," I say; '*und* I see pins; I take out pins, I sweep carpet, I put back pins. You put pins in corners yourself, you can take out!' "[31]

The stories of three domestic servants reveal in greater depth their odysseys and experiences. Almira came from New Hampshire to work in New York just after the Civil War, while the washerwoman and Lillian Pettengill worked in households just before and after the turn of the twentieth century.

Almira came from a rural New Hampshire village and grew up with the ambition of living in New York City. "Boston won't do," she told Helen Campbell, who recorded Almira's story in *Prisoners of Poverty*. "I want the biggest an' the stirringest thing there is in the United States." After her parents died, the mortgage was foreclosed on the family farm and she received forty dollars and the old furniture; she gave the latter to her boyfriend Leander's folks. Then she traveled to Boston by train and to New York by boat. She was seventeen.

For five years Almira worked piece-rate as a fur sewer. The work was seasonal. She could earn ten to twelve dollars a month for half the year, and then five to six dollars a month, if work was available, the rest of the year. Leander had followed her to New York and had found success as a clerk at eight hundred dollars a year. After a two-year engagement, they were married. But six months later Leander "had a hemorrhage an' just went into quick consumption." The burden of supporting both of them fell on Almira.

"You're not to worry," Almira told Leander. "there's more ways than one of earning, an' if my eyes is bad, I've got two hands an' know how to use 'em. I'll take a place an' do housework if I can't do nothing else."

"You'd never believe how the thought o' that weighed on him. He'd wake me up in the night to say, 'Now, Almiry, jest give up that thought an' promise me you'll try something else. I think I'd turn in my grave if I had to know you was slavin' in anybody's kitchen.'"

She promised him "I would n't do it unless I had to." Soon after he died. She had pawned everything in the month before Leander died, so now she had to seek work.

"Sewing was no good. My eyes went back on me like everything else, an' in a fortnight I knew there was n't anything for it but getting a place. I left such things as I had in charge of the old ladies an' answered an advertisement for 'a capable girl willing to work.'

"Well, it was a handsome house an' elegant things in the parlors an' bedrooms, but my heart sunk when she took me into the kitchen. The last girl had gone off in a rage an' left everything, an' there was grease and dirt from floor to ceiling. It was a deep basement, with one window an' a door opening right into the area with glass set in it, an' iron bars to both; but dirty to that degree you could n't see three feet beyond; cockroaches walking round at their ease an' water-bugs so thick you did n't know where to lay anything.

" 'You'll have things quite your own way,' the lady said, 'for I never come into the kitchen. Bridget attends to upstairs, but you attend to fires and meals and washing and ironing, and I expect punctuality and everything well done.'

" 'At least it sounds independent,' I thought, and I made up my mind to try it, for the wages were fifteen dollars a month, an' that with board seemed doing well.

" 'It's the bell,' said Bridget who was seventeen and looked 'fit to drop.' 'The comin' an' goin' here niver ceases, an' whin 't is n't the front door it's her own bell, an' she'll jingle it or holler up the tube in the middle o' the night if she takes a notion."

Almira found her room disappointing:

"A hall bedroom, with a single bed an' a small table, with a washbowl an' small pitcher, one chair an' some nails in the door for hanging things; that was all except a torn shade at the window. I looked at the bed. The two ragged comfortables were foul with long use.

"I started down the stair an' came right upon Mrs. Melrose, who smiled as if she thought I had been enjoying myself.

" 'I'm perfectly willing to try an' do your work as well as I know how,' I said, 'but I must have a place to myself an' clean things in it.'

" 'Highty-tighty!' says she. 'What impudence is this? You'll take what I give you and be thankful to get it. Plenty as good as you have slept in that room and never complained.'

" 'Then it's time some one did,' said I. "I don't ask anything but decency, an' if you can't give it I must try elsewhere.'

" 'Then you'd better set about it at once."

Almira went to another household, where after examining the room, which "was bare enough, but clean," she was hired. A wealthy but eccentric family of three occupied the house. The eccentricity didn't bother her, but the way she was treated did. "What I did mind was that from the time I entered the house till I left it there was never a word for me beyond an order, any more than if I had n't been a human being. . . . That house shone from top to bottom; but a dog would have got far more kindness than they gave me." After two years, she gave a month's notice and left.

After six years of service, Almira had been in seven places.

"I could have stayed in every one, an' about every one I could tell you things that make it plain enough why a self-respecting girl would rather try something else. . . . But out of these seven places there was just one in which the mistress seemed to think I was a human being with something in me the same as in her. I've been underfed an' worked half to death in two of the houses. The mistress expected just so much, an' if it failed she stormed an' went on an' said I was a shirk an' good for nothing an' all that. There was only one of them that had a decently comfortable room. . . . As long as I had a trade I was certain of my evenings an' my Sundays. Now I'm never certain of anything. . . . In ten hours I earn more than I ever get. But I begin my day at six an' in summer at five, an' it's never done before ten an' sometimes later. . . ."[32]

In 1904 another young woman recounted her odyssey, after her father's death, from store clerk to domestic to washerwoman. She was twenty-four when she went to work outside her home for the first time. She worked for eleven weeks in a department store, and while she found the position "confining and tiresome," the work conditions were not particularly bad. But at $4.50 per week she found herself with nothing left over after she paid her room, board, and carfare. With no prospects for a raise and unable to find another position (she had gotten the first through her uncle's influence), she turned to the long list of ads for servants in the newspaper.

She responded to the advertisement.

"I avoided all places where more than one maid was kept, for I knew two would mean a room-mate, but I answered seven ads for general housework. Every one of the seven would have taken me on my face without a word of reference as to character or ability, but I continued on my way until I found what seemed ideal—a clean, tidy, little house with a family of two—mother and son. . . . She promised to have a woman come in for half a day to wash if I would do the ironing, and pay me four dollars a week [plus room and board]. . . . .

"Now, as far as the work went I knew my business. I had been housekeeper at home for many years, and had for short periods been without a servant, but the steady continuity of my duties now overwhelmed me. My feet had been seasoned to ten hours a day, but here fourteen and fifteen were required, with but little Sunday rest. The long continuance of work was in some degree due to my inexperience, but even when I became wonted and trained to my duties there was no hour from six a.m. to ten p.m. wholly my own for rest. The hot, sweaty kitchen work made me long for a daily bath, but, of course, the bathroom was denied me; and after carrying water up two flights of stairs to my room and preparing for a bath the door bell was sure to ring. . . .

"I had money in plenty; had bought not only stockings, but shoes, gloves, etc., and was saving up a little sum for emergencies. One Thursday afternoon after about three months of this I went to call upon a friend. She was packing for a summer trip and my heart grew sick at the thought of *my* prospects.

" '*I* want to get away,' I said, 'I want just a breath of vacation.'

"Can't you have it?' she asked.

"I shook my head. 'Mr. Holmes takes his mother away for two weeks, but I'm to stay and care for the house and dog.'

" 'That will give you a good rest.'

" 'Oh, I suppose so, but then it will all begin again, and—and—I can't see any of my friends. I'm ashamed to tell them where I am.' Now, this was the worst of it. I had many dear friends from whom I was drifting because I could not receive them in my kitchen."

Thus she left live-in service to become a washerwoman. Although doing laundry by the day in people's house was another form of domestic work just as low in status as household work, it gave her greater independence than had live-in housework, and she now had Saturdays and Sundays off. "The pay is good—equal to ten dollars a week without board—the hours are definite, and one is entirely free from working surroundings out of hours. The vigorous labor makes muscle and digests food, and a pleasant Saturday and Sunday are always ahead of one."[33]

At about the same time, Lillian Pettengill entered domestic

Miss Lillian Pettengill, the Mount Holyoke graduate who entered domestic service. Authored *Toilers of the Home*. This photograph appeared as the frontispiece in the March 1903 issue of *Everybody's Magazine*.

service and found her first position dull and isolating. "As time passed," she wrote, "I chafed under the monotony; I felt my isolation, alone in a big house full of people, with whom, though kindly and friendly, I could not feel one. . . . Personal devotion might have grown in time, I suppose, but in four weeks the germ had not sprouted. I had no visiting friends, and no chance for any sort of society such as I would have chosen." In this dreariness, there were of course bright spots: "My 'every Thursday and every other Sunday.' What a jolly click was that of the gate behind me about three o'clock! What a sense of freedom came with the turning of the corner!"

She left the Barry household the following week.[34]

Pettengill's next employer made her long "for the blessed sanity and isolation of the Barry kitchen!" Her new mistress, Mrs. Kinderlieber, was forever at her side. "She followed me about constantly. She looked into the cupboard when I was by to see if I had washed the dishes clean. She addressed me with emphasis for having scraped the wooden potato-masher with a knife, whereas I had used the side of a fork. . . . She nagged me continually about the opening and shutting, the locking and unlocking of the doors, windows and gates; about the lights, and the animals. She was forever at my heels." That Mrs. Kinderlieber was lonely, an excessive talker, and a hypochondriac added to Pettengill's burdens.[35]

While she had left the Barry household with some regrets, leaving the Kinderliebers' was an act of flight: "The shutting of that front door snapped a thread somewhere. The strain was over. . . . By every possible way in which Mrs. Kinderlieber could insult me by word or deed, she had done so. Her passions had been more exhausting than a whole Barry ironing, and the time I spent in her house was as one long horrid nightmare. Go back again? Stay longer? It was not in human endurance. Tired? To the very death. Even the street was hateful."[36]

Pettengill's next position was with the three Wetherly sisters. Miss Margaret, "unmistakably a professional woman," had hired her and treated her as a professional. "If you want to arrange your kitchen more conveniently, why do so," Miss Margaret had told her. And the ironing?

"Yes'm; when shall I have them done?" Pettengill asked.

"Oh, any time, as you can; it doesn't matter so that they are done," Miss Margaret said, deferring to the domestic's judgment. This treatment had been unexpected. "Experience had not prepared me for the courteously considerate, appreciative and friendly Miss Margaret. . . . It was strange to be in working-dress and yet a recipient of the common decencies. . . ."[37]

Even in the Wetherly household, however, not everything was perfect, although "I fared exactly as the three woman whom I served, and at the first it seemed substantially enough for the work I had to do. But as the days passed and I became more accustomed, the work dragged. For my life I could not finish the washing before half-past three . . . [while] just over the fence . . . a little undersized coloured girl with a family of five hung out her last piece by twelve o'clock. . . . I grew thin. . . . I was always more tired than I ought to be. . . ." Although Pettengill enjoyed the same diet as her employers, it was not nutritious enough for the physical labor that she had to perform.[38]

Overall, however, it was an appealing position. "It was pleasant. . . . There was a rocking-chair in the kitchen. On sunny days there was the pleasant outdoor workroom beyond the kitchen door. . . . I did enjoy working for the Wetherly sisters. Miss Margaret and Miss Eleanor so managed that the work appealed to my pride and sense of dependableness. . . . I began to feel the dignity of my position as an independent worker, and to outgrow the shame of being only a housework girl, felt in spite of myself."[39]

While servants nationally shared certain common experiences, household labor in the South differed from such work in the North. In the South, "domestic servant" was synonymous with "black woman." In 1912 the *Independent* published the autobiography of a black Southern domestic who had told her story to one of the magazine's reporters:

I am a negro woman, and I was born and reared in the South. I am now past forty years of age and am the mother of three children. My husband died nearly fifteen years ago. . . . For more than thirty years—or since I was ten years old—I have been a servant in one capacity or another in white families. . . . In my early years I was at first what might be called a 'house-girl.' . . . Later on I became a chambermaid. . . . Still later I was graduated into a cook. . . . During the last ten years I have been a nurse. I have worked for only four different families during all these thirty years. . . .

"More than two-thirds of the negroes of the town where I live are menial servants of one kind or another, and besides that more than two-thirds of the negro women here, whether married or single, are compelled to work for a living,—as nurses, cooks, washerwomen, chambermaids, seamstresses, hucksters, janitresses, and the like. . . . Tho' today we are enjoying nominal freedom, we are literally slaves. . . .

"I frequently work from fourteen to sixteen hours a day. I am compelled by my contract, which is oral only, to sleep in the house. I am allowed to go home to my own children, the oldest of whom is a girl of 18 years, only once in two weeks, every other Sunday afternoon—even then I'm not permitted to stay all night. . . . I don't know what it is to go to church; I don't know what it is to go to a lecture or entertainment or anything of the kind; I live a treadmill life: and I see my own children only when they happen to see me on the streets when I am out with the children, or when my children come to the 'yard' to see me, which isn't often, because my white folks don't like to see their servants' children hanging around their premises. You might as well say that I'm on duty all the time—from sunrise to sunrise, every day in the week. I am the slave, body and soul, of this family. And what do I get for this work—this lifetime bondage? The pitiful sum of ten dollars a month! And what am I expected to do with these ten dollars? Pay my house rent, which is four dollars per month, for a little house of two rooms, just big enough to turn around in; and . . . feed and clothe myself and three children. For two years my oldest child, it is true, has helped a little toward our support by taking in a little washing at home. She does the washing and ironing of two white families. . . . For six months my youngest child, a girl about thirteen years old, has been nursing, and she receives $1.50 per week but has no night work.

"Of course, nothing is being done to increase our wages. . . . We have no labor unions or organizations of any kind that could demand for us a uniform scale of wages for cooks, washerwomen, nurses, and the like; and, for another thing, if some negroes did here and there refuse to work for seven and eight and ten dollars a month, there would be hundreds of other negroes right on the spot ready to take their places and do the same work, or more, for the low wages that had been refused. So that, the truth is, we have to work for little or nothing or become vagrants! And that, of course, in this State would mean that we would be arrested, tried and despatched to the 'State Farm,' where we would surely have to work for nothing or be beaten with many stripes! . . .

"I remember very well the first and last place from which I was dismissed. I lost my place because I refused to let the madam's husband kiss me. He must have been accustomed to undue familiarity with his servants, or else he took it as a matter of course, because without any lovemaking at all, soon after I was installed as cook, he walked up to me, threw his arms around me, and was in the act of kissing me, when I demanded to know what he meant, and shoved him away. I was young then, and newly married, and didn't know then what has been a burden to my mind and heart ever since: that a colored woman's virtue in this part of the country has no protection. I at once went home, and told my husband about it. When my husband went to the man who had insulted me, the man cursed him, and slapped him, and—had him arrested! The police judge fined my husband $25. . . . I believe nearly all white men take, and expect to take, undue liberties with their colored female servants—not only the fathers, but in many cases the sons also. Those servants who rebel against such familiarity must either leave or expect a mighty hard time, if they stay. By comparison, those who tamely submit to these improper relations live in clover. . . .

"Another thing—it's a small indignity, it may be, but an indignity just the same. No white person, not even the little children just learning to talk, no white person at the South ever thinks of addressing any negro man or woman as _Mr._ or _Mrs._, or _Miss._ The women are called, 'Cook,' or 'Nurse,' or 'Mammy,' or 'Mary Jane,' or 'Lou,' or 'Dilcey,' as the case might be. . . . In many cases our white employers refer to us, and in our presence, too, as their 'niggers.' No matter what they call us—no matter what they teach their children to call us—we must tamely submit, and answer when we are called; we must enter no protest; if we did object, we should be driven out, . . . and, in applying for work at other places, we should find it very hard to procure another situation.[40]

Sexual exploitation of domestics was a common theme in Victorian literature, but in the American South it was compounded by racial tension. "A Southern Colored Woman," an anonymous granddaughter of a plantation master and daughter of an ex-slave who owned large grocery and feed stores, wrote: "My mother and her children never performed any labor outside of my father's and their own homes." Educated in private schools and married to a physician, she had the same feeling towards her three children that her parents had toward their children. "There is no sacrifice I would not make, no hardship I would not undergo," she wrote in the _Independent_ in 1904, "rather than allow my daughters to go in service where they would be thrown constantly in contact with Southern white men, for they consider the colored girl their special prey."[41]

Racial friction between an employer and employee was not uncommon. C. W. Hines, Sr., the Louisville, Kentucky, correspondent of the *New York Freeman*, reported a conflict between a black domestic and her white employer over the *Freeman*. It is possible that Hines may have invented the episode to boost T. Thomas Fortune's *Freeman*, but it nonetheless represents what must have been a frequent occurrence when a servant's interest in issues involving race came to her employer's attention. The employer

said he had read an article clipped from the *The New York Freeman* by a white paper urging the freedmen to demand this, that and the other.

"It's an impudent paper," he said, "full of slanderous publications. The whites are the freedmen's best friend, and if you want to be popular with the white employer stop reading the paper, it's a one-sided concern. . . ."

"THE FREEMAN is the paper to tell the truth, [she responded] and I shan't work for . . . anybody who objects to me patronizing Mr. Fortune's paper. Its writers are free speakers in defense of our race and that's the kind of paper I want to read, and it shall come wherever I go."[42]

In the cities of the Northeast, household positions were filled by immigrants from Ireland, black women from the South, and migrants from the rural hinterlands. In Maine, the shortage of household help reached crisis proportions as young women entered New England factories or went to the cities to work as domestics. In 1892 the Main Bureau of Industrial and Labor Statistics investigated the condition of "women wage-earners" in the state. Interviewers from the bureau spoke with women workers, including a group of "house girls," and in the bureau's report a balanced view of domestic working conditions is presented.

"I don't know how to do anything but wash dishes, etc.," a domestic said, "if I did I should not be at housework. Decent girls can find something better than slaving in any-

Woman washing dishes in turn-of-the-century Maine. (Photograph by
Chansonetta Emmons. Culver Pictures.)

body's kitchen." "I have as good a place as any," reported another, "for any place at housework is poor enough. People don't know how to treat you decently well and if they do know they won't. A girl is a fool to do housework if she can do anything else in the world." One servant was indifferent: "I have not much fault to find, though I have a poor room and generally do wherever I work, but $3.00 a week and board is better than hunting for work."

Other women, however, preferred domestic work. "I like housework and would not do anything else," one women testified. "I have been here a long time and attend to my business and let the family attend to theirs." Another house servant agreed: "I have been ten years with this one family, and they are nice people, and I have over $500 saved in the bank, and have many privileges that girls don't usually have."

Finally, the report presented a dialogue between two girls comparing household work to factory work, although the statements had originally been made separately:

"It is better than being hurried up in a factory, and wages with board are about as good. Health is worth something and once in a while I can arrange to have an afternoon out."

"I don't like it, and never did, and if I knew of any place where I could go into a shop or factory I would go this minute. One thing sure, that the first chance I get I shall leave."[43]

For domestics who migrated, the uprooting experience could be a difficult one. Black women coming from the South into the cities of the North faced difficult cultural adjustments. One Richmond, Virginia, woman who worked "off and on" in her new home of New York City found Northern urban life too materialistic. While she had been active in voluntary associations in the South, she seldom went out in New York City because she knew too few people. Another cook and laundress from Richmond who moved to New York also found her social world much less extensive in the North than it had been in the South. She complained that Northern churches were "lacking in the spirit."[44]

In the Midwest, domestic servants also expressed dissatisfaction with their positions. A Swedish woman, twenty-two years old, told the Kansas Department of Labor and Industry that she was "very dissatisfied with housework and thinks some of trying to secure work in a packinghouse." She reported that she worked from thirteen to fourteen hours a day, seven days a week, often working extra time with no additional pay. She had been with a family for ten years. Another Kansas servant, Mrs. Mc——, was a forty-eight-year-old domestic who disliked the living-in system and the restrictions on privileges.[45]

To the north, in Minnesota, working women agreed with their sisters elsewhere in the country. Factory workers shunned household work; "Housekeepers do not pay enough for the work," a bag-factory employee told the investigator from Minnesota's Bureau of Labor Statistics. "They think you never do enough, and will require more work than a girl is able to do." Another bag-factory worker said, "The hours are too long for the wages paid, and a girl is treated as an inferior." A third woman agreed: "I do not like to do housework because people look down upon you. Girls who work in factories are more respected.

A bookbindery employee was adamant. "I would not do housework under any consideration. In the first place, I would not be any one's servant. In the second place, I am not obliged to. In the third place, girls as a rule, are not treated properly. I know a woman who compels her girls to eat in the back shed."

Shirtmakers voiced their agreement:

"Don't like the idea of living in a kitchen and sleeping in an attic or basement."
"Housekeepers too hard to get along with."
"Dirty, nasty work."
"It is degrading—the way girls are treated."

Obviously these opinions reflected a prejudice against working in service, but the Minnesota report revealed that some of the factory workers' coworkers had had experience as domestics and might have provided their fellow employees with the basis for rejecting household work. "Washing was too hard, when I did housework," a knitting factory employee said. "I always had more to do on Sunday than any other day." A woolen-mill operative told the investigator that she "worked for one family who used me like a dog around the house. I will never do that kind of work again."

"My objection to housework is that in many places a hired girl is much less than a dog," a shirtmaker stated. "All hours are working hours; never any pay extra for any kind of extra work. Have had many years of personal experience at housework."

The views of Minnesota domestics currently engaged were only slightly more favorable. Few girls had positive things to report. "Sometimes the treatment is good; sometimes it is bad" was the most favorable view expressed. Among the comments:

"The last place I worked they did not pay me."
"Won't average more than one hour's spare time each day."
"I feel like a slave on account of the way I am treated."
"I worked in a place three months where I had to get up at five o'clock a.m. and work until 9:30 p.m. It nearly killed me. Then I worked in another place for nine months, and was well treated. Have had three and a half years' experience at family work, and I do not want any more family places."
"I worked four weeks for a family in Minneapolis. I used to get up at four o'clock every morning and work until ten p.m. every day in the week. Mondays and Tuesdays, when the washing and ironing was to be done I used to get up at two o'clock and wash or iron until breakfast time. I was paid $3.50 per week."

A more elaborate and retrospective view was offered by an older woman:

"When I came to this country and could not speak good English, I could not get a place at housework. Girls who cannot speak English have to take the poorest and roughest places, chiefly in boarding houses. Generally I pay for my sewing; sometimes I do it in the evenings; but it is too hard after working all day. Young girls sometimes do their [own] sewing and washing in the evening after working all day, but they do it at the expense of their health, which breaks down under the strain in time, and they do not realize that they are losing their health until it is gone, and then it cannot be replaced. When they reach middle age, as I have, with broken health, they realize the danger of such overwork. When I came to this country, I used to take care of a sick baby all night and do the housework in the day. Sometimes it would be past midnight when the housework was finished."[46]

In 1901 Inez A. Godman, curious about the servant problem, left her comfortable middle-class home to enter service to find out "who is to blame, the maids or the mistresses." She probably worked in a Midwestern city; in any case, her remarks would later be augmented by a Chicago domestic. Godman went to an employment office where she negotiated with a mistress for a position, agreeing to $2.75 per week for general housework and cooking without laundry. Her expectations for success were high because "my lady was newly married and her furnishings were fresh from cellar to attic."

Godman described her first full day as a domestic:

I rose at six and served breakfast promptly at seven. By half-past nine the downstairs work was finished.

"Thursdays you will clean the sitting room," said my lady, "but you must tidy your own room first. I wish you always to put your own room in order before noon." So I spent ten minutes in my room and two hours in the sitting room. I could not finish in less time. . . . Five times during the two hours I was called off by the door bell and twice I went down to look after my bread.

I finished soon after twelve, and hurried down to prepare luncheon; this I served at one. I had been on my feet steadily for seven hours and they began to complain. I was thankful for a chance to sit, and dawdled over my lunch for half an hour. It was half-past two, everything was in order, and I was preparing to go to my room when my lady appeared saying that the kitchen floor ought to be wiped. She was right. The floor was covered with oilcloth and it was getting dingy. The kitchen was large, and it took me half an hour; then I went to my room. I was very tired. In my own housekeeping I had taken frequent opportunities for short rests, here the strain had been steady. I was too much heated to dare a bath, but I rocked and rested, did a little mending, and tidied myself up a bit. It was astonishing how soon four o'clock came. It did not seem possible that I had been upstairs forty minutes.

There was a roast for dinner and I hastened down to heat the oven. Then came three hard hours. Dinner was a complex meal, and coming at night when I was tired was always something of a worry. To have the different courses ready at just the right moment, to be sure that nothing burned or curdled while I was waiting on the table, to think quickly and act calmly; all this meant weariness, and by the time the dishes were washed my whole being was in a state of rebellion. I had started upstairs with a pail of hot water for my tired feet when I remembered the ice water [for the mistress]. For a moment I hesitated. It meant another trip and had not been asked for. Nevertheless I took it up and my lady smiled again, but not surprisedly this time. I assured you that I did not dally an hour with my toilet but was in bed and heavily asleep in twenty minutes.

Although she didn't have to do the wash, she found ironing an impossible task.

When I told the laundress that I had never ironed shirts she stayed long enough to starch them for me. There were two shirts, two pairs of cuffs, and three collars. It took me all the afternoon to do them, but they were acceptable to my lady and I felt pleased, although I had no afternoon hour and was very tired.

Wednesday I ironed all day, every moment I could spare from the meals. My feet gave out, and I placed a chair where I could rest one knee at a time as I ironed. My wrists and shoulders began to join my feet in protest, but I held on steadily till dinner time. Had I been able to iron two hours after dinner I could have finished, but I was exhausted and clambered upstairs without a thought of the ice water.

On Thursday her mistress went to town. After finally finishing the ironing, "I settled down in an easy chair and rested an hour. . . . Well, the week had passed, and the others passed much in the same way."

After time, however, things did not ease. "Instead of toughening I was breaking; each week I lost something that I did not regain."[47]

A domestic servant from Chicago with twenty years' experience responded to Inez Godman's article describing her experiences. According to the editorial note in the *Independent*, the "servant girl's letter" was simply a letter to a brother, not something written for publication.

> I am sorry, but under the present conditions it is impossible for me to write anything on any subject. This may seem incredible, but it will not be when I tell you that from six A.M. to eight P.M. I don't get time to write so much as a postal card. After the day is over I am too tired, confused and nervous to do anything except look over the paper and go to bed. . . .
>
> The negroes in the South have as much chance of social recognition as have those who do domestic service in the North. Between them and society there is a great gulf fixed. Of course I don't mean fashionable society, but any that a respectable, intelligent person would desire to be recognized by. The very name servant girl carries along with it a degrading sense of servility and serfdom that is resented by the most ignorant of them.
>
> Lately some enterprising and well meaning women have formed a union here in the hope of bettering the condition of those whose lot it is to do housework. It is not called the "Servant Girl's Union." I believe it is the "Household Workers of America." What's in a name? Ask Shakespeare. A good deal sometimes.
>
> I am extremely optimistic of the servant girl problem. I think it will be solved some time—in the millennium.[48]

Employment or intelligence agencies played an important role in the employers' search for servants and vice versa. Newspaper advertisements and word of mouth were the other two ways in which one could broadcast open positions. Newcomers to cities were especially dependent on the agencies. Sometimes the offices recruited household workers from outside of the city, as in the recruitment of Southern black women to work as domestics in New York and other cities. The abuses and corruption of the agency system were so widely known by the turn of the century that Frances A. Kellor headed an investigation of employment agencies in Boston, Chicago, New York, and Philadelphia in 1902 and 1903. In studying 834 licensed agencies in the four cities, the investigators assumed the role of participant-observer, since the agencies and the employers often refused to cooperate. Although the employment-agency system will be analyzed in Chapter 3, Kellor's study, *Out of Work*, will be used here for the experiences of servants and investigators that it reported.[49]

The investigators experienced the radically different treatment of employers and employees in the same agencies. "Occasionally we went into 'ladies' rooms," Kellor wrote, "and allowed them to talk to us politely for a few minutes. Then we said we were looking for places, and they had misunderstood us." The reply? " 'Well, why didn't you say so? get in the other room.' " The tone in the employers' room was "modulated, polite, smooth, pleasing, courteous"; in the servants' chamber they found it "rough, arrogant, and discourteous, and often nothing expresses it but 'fresh.' "

They also found themselves powerless. "We fixed our wages—the office said 'Change it or get out.' We stated the kind of work we wanted—the office said 'Do something different.' We wanted work in a private family—the office cajoled us into going into a hotel. . . . We stated we were twenty-five years old, and the office replied, 'You are only twenty for our business.' "[50]

In theory an employment agency offered servants a way of screening employers. But in removing one risk, it created another: the possibility of wasting the registration fee. The agencies insisted, and indeed coerced the job-seeking domestics into paying their placement fee in advance.

The first thing that usually happened to us on entering the "servants" room was an attendant pouncing on us with "Have you paid your fee?" If we had not, many roughly told us to "pay or get out." If we still refused, we were sometimes let alone, but no positions were offered, and the clerk would sneeringly remark, "If you knew enough to pay your fee you would be getting these." In some they said it was "no day hotel," and we could not wait unless we paid, and they were so disagreeable we were actually forced out.[51]

Part of the domestic servants' problem with employment agencies resulted from the general powerlessness of household workers. Unorganized and faced with millions of separate employers, relatively few of whom hired more than one worker at a time, domestics had little control over the hiring market and even less bargaining power with their employers in spite of the shortage of household workers. Among the most frequent complaints of domestics were those of being fired without adequate notice and being cheated of pay or their afternoons off. Lillian Pettengill discovered that her employer felt no inhibitions about challenging her right to an afternoon off:

"Er—Eliza," said Mrs. Scharff on Thursday morning, seemingly a bit uneasy in her mind, "I can't let you go out this afternoon on account of the workmen who are coming."

I had expected something of the sort, being warned by Frieda, who had been interviewed on the subject of my intentions. . . . I looked her in the eyes a full minute before I reminded her that Thursday was my day, and that I wished to take that afternoon.

"I gave you a Thursday of one week and a Sunday of the next," she explained gently. "You have been here only a week and are entitled to either day, whichever I choose to allow you. It does not suit me to give you the Thursday of this week, because of the strange workmen who are coming. I cannot stay at home myself on account of my business."

"I wish to go out this afternoon as I had planned," I insisted quietly.

"But how can you go?" she returned. "Don't you see that you've got to stay? I can't have those strange men here by themselves. . . . You understand how it is—now do be sensible about it."

They parried back and forth. Pettengill resisted giving in.

Had she asked for the favour pleasantly, as one woman of another, I should have granted it in spite of personal disappointment or previous infelicities. But to be told as if I were a young child and she my guardian, that she chose not to give me what I had a right to demand, that it wasn't necessary that I have it, was insulting to my dignity as an adult. I was not ready to say my final good-by, so I saw nothing left me but to go about my work, which I did, looking sullen and saying nothing.

Work is a splendid reconciler. In less than an hour I was able to say, in my second-best manner, that I would "go out that evening and Sunday afternoon, thank you," thus foregoing the afternoon off.[52]

Not all domestic work was as hard as that done in the middle-class urban home. Anne Ellis described her first job

as rather easy when she entered the employ of a prostitute in
the Colorado mining frontier in the 1880s:

My first job was with her—I got twenty-five cents each day, and
this was far more than I earned, as I did little, except eat; she said
she was afraid to stay alone; her husband was on the night shift [in
the mines].

We put in the day stringing beads, working on cardboard or anything except cleaning house; then at meal time I would be rushed
to the store for a steak, canned corn, and gingersnaps. In the evening she would read "Peck's Bad Boy" to me. Over this we giggled
a great deal. Many nights I would be awakened by the sounds of a
man in the house, but this neither amused, interested, nor
disgusted me; my only thought was never to let Mama know,
because she would make me come home.[53]

An Irish immigrant found her life's work as a domestic
cook after a brief, upsetting encounter with American plu-
ralism. The "Irish cook" who recounted her autobiography
to the *Independent* had been brought to the United States by
her sister, a domestic in a Philadelphia home. Upon arrival
she moved in with her sister for two months to learn the
work, "me bein' such a greenhorn." She got her first place,
but it was unsuitable.

They were nice appearing people enough, but the second day I
found out they were Jews. I never had seen a Jew before, so I
packed my bag and said to the lady, "I beg your pardon, ma'am,
but I can't eat the bread of them as crucified the Saviour." "But,"
she said, "he was a Jew." So at that I put out.

Then I got a place for general housework with Mrs. Carr. I got
$2 till I learned to cook good, and then $3 and then $4. I was in
that house as a cook and nurse for twenty-two years. Tilly [her sis-
ter] lived with the Brents till she died, eighteen years. . . . Mrs.
Carr's interests was my interests. I took better care of her things
than she did herself, and I loved the children as if they was my
own.[54]

By and large, discussions of household service tended to be
one-sided. Despite the experiences of servants presented
here, their voices were heard and their words read only
rarely in public. The "servant problem"—the shortage of servants—was pressing enough that in July 1910 the Maine

Bureau of Industrial and Labor Statistics circulated the following announcement to five hundred daily newspapers from coast to coast:

WANTED—10,000 girls to help around the house. Must be honest and willing to work. Good homes for those who suit.

The response—less than twenty-five inquiries for positions, and not one which actually resulted in a job. But there was no shortage of solutions proposed.[55]

In the late nineteenth century, household work became "domestic science" and was introduced into college curricula; during the same period, training schools for domestics were established in major cities. There is no evidence that domestics themselves were ever consulted about curricula, or even the utility of such training programs; they were essentially designed to meet the needs of employers.

Frances A. Kellor, however, questioned some domestic servants about the programs. One opposed it by noting, "I can get just as good without it." A Boston Irish servant agreed, "Shure, now, why should I be l'arnin' when I kin shove me ear in anywhere and get a good job?" Even if instructions had been free, many said they were a waste of time or "we know enough for what we have to do." A few recognized that "those schools are not for us; no one ever finds out what we want to learn; they start out with a theory and everything must fit that, and we won't fit—that's all."[56]

Good Housekeeping, like other women's magazines, tended to stress the role of the employer in focusing on the servant problem. In doing so, it affirmed its belief in the self-improvement advice it frequently printed and reflected its generally positivist outlook. To dwell too much on the depravities of servants or the inherent conflict between servant and mistress would be nihilism; it would leave no room for improvement, betterment, or progress. In support of this view, Helen Campbell, editor of the "Woman's Work and Wages" section, found a forty-year-old Irish-American factory worker who had been a domestic for fifteen years. She testified that servants "say the trouble is first with the mistresses that don't know any more than babies what a day's work really is. A smart girl will keep on her feet the whole time to prove she isn't lazy, for if her mistress finds her sitting down, she thinks there can't be much to do, and that she doesn't earn her wages. Then if a girl tries to save herself, or is deliberate, they call her slow. They want girls on tap from six in the morning to 10 or 11 at night." The answer to this problem: "Women make hard mistresses, and I say again I'd rather be under a man that knows what he wants. That's the way with most of us!" Presumably, *Good Housekeeping* readers were not to turn their mistress duties over to their husbands, but instead were to become better mistresses.[57]

Two weeks later, Campbell reiterated this view by printing responses from Philadelphia domestics gathered in an investigation by the president of the New Century Working Woman's Guild. The five daughters of an Irish woman who had served for ten years as a cook in a family all chose to work in a jute mill rather than follow their mother into service. The eldest spoke for the daughters:

"I hate the word service," she said. "We came to this country to better ourselves, and it's not bettering to have anybody ordering you around."

"But you are ordered in the mill."

"That's different. A man knows what he wants and never goes beyond it. A woman never knows what she wants, and sort of bosses you everlastingly. If there was such a thing as fixed hours and some time certain to yourself, it might be different, but now I tell every girl I know, 'Whatever you do, don't you go into service.' "[58]

Rarely did domestics have an opportunity to suggest reforms in domestic service. The debate over the servant problem was usually among employers; the point of view of servants was only infrequently solicited. In the 1880s, the Minnesota Bureau of Labor Statistics recorded the thoughts of one servant, "a girl of fifteen years experience at all kinds of general housework—exceptionally intelligent and sensible."

"I think that about half the people who hire help do not treat them properly. In some places the treatment is shameful. I believe that an organization for domestics would do a great deal of good. I wish to say that if employers would assist their help in acquiring knowledge of the world, through newspaper reading and books, that they would have a much more efficient class of help. Many employers seem bent on preventing their help from acquiring knowledge, rather than in aiding them. . . . Nine housekeepers out of ten require a girl to do the work according to their ideas, although a girl may be able to accomplish twice as much by working in her own way. I do not consider housework especially injurious to health, if a girl knows anything about the laws of health when she begins, and will take care of herself. The exposure which a girl has to undergo on washing days in Winter [in Minnesota and other Northern states] is due either to her own neglect or the driving disposition of the employer. . . . There is too much of a disposition to overwork help. I believe in severe rules so far as proper discipline is concerned; but I do not believe in abusive language, petty meanness, or slave driving. In a majority of places there is such an anxiety about getting through with the work, that many young girls neglect to take regular meals and thereby seriously injure their health. I brlieve that working girls ought to be taught to take care of their money, and I believe they would accept such advice and profit by it; if it was given them by people whom they knew to be their friends."[59]

In suggesting reforms an articulate domestic servant wrote at the turn of the century to Gail Laughlin, who investigated the occupation for the United States Industrial Commission:

I would suggest that there be schools established all over the United States free, where every girl that enters the domestic service should be compelled to attend at least 6 months and pass an examination successfully, and that each girl should be graded according to her work and her ability, and no girl should be allowed to enter any house as a domestic without a certificate from such a school.

I would suggest that the families that apply for help be graded according to their way of living and the wages they pay for amount of work done.

I would have the schools compulsory because a great many of the girls would not attend unless compelled to.

The majority of us housework girls are ignorant * * * Our position is something like that of a slave at the mercy of the mistress. If she should be a kind woman, we fare pretty well, if not, we fare worse. It is a shame that housework has no system. * * *

The ladies that I worked for have generally been kind, and some of them are my friends. They did about their best under the present circumstances. I mean the household needs different regulations also. I feel certain that would come out all right if the schools were established, and the girl would have regular hours on duty and regular hours off, and housework was given the dignity that education gives.[60]

A forty-nine-year-old Chicago woman who had been working in private families since age sixteen responded to a series of articles on the servant problem in the *Outlook*. Her letter mixed suggestions for other reforms in household work with complaints from her own experiences, especially concerning the depersonalization of the mistress-servant relationship.

If the housewives would apply some sort of business system to the conduct of their housekeeping, the answer would be simple. But no. . . . Their most common phrase is: "That is my business; this is my house." If anything goes wrong, their first word is: "You will walk out of this house this minute, or I will get a man to put you out." . . .

Then, again, there are not enough tools to work with. Perhaps there is an old worn-out can-opener or none at all, knives that are not sharp, no sleeve-board for ironing—little necessary things that could be bought at the ten-cent store. When I ask if I can have a new one, the answer is: "Well, we have used that one" or "done without it," as the case may be, "for the last forty years, and I guess you can make it do for the little while you are here." . . .

Then, again, if a girl could work under a legal contract agreement, say, from three to six months, it would improve conditions immensely. The girl would know she had a good permanent home and steady work, and the lady would know that she had a contract agreement that she could depend upon. The leisure time of the girl should be fixed in this contract.

Ladies are sometimes not honest in money matters concerning the girls they employ. I have known many nice girls to work for little money—two dollars and a half or three dollars a week—and one week out of five or six the lady would forget, or pretend to forget, to pay her.

If the mistress of the house would only write out the work of the week, day by day, would put down on paper the work required, certain work for certain days, would treat housework like a business, and treat their maids like the employees of a business, many of the problems of domestic service would be solved.[61]

A few years later, in 1915, domestic servants affiliated with the YWCA reform efforts focused primarily on working conditions: "Systematize the work so as to get about eight hours a day," a woman wrote. "Arrange so that there would be one room where she could entertain her friends with an 'at home' feeling. . . . Give her more privileges, be more companionable. . . . She should be made to feel that her work was just as important to keep the machinery of her household in perfect running order as the man in business feels is necessary to be at his point of duty."

A room should be arranged for in every home," advised a second servant, "for a maid to sit and entertain a friend. More consideration on the part of the mistress. Treating their maids as they would like to be treated had their lot been cast in the same place. Arrange for shorter hours. Have an hour set for meals and be prompt. If women desire more efficient help in their homes, it is in their power to have it. Treat them as human beings, not machines."

A third domestic sent a separate letter with her questionnaire detailing changes she would like to see:

In my experience, the first item towards producing cheerful, willing and efficient help in the house, is a light, airy and well-ventilated kitchen. The kitchen *should* be the best room in the house. Windows large and easily opened—good lights. . . . Then there should be a couple of small rocking chairs to use while peeling vegetables, etc., or rest between work. . . .

The next item is the hours of labor. Those working at housework should require certain hours of rest and recreation every day, as women working at other trades and business. They should have a full half hour for meals, an hour in the afternoon, and two hours at least every evening to call their own before retiring for the night, one-half day on Sunday, either morning or evening, and half a day in the week, which should be religiously kept on the mistress' side, whether the maid wishes to go out or not.[62]

In spite of all the suggestions for reform and the pleas for change, domestics remained servants—in service—with all the stigmas attached to servile and menial work, to woman's work, to black and immigrant work, to work the middle and upper classes wanted done but didn't want to do themselves.

❧ II ❧

DOMESTIC SERVANTS

DOMESTIC SERVANTS WORKED IN PRIVATE FAMILIES, PERFORM-
ing tasks commonly done by the housewife/mother without
compensation. The occupation included general servants
(maid-of-all-work), chambermaids, child nurses, cooks,
waitresses in families, day workers, laundresses, and other
similar workers in private households. Females predominated
overwhelmingly among paid household workers, and
throughout the late nineteenth and early twentieth centuries
it was the single most important class of women's gainful
employment. As a low-status occupation without any educational, experiential, or skill requisites for entry, it tended to
be shunned by the native-born, and thus it was work performed disproportionately by immigrants and blacks. The
overall importance of domestic service within the female occupational structure declined as industrialization and modernization opened up work in factories, shops, and offices to
women. At the same time, household employment slowly
evolved from an occupation in which the worker lived in her
employer's home to one in which the servant lived elsewhere.
World War I accelerated this change, and by the 1920s live-
out work had become the predominant pattern.

Available national data on domestic servants permits only
an approximation of the number of women who could be

classified as domestic servants—women performing labor in private households for pay. The decennial census provided the only series of data over time, and it grouped servants under the category of "Domestic and Personal Service" (see table A–1*). Domestic workers within this classification included laundresses, untrained nurses, housekeepers and stewards, cooks, waitresses, and other servants. For this study, servants, cooks (after 1910), and sometimes laundresses will be used as the census categories best approximating domestic servants in middle-class homes.[1]

Traditionally, domestic service—work within the household—has been work performed by women. The tasks of cooking, cleaning, child care, and laundry have generally been relegated to women in American society. Where the work was transferred from unpaid labor—wives, female children, and grandmothers, for instance—to paid workers, women workers were hired. Census data suggests that the percentage of women in domestic service compared to all servants between 1870 and 1930 fluctuated within a narrow range of 83.8 and 87.5 percent. These statistics are misleading, however, and females probably comprised more than 90 or 95 percent of all servants. Only in rare cases did male cooks and waiters work in households, yet these categories predominated among the census classification of male servants before 1910 (see Table A–2). Moreover, most males in household labor were not in competition with women for jobs and were not considered domestic servants. The general category of servants included men hired to do heavy physical household work, or gardening, or house maintenance. Only in upper-class homes, where male servants were common, and in California, where Chinese menservants sometimes outnumbered women servants, were women and men competing for the same jobs. Finally, the data for men was inflated by the inclusion of porters in the servant category prior to 1900.

A more accurate estimate of the predominance of women

*Tables A–1 through A–24 are to be found on pages 281–314.

in service work can be obtained by comparing the number of female and male servants and launderers from 1910 through 1930. While this excludes male cooks and waiters in private homes, it assumes that this loss is balanced out by the inclusion of handymen, gardeners, and so forth in the servant classification. Within these categories, women comprised 92 percent of servants in 1910, 90.9 percent in 1920, and 91.8 percent in 1930; these percentages represent the lower range of female representation among domestic servants. In these same years, women servants comprised 24.6, 16.2, and 18.5 percent of all gainfully employed female workers ten years old and over. From 1910 through 1930, men in domestic service represented about 0.5 percent of all male workers. Thus within the male occupational distribution, household workers were an insignificant factor.

From 1870 through 1910, the number of female domestic servants rose from 960,000 to 1,830,000. Between 1910 and 1920 this number declined to 1,400,000, but it rose again to nearly 2,000,000 in 1930 (see Table 2–1). Although some of the erratic fluctuations in the census counts can be attributed to the difficulty of accurately enumerating the more than one million employees and employers, the growth between 1870 and 1910 nonetheless reflected effects of immigration and rapid urbanization in the United States. Women entering the United States often found no other work than household labor, and they replaced the large number of women leaving service to marry, have children, or enter other occupations. During this period the relative number of native-born white women entering service declined, but the foreign-born women more than compensated for the departure of native-born ones. At the same time, the number of laundresses increased as more families could afford to hire washerwomen as well as other servants. The expansion of the urban-based middle class—a result of the rapid industrialization and accompanying urbanization—constantly increased the demand for household labor. Nearly all observers and analysts of the time agreed that the number of domestics was limited not by the demand, but by the inadequacy of the supply. Between

Table 2–1. Female Household Workers, 1870–1930 (10 Yrs. and Over).

	1870	1880	1890	1900	1910	1920	1930
Servants	901,954	970,257	1,216,615	1,283,727	976,113	743,515	1,263,864
Cooks					333,436	268,618	371,095
Laundresses	58,102	108,198	216,631				
Laundresses (not in laundry)				335,282	520,004	385,874	356,468
Subtract:							
Waitresses				(42,839)	Not included in above		
Laundry operatives				(9,933)	Not included in above		
Total domestic servants	960,056	1,078,455	1,433,246	1,566,237	1,829,553	1,398,007	1,991,427

Sources: Servants, cooks, laundresses: *Sixteenth Census: 1940, Population*, Alba Edwards, *Comparative Occupation Statistics for the United States, 1870 to 1940*, p. 129. Waitresses, laundry operatives: *Twelfth Census: 1900, Occupations*, p. 7.

1910 and 1920, the number of servants fell sharply, declining by about 25 percent. This sharp decline has been attributed to the 1910 census overcount of women working and the 1920 undercount. The overcount resulted from special instructions to record an occupation for every women enumerated, and the undercount from the dropping of those instructions in 1920. There is compelling evidence, however, to suggest that the decline in household workers between 1910 and 1920 was a real one and not the result of enumeration error in the census.[2]

After a steady rise for more than a century and then the aforementioned sudden drop between 1910 and 1920, the number of household workers increased until the 1930s and 40s, when diminished immigration and the radical changes in women's work wrought by World War II brought an end to domestic service as a significant employer of women. The drop in servants from 1910 to 1920 reflected the acceleration during World War I of long-range shifts in women's work, the deep decline in immigration, and the gradual disappearance of child employment. By World War I, manufacturing, professional, trade, and clerical occupations were becoming the mainstays of women (see Table A–3). Between 1910 and 1920, the largest increases in numbers of women workers occurred in professional service, trade, and clerical occupations, reflecting intensified urbanization and the long-range modernization of education. The latter condition created jobs for women teachers and qualified greater numbers of women to hold clerical and sales jobs. To a great extent, these trends affected native-born younger women newly entering the job market; the expansion of women's occupations permitted them to work in jobs other than manufacturing or domestic service. Often the daughters of women who had been servants worked in offices or shops.

While more than one million new white-collar jobs for women were created between 1910 and 1920, the supply of potential domestic servants declined sharply as the tide of female immigrants from Europe ebbed during World War I. In the four years from July 1910 through June 1914,

1,426,000 female immigrants entered the United States. In the next five and a half years, through December 31, 1919, 561,000 women entered the country. Given the high turnover among servants and the tendency of white women to leave service once married, the number of foreign-born servants—the largest group next to blacks—fell in 1920. Moreover, the immigrants who entered between 1910 and 1920 were from groups with little inclination to enter domestic service. During the 1910s, immigrants from Ireland, Scandinavia, and Germany comprised 8.5 percent of all immigrants, while those from Russia (including Poland) and Italy amounted to 35.5 percent of all immigrants. The 1900 census showed that among those employed, 60.5 percent of Irish-born women, 61.9 percent of Scandinavian-born women, and 42.6 percent of German-born women worked as servants or laundresses. Russian-, Polish-, and Italian-born women, on the other hand, had relatively little inclination to work as servants: 20.6 percent of Russian and Polish women and 11.6 percent of Italians.

The fall in total immigration led to an older foreign-born population. Thus, while the number of foreign-born women in the United States increased between 1910 and 1920, the number of single immigrant women declined, as did the percentage of all foreign-born women employed. In 1920 there were 175,000 fewer foreign-born women employed than in 1910. The overall effect of this decline and shift in immigration was to reduce the number of foreign-born women in domestic service from 386,500 in 1910 to 240,600 in 1920, a 38 percent decline. During the 1920s, the supply of foreign-born women available for work in households rose sharply in comparison with the period from 1914 through 1920. From 1921 through 1930, the number of female immigrants averaged 182,000 per year, nearly twice as high as the average during World War I (1915–1919) of 97,000 per year. The number of Irish, Scandinavian, and German immigrants during the 1920s increased to 20.2 percent of the total, whereas the proportion of Polish, Russian, and Italian immigrants fell to 18.1 percent. The number of Italians, the

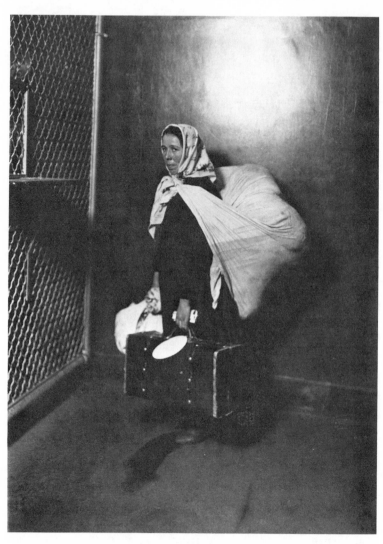

Slovak woman, Ellis Island, 1905. (Photograph by Lewis W. Hine. George Eastman House-International Museum of Photography, Rochester, New York.)

group least likely to work as domestic servants, fell from one-fifth of all immigrants during the 1910s to one-tenth during the 1920s.[3]

The greatest impact of World War I on women's employment was in the residual jobs created in the expansion of large bureaucratic firms and the continued growth of large retail outlets. Manufacturing occupations, however, offered the most readily available alternatives to those otherwise bound to household labor, because many domestics lacked the social status, education, or knowledge of English and/or commercial skills to enter offices or shops. Although the number of manufacturing jobs for women stabilized between 1910 and 1930, the opportunities for factory employment expanded. In 1910 women in manufacturing and mechanical industries had been concentrated in nonfactory handwork such as dressmaking and millinery; that year only 28 percent of all women in the clothing industry worked in factories. As clothing-industry employment declined, factory work increased, so that in 1920, 44.4 percent of women in the industry worked in factories, and in 1930, 61.7 percent. While the overall number of female manufacturing workers remained stable, the number of female factory workers continued to rise, with the greatest increase occurring between 1910 and 1920 when women factory employees increased 33 percent. In 1910, 52 percent of women in manufacturing had worked in factories; in 1920, 66 percent.

The expanding factory work generated by new technologies—initiated by the war and spurred on by the consumer society of the 1920s—compensated for the decline in traditional women's jobs in manufacturing. Chemical, electrical, food-processing, and automobile-factory employment, for instance, increased dramatically. But immigrant women and married women had relied heavily on the traditional handwork, and factory work posed language barriers or was incompatible with raising children for the minority of married women wage earners. On the other hand, by the 1920s live-out work predominated in household labor, offering opportunities for work once found in the sewing trades. The shifts in immigration and within manufacturing during the 1920s, then, served to increase the pool of potential servants, a fact reflected in the large increase in household workers during the 1920s.[4]

Other factors influenced the fluctuations in domestic service during World War I and the 1920s. The number of girls younger than sixteen who were gainfully employed continued to decline. An important source of servants in the nineteenth century, girls ten to fifteen composed 9.9 percent of servants in 1880 and 9.4 percent in 1900. Thereafter, child labor became a focal point of reformers, and as state compulsory education laws spread, the proportion of young girls in service dropped to 5.8 percent in 1910 and 3.0 percent in 1920. (see Table A–16). The latter decline occurred as the overall total of servants fell by nearly one-fourth.

Other traditional sources of domestic servants grew during the 1920s. Rapid urbanization, fed by the resumption of immigration, the continued black migration to cities, and an estimated migration of nearly twenty million whites from the rural areas to the cities, further served to swell the pool of potential servants. At the same time, the number of married women working rose, and live-out or day work allowed them to work four or five days part time. This does not imply that women in offices and shops or even factories shifted to household work, for they didn't; instead, the shift to live-out work enabled unskilled married working-class women to work outside their own households while still managing to fulfill their roles as housewives and mothers.

Finally, the decline in hand laundresses outside commercial laundries was a significant factor in the overall decline in servants between 1910 and 1920. This was part of a process in which work formerly done within the home was now transferred to outside commercial establishments or to innovations and new inventions within the home—washing machines and electric or gas irons, which eased the physical burden and made it possible for middle-class mistresses or maids-of-all-work to do the wash. Outside of the South, washerwomen were beginning to disappear. By 1920, 66 percent of laundresses not working in laundries were concentrated in the sixteen states plus the District of Columbia which made up the South Atlantic and South Central census divisions.

In 1870, one-half of all women wage earners in the United States had been domestic servants. In the ensuing sixty years, while the number of servants doubled, the proportion of working women in service fell. By 1930 only 20 percent of all working women were domestics (see Table 2–2). The decline of household labor outside of the agricultural sector was even more precipitous. In 1870, 65.6 percent of all female nonagricultural workers had been servants; in 1930, only 20.6 percent. In 1870, 50 percent of women wage earners had cleaned house, cooked meals, or scrubbed clothes, but by 1920 nearly 40 percent worked as teachers, shop women, or office workers. Demand and opportunities for women in offices, shops, and factories had expanded more rapidly than the demand for household labor.

The greatest gains in women's employment occurred in seven specific occupations whose expansion had resulted from modernization and innovation in education and commerce and from the rise of the modern bureaucratic corporation. In 1870, 97,000 women had been employed as saleswomen or store clerks; teachers; trained nurses; bookkeepers, cashiers, accountants; office clerks; and stenographers or typists. By 1930 these six occupations plus telephone operators

Table 2–2. Percentage of Women Wage Earners in Household Labor, 1870–1930

	1870	*1880*	*1890*	*1900*	*1910*	*1920*	*1930*
Household workers* as a percentage of all women wage-earners	50.1	40.7	35.8	29.4	24.6	16.2	18.5
Household workers* as a percentage of nonagricultural women workers	65.6	53.4	44.7	36.3	29.2	18.7	20.2

*For definition of household workers, see Table 2–1.

Source: See tables 2–1 and A–3.

had risen more than fortyfold, to 4,075,000. During the same period, employment of women in manufacturing and mechanical industries increased only fivefold, from 364,000 to 1,886,000. In 1870 these seven occupations comprised 5 percent of all women workers and 6.6 percent of those outside of agriculture, whereas in 1930, 37.9 percent of all working women and 41.4 percent of nonagricultural workers held these jobs. Manufacturing, on the other hand, declined in importance from 19 to 17.5 percent among all employed females and from 24.9 to 19.2 percent among those in the nonagricultural sector.

Part of the relative decline in importance of household labor within the women's occupational structure was due to the transfer of household tasks to the commercial or industrial sector. Some of the employment in factories, offices, and shops was generated by this shift in work. In the nineteenth century, the appearance of soap and commercially prepared cleaning solutions had led to the manufacture of items formerly produced in the home. At the turn of the century, the increased sales of commercially baked bread and canned foods, steam laundry, cleaning and pressing services, and restaurant meals led to an enormous expansion of female employment in these industries. Between 1910 and 1930, female employment in six occupations affected by the transfer of household tasks to commercial industries increased by nearly 500,000 (see Table A–4). This figure is slightly inflated by the inclusion of waitresses, some of whom continued to work in private homes, as well as restaurant, lunchroom, and café keepers. At the same time, an indeterminate number of office and retail workers in food industries and laundries filled jobs created by the transferal of household work to commercial industries. Similarly, factory workers manufacturing washing machines, vacuum cleaners, and so forth benefited from the decline in servants. Most workers in the latter industries were probably men, and most of the new jobs created in the process were also held by men. In 1910, for instance, men in the food industries comprised 84 percent of the workers; by 1930 this fell only to 77.8 percent. The general rule was that men occupied the more skilled, better-paying jobs created in the new industries, while women were relegated to the lower-status, low-paying jobs requiring fewer skills. The physical labor involved was irrelevant; consequently, after 1910 women began to dominate as laundry operatives, and, in fact, about 67 to 68 percent of those employed between 1910 and 1930 were women. On the other hand, among laundry owners, managers, and officials, women comprised only 5.5 percent in 1910, 10.6 percent in 1920, and 8.4 percent in 1930. Similarly, as lunchrooms flourished, women ran less than one-quarter of them, yet in 1920 waitresses exceeded waiters for the first time, and by 1930 women comprised 59 percent of all waiters and waitresses.

Between the Civil War and World War I, the growth in the number of domestic servants lagged behind population growth and the increase in number of individual families in the United States. From 1880 through 1920, the ratio of servants per thousand families fell by more than one-half (see Table 2–3). During the same period, average family size shrunk as well, so the number of servants per thousand population fell by a slightly smaller margin (see Table 2–4). The result was that by 1920 servants were available to only about half as many families or individuals as they had been in 1870.

The Western states experienced the most rapid growth in domestic servants during the late nineteenth and early twentieth centuries. The number of female servants nearly tripled between 1880 and 1900, and the ratio of servants to families and population increased (incidentally, the only section after the Civil War to experience a relative growth in the ratio of servants to families). (See Table 2–3.) The demand for servants was greatest in the West because of its distance from the ports of entry of European immigrants and from the source of black servants in the South. This resulted in a unique situation: in 1880 California and Washington were the only states in which a majority of domestic servants were men. As the Western states began to urbanize and industrialize, Chinese migration slowed to a trickle and the

Table 2-3. Female Servants by Regions, 1880–1920 (16 Yrs. and Over).

	1880	1900	1920	Per 1,000 families		
				1880	1900	1920
United States	845,699	1,165,561	981,557			
The North	583,908	812,544	585,179	92	80	39
New England	91,461	118,569	76,478	105	96	45
Middle Atlantic	255,894	327,773	249,636	121	99	49
Eastern North Central	164,773	235,896	166,674	74	68	32
Western North Central	71,780	130,306	92,391	61	61	32
The South	245,907	309,548	333,611	78	63	46
Northern South Atlantic	82,769	91,133	81,101	131	104	64
Southern South Atlantic	58,086	70,246	87,411	70	59	51
Eastern South Central	72,034	92,547	83,734	68	61	42
Western South Central	33,018	55,622	81,365	51	43	36
The West	15,884	43,469	62,767	43	49	28
Mountain, Basin, and Plateau	4,713	15,795	19,913	33	43	25
Pacific	11,171	27,674	42,854	49	53	29

Sources: *Tenth Census: 1880, Population*, vol. I, pp. 669, 724. *Twelfth Census: 1900, Population*, vol. II, pt. 2, p. clx. U.S. Bureau of the Census, *Statistics of Women at Work* (Washington, D.C., 1907), p. 42. *Fourteenth Census: 1920, Population*, vol. I, pp. 34–39. Joseph A. Hill, *Women in Gainful Occupations 1870 to 1920*, Census Monographs IX (Washington, D.C., 1929), p. 119.

number of women servants increased to fill the urban demand and to replace Chinese menservants. The wages in domestic service on the West Coast—the highest in the nation—reflected the insatiable demand. But the pace of Western industrialization was slower than that of the Midwestern states—Ohio and Michigan, for instance—and opportunities for working women outside of household labor expanded proportionately less. In 1880, for instance, a greater proportion of California women than of Michigan or Ohio women had worked outside of service; in 1900 the situations were reversed. Thus California in the late nineteenth century was experiencing an increase in the ratio of female domestics per family and population similar to the mid-century growth experienced in the North Central and Middle Atlantic states. After 1900, however, the West Coast underwent a relative decline in servants similar to the rest of the country, although at a level much below that of Northern and Southern states because of the smaller proportion of blacks and immigrants in the population (see tables 2–4 and 2–5).

In the North and South, the number of servants grew until the turn of the century, but the relative number of

Table 2–4. Ratio of Female Household Workers per 1,000 Population, 1900 and 1920, by Region (16 Yrs. and Over).

	1900		1920	
	Per 1,000 population	Per 1,000 white population	Per 1,000 population	Per 1,000 white population
The North	20	21	11	11
The South	21	31	18	24
The West	13	13	8	8

For definitions of regions, see Appendix 1.

Table 2–5. Ratio of Female Servants and Laundresses per 1,000 Families, 1900 and 1920, by Region (16 Yrs. and Over).

	1900			1920		
	Servants	Laundresses	Total	Servants	Laundresses	Total
The North	80	12	92	39	8	47
New England	96	12	108	45	5	50
Mid-Atlantic	99	13	112	49	8	57
Eastern North Central	68	10	78	32	8	40
Western North Central	61	11	72	32	9	41
The South	63	41	104	46	35	81
Northern South Atlantic	104	44	148	64	33	97
Southern South Atlantic	59	52	111	51	48	99
Eastern South Central	61	40	101	42	36	78
Western South Central	43	30	73	36	25	61
The West	49	10	59	28	4	32
Mountain, Basin, and Plateau	43	12	55	25	7	32
Pacific	53	8	61	29	3	32

Source: See Tables 2–3 and A–7.

domestics diminished (see tables 2–3 and 2–4). The increase in number of servants was so rapid in the relatively urbanized North that it almost kept pace with the tremendous surge in population between 1880 and 1900. The number of domestic servants (excluding laundresses) per thousand population in the North fell only from eighteen to seventeen in the twenty-year period. At the same time, the number of servants per thousand families fell only 13 percent.

In the North after 1900, the number of servants declined sharply. As women left service for marriage or other jobs, their numbers were not replenished. The fall in immigration and the expansion of factory employment further served to reduce the number of servants. Given the increase in families between 1900 and 1920, potential employers had only half as many servants available in 1920 as in 1900.

Although the ratio of servants per thousand families fell in the South as well, the ratio of servants to households was still more than 40 percent higher than in the North. The population of the South grew less rapidly than that of the North, and family size remained larger, so the decrease in number of servants per thousand population was more modest than in the North. More importantly for potential white employers, the number of servants available per thousand white population in 1920 in the South was more than twice as high as elsewhere. This represented the real discrepancy in servant employment between the South and other sections of the country. While there were elite black families who employed servants, their overall numbers were small. Thus the relatively large black population concentrated in the South provided white mistresses with a pool of servants much larger than the servant-to-family ratio would seem to indicate. As whites outnumbered blacks and blacks had larger families than whites, the ratio of servants per white family would probably have been from 30 to 40 percent higher than the ratio of servants to all families. By Northern standards, then, Southern white families had as many servants available in 1920 as Northern white families had had two generations before.

While regional patterns in household labor were important, rural-urban differences were equally significant. The
employment of domestic servants was predominantly an
urban phenomenon reflecting the growth of the urban middle
class. In 1880, 15 percent of the U.S. population lived in the
50 largest cities, yet this 15 percent employed 32 percent of
all servants and 49 percent of all laundresses (outside laundries, in this and all subsequent examples). In 1900 the 78
largest cities—each with a population of at least 50,000—contained 22.2 percent of the total population, 37.1 percent of all
servants, and 35.4 percent of all laundresses. In 1920 the 68
cities whose population exceeded 100,000 had 26 percent of
the population, 38 percent of all servants, and 29 percent of
all laundresses. In 1920 the next 219 largest cities—all in the
25,000 to 100,000 population range—had 9.7 percent of the
population, 9.7 percent of all servants, and 15.9 percent of all
laundresses.

Within states, there were significant differences in the patterns of employing servants. The greatest rural-urban gaps
were in such states as Louisiana and Georgia, where large
rural black populations hired few servants and dominant
urban centers such as New Orleans and Atlanta had extremely high ratios of servants per thousand families. In 1900
servants per household were nearly four times as plentiful in
Atlanta as in the rest of Georgia (see Table A–5). In
Michigan and Colorado, the low ratios of servants per thousand families in 1880 in the areas outside Detroit and Denver
reflected the low level of outstate urbanization. In New York
State, where the ratio of servants per family excluding Buffalo and New York City was greater than that of Denver, the
high ratio resulted from the large urban population throughout the state. By 1920 the rural-urban gap had narrowed, although servants remained disproportionately urban based
(see Table A–5). The narrowing of the gap did not reflect
any increase in rural household labor; it represented the
growth of other urban centers within states, the growth of
suburban cities (e.g., Brookline, Massachusetts; New Rochelle, New York) with relatively high servants-per-family

ratios, and the diminishing tide of foreign immigration into the great cities during the 1910s. The Louisiana and Georgia patterns also suggest that the employment of domestics in the South was even more heavily urban than in the North, and that the association of the Southern white life-style with servants was more of an urban pattern than a universally Southern one.[5]

The decrease in number of servants in Southern cities, however, was significantly less than the decrease elsewhere. Atlanta, Nashville, New Orleans, Richmond and Washington, D.C., had ratios of servants per thousand families two to three times those in the North and West (see Table 2–6). Although the ratio per thousand families had fallen by more than a half in Atlanta between 1880 and 1920, it was still at a higher level than that of any Northern or Western city in 1880. At more modest levels, the other Southern cities had ratios of servant-laundress per family competitive with those of Northern cities of forty years before. Among Northern cities, the most rapidly growing boom towns at the beginning of the century—Cleveland, Detroit, Los Angeles—lagged far behind cities whose greatest relative expansion had occurred in the nineteenth century. In part this was because these boom towns experienced their greatest growth from rural-to-urban migration rather than from foreign immigration. And in Northern and Western cities—especially in such expanding industrial cities as Cleveland and Detroit—women had more opportunities for work other than household employment than did their Southern urban sisters.

By 1920 no Northern or Western city had *more* than 19.3 percent of women wage earners employed as domestics and laundresses, whereas in the South no city had *less* than 21.2 percent of employed women in service (see Table A–6). In Nashville and Atlanta, 38 percent of all employed women worked as domestics and laundresses—a level higher than that of any northern city of twenty years earlier except Kansas City. In the South, the persistence of washerwomen was an important factor in the high level of domestic service employment (see Table A–7). The spread of commercial

Table 2–6. Ratio of Female Servants and Laundresses per 1,000 Families, 1880–1920, for Selected Cities (10 Yrs. and Over)

	Servants per 1,000 families			Laundresses per 1,000 families			Servants and laundresses per 1,000 families		
	1880	*1900*	*1920*	*1880*	*1900*	*1920*	*1880*	*1900*	*1920*
New England									
Boston	219	167	74	20	25	8	239	192	82
Hartford	200	160	59	20	21	6	220	181	65
Mid-Atlantic									
Buffalo	145	118	47	12	15	8	157	133	55
New York	188	141	66	29	22	8	217	163	74
Philadelphia	183	138	70	20	16	11	203	154	81
Rochester	132	100	36	12	18	6	144	118	42
North Central									
Chicago	138	98	57	15	18	11	153	116	68
Cincinnati	150	122	64	25	40	28	175	147	92
Cleveland	129	97	35	14	18	11	143	115	46
Detroit	147	115	35	14	17	6	161	132	41
Indianapolis	136	104	49	37	34	22	173	138	71
Kansas City, Missouri	174	121	58	58	59	21	232	180	79
Minneapolis	206	138	58	14	25	6	220	163	64
St. Louis	189	117	63	38	42	31	227	159	94
South Atlantic									
Atlanta	331	214	136	233	238	113	564	452	249
Baltimore	212	159	91	65	74	48	277	233	139
Richmond	324	226	137	120	141	71	444	367	208
Washington, D.C.	299	269	152	87	127	63	386	396	215
Wilmington, Delaware	205	181	77	18	20	25	213	201	102
South Central									
Louisville	204	156	73	69	85	66	273	241	139
Nashville	310	196	110	135	193	116	445	389	226
New Orleans	206	157	121	80	101	86	286	258	207
West									
Denver	109	101	50	18	20	8	127	121	58
Los Angeles		71	43		11	5		82	48
San Francisco	125	95	45	11	15	2	136	110	47

Sources: *Tenth Census: 1880, Population*, vol. I, passim. *Twelfth Census: 1900, Population*, vol. II, pt II, pp. clxi–clxiv; *Occupations*, passim. *Fourteenth Census: 1920, Population*, vol. III, pp. 40–46; *Occupations*, passim.

laundries reduced the number of washerwomen in all urban centers everywhere except in the South, where laundry firms never appeared in large numbers until after World War II. It is most likely that the Southern preference for hiring servants retarded the development of commercial laundries. The Southern white pattern was to hire black servants, a custom that was an integral part of Southern white urban life and that served to define black-white relations and signify class and status within the white community. The low wages of black men, which forced their wives to work, and the barring of black women from office, shop, and most factory work sustained this system in the South. Thus, in the South race and domestic service were inseparable, and in the North, with the decline of foreign immigration and the in-migration of southern blacks, race was becoming an integral factor in domestic service as well.

While the disappearance of native-born women from service was widely lamented by housewives in popular literature of the nineteenth century, native-born women continued to comprise a significant proportion of servants. Native-born women still provided the largest group of servants nationally until 1920, although their numbers fell after the turn of the century and they were disproportionately underrepresented in household work (see Table 2–7). In sheer numbers alone, American-born women remained an important element; in 1920 native-born women comprised 69 percent of all women

Table 2–7. Nativity and Race of Female Servants, 1890–1920 (16 Yrs. and Over)

	*1890**	*1900*	*1910*	*1920*
Native-born white	507,120	529,210	510,516	381,565
Foreign-born white	366,097	322,062	333,011	207,811
Negro†	272,038	313,078	388,659	389,276
Total‡	1,145,255	1,165,561	1,234,758	981,557

*1890: 15 years and over.

† 1890 includes all nonwhites.

‡ Totals include Indian and Oriental servants.

Sources: U.S. Bureau of the Census, *Statistics of Women at Work* (Washington, D.C., 1907), pp. 159, 185. Joseph Hill, *Women in Gainful Occupations 1870 to 1920*, Census Monograph IX (Washington, D.C., 1929), p. 38.

wage earners. Regionally they were the majority in the West and North (see Table 2–8). Indeed, in the Western sections, in New England, and in the Western North Central states the proportion of native-born domestics rose between 1900 and 1920. The discrepancy between the actual presence of native-born servants and the popularly held belief that they had disappeared reflected their concentration in the small towns and rural areas. In both 1900 and 1920, native-born women servants were more numerous than foreign-born ones in the small urban cities and rural areas of every section of the country (see tables A–8 and A–9). The greatest contrast

Table 2–8. Distribution of Female Servants in Regions, by Nativity and Race, 1900 and 1920 (16 Yrs. and Over)

	1900			*1920*		
	Native-born white	*Foreign-born white*	*Negro*	*Native-born white*	*Foreign-born white*	*Negro*
United States	45	28	27	39	21	40
The North	54	37	9	50	31	19
New England	36	59	5	41	51	8
Mid-Atlantic	44	43	12	39	37	24
Eastern North Central	69	25	6	63	21	16
Western North Central*	68	23	10	69	14	17
The South	20	3	77	15	3	82
South Atlantic	19	3	78	13	2	85
Eastern South Central	21	1	78	14	1	85
Western South Central*	24	5	70	19	6	75
The West *	60	35	3	58	30	9
Mountain, Basin, and Plateau*	61	32	6	67	22	9
Pacific	59	37	3	53	34	9

*Distribution does not equal 100 percent due to rounding off, or in the West because of small percentage of Asians.

Sources: 1900: U.S. Bureau of the Census, *Statistics of Women at Work* (Washington, D.C., 1907), p. 42. 1920: Joseph Hill, *Women in Gainful Occupations 1870 to 1920*, Census Monograph IX (Washington, D.C., 1929), p. 89.

between the two groups occurred in the New England and Mid-Atlantic states, where native-born white women comprised the majority of servants in the smaller cities and country districts, while the foreign-born formed the majority in the largest cities. Nationally, native-born white women formed the majority of servants outside the largest cities in 1900 and a plurality in 1920, and they predominated in areas with relatively small foreign-born and black populations. In part this explains the relatively low ratios of servants per thousand families in the West and North Central regions. Dependence on white native-born women as a servant class meant that there were fewer servants available in these regions than in metropolitan cities and the South, where large foreign-born and/or black populations provided ample labor pools for household work.

In general, the higher the proportion of native-born among servants in cities or states, the lower the ratio of servants per thousand families. Outside of the South, urbanized and industrial states had higher servants-per-family and servants-per-population ratios than other states. This resulted not only from the growth of an urban middle class demanding household labor but also from the cities' ability to attract migrants—both immigrants and blacks.

Comparing the percentages of native-born in the servant population of major cities with percentages for outstate areas reveals the continued domination by native-born women outside large metropolitan areas. In New York State, for instance, native-born women comprised 63.2 percent of servants outside of New York City in 1900 and 60.5 percent in 1920, yet were only 21.7 and 17.8 percent respectively within New York City. Similar differences occurred in Illinois, Indiana, Michigan, and Maryland. In the South, white women were such a small proportion of servants as to be irrelevant (see Table A–9). In smaller metropolitan areas such as Albany, Buffalo, Rochester, and Syracuse, native-born servants comprised a majority of all servants, and their proportions increased between 1900 and 1920. This resulted from the precipitous decline in domestic servants in small industrial cities. With new occupations opening up to women, the total number of native-born servants fell, but the decline in numbers of foreign-born servants in these cities was even greater. Foreign-born women tended to concentrate in larger cities and in any case the new immigrants—Italians, Russians, Poles—had lower propensities to work than the previous generations of immigrants. At the same time, the proportion of blacks in service rose dramatically to 39.7 percent of all servants in 1920.

While the number of white women in service declined by 30 percent between 1910 and 1920, the number of black women remained virtually the same. But the regional distribution of black women servants shifted, and the number in the North increased 17 percent. More importantly, the proportion of black servants in the nation's largest cities rose even more. Since black migrants tended to move to the largest metropolitan areas, smaller cities suffered a decline in both foreign-born and black women. Thus the proportion of native-born among servants in the largest cities continued to decline, while their percentage in smaller cities grew.

The domination of household labor by immigrants was the obverse of the folklore of the disappearance of American-born women from service. But while housewives and state labor commissioners despaired of their seemingly involuntary dependence on immigrant servants, after 1890 the number and proportion of immigrant servants declined, while the number of native-born domestics was still growing (see tables 2–7 and 2–8). What heightened the sense of service as an exclusively foreign-born domain outside of the South was the concentration of immigrant servants in large urban centers in the industrial Northeast. In 1900, immigrants were only 28 percent of all servants, but they were 45 percent of servants in cities of more than 50,000 population. In the New England and Mid-Atlantic states, they were 61 percent of servants in metropolitan areas (see Table A–8). In the New England cities of Boston, Bridgeport, Cambridge, Fall River, Hartford, Lawrence, Lowell, Lynn, New Bedford, New Haven, Portland, Providence, Somerville, Springfield, and

Worcester, they exceeded 60 percent of all servants. Outside of New England, only in New York City, Hoboken, New Jersey, and Duluth, Minnesota, were as many as 60 percent of domestics foreign-born. By 1920 the proportion of foreign-born servants had dropped sharply, but in that year immigrant women still comprised a majority of servants in the above New England cities. At the same time, foreign-born servants were virtually absent from the South, providing only 3 percent of all domestics in that area in 1900 and 1920. In most areas of the country, Irish-born women formed the largest single group within the foreign-born servant class, and it was this factor which gave rise to the image of the Irish domestic as the typical American servant.

The image of the Irish servant woman in the United States was not unearned. Of the 320,000 foreign-born servants in 1900, 41 percent had been born in Ireland. In New England in 1900, where the Irish were clustered, Irish-born women or those whose parents had been born in Ireland comprised a majority of servants in Boston, Cambridge, Hartford, Lowell, New Haven, Providence, and Springfield. In New York City they comprised 42 percent of servants; in Philadelphia, 38 percent; and in Chicago, 21 percent. Although comparable date for previous years is not available, the 1880 census recorded the birthplace of servants (male and female combined) in the nation's fifty largest cities. Irish-born servants comprised 44 percent of all servants in 1880 in New York City and the then independent Brooklyn, 34 percent in Philadelphia, and 19 percent in Chicago. In Boston, Cambridge, Fall River, Hartford, Jersey City, New Haven, Providence, and Troy, Irish-born servants exceeded 40 percent of all servants. Yet this period was long past the major era of Irish immigration to the United States. The peak had been reached during the famine period in Ireland, approximately 1846 through 1854, when from 100,000 to 200,000 Irish immigrants a year entered the United States. Irish immigration fell during the Civil War, rose slightly afterward, and then fell again in the early 1870s. This was the "end of the period of the closest connection between the Irish immigrant and domestic service," as Blaine McKinley has described it. Although Irish immigration surged again during the 1880s, reaching a level surpassed only by immigration during the famine era, Scandinavian and German immigration exceeded that of the Irish, and the Irish were a declining percentage of all immigrants. From 1821 through 1860, 39 percent of all immigrants had come from Ireland; in the 1860s, 19 percent; in the 1870s, 16 percent; in the 1880s, 12 percent; and in the 1890s, 11 percent. And while Irish immigration declined, the number of Irish-born servants in the United States increased. The persistence of large numbers of Irish domestics was maintained by the Irish female immigrant's preference for household labor; in 1900, 54 percent of all Irish-born working women in the United States were servants, and another 6.5 percent were laundresses.[6] The decline of the foreign-born in domestic service resulted not only from diminished immigration but also from changes in the countries of origin. Central European and Scandinavian women had high propensities for household work, while the newer immigrants in the 1890s—Russians, Poles, and Italians—had relatively low inclinations toward household work (see Table 2–9). After 1892, immigration from Central Europe, Scandinavia, and

Table 2–9. Propensity of Immigrant Women for Household Labor, 1900

	Servants		Laundresses		
Place of birth	Number	Percent of group's wage earners	Number	Percent of group's wage earners	Percent in domestic service
Sweden	35,075	61.5	3,501	6.1	67.6
Ireland	132,662	54.0	15,925	6.5	60.5
Norway	10,440	45.6	1,385	6.0	51.6
Denmark	3,970	45.3	485	5.5	50.8
Hungary	5,837	46.3	308	2.4	48.7
Germany	58,716	36.3	10,174	6.3	42.6
Austria	7,866	38.6	482	2.4	41.0
Poland	6,292	24.1	1,098	4.2	28.3
England and Wales	13,620	21.9	1,937	3.1	25.0
Russia	4,850	13.8	364	1.0	14.8
Italy	1,840	9.1	505	2.5	11.6

Source: U.S., Senate, 61st Congress, 2nd session, Document No. 282, *Reports of the Immigration Commission, Occupations of the First and Second Generations of Immigrants in the United States* (Washington, D.C., 1911), pp. 71–79.

Servants en route to the New World huddle on the steerage deck of the S.S. Pennland, c. 1893. (Photograph by Byron. The Byron Collection, Museum of the City of New York.)

Ireland never attained the levels it had reached before, while Italian, Polish, and Russian immigrants after 1900 provided about 40 percent of the annual stream to the United States. Not only did Italian women constitute a low proportion of domestic servants, but they also had the lowest propensity among women for holding gainful employment. In 1900 only 8.9 percent of Italian-born women or those with Italian-born parents were wage earners. Similarly, only 12.3 percent of Polish-born and 12.7 percent of Russian-born or Russian parentage women were employed. Irish women, on the other hand, topped the list, with 24.8 percent employment.[7]

The propensities of immigrant women in the United States to work at domestic labor reflected a complex set of factors. For many, the cultural matrix they brought to the United States was an important determining element. Italian women, as Virginia Yans McLaughlin has shown in her excellent study of Buffalo, New York, avoided work incompatible with their family roles. Few Italian women worked outside their own households, and fewer still worked in domestic service, which was still predominantly live-in work in the North in 1900. Interestingly, among all foreign-born women, Italians had the highest ratio of laundresses to servants in 1900. Washerwomen who collected laundry to be washed in their own home would have the least conflict between work and family roles of all working women. Similarly, Jewish women who came to the United States—mostly from Russia or Poland—tended to avoid household work. Their preference for home manufacturing—piecework in the needle trades—suggest that they too sought work compatible with the traditional family role. Moreover, Rose Cohen's experience of her mother's disgrace at her employment as a servant—even when the family had no alternative source of income—suggests that such work was culturally objectionable. Irish women immigrants, on the other hand, brought with them a service tradition: domestic labor had been the single largest employer of women in Ireland. Most were single, tended to marry at a later age than other women in the United States, and knew English; as a consequence, they entered household labor and probably continued to work longer at it than other white women. To work a lifetime in an employer's family without marrying was an accepted custom on the Emerald Isle. America's gain in servants was Ireland's loss. In the 1880s the *London Times* Donegal correspondent reported that female domestics were becoming scarcer because they were going to America "in search of service and husbands." In 1889 the *Tuam Herald* complained that as soon as girls attained working age they left Ireland to "slave and scrub and stifle in American cities." Likewise, Scandinavian women entering the United States were participating in the traditional rural-urban migration wherein young farm women entered town households as servants. The only difference was that they moved a longer distance—from Sweden, Norway, or Denmark to Scandinavian communities in the American Midwest.[8]

The preference of mistresses for servants of a given nationality or race became part of the folklore of household labor. Previous experience with one or more servants from a group, anti-Catholicism, Anglophilia, Negrophobia, or any other personal prejudices influenced likes and dislikes. The Maine Bureau of Industrial and Labor Statistics polled a group of mistresses in 1910 on their preferences for women servants by nationality or place of birth. American-born women were preferred, but when mistresses were questioned about what national group they would prefer their foreign-born servants derive from, 43 percent favored Scandinavians and 27 percent, Irish. At the same time, Scandinavians comprised only 7 percent of the foreign-born servants employed, while 36 percent were Irish. Obviously the existing pool of available workers did not coincide with the preferences of the housewives. In fact, the Maine poll reflected the tendency for the mistress/servant relationship to be an unsatisfactory one. Thus mistresses, generalizing from their own experiences, preferred servants of nationalities or racial groups other than those available. A Minnesota employment agent reported that Swedish girls—the largest element among servants in Minnesota in the 1880s—were considered less able and clean than other nationalities.[9]

Whatever effects the cultural matrix had on the Irish-born woman's propensity for domestic service, the next generation—the first to be born in the United States—had adapted sufficiently to the American experience to avoid household labor. While in 1900 60.5 percent of Irish-born women wage earners in the United States were servants or laundresses, only 18.9 percent of the next generation worked in household labor. In Massachusetts in 1900, 53 percent of Irish-born women worked as servants (excluding laundresses), while only 11.2 percent of the second generation were domestics. In New York, the difference was 60 and 17 percent between first- and second-generation domestics. Clearly, for Irish immigrants service had provided the vehicle for entry into American society and for upward mobility. Among women of Scandinavian parentage, the proportion of servants also declined (although only marginally among Norwegians). (See

Table 2–10.) Nonetheless, with only 13 percent of women of Norwegian parentage gainfully employed in 1900, it is certain that no foreign-born group had formed a permanent service class in American society. The decline in immigration and the increasing tendency of native-born women, whether of native or foreign parentage, to avoid household labor left the work mostly to black women.[10]

The composition of the servant labor force changed significantly during the nineteenth and twentieth centuries. In the early part of the nineteenth century, immigrants had replaced native-born white women in the urban North and West, meeting the great increase in demand in the growing cities. Blacks dominated household labor in the South. Toward the end of the century, however, the proportion of native-born white women—still the dominant group outside the great cities—declined further as American-born women entered offices and shops. The number of foreign-born servants tended to fluctuate with the level and character of immigration. By the end of World War I, the drop in the number of

Table 2–10. Propensity of Second-Generation Women for Household Labor, 1900

	Servants		Laundresses		
Birthplace of one or both parents	Number	Percent of group's wage earners	Number	Percent of group's wage earners	Percent in domestic service
Sweden	10,728	44.5	430	1.8	46.3
Ireland	62,159	16.0	11,338	2.9	18.9
Norway	12,088	48.2	413	1.6	49.8
Denmark	2,889	42.4	84	1.2	43.6
Hungary	247	12.2	14	.7	12.9
Germany	102,109	27.1	10,091	2.7	29.8
Austria	1,041	20.0	72	1.4	21.4
Poland	2,521	20.4	509	4.1	24.5
England and Wales	14,931	15.5	1,810	1.9	17.4
Russia	1,001	17.3	41	.7	18.0
Italy	536	9.3	93	1.6	10.9

Source: U.S., Senate, 61st Congress, 2nd Session, Document No. 282, *Reports of the Immigration Commission, Occupations of the First and Second Generations of Immigrants in the United States* (Washington, D.C., 1911), pp. 71–79.

white women servants, whether native- or foreign-born, was enormous. At the same time black women were migrating from the South into Northern cities. Once almost exclusively a regional servant class, they began replacing whites in the nation's largest cities, where they formed an urban servant population. Soon black women comprised nearly a majority of all servants and laundresses nationally. Unlike white women, for whom household labor provided a bridge between leaving their parents home and getting married, many urban black women could expect to be wage earners most of their lives, regardless of whether or not they married. And by 1910, when household labor had lost most of its significance within the white female occupational structure, approximately three-quarters of black women wage earners worked as domestic servants or washerwomen. Discrimination barred black women from most other work, but many favored domestic service anyway, for live-out work was relatively compatible with marriage. As blacks began to dominate household labor in cities, they were the most important element in shifting domestic work from a live-in to a live-out occupation. Within a hundred years the image of the household servant had changed from rural "help" to the Irish "biddy" of the nineteenth century to the black "cleaning woman" of the twentieth.

Between 1890 and 1920 the number of white female servants declined by one-third, while black female domestics increased in number by 43 percent (see Table 2–7). In 1920 black women comprised 40 percent of all domestic servants. The number of washerwomen, having peaked in 1910, began to decline thereafter as commercial laundries and ordinary servants assisted by machine power took over the doing of the wash. As all women left hand-laundry work, the proportion of black laundresses steadily increased, and in 1920, 73 percent of all laundresses outside laundries were black. The expansion in woman's work in offices and shops, however, only had a slight impact on black women. While the proportion of black women working as office clerks, stenographers, typists, bookkeepers, cashiers, accountants, store clerks and saleswomen, and telephone operators tripled between 1910 and 1920, only 0.5 percent in 1910 and 1.4 percent in 1920 of black women in nonagricultural occupations were employed in these occupations. Among native-born white women, 23.2 and 36.1 percent worked in these five occupations in 1910 and 1920 respectively, while 7.1 and 13.7 percent of foreign-born white women held these jobs. On the other hand, household labor became relatively unimportant as a form of employment for white women. Between 1890 and 1920, the proportion of native-born white women outside of agricultural occupations working in service fell by more than two-thirds, and among immigrants, it fell by 60 percent (see Table A–11). In 1920 only 7 percent of native-born wage earners and 20 percent of immigrant women worked as servants. Household laundry work also had lost nearly all importance as a form of employment for white women; in 1920 only 1 percent of native-born women and 3 percent of the foreign-born did this work.

On the other hand, while the proportion of black women

Table 2–11. Percentage Distribution of Female Servants and Laundresses by Nativity and Race, 1890–1920 (16 Yrs. and Over)

	1890*	*1900*	*1910*	*1920*
Servants				
Native-born white	44	45	41	39
Foreign-born white	32	28	27	21
Negro	24	27	32	40
Laundresses				
Native-born white	15	21	20	18
Foreign-born white	15	13	10	9
Negro	70	65	69	73
Servants and Laundresses				
Native-born white	40	40	35	33
Foreign-born white	29	24	22	18
Negro	31	35	43	49

* 1890: 15 years and over.

Sources: U.S. Bureau of the Census, *Statistics of Women at Work* (Washington, D.C., 1907), pp. 159, 185. Joseph Hill, *Women in Gainful Occupations 1870 to 1920*, Census Monograph IX (Washington, D.C., 1929), pp. 38, 90, 96, 105, 117.

outside of agriculture working in service declined between 1890 and 1920, 41 percent still worked as servants and 30 percent as laundresses in 1920. Thus 71 percent of all non-agricultural black women wage earners performed household labor. At the same time, black women represented only 13 percent of all women in nonagricultural occupations. The degree to which black women disproportionately formed a servant class is graphically illustrated in the charts below. The index represents the relative degree to which a group was over- or underrepresented among servants and laundresses by comparing its percentage in service or laundry work to its representation among all nonagricultural workers. One hundred would be the level at which a group's proportion in service equaled its proportion among all nonagricultural wage earners. In 1920 then black women were more than threefold overrepresented in service, while native-born whites were underrepresented by nearly a half. Among laundresses, blacks were nearly six times more numerous than their dis-

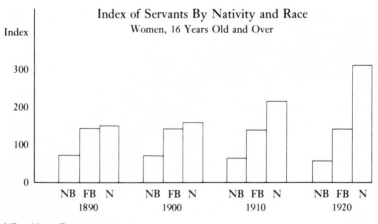

Index of Servants By Nativity and Race
Women, 16 Years Old and Over

NB = Native Born
FB = Foreign Born
N = Negro (1890 includes All non-white)
1890 = 15 Years Old and Over

$$\text{Index Number} = \frac{\text{Percent of Servants of Given Nativity and Race}}{\text{Percent of Non-Agricultural Workers of Given Nativity and Race}} \times 100$$

tribution in the nonagricultural wage-earning population
would warrant.

By 1920 black women servants were no longer confined
mostly to the South. In 1920, 29.3 percent of black servants
worked outside of the South and comprised 19 percent of
Northern servants and 9 percent of Western ones (see Table
2–8). More importantly, migration had brought them to the
nation's largest cities. Nationally they constituted 39 percent
of all servants in metropolitan areas of population 100,000 or
more. A comparison of cities of more than 50,000 in 1900
with cities of more than 100,000 in 1920, shows that the
proportion of blacks among servants more than doubled in
large cities between those years (see tables A–8 and A–9). By
1920 black women comprised a majority of servants in such
Northern cities as Camden; Indianapolis; Kansas City, Kansas; Kansas City, Missouri; and Philadelphia. In 1920 black
women comprised 25.6 percent of servants in North Atlantic
cities and 28.1 percent in North Central cities, more than

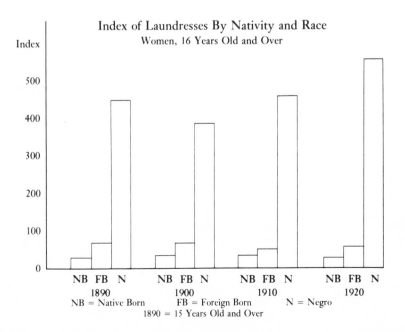

Index of Laundresses By Nativity and Race
Women, 16 Years Old and Over

NB = Native Born   FB = Foreign Born   N = Negro
1890 = 15 Years Old and Over

doubling their representation in these regions. Black migrants were concentrated in the largest cities, and their representation in household work rose more rapidly in larger cities
than in small cities and country districts (see tables A–8 and
A–9). Blacks eventually came to dominate hand-laundry
work in the North and West as they already did in the
South. In 1920, black women made up 47.9 percent of the
washerwomen in New England and Mid-Atlantic metropolitan areas and 59.5 percent in North Central cities of more
than 100,000 population. Of the nation's sixty largest cities
in which the race of laundresses was reported in the census,
black women formed a majority in thirty-seven of these
cities.

The sharp increase in the number of black servants resulted from black migration to the North and from black
women having the highest propensity to work and to work as
servants. Migrants—whether from rural districts or from
abroad—had always provided urban households with a significant if not the major source of household labor. With immigration virtually halted during World War I, the steady
stream of black migration Northward accelerated. With
white women finding other work in demand, the number of
white servants fell; at the same time, most black women entering the cities to work found only household work available to them. Thus the black increase in service was not
merely a relative one; the total number of black servants in
Northern cities increased while the total number of all servants was declining.

Two cities in particular—Detroit in 1880 and Philadelphia
in 1897—revealed the role of migrants among black service
workers. In Detroit in 1880, 20 percent of the 160 black servants and cooks had been born in Michigan. Fifty-one percent came from the surrounding hinterland (Ohio, Indiana,
and Canada), while 17 percent had been born in the South,
mostly the South Central region. This latter group reflected
the importance of Kentucky and Tennessee as a source of
black migrants to Michigan. Similarly, among the 110 black
washerwomen, only 7 percent were Michigan-born, while 29

percent had been born in the adjoining states or Canada. Nearly half (49 percent) had been born in the South, with Kentucky alone providing 22 percent of all laundresses. As a group, washerwomen tended to be older than servants and more were married. The Michigan-born black population provided few working wives, and the Kentucky-born black washerwomen were from a poorer group of blacks who had migrated to the city after the Civil War. More than half of the servants (54 percent) and nearly half of the washerwomen (48 percent) were unable to provide the census taker with their parents' places of birth, and this suggests their close ties with slavery. Indeed, it is not unlikely that nearly all of the Southern-born among these servants and washerwomen had been born slaves.[11]

A study of black domestics in Philadelphia, part of W. E. B. DuBois's social survey of the Philadelphia black community, was undertaken at a time when black women were migrating to the largest Northern cities, where they would work as domestics. In 1900 in Philadelphia, 84.2 percent of all black women worked as servants or laundresses, and they comprised 29 percent of all women in domestic service. Isabel Eaton studied the black servant group in Philadelphia's Seventh Ward in 1897, and among the 1,540 respondents who reported their place of birth, only 14 percent had been born in the city. Another 11.5 percent came from other parts of Pennsylvania or from the adjoining states. Nearly all of the rest (73 percent) had been born in the Southern Atlantic seaboard states or in the District of Columbia. Maryland and Virginia provided 23 and 29 percent respectively of all servants. The Philadelphia pattern revealed the prevalence of the coastal migratory route among black women servants and the Southern flavor among black urban life in the North. Most importantly, it again demonstrated the ties between migration and service.[12]

As migration increased the Northern urban black population, as white women took office and shop work, and as immigration declined, the growing black communities became the major source of household labor. In Philadelphia in 1900 black women comprised 28.6 percent of all female domestic servants. In 1910, 38.6 percent of servants were black, and in 1920 they formed the majority—53.9 percent were black. Across the Delaware River in Camden, New Jersey, 46.7 percent of servants were black in 1900, and by 1920 their proportion had risen to 69.4 percent. Philadelphia and Camden, like Indianapolis and the twin Kansas Cities, had been the focal point of a large black migration before World War I, so before the Great Migration blacks had comprised the largest single group of servants. Among Northern cities in 1900, Philadelphia had the largest black population. The period 1910 to 1920 was the great period in urban black community growth. Leading the relative expansion was the black community in Detroit, which grew 600 percent; the one in Cleveland, which grew 300 percent; and the one in Chicago, which grew 150 percent. By 1920, ten Northern cities had black populations exceeding 30,000, with New York's black community the largest, at 152,000.

After World War I, black women made up a significant proportion of servants in nearly all major cities regardless of region. In Philadelphia in 1920, for instance, blacks were 8 percent of all women ten years old and over, and 13 percent of all women wage earners; yet they accounted for 54 and 78 percent of all servants and laundresses respectively. In Camden black women were also 8 percent of the population and 12 percent of wage earners, but 69 and 86 percent of servants and laundresses respectively. In Philadelphia 68 percent and in Camden 82 percent of all black women wage earners were either servants or laundresses. More importantly, in both cities approximately *one-third* of all black women ten and over worked as paid household labor. In other words, one in every three black women, including students, housewives, and the aged, worked as servants or laundresses. Among white women ten and older, only 2 percent in Philadelphia and less than 1 percent in Camden were household workers. Even in cities where black women comprised only a small fraction of the population, they formed a significant servant class. In Chicago, Cleveland, and Detroit, black women were

4 percent of all women, yet comprised from 23 to 30 percent of servants and from 43 to 54 percent of laundresses. A majority of black female wage earners worked as servants and laundresses in all major cities except for the most rapidly expanding industrial ones, such as Chicago and Detroit (see Table A–12).

More importantly, urban black women tended to form a servant and laundress class. In Southern cities, from one-third to two-fifths of all black women ten and over worked in paid household labor. In Richmond, where only 31 percent of all black women worked as servants and laundresses, work in tobacco and cigarette factories was available to some black women. Even in the North, however, from a fifth to a third of black women worked in households. In cities such as Rochester and San Francisco, where black women made up less than 1 percent of the population, about 30 percent of all black women worked as domestics or laundresses. Only in Detroit and Chicago did less than one-fifth of black women work as household labor, and in these cities, as in Richmond, some industrial work was open to black women (see Table A–12).

That so many black women were available for household work reflected the degree to which a greater proportion of black than white women held paid jobs. Although the proportion of women wage earners gradually increased between 1890 and 1920, the gap between black and white did not significantly narrow. In either year black women were at least twice as likely to be employed as white women (see tables A–13 and A–14). Nationally, in 1920, 43 percent of black women sixteen and over were employed, while less than 20 percent of native- or foreign-born white women held gainful employment. Women in large cities were more likely to be employed than their sisters in smaller cities and country districts. Yet while a substantial percentage of white women in large cities worked, half of all black urban women in 1900 and 1920 were gainfully employed (see table A–15). The high proportion of black women who worked reflected the essential differences between white and black life cycles, which in turn greatly affected the household servant population.

For many young white women, as has been pointed out earlier, domestic service was but a temporary stage in their lives. Michael Katz, in studying Hamilton, Ontario, of the 1850s, described this as a period of semiautonomy. "It consisted of the span of years," Katz concluded, "between leaving home and marrying during which young men and women frequently worked and lived as members of a household other than that of their parents." In his study of Buffalo in the 1850s, Lawrence Glasco concluded that domestic service "was almost a universal experience of foreign-born girls." Irish girls in Buffalo, Glasco found, began leaving home at age eleven, and by age seventeen to eighteen, 90 percent had left. The propensity of Irish girls to work in service was so high that Glasco concluded that "virtually *every* Irish girl during adolescence spent several years as a live-in domestic." As young women married, however, they left service to establish their own households. By age twenty-one nearly 50 percent were married, and by twenty-six only 12 percent were classified as servants. German girls in Buffalo also left home beginning at age twelve but at a slower rate for the whole group, so the process was not completed until age twenty-three. As with the Irish, nearly all German girls worked at some time as domestics, although for shorter periods, since they tended to leave home later and marry earlier. Native-born women, however, began to leave home at age sixteen, five years later than Irish and German girls, and relatively few entered service. The modal age for native-born girls in domestic service was eighteen, and at that age less than 20 percent were domestics, whereas at the modal ages, two-thirds of Irish and German girls were servants. In studying Pittsburgh after the Civil War, Susan J. Kleinberg found the same patterns as had Katz and Glasco. Pittsburgh included a sizable black population, and Kleinberg concluded that "black and Irish women went out to service earlier and remained as servants longer than did any other group." While domestic service was a "transitional period" for white women, a large proportion of black women would continue working after marriage.[13]

Why were girls so young—age thirteen or younger—sent out to work? In most cases it was probably an economic question; they were a financial liability to their families. In a rural farm community, children, especially males, were an important economic asset as extra hands. In towns or cities, however, children could only contribute marginally to family productivity. Thus girls were sent out to other people's homes to work as servants, sometimes with no more pay than room and board.

After 1900, however, very young girls played a declining role as a source of domestic servants. Child-labor reform, compulsory education, and increased prosperity among many families reduced the number of girls in their early teens leaving their parents' homes. In 1880 nearly 10 percent of all female servants (93,000) had been fifteen or younger. In 1900, 120,000 girls ages ten to fifteen worked in service, comprising 9.4 percent of women servants. Thereafter their numbers diminished, so that in 1920 only 31,000 young girls were servants. That 12.4 percent of all native-born servants in 1900 were ten to fifteen years old testified to the persistence of this semi-autonomous life cycle among young American-born girls in rural Midwestern states. By 1920, however, only 4.2 percent of native-born servants were fifteen years old or younger (see Table A–16).

Among white women, gainful employment was an interlude. While the proportion of white women who worked fell off sharply beyond age twenty, black women did not experience the same decline in their propensity to work. Foreign- or native-born, urban or rural, as soon as white women reached marrying age, they tended to stop working. The older they were, the less likely they were to work (see tables A–13, A–14 and A–15). Marriage, not age, was the important factor here. In 1900 only three out of every hundred married white women held paid employment; in 1920 still only six out of every hundred were gainfully employed. Nearly all white women, then, worked until they were married, and gainful employment represented a stage in their life before marriage. Work was but a temporary station between adolescence or early adulthood and an independent family role as wife and mother.[14]

Nearly half of all black women, however, could expect to work most of their adult life. The proportion of black women gainfully employed did not drop significantly with age until after sixty-five. In 1900 and 1920, more than 40 percent of all black women regardless of age worked. And in the nation's largest cities in 1900, a majority of black women between fifteen and sixty-five worked. Among women over twenty-five, blacks were two to four times more likely to be employed than whites. In cities black women outnumbered black men to a much greater extent than white women outnumbered white men. Blacks also tended to marry at a later age, thus increasing the chances of a black woman working until an older age. In part this imbalance between black men and women was created by the great demand for black servants— women migrants could find jobs more easily than men. Equally important, however, was the tendency of black married women to work. In 1900, twenty-six out of every hundred black married women worked; in 1920, thirty-three out of every hundred. In cities of 100,000 or more in 1920, forty out of every hundred black married women worked, whereas only eight of every hundred white married women were gainfully employed. In 1920, there was more than 40 percent employment among black married women in Hartford, Springfield, New York City, Paterson, Yonkers, and San Francisco, cities outside of the South. In Atlanta, Baltimore, Dallas, Louisville, and Wilmington, Delaware, more than 50 percent of black married women worked.[15]

Most married women worked out of economic necessity. In the early 1870s, "the inadequate wage paid to unskilled and, to a lesser degree, to semi-skilled urban workers," Herbert Gutman concluded, "partly explained why so many women and children worked." Wages were so low that escape from poverty was a responsibility of all, not just that of the adult male worker. A study of working mothers in Philadelphia from 1918 to 1919 revealed the ties between financial necessity and work. Gwendolyn Hughes studied 728 wage-earning Philadelphia white mothers and found that in 29 percent of the cases their husbands' insufficient wages forced them to work, while another 60 percent worked because of death, illness, or desertion of, or nonsupport by, their husbands. Only 11 percent reported a preference for gainful employment outside of their home as a reason for gainful employment. Hughes's study was in part motivated by the charges that women provided unfair competition to men, since they were often depicted as working only to earn the proverbial pin money. In the 1920s the Women's Bureau of the Labor Department reported in a number of studies that about 90 percent of employed females went to work because of economic need. Black women in particular faced these conditions. In his 1897 survey of the black community in Philadelphia's Seventh Ward, W. E. B. DuBois concluded that "the low wages of men make it necessary for mothers to work." In New York, Mary White Ovington observed that among blacks "the wage of the husband . . . is usually insufficient to support a family, save in extreme penury, and the wife accepts the necessity of supplementing the husband's income." The solution: "this she accomplished by taking in washing or by entering a private family to do housework."[16]

Among poorer families in which the husband's income alone was insufficient to provide for the family, the children, if old enough, and/or the wife-mother could work to provide additional income. In her study of Boston during the late nineteenth century, Elizabeth Pleck noted that in white families children were used to supplement or provide the basic family income, while among blacks the mother was more likely to work. In Cambridge in 1900, for instance, Pleck found 5 percent of white mothers employed and 80 percent of white children in families working. In black families, on the other hand, 39 percent of mothers worked, as opposed to only 6 percent of children. Unfortunately, the census does not provide sufficient data to explain these differences. Traditionally, black women—both as slaves and as freed women—had been accustomed to working outside of their own household. Moreover, by specializing in household labor and selecting live-out work, they could at least continue to run their own homes and families. Part of the black preference for working as washerwomen was their ability to collect laundry and do it in their own homes. In Boston in 1900, 33 percent of black laundresses were married; in Baltimore and Washington, 47 percent; in New York, 36.5 percent. And with live-out work common among black women and cooks having the opportunity to return home during the day, black married women could more easily reconcile paid employment with running their own households.[17]

On the other hand, it is not certain that black women, if given the choice, would have preferred working to sending their children out to work. Black children, as Elizabeth Pleck noticed, had employment opportunities only in "menial and temporary jobs." Moreover, if they were sent out to work as servants, as many were, they would not have been recorded in the census as part of their parents' family. Furthermore, married working women conflicted with the idealized role of the wife as mother and homemaker. While some married women—white and black—were motivated to work for the fulfillment an independent career provided or for extra spending money for their families, the small percentage of married white women who worked before the 1920s suggests that this was not the norm. For blacks, with 40 percent of urban married women working, the situation was not a desirable one but an economic necessity. The family was the basic institution in black life, and "the Negro male," according to John Blassingame, "contended that a woman's sphere of action was the home." With such a large proportion of black married women working, many blacks sought to win community respect for the black working wife and mother. Katherine Tillman in the *A.M.E. Church Review* described the nobility of the domestic servant who struggled to earn a living and to raise a family at the same time. Similarly, E. Azalia Hackley praised the black women who worked: "No one should ever scorn a colored working woman," she wrote in 1916. "She has been the bone and sinew of the race." Both women, however, stressed the ideal fulfillment of black women as mothers and wives in bringing up their children and in running their own homes.[18]

Hand-laundry work was the mainstay of married working women in service, especially black women. Few washerwomen lived in; even in the North where live-in service predominated, a washerwoman could live with her own family or board and have the same independence and freedom as other working women. These women were the forerunners of the post–World War II domestic cleaning women. A washerwoman had several mistresses, visiting each one once or twice a week. This allowed laundresses to work six days a week at the maximum and less if they wished. Servants, cooks, or even office, shop, and factory workers could not regularly work less than the full work week fixed by the employer, whereas the washerwoman determined the number of days she would work by choosing the number of employers. Moreover, if she needed to be home to care for young children, she could take wash to her own home rather than doing it in mistresses' households. Mary White Ovington found this a common pattern in New York City. At the same time, laundry work was more physically demanding than other forms of household labor. Many of the maids-of-all-work, in the period before washing machines became widespread, would not do laundry work. Inez Godman, for instance, accepted a weekly wage of $2.75 instead of $3.50 so that she would not have to do the wash.[19]

As the occupation most compatible with running an independent household, laundry work attracted married women. In 1900 approximately one-fifth of white women and two-fifths of black laundresses were married (see Table 2–12). The number of washerwomen declined between 1910 and 1920, and more single women than married ones left the occupation, so the proportion of married women increased from 34 to 49 percent. Indeed, divorced and widowed women outnumbered single washerwomen. By 1920 in Atlanta, Baltimore, Cleveland, Detroit, Indianapolis, and New

Table 2–12. Percentage of Laundresses and All Female Wage Earners Married, by Race and Nativity, 1900 and 1920

	Native-born white	Foreign-born white	Negro
1900*			
Percent of laundresses married	21.2	21.8	40.5
Percent of all female wage earners married	10.0	12.2	33.6
1920*			
Percent of laundresses married	39.6	35.7	52.4
Percent of all female wage earners married	16.6	26.6	44.9

*Figures for 1900 based on females 16 years and over; those for 1920, 15 years and over.

Sources: U.S. Bureau of the Census, *Statistics of Women at Work* (Washington, D.C., 1907), pp. 15, 59. *Twelfth Census: 1900, Occupations*, p. ccxxiv. *Fourteenth Census: 1920, Occupations*, pp. 694, 714–715, 722–723, 730–731, 738.

Orleans, more than half of all washerwomen were married. Laundry work attracted the highest proportion of black married women; in 1920, 52.4 percent of all black laundresses were married.

Domestic service as employment for married women began to change significantly after the turn of the century. Between 1900 and 1920, the gap between the proportion of servants who were married and the proportion of all wage earners who were married began to narrow. (see Table 2–13). This reflected the increase in the number of blacks among servants, since so many black working women were married. But the percentage of married women in each group of servants (native-born, foreign-born, Negro) increased between 1900 and 1920, and rose more rapidly than the percentage of married women among all wage earners. In nearly all of the nation's largest cities in 1920, the proportion of married women in service exceeded the proportion of married women among all female wage earners in the city. In Southern cities such as Atlanta, 34.8 percent of all female wage earners were married, as opposed to 40.7 percent of servants. In 1900, 24.5 and 22.4 percent of female wage earners and servants had been married. Baltimore, Washington, and New Orleans experienced the same reversal, as did other large Southern cities. In the North, in the metropolitan cities of Boston, Chicago, Cincinnati, Cleveland, Detroit, Indianapolis, New York City, Pittsburgh, and St. Louis, the proportion of servants who were married changed from being below that of female wage earners who were married in 1900 to being above it in 1920. In a few cities in 1900—Camden, Louisville, Newark, and Wilmington, Delaware—the proportion of servants who were married had exceeded the general average, and it continued to do so in 1920. More importantly, in a few large cities in 1920—Fall River, Minneapolis, Providence, and Rochester—the proportion of servants who were married continued to be below the average of all women in the city. These cities in which the proportion of married domestic servants was below the average for all working women had two interrelated factors in common: a very low percentage of black servants and the persistence of live-in service among a majority of domestics.[20]

Domestic service was in the process of changing from predominantly live-in to predominantly live-out work. Live-in service persisted in cities where relatively few married women engaged in service and where there were very small

Table 2–13. Percentage of Female Servants and All Female Wage Earners Married, by Race and Nativity, 1900 and 1920

	Native-born white	Foreign-born white	Negro
1900*			
Percent of servants married	6.5	4.7	22.3
Percent of all female wage earners married	10.0	12.2	33.6
1920*			
Percent of servants married	14.5	14.0	35.7
Percent of all female wage earners married	16.6	26.6	44.9

*Figures for 1900 based on females 16 years and over; those for 1920, 15 years and over.

Sources: U.S. Bureau of the Census, *Statistics of Women at Work* (Washington, D.C., 1907), pp. 15, 60. *Twelfth Census: 1900, Occupations*, p. ccxiv. *Fourteenth Census: 1920, Occupations*, pp. 694, 714–715, 722–723, 730–731, 738.

black communities. Conversely, day work was a direct result of a large number of blacks and married women in household labor. Data exists for examining the patterns in eleven cities in 1920. In all eleven cities, most married female servants lived out, and only in two—Paterson and Rochester—did more than one-quarter of married women servants live in their employers' households. The greatest disparities among the cities were in the tendencies of single women to live in and in the proportions of single women in the servant population. These factors were inversely related to the percentage of black women in service (see Table A–17).

In the Southern cities—Atlanta and New Orleans—live-out work was firmly established. Overall, 95.5 percent of servants in Atlanta were black; the figure was 86.1 percent in New Orleans. Only 10 percent of all household workers were live-in servants in these two cities (see Table A–18) and live-out work predominated among both married and single women.

Three cities outside of the South with a sizable majority of servants living out—Louisville, Indianapolis, and Kansas City, Missouri—had a Southern ambiance brought by the black migrants. In 1920 Indianapolis and Kansas City had black majorities in service, while in Louisville they formed a plurality. In all three cities, single women formed a minority of all servants. Although live-out work had not yet become the norm among Kansas City's single servants, the dominance of married, widowed, and divorced women in service meant that live-out work was most commmon. Cincinnati had a lower proportion of black servants, but since 1900 the proportion of blacks in service had increased 2½-fold. The proportion of married women in day work was lower than in Kansas City and only marginally higher than in Atlanta, yet only a bare majority of all servants lived out. The preponderance of single women in service—a function of the smaller black proportion among servants—determined the difference between Cincinnati and Indianapolis and Kansas City. Among the remaining Northern cities, live-in service was still the norm. In four of these cities—Fall River, Paterson,

Providence, and Rochester—the proportion of married women in the working population at large exceeded that among servants. In all five of the cities plus Cincinnati, single women formed a majority of the servant population. More importantly, in all these cities except Paterson, only a relatively small percentage of servants were black women. None of these cities had been a recipient of the northward migration of blacks; contrary to the trend among cities, the number of black servants in Paterson, Fall River, and Providence decreased between 1900 and 1920. While the number of black servants in Rochester and St. Paul increased, there were still too few of them for them to have any significant effect on the overall work pattern (see Table A–17).

When data for the eleven cities in 1920 is compared with similar data for 1900, the trend toward live-out service becomes apparent. Joseph Hill retabulated 1900 census data to permit a loose comparison. In order to compare 1920 with 1900, the categories of servants and waitresses must be combined for the 1920 data, since the 1900 data included both categories. The 1900 data was also slightly inflated by the inclusion of charwomen and cleaners. Finally, in the 1900 data, no distinction had been made between servants boarding and those living with their employers. Thus the only meaningful comparison possible is between the proportions of servants and waitresses living at home in 1900 and in 1920. This provides a trend that represents the minimum percentage of servants living out, since it excludes servants living out but boarding. In 1920 in the eleven cities, for instance, 49.6 percent of servants and waitresses lived at home, while another 16.9 percent boarded or lodged outside of their employers' homes. Unfortunately the 1920 data cannot be interpolated to fit the 1900 statistics; too many factors had changed. Nonetheless, Hill found that in every one of the eleven cities the percentage of servants and waitresses living at home had increased between 1900 and 1920 (see Table A–19). This suggests an increasing tendency toward live-out service work. The 1900 data indicates that a majority of servants and waitresses in Atlanta and New Orleans were living at home.

This substantiates the degree to which live-out domestic service had been prevalent at an earlier period in the urban
South.[21]

Finally, 1900 census data makes it possible to compare
live-in and live-out service by the nativity and race of married domestics. In large cities of 100,000 or more, only in
Newark did a smaller percentage of white married servants
and waitresses than black ones live in with their employer or
board out. In all other cities, more black married women lived
at home than did white ones. In Atlanta a majority of white
married servants boarded or lived in while only one-quarter
of blacks lived outside their own home. In Baltimore among
white married servants nearly 70 percent boarded or lived in;
only 41 percent of blacks did not live at home. Similarly, in
Cincinnati, Indianapolis, Louisville, Minneapolis, New Ore-
leans, Providence, and Washington, D.C., a majority of
white married servants lived in or boarded while a minority
of blacks did.[22]

In the early 1920s, investigators interested in domestic service noticed the trend toward day work. One study by Mary
V. Robinson used the records of the Domestic Efficiency Association of Baltimore, a nonprofit employment agency. The
association recorded the servants' preferences for live-in or
live-out work. Among 416 white women, 80 percent preferred to live in, while only 36 percent of the 1,385 black
women indicated such a preference. The Baltimore study is
also the first to explicitly deal with the "day worker." The
position of day worker was different from that of cook or of
general servant wishing to live out; the day worker herself
was the forerunner of the modern domestic cleaning women
who divides her work among a number of employers. Robinson found that 15.4 percent of women applied to the association for day work. "This tendency is traceable," she concluded, "to the desire on the part of the workers to be more
independent in regard to days off, to work shorter hours—
and usually at higher wages—per day, and to escape the monotony of a regular household position." Among housewives
there was an increasing demand for day service because

apartment living and household innovations had made it possible "to dispense with the continuous service of domestic
employees." Among the day workers whose race was reported, 93 percent were black, while only 66 percent of all
female applicants were black. Among the black day workers,
71 percent were married; among the white ones, 45 percent.
Black day workers were one-third more likely to be married
than all black servants; white day workers were one-half
more likely to be married than all white servants. These
women were seeking the advantages that laundresses already
enjoyed. As Lillian Pettengill had learned, washerwomen
would not trade day work even for living-out service.

"Why don't you live out, instead of working out by the
day?" Pettengill had asked Sophie, the laundress for the
Barry family. "I should think you'd like it better."

"Oh, no; I'd rather work by the day, because then I can
earn more money and be at home."[23]

Pettengill's anecdote about Sophie demonstrates that by
the turn of the century there was a clear distinction between
live-out work—living at home or boarding and working full
time for one employer—and day work, where the servant
worked regularly on given days for a number of employers.
For women servants, day work was not casual labor. Unlike
day laborers, who worked for some limited time period for
an employer and then had to seek other employment, day
workers in household labor had a regular schedule of employment. Laundresses, for instance, might work Mondays
and Tuesdays for one family, Wednesdays and Thursdays
for another, and Fridays and Saturdays for a third. Laundresses who did no ironing might have six employers if they
worked full time, four or five if they worked a shorter week.

The seemingly insatiable demand for servants provided security to domestics. Household day work also had the effect
of increasing the number of servants available per household.
In Atlanta in 1900, for instance, there were 238 laundresses
per thousand families (see Table A–5). If each laundress
worked for an average of three families per week, 700 families per thousand in Atlanta would have employed a washer-

women. If it is assumed that the ratio of white to black families was approximately the same as the proportion of whites to blacks in the population (60 to 40 percent), 700 laundresses per thousand families would have provided every white family with a laundress with enough remaining for every fourth black family to hire a washerwomen. While this is purely speculative, it is likely that nearly every white household had a washerwomen. Thus day work, the prevalent pattern among black laundresses and the growing preference of black servants, eventually would become the solution to the decrease in the number of full-time servants and would permit the retention of household workers by more families than live-out work would have allowed. Initially, the pattern of day work was common only among laundresses, an overwhelming majority of whom were black and married; it spread slowly as black women brought it to Northern and Western cities. As the proportion of black and married women in service increased, so did day work.

Passaic, New Jersey, reflected many of the national trends in domestic service. The Women's Bureau sponsored a detailed study of women wage earners in Passaic based on unpublished 1920 census tabulations. The city was an industrial community in which 46 percent of all women fourteen and over were gainfully employed. Of the nearly 10,000 working women, almost 60 percent were of foreign birth, and a majority of these were Polish and Hungarian. Only 1.4 percent of the female labor force was black. In 1920 there were 444 domestic servants; 59 percent lived in, 23 percent lived out, and 18 percent were day workers. Together they comprised 4.5 percent of all women wage earners. Of the single women in service, 77 percent lived in. Among married women, on the other hand, only 21.7 percent lived in, while 42.4 percent of widows and divorced women lived with their employers.

In Passaic the few black wage earners formed a service class; 61.2 percent of employed black women worked as servants, while another 26.2 percent did kindred work—did washing, served as restaurant or kitchen help, or took in boarders or lodgers. Blacks comprised 19.1 percent of all domestic servants and day workers; among live-out servants and day workers alone they made up 34.8 percent. Black women played an important role in providing day work; they comprised 43.9 percent of that group. Only one-quarter of black domestics lived in. Although a majority of servants were foreign-born women, only 4.7 percent of immigrants worked in domestic service. Among the immigrants, 19.3 percent of Germans and 10.0 percent of Austrian female wage earners worked as servants. Among Italians, Poles, and Russians, on the other hand, 0.4, 1.4, and 0.3 percent respectively worked in service. No data on Irish women was provided. Polish women were the only significant group other than blacks who favored live-out or day work; 53 percent of the Polish servants did not live with their employer. Of those servants who had been in the United States less than ten years, 80 percent lived in; of those who had resided here ten years and over, 57 percent lived in. This resulted from the factor that the longer the period of time a woman had been in the United States, the older she was likely to be and the more likely she was to be married. Of all servants between thirty and fifty years of age, a majority lived out or worked days. Overall, then, black and married women favored live-out service; single women, live-in. Black women favored day work over live-out work, and preferred both to live-in work. The trend in Passaic, then, was away from live-in service and toward live-out and day work.[24]

Within a century, domestic service had changed from the major form of female employment to an occupation statistically unimportant among all but black women. Once a field dominated by immigrants in cities, by native-born girls in smaller towns and rural areas, and by blacks in the South, it became a predominately black occupation throughout urban America. As the level and source of immigration began to shift, the number of foreign-born women in service began to decrease. As shops and offices opened to women, fewer native-born women entered service, while child labor laws and compulsory education reduced the number of young girls under fifteen in service, so that by 1920 they virtually disappeared as a source of domestics. The absolute number of black women in service remained relatively stable as the absolute number of white domestics declined; in time, blacks became the dominant group in domestic service. Accordingly, the percentage of all servants who were married rose as black married women entered service in large numbers. This was probably further accelerated by the decline in washerwomen after 1910; many married black women who had been or would have become laundresses entered domestic service. As black women migrated into the urban North, they brought with them their preference for live-out household work, which was most compatible with marriage. By the 1920s, as the proportion of black and married servants increased, live-in service was dying out. At the same time, day work was beginning to replace live-out employment. By the 1920s, then, the modern system of domestic service in the form of day work—prevalent after World War II—had become entrenched.

III

HOUSEHOLD WORK

UNTIL WORLD WAR I, MOST AMERICAN SERVANTS LIVED IN their employers' homes; the work environment and tasks were thus central to their personal lives. Their employment, living conditions, work tasks, roles, hours, and wages had decided effects on their roles outside the work environment. This complex interrelation of work, environment, and personal life was an anachronism in an industrializing and modernizing society in which workplace and home had become separate and the daily hours of work were rapidly diminishing. About the time of World War I, however, live-out and day work became more prevalent than live-in service, and household work came to resemble other occupations. Nonetheless, for all the changes wrought by the separation of work and home, by the decline in the number of servants, and by the changes in the work tasks, the impersonal work relationship characteristic of a modern society was rarely present between mistress and servant. Modernization, urbanization, and technology may have altered the structure of service and many of the tasks, but they failed to significantly alter the personalized work relationship. Thus the contemporary pattern of day work that would become common around World War II is, in fact, rooted more in the ways of the eighteenth century than in those of the twentieth.

From the eighteenth century on, free servants and mistresses relied on three mechanisms as a means for finding one another: informal personal contacts, newspaper advertisements, and intelligence offices (employment agencies). For free labor, the basic ways of entering domestic service remained unchanged during the nineteenth and twentieth centuries. The single significant overall change was in the abolition of slavery; the purchase and ownership of servants had ended. By the time of the Civil War, gradual emancipation had already occurred in the North (except, most notably, in New Jersey), so the Southern system of household service was most radically affected by the ending of slavery.

Involuntary servitude, however, had not been completely abolished by the Reconstruction constitutional amendments. Peonage not only could hold a black man to the land as a sharecropper but also could tie a woman to a mistress's kitchen. Furthermore, some Southern states had vagrancy laws that compelled blacks to work. In 1895, two black women were convicted of vagrancy in Georgetown, Kentucky, and the circuit court ordered their labor sold at a public auction in front of the courthouse. Two black men bought the women for $1.05 and $2.00 respectively. The Chicago Commission on Race Relations reported that immediately after World War I, Chicago housekeepers had secured black women from the South and from the British West Indies. The employers provided transportation and clothes and expected the women "to work out this indebtedness." Moreover, the study reported a number of cases in which the employers used physical force to retain their servants. In one such case:

One colored woman was brought from a small town in Florida to a Chicago suburb by a white family. . . . After a few weeks' service the employer complained that the work performed by the woman as a general maid was unsatisfactory. Abuse followed. The woman sought to go to a Negro family under the pretence that she wished to return a pair of borrowed shoes. Her employer, fearing that she wished to escape, drove her to the home of the Negro family in his automobile. Once inside the home, she told a story of how her employer had kicked, beaten, and threatened her with a revolver if she attempted to leave.

The Negro family gave her shelter, and the employer left "after threatening to take her away by force." Assault and battery charges against the employer were dismissed for lack of evidence.[1]

Although the demand for servants always exceeded the supply, finding a job was not easy for a household worker. Between the Civil War and World War I the number of women looking for such jobs on any one day could exceed a million, while the potential number of individual employers was even greater. Given the very high turnover in household employment—the brief job tenure and the steady stream of women leaving domestic work—the number of actual hirings could easily have exceeded a million in any year around the turn of the century. The vast number of workplaces in service differentiated it from other occupations. While industrial workers were more numerous than servants, specialization, the large-scale work forces, and the centralized role of factories as workplaces enabled worker and employer to come together with relative ease. The atomization of the workplace in the building trades resembled that of domestic service, but in the early stages of industrialization taverns and specified streets in cities functioned as centralized hiring markets. Later, craft unions assumed control of job placement and the unions' offices became hiring halls. Servants faced greater difficulty. As women they could not loiter in saloons or on streetcorners and still maintain their respectability as potential employees. Moreover, their powerlessness and their confinement and isolation in the workplace prevented them from mastering the hiring process.

The informal process, the traditional use of personal contacts, offered the servant and mistress the most control and remained the most desirable system for both. For a servant in search of work it meant asking friends, acquaintances, other domestics, and employers whether or not they knew of a vacancy. Employers would undergo a similar search. This process enabled employers to find respectable employees, and vice versa. Its origins lay in the preindustrial society before the Civil War when servants "were socially the equal of their employers, especially in New England and in the smaller towns." Employer and employee—more properly termed housewife and "help"—came from the same community, ate at the same table, and attended the same church. A hired girl's parents often participated in the process of finding a suitable place, and the employer would fulfill a parental role. For the employing family this alleviated some of the tension involved in having strangers work and live in their private household. Probably this pattern was less widespread than most historians of domestic service have assumed it to be, but it did exist and persisted in rural communities where informal personal contacts provided the only hiring mechanism.[2]

Urbanization, immigration, and migration rendered the personal-reference system ineffective. Servants were concentrated in the largest cities, and by the late nineteenth century the urban areas were too populous for the personal-referral system to be widely effective in bringing together servants and mistresses. In the great cities, migrant groups—whether foreign immigrants, Southern blacks, or whites from rural areas and other cities—provided the majority of servants, and these individuals lacked the proper contacts to utilize such a system even if it could have been effective. Women as well as men migrated long distances, and reliance on personal contacts in hiring would have restrained their ability to move.

Even if the system was no longer adequate, most servants and mistresses gave it up reluctantly. Frances Kellor's investigation at the turn of the century concluded that "securing help through friends or acquaintances of either employer or employee . . . is universally preferred." Dependence on personal contacts in hiring seemed most appropriate for an occupation involving intense personal relationships on the job. It offered not only a more trustworthy source of information than impersonal third parties—employment agencies—but also security in work. Servants reasoned that they might be better treated if the employer knew their family or friends. Even migrants or immigrants could use this process through relatives or close friends who assisted their journey by arranging a place in advance. Thus in the hiring process at least, servants wished to maximize the degree of personalization involved. This was in sharp contrast to the personalized relationship of live-in work, which most servants came to view as oppressive. By maintaining the traditional hiring process, household workers and mistresses were also resisting the impersonal work relationships that came to dominate within industrial society. Powerless to change the essential structure of their work, domestic servants who remained in household labor constantly sought the benevolent family, and the high turnover implies that it was rarely found. Nonetheless, the personalized hiring system offered the best hope of finding such an ideal family—the family of an idealized time before the Civil War when help and housewife had been equal. But while servants and mistresses yearned for the past, they had to confront work in the present, and they often turned to employment agencies and newspaper help-wanted advertisements.[3]

Newspaper advertising served to bring together mistress and servant. Without a physical marketplace for centralized household employment, employers advertised for servants in the eighteenth century. During the following century servants occasionally placed their own situations-wanted notices. In 1874 *Frank Leslie's Illustrated Newspaper* featured a pictorial article on servant girls and the help- and situations-wanted columns. "The rosy-cheeked German, the bright-eyed Irish girl, the French *bonne*, and the ebony daughter of Africa," the weekly reported, "go to make up the varied crowd" studying the newspapers. Advertising columns were the literature of the servant class, and in New York City during the 1870s, the *New York Herald* was the favored newspaper.[4]

Servants and mistresses disagreed on the benefits and disadvantages of newspaper advertising, and its popularity rested mostly on its accessibility as an alternative to employment agencies. Women looking for new positions found that newspapers contained a readily available list of potential employers. Advertisements provided the domestic thinking of changing positions with an opportunity to review openings without paying a fee or committing herself to leaving; going to an agency involved taking time off to register and interview. Servants could also make direct contact with possible employers in their homes. Thus advertisements provided a middle ground between the personalized referral system and impersonal agencies. Some newspapers refused to carry help-wanted ads if they thought them not bona fide. Unfortunately, Frances Kellor found that the newspapers with the most ads exercised the least care.

For the job hunter, it required much time, energy, and money to travel around a city answering ads for jobs that already might have been filled or were perhaps unsuitable. Domestics themselves placed situations-wanted ads, which they considered preferable to using agencies because, as one domestic testified, "no sober, competent, respectable girl goes to a public office if she has friends or a home from which to advertise." Others thought it "cheaper and quicker than to pay big fees and wait in offices," and felt that "ladies who look up a girl are particular and we get into good houses." It offered some protections similar to the traditional referral system: "we are better protected," a domestic told Frances Kellor, "if the employer knows we have respectable friends and a home to receive us." Although the cost of advertising kept some domestics from placing a newspaper notice, the lack of a household in which to receive potential employers was the most inhibiting factor. There is no evidence that an employer ever permitted a domestic to use her home for interviews. Moreover, most domestics did not have a suitable family home or, among migrants, even a place to interview. And their relative isolation as live-in servants did not permit the development of friendships with other women who could let them use their homes for interviewing. Even more seriously, they faced employer reluctance to answer servants' ads.[5]

In general, employers would not answer situation-wanted ads by domestics and had mixed reactions about advertising themselves. Most mistresses did not think it worth the trouble to answer ads. They complained that they found that "the girls have just taken a place," or they had difficulty in finding the places. Most seemed to agree with the statement that answering ads "requires more exertion than going to an office." Indeed, agencies also advertised, sometimes placing blind ads to bring employers to their offices. Employers generally thought that placing advertisements themselves was worthwhile, but it depended in part on local custom. In New York City, employers favored this practice, while "in Chicago employers insist that they receive better employees from offices and that advertisements are unsatisfactory." Advertising enabled the employers to do their own screening, and thus it was common for employers to state preferences or prejudices in their advertisements. Ads expressing a preference for Irish, colored, white, Protestant, or native-born women were as common as those in which Irish or Catholic or colored servants were advised not to apply. Some employers complained that advertising turned their parlors into offices and brought all types of women to their homes, including many undesirable ones. Overall, however, advertising was considered better than going to the noisy, rabble-filled chambers of an intelligence office. With the demand for servants outstripping the supply everywhere but in the South, mistresses eventually had no choice but to patronize an employment agency.[6]

Although few servants or mistresses expressed satisfaction with intelligence offices, increasingly these provided the primary marketplace for urban domestic jobs. A woman looking for work would register with a number of agencies, generally at a fee from 10 to 25 percent of a week's wages each. The relatively poor record of agencies in placing servants required multiregistration. The agencies would send girls to interview in prospective mistresses' homes or provide a room for interviews in their offices. Employers also paid a registration fee, usually double that of a servant. In cities such as New York,

Employment agencies for servants in a New York City tenement district.
(Brown Brothers)

both parties often had to pay a fairly small fee for each interview and a larger amount when a hiring occurred. Most
agencies handling household labor dealt with no other kinds
of workers, and in her 1903–1904 study Frances Kellor found
that three-fifths of all agencies in the nation's four largest cities specialized in household positions. Many agencies repre-

sented servants of one particular ethnic group, acting as a conduit between immigrants and middle-class housewives. Larger cities were filled with Bohemian, German, Hungarian, Irish, Jewish, Polish, and Swedish agencies. "American" agencies tended to serve only white native-born women, while colored offices enrolled both black and white servants.[7]

Though they provided a service to both servant and mistress, agencies tended to favor the employer. Employers provided the greater part of an agency's income—they paid higher fees—and could more readily place their own advertisements than could domestics. Agents seemed to be more sensitive to the middle-class sensibilities of housewives and treated them with respect, while servants were crowded into small rooms and made to wait around all day. To meet the demand for servants, agencies often worked to stimulate migration to the cities and played an important role in recruiting women both from abroad and from the South. Agencies valued the trust of mistresses more than they did the confidence of individual servants. The high rate of turnover among domestics made this inevitable; servants were always leaving paid household labor, while the same mistresses would be looking for domestics year after year.

Nonetheless, agencies did serve working women as well. Domestics just coming to a city or between jobs needed a place to room or to leave their trunks, and many offices offered these services at a fee. Moreover, in theory agencies screened employers, providing a degree of security for servants. They also offered servants the one place where they could meet other household workers, make friends, and discuss and compare wages, work conditions, and employers.[8]

The abuses of disreputable employment agencies were well known. An 1887 guide to job hunting referred to an employment agency as a "swindling trap." Agencies promised quality jobs they did not have to offer, and fees were frequently wasted. Servants reported to the New York Bureau of Statistics that they repeatedly had to pay reregistration fees. In her study of employment offices Frances Kellor interviewed servants and sent investigators into agencies, and she produced a long inventory of unscrupulous practices. Some firms were bogus: the agents disappeared after collecting fees. As a group agents became notorious for cheating servants—charging fees in cases where the employer had paid the fee, failing to remit money when they acted as agents, obtaining workers at lower wages to win mistress loyalty, and demanding bribes to furnish employment to women who had already paid fees. As a screening mechanism they were totally unreliable. In collaboration with the agencies, employers frequently misrepresented the working conditions. Kellor estimated that 75 percent of agencies in New York were "not averse to sending women as employees to questionable places," while 40 to 60 percent would send them out to be prostitutes under the ruse of service positions. In Philadelphia, Kellor found a number of intelligence offices financially backed by "sporting houses."[9]

Mistresses too were troubled by the practices of employment agencies. They were more concerned with their own role as employers, however, than with the victimization of working women. At the turn of the century, such reformers as Frances Kellor exposed the exploitation of working women, and they were moved by genuine sympathies for the workers. Kellor's exposé of employment agencies was a natural result of these sympathies. Traditionally, employers shared the reformers' concern about intelligence offices while also blaming the agencies for servant inefficiency and employee turnover. In 1866 the New York Association for Improving the Condition of the Poor blamed intelligence offices for the deteriorating character of servants and claimed that these offices produced instability in homes by encouraging servants to change jobs in order to create employment-office profits. From an early date the solution to this problem was the creation of an employment exchange, a nonprofit agency to bring together servant and mistress in a respectable place and to encourage loyalty and moral uplift among servants. In 1825 a group of New Yorkers formed the Society for the Encouragement of Faithful Domestic Servants in New-York, which in turn opened an intelligence office. The office was intended to recruit and develop faithful and respectable servants—the major concern of the employers. In imitation of a similar London society, it also was to award prizes to servants "who have distinguished themselves by their good conduct, and by having remained in their respective places one, two and three or more years." The employment office was a most successful innovation, and similar exchanges would subsequently be opened in other American cities.[10]

Nonetheless, these exchanges had little overall impact on the marketplace. Compared to private agencies they were never very numerous. Moreover, though they frequently had a paid manager, they were products of voluntary associations whose members' interests in the project would eventually wane. Most importantly, they were even more closely allied with the interests of employers than were the private agencies. The New York society took seriously its mission to screen out risky employees and only send out worthy ones. It declared letters of recommendations to be essential requisites for servants seeking a place, although no thought was given to having servants evaluate their mistresses. The information was compiled into a list "of those who may be reported as unworthy." "This species of intelligence," the society's report declared, "is really *more important* than the more gratifying information of fidelity. . . . Already several have been reported as intemperate, or otherwise vicious, to whose names the Agent has affixed a mark, which will effectually prevent them from imposing a second time upon subscribers." This blacklisting, based on an unreliable system of personalized and impressionistic employer reports, could hardly have been acceptable to most domestics. Some servants were quick to grasp the society's interests, and the agent sometimes received reports that the objects of the society were opposed to the interests of servants. Societies also kept records on their offices' activities, classifying servants by race and place of birth. Their open objective was to encourage white native-born women to enter service. This concern could easily have discouraged the many immigrant and black women who comprised the majority of servants seeking places. Moreover, while some women probably found security in the moral concerns of the exchanges, others probably felt questions about morality were an invasion of privacy. At least private agents respected their privacy by ignoring personal morality or religion. In any case, employment exchanges never offered sustained competition to private agencies.[11]

Having found a position through a personal reference, a newspaper ad, or an employment agency, the live-in domestic reported to her employer's home. The first contact between servant and mistress established the tone of the relationship; the mistress was addressed as "Mrs. ——" or "ma'am," the servant by her given name. Frequently the servant started work the next day, the employer allowing her a short period to collect her baggage. The work agreement was a verbal one, generally specifying wages, time off, and the general area of work tasks—whether or not the servant cooked, washed, ironed, and so forth. The specific nature of the work and living conditions were worked out on the job. Often a girl entered employment without any time for adjustment. Lillian Pettengill more often than not found herself left on her own to begin work immediately. Mistresses left the housecleaning and kitchen chores to the new servant, which meant entering the kitchen for the first time with the sink piled high with dishes, and with pots and other things left lying around. For example, a servant reported to Helen Campbell of her first position: "It was a handsome house an' elegant things in the parlors an' bedrooms, but my heart sunk when she took me into the kitchen. The last girl had gone off in a rage an' left everything, an' there was grease and dirt from floor to ceiling."[12]

Generally the first week was considered a probationary period for both employer and employee, and either could end the contract after the week was up without prior notice. Thereafter some advance notice was expected. The verbal contract with all of its ambiguities persisted, although reformers pushed for written contracts to spell out the mutual responsibilities. Because domestic service involved the hiring of a person rather than just the obtaining of her labor, both servant and mistress probably felt that the complex interrelationships could not be adequately defined. The atomization of the work and the lack of commercial experience of the women involved also worked against the introduction of set contracts. Legal enforcement of contracts would have meant dependence on attorneys and the judicial system, and courtroom litigation was an expensive process inappropriate to the small sums or damages that might be involved. Finally, legal action would have established legal principles of servants' rights, which mistresses preferred to treat, if and when granted, as privileges. Contracts, then, would have restricted the employer's potential control and power.[13]

The live-in servant had to be very concerned about her living conditions in her employer's home, since workplace and home were combined. This was somewhat similar to the situation during the preindustrial period, when much industry had been based in the household. Industrialization moved most manufacturing outside the home but left very little mark on domestic service. More accurately, service was a nonindustrial rather than a preindustrial occupation. While some activities were done outside the home, such as breadbaking and washing, the household necessarily remained the essential base, since domestic service by definition was work within the home. The distinctive structure of domestic service centered on the unique personalized mistress/servant relationship between women. Whether the servants lived in or were day workers, that intense personal interaction remained and had no comparable counterpart in any other occupation. (See chapters 4 and 5 for a discussion of the mistress/servant relationship.)

The process of getting a job was inadequate preparation for a servant's entry into her new household. Mistresses and employment agencies often misrepresented the conditions under which an employee would be living. The strategy in hiring servants seemed "to be to resort to any means to get an employee and trust to other devices to keep her." Almost

every ad promised a good home. An Irish servant reported
that she "kept shy" of such advertisements. Even a personal
interview with the prospective employer in her own home
could be misleading, as one servant discovered: a handsome
and elegant parlor shielded dirty and depressing servants'
quarters and kitchen.[14]

The quality of a servant's living quarters depended upon
the class, wealth, values, life-style, and benevolence of the
employer family. As Lillian Pettengill discovered, a single
domestic could encounter a wide range of differences in servant living space from comfortable, clean, airy rooms and
kitchens to third-story rooms with hardly more space than a
closet. In the best households, a servant would have a room
fit for a daughter of the family. In the worst, servants had no
room of their own. Frances Kellor found cases where "the
only sleeping quarters provided are such as an ironing board
placed over the bath-tub; a bed made up for two on the dining room table." Gail Laughlin reported cases of a maid
sleeping in a closet, without light or fresh air, while another
slept in the kitchen. More typically, servants' quarters were
rooms in the third-story attic filled with worn-out family furniture. The water closet for servants was, in most houses, in
dark, poorly ventilated corners of the basement. And when
more than one maid worked in a household, two or more
women often had to share facilities inadequate for one. Almira, a servant in New York City in the 1880s, found that
she was expected to share a single bed in a sparsely furnished
room with another servant. On examining the bed, she saw
that "the two ragged comfortables were foul with long use."
The other servant told her that there was a better room available, and she asked the mistress for her own clean room.
"What impudence is this," the employer retorted. "You'll
take what I give you and be thankful to get it. Plenty as good
as you have slept in that room and never complained." Almira left that day.[15]

It is difficult to evaluate objectively the living conditions of
servants between the Civil War and World War I. Most servants were very critical of the inadequate and undesirable

conditions they found, while less commonly, some expressed satisfaction with their situations. Mistresses defended their own servants' quarters, yet the poor conditions to be found in other employers' houses were widely acknowledged. Part of the problem lay in the nature of the sources. The most extensive writings on domestic service come either from mistresses, who almost always present themselves as ideal employers, or from middle-class women who have worked as servants. The latter group tended to be older than most domestics and perhaps were less adaptable to change. Moreover, they tended, either implicitly or explicitly, to compare the conditions under which they lived as servants to the comforts of their own middle-class homes, which they inevitably reported were superior. Yet at the same time they often expressed a sympathetic understanding of the mistress's efforts, since they themselves shared so much of the employer's point of view. State labor bureaus and such independent investigators as Kellor recorded extensive criticism by servants of the conditions encountered, with only an occasional reference to an employee finding better living conditions in her workplace than she had in her own family. Yet surely many domestic servants—especially many poor black and immigrant girls who were sent out to work in their early teens—must have found their employers' homes more comfortable than those of their parents'. If servants tended to be overcritical (and probably they were) it was a justifiable reaction. To a great degree the unhappiness expressed in condemnations of their living conditions reflected two conditions they could not change: whatever the standard of living for the servants, it was inferior to that of the employing family, and unlike all other workers servants were powerless to determine their living environment.

No servant expected to live at the same level of comfort as the family employing her, but every distinction between the world of family and that of the servant served as a reminder of her inability to control her own living conditions. Although a servant would work in every room of the house, her living area was clearly restricted. At the least it included a bedroom, the kitchen, a basement water closet, and possibly a back porch. Privileges might extend to the dining room and sewing room, and occasionally though less frequently, to the bathroom. Mistresses required their servants to meet the hygienic standards of the household, but not by using the same facilities as the family. In the Kinderlieber household, Pettengill was not permitted to use the bathroom but instead had to use the kitchen sink for taking a bath. The servant was not provided with towels. In another case a servant denied access to the bathroom carried water up three flights from the kitchen to her room. The interruptions while she was bathing were so numerous, however, that she "soon ceased to bathe with any regularity."[16]

The servants' diet also depended upon the wisdom, generosity, and eating habits of their employers, and this was true for day workers as well as live-in servants. Most commonly, mistresses had their servants eat foods less expensive and elaborate than those served on their own table. But even in households where the domestic ate what her employer did, this might prove inadequate. Lillian Pettengill worked for three generous sisters who shared their food with her, but she found herself getting weaker and growing thinner. While the food her mistresses ate was adequate for their needs, it provided insufficient nutrition for the heavy physical labor that the servant had to perform. Another servant encountered the same situation: "her table did not give me strength to do my work." Some mistresses kept and measured out food as a family treasure. A servant told how her employers "were set in their ways an' they had some money. But every day . . . the lady cut off herself from the meat what she though I ought to have, an' ordered me to put away the rest. She allowed no dessert except on Sunday, an' she kept cake and preserves locked in an upstair closet."[17]

Another aspect of limited freedom was the extremely long workdays. Servants averaged about two more hours of work daily than other working women, and long after the 5½-day workweek had become prevalent, household workers continued to work seven days a week. For many domestics the workday ran from before dawn until after nightfall. "I used to get up at four o'clock every morning," a Minneapolis housemaid recalled of her four weeks with a family, "and work until ten P.M. every day of the week. Mondays and Tuesdays, when the washing and ironing was to be done, I used to get up at two o'clock and wash or iron until breakfast time." Another Minnesota domestic arose at 5:00 A.M. and worked until 9:30 P.M. "It nearly killed me," she commented. A servant in Kansas, twenty-two years old, had worked for ten years with one family, laboring thirteen to fourteen hours a day, seven days a week. In Virginia, Orra Langhorne reported in 1890 that household workers worked from five or six in the morning until ten at night. These long working days and weeks were not atypical; investigations of hours of service gave the range of hours from part-time labor at five or six hours daily to live-in servants working fifteen- to eighteen-hour days.[18]

Nearly all domestics in the nineteenth century worked at least ten hours a day, with a full working day averaging eleven to twelve hours (see Table 3–1). As the number of hours in the average workday in industry and commerce decreased, so did the length of a servant's average working day, but a gap still remained. The eight-hour day in manufacturing and offices was equivalent to the ten-hour day in household work. Outside the South, however, day workers tended to work the same hours as women in other nonservice occupations until it gradually was reduced to an eight-hour day. In the South, day workers probably worked the same hours as other servants. Cooks, on the other hand, worked considerably fewer hours than other Southern household workers. Generally the cook only worked until late afternoon, leaving after she had cooked breakfast, the traditional midday dinner, and a light supper to be served after she was gone. Long work hours were considered an inherent part of domestic work, and at the turn of the century, when state legislatures began to put restrictions on women's work, household employment was excluded. In 1906, Josephine Goldmark reported that four states—Indiana, Massachusetts,

Seven Days a Week

Table 3–1. Daily Hours of Work, Female Servants

Year	Sample	N	Range of hours	Percentage working ten or more hours	Average daily hours
1887	Minnesota	36	8–15	94	12:24
1889–90	United States	1,434	5–18	75	
1894	Kansas	241	8–14*		10:36
1894	Baltimore slums	149	5–15	93	11:42
	Chicago slums	192	4–17	70	10:30
	New York slums	168	4–15	82	10:54
1898	Massachusetts				
	All servants	245	8:26–12:47†	84	10:29‡
	General housework only	127	9:30–11:24†	91	10:23‡
c. 1900	United States				
	Employer response				9:05
	Employee response				12:12
1900	Boston	20	7½–15½		11:36
1910	Maine	117	6–24	55	9:56

*Range of average hours worked in fifteen cities.

†Range of hours averages of classes grouped by job and wages.

‡Average hours daily computed in report by dividing total weekly hours by seven. Thus actual daily average on a typical workday (excluding Sunday or day off) was 11:25 for all servants and 11:20 for general housekeepers.

Sources: 1887 Minnesota: Minnesota, Bureau of Labor Statistics, *Biennial Report 1887–8* (n.p., 1887), p. 140. 1889–90 U.S.: Lucy Maynard Salmon, *Domestic Service* (New York, 1897), pp. 143–144. 1894 Kansas: Kansas Bureau of Labor and Industry, *Annual Report 1894* (Topeka, 1895), pp. 178, 198. 1894 slums: U.S. Commissioner of Labor, *Special Report 1894: The Slums of Baltimore, Chicago, New York and Philadelphia* (Washington, D.C., 1894), pp. 220–221, 271–274, 341–343. 1898 Massachusetts: "Hours of Labor in Domestic Service," *Massachusetts Labor Bulletin* No. 8 (October 1898), pp. 2–6, 22. 1900 U.S.: Gail Laughlin, "Domestic Service," *Report [and Testimony] of the Industrial Commission . . .* , vol. XIV (19 vols.; Washington, D.C., 1901), p. 756. 1900 Boston: [Mary E. Trueblood], "Social Statistics of Workingwomen," *Massachusetts Labor Bulletin* No. 18 (May 1901), pp. 37–38. 1910 Maine: Maine Bureau of Industrial and Labor Statistics, *Annual Report 1910* (Augusta, 1910), p. 333.

Nebraska, and New York—prohibited the employment of women at night. In Indiana and Massachusetts, the ban was confined to manufacturing occupations; in the two other states, to both industry and commerce. Nineteen states had laws limiting the number of hours per day and per week that women could work. Most laws applied exclusively to manufacturing, but some, such as Pennsylvania's more general legislation, specifically exempted domestic service, as did California's eight-hour-day law.[19]

When she wasn't asleep, a live-in domestic was at the beck

and call of her mistress. Work and rest time, other than time outside the house (discussed below), were allotted at the discretion of the employer. The ten, eleven, or twelve hours of work—"busy time"—were spread over twelve to fifteen hours, allowing the servant time for meals and perhaps, as in the household where Inez Godman had worked, an hour or so of rest each afternoon before preparing dinner. The remainder of the day, from quitting time to bedtime, could be used for rest, or if she had enough energy, for reading, sewing, and so forth. For a few hours of that time, the servant was "on call"; she had to be available to answer any summons from the household. During rest time in which a servant was not on call, she still could be summoned to work, but unless she had been notified in advance, only an emergency would justify an encroachment on this time off. Realistically, then, call time should be added to busy time to measure accurately the length of a servant's work day. The only study to examine call time, the 1898 Massachusetts study of domestic working hours, reported an average-day call time of one hour, forty-one minutes the first week and one hour, thirty-nine minutes the second, raising the average working day to twelve hours, ten minutes and twelve hours, four minutes during the first and second week respectively. If busy and call time are combined and days on which servants had time off or a half-day holiday are excluded, the average working day was thirteen hours, thirteen minutes the first week and thirteen hours, nine minutes the second.[20]

The only time a servant fully controlled was that spent outside her employer's house. Since few live-in servants were free to leave the house when not actually working, it was only during their time out that they had the same independence enjoyed by other working women. By the 1880s most urban and governmental employees worked 5½-day weeks; Saturday had become a "half-holiday." According to Blaine McKinley, household workers' time out also increased at about that same time. Prior to the 1870s, regular servant holidays had been limited generally to one evening or half-day (part of an afternoon and all the evening) per week or every other week. By the 1880s part of a Sunday and one other evening out per week had become customary. Maud Nathan recalled that in New York City during the 1880s "every other Sunday afternoon and evening and one evening a week was the invariable rule." By the turn of the century, Thursday afternoons and Sunday evenings became stereotyped as servants' time out. Mary Trueblood confirmed this pattern in her study of twenty Boston domestics. The two most prevalent holiday patterns she recorded were: every other Sunday and Thursday afternoon off, and part of every other Sunday and Thursday. Lucy Maynard Salmon, on the other hand, recorded 1,000 employees with at least one afternoon out a week and 400 with part of a Sunday off. Thursday, she concluded, was not a servant's universal holiday. At the same time, 3 percent of the employers Salmon questioned said that they did not give their domestics any specific time off. Similarly, the Massachusetts study of 1898 reported that 91 employees the first week and 80 employees the second week out of a total of 245 had received no day off. Even servants with time out as part of their oral contract of employment found it difficult to consistently take the free time. As Lillian Pettengill found out, employers occasionally demanded that servants forgo their day off because of some household crisis—workmen coming to do repairs or to paint, last-minute guests for dinner, and so forth. Thus the regular day out was somewhat less than regular, and less frequent than the Thursdays and Sunday off associated with service.[21]

Sundays and days on which they had afternoons out were anything but days of rest for domestics. Their time out of the house came after working what would have been nearly a full's day work in any other occupation. The 1898 Massachusetts study investigated the actual time domestics labored on days out and Sundays. On both days the domestics averaged between seven and seven and a half working hours (see Table 3–2). The range of hours worked was wide, with seamstresses, cooks, and a single waitress working the fewest hours. Nursemaids and general houseworkers tended to labor the longest. Indeed, some servants found Sunday and holi-

Table 3–2. Hours Worked, Day Out and Sunday, Female Servants, Massachusetts, 1898

	First week	*Second week*
Day out		
Number with time out (n = 245)	154	164
Average hours worked	7 hours, 30 minutes	7 hours, 12 minutes
Range of hours	4:45–9:00	5:00–9:00
Sundays		
Average hours worked	7 hours, 24 minutes	7 hours, 18 minutes
Range of hours	2:30–12:00	2:00–11:30

Source: "Hours of Labor in Domestic Service," *Massachusetts Labor Bulletin* No. 8 (October 1898), pp. 14–17.

day work (Thanksgiving and Christmas) especially trying. "Sunday in a private family," a servant wrote Lucy Maynard Salmon, "is usually anything but a day of rest to the domestic, for on that day there are usually guests to dinner or tea or both, which means extra work."[22]

Long workdays seven days a week and restricted free time left servants isolated from ordinary social interaction. More than anything else, servants felt this loss of freedom. It was further compounded by the restrictions on their right to receive friends in their living quarters. In a study of 181 families employing 231 servants in 1899, Mary Dewson found that 86 percent of the servants were free to entertain women friends, and 81 percent male acquaintances. Yet in actual practice, 51 servants received no visitors during the weeks of investigation, while 64 had no women callers and 118 no male visitors (see Table 3–3). Mistresses severely restricted where a servant could entertain. Dewson found that 150 servants could use only the kitchen to entertain, while 30 could use the kitchen or their room. Only one was permitted to use the parlor. An employer often expressed her dissatisfaction at a servant's "company," even when she permitted her to entertain. Male visitors of course were nearly always discouraged, but so also were other women visitors and even parents. Inez Godman recounted that "during my ten weeks

Table 3–3. Visitors to Live-in Servants per Week, Boston, 1899

Average number of women callers per week	Number of replies	Average number of men callers per week	Number of replies
1	28	1	48
2	39	2	9
3	29	3	5
4	13	4	—
5	3	5	2
6	3	6	1
7	2	7	—
Few	13	Few	12
Not any	64	Not any	118
Unknown	37	Unknown	36
	231		231

Source: "Social Conditions in Domestic Service," *Massachusetts Labor Bulletin* No. 13 (February 1900), p. 11.

in a kitchen my father and mother dropped in twice for a few minutes in the evening and the lady was annoyed." Godman, when not masquerading as a servant, employed domestics in her own home, and she recognized that it could be "disagreeable" to have visitors in her own kitchen. Another servant reported: "In some families no acquaintances can call on the servant; she may have one or two friends, but the number is always limited, because, says the lady of the house, not without truth, 'who wants a dozen strange girls running in and out of one's back door?' " Finally, mistresses generally made it clear that whatever freedom a domestic had was a privilege granted by the mistress. As an incentive to insure tenure of service, one employer said, "I allow my girls to invite their female friends to afternoon tea and dinner, and I give their male friends the freedom of my kitchen for purposes of courtship." In allowing this practice, she of course could as easily arbitrarily withdraw it.[23]

Living in one's employer's home was not the same as living in one's own home. "Home is the place where the loved ones lived," a servant said, "a place of freedom, with the companionship of equals on equal terms. Home is not the kitchen and back bedroom of a house belonging to another." The employer independently determined the quality and structure of the home environment provided to the servant. Other working women could order their priorities and arrange their periods of freedom; servants were powerless to do so. A factory or shop worker could improve her home or diet; the servant could not exercise such an option. Other women were free to see friends whenever they wished and under the conditions they wanted; domestics had little choice in such matters. Indeed, industrialization and urbanization increased the free choices available to shop, factory, and office workers as the number of hours worked per week decreased and more and more single women lived apart from their families. A report in the *Massachusetts Labor Bulletin* astutely summarized the ambiguous position of domestics: "She is in the family, but not of it," read the report. "There is neither the clear recognition of mutual responsibility and reciprocal rights and duties which marked the old relation of mistress and servant, nor the equally well-defined relations which in industrial or mercantile employment exist between employer and employee. The domestic has ceased to be a servant as that term was formerly used ["help"]; she has not yet become an employé, as that term is now used in industrial occupations." Domestic service, though, was changing as live-in service gave way to live-out work by the time of World War I. But while living out transferred control over servants' nonworking time to them, the personalized mistress/servant relationship remained, as did employer control over the work.[24]

When a servant entered a household to live and work, usually she found herself alone as the only full-time paid employee, and she worked doing general household work—the "maid-of-all-work." If two servants were present—the next most common pattern—the second would be a cook. Nearly all families with servants employed a laundress or washerwoman, either as a once-or-twice-weekly day worker or as an independent contractor who took the wash home. In the South, it was most common to have both a general houseworker and a cook as well as a regular washerwoman. As day workers replaced live-in servants among the urban middle class, the maid-of-all-work remained as the essential servant.

Although job titles proliferated among domestic workers toward the end of the nineteenth century, in middle-class households the work was not significantly specialized. Maintaining a large household staff, each servant with a specific task, was a European upper-class pattern adopted by the American upper class. These American aristocrats, who built castles and forty-room "cottages" in such places as Newport, Rhode Island, and whose mansions lined New York City's Fifth Avenue, filled their vast domains with butlers, valets, coachmen, footmen, housekeepers, lady's maids, cooks, waitresses, scullery maids, nurses, parlor maids, chambermaids, and laundresses, most of whom were brought from Europe. Middle-class families with three or more servants emulated this pattern, so that the movement appeared to be toward specialization of household work. In theory, work would be divided among specialists who had developed defined skills; in reality, however, the division of labor was arbitrary and ever-changing, and specialization never developed to any significant degree. Except for a small group of urban cooks whose skills approached those of a chef (a title not applied to female cooks), servants moved from one job to another, regardless of the specialized title. Even in the South, where there were four distinct and common servant roles—cook, servant, child nurse, and washerwoman—the worker's age and marital status and the availability of positions were more important than her experience or training in determining her area of specialization. Teenagers tended to be nurses; young single women, maids-of-all-work; and married women, cooks and laundresses. At the same time, women were free to move back and forth among the jobs. Thus regardless of job title nearly all servants were general household workers. Perhaps the growth of specialized jobs reflected the desire for upward mobility of some middle-class families.

Although most families with servants employed only one maid-of-all-work, often they expected a specialized work performance similar to that encountered in upper-class households. "Families employing but one domestic servant, in

Staff of Stevens family at Castle Point, Hoboken, New Jersey, 1895. (Photograph by Byron. The Byron Collection, Museum of the City of New York.)

many if not in most cases," Gail Laughlin concluded, "want as varied and elegant service as is enjoyed by families which employ more than one servant." In analyzing American occupations in 1903 Gilson Willets concurred when he noted that "most employers insist on maintaining a degree of style compatible with the employment of several servants." It was simply impossible for most servants to meet the ceaseless demands of their mistresses, even working from before dawn to after nightfall.[25]

Domestic work differed from region to region and between urban and rural areas in the United States. Just as home furnishings and family values vary according to class, race, ethnicity, tradition, and the personalities of family members, so too did the conditions under which servants labored. Nonetheless, certain general patterns emerge from the literature on servants, the servant problem, household technology, and household architecture. Domestic work was really three jobs in one. Each of the first two discussed below would have been a full-time job in itself; yet more often than not a single employee performed all three. The first set of duties consisted of the ordinary routine of household tasks, performed daily. The second set included the weekly chores, each segment taking one day but collectively requiring six days' work. The last job was monthly or seasonal work, performed occasionally, but nonetheless adding another burden to the already full day of daily and weekly work.

The best way of illustrating the daily and weekly cycles is to follow a general household worker through a part of her week's work. Inez Godman recorded her activities on a typical workday in 1901. She worked in a Northern home, doing all of the work except the wash. She had negotiated a 75¢-a-week reduction in wages to $2.75 in return for her mistress hiring the wash out. Godman began work on a Wednesday afternoon and immediately prepared the dinner. Apparently no time was allotted for her to adjust to her new work and living environment. Wearing the apron and cap provided her, she served the meal. After cleaning up the kitchen and dining room, she prepared bread dough; her mistress had become "weary of baker's stuff." At 9:00 P.M. she was through for the day.[26]

On Thursday she rose at 6:00 A.M. and served breakfast an hour later. By 9:30 A.M. the kitchen and dining room had been cleaned, and her weekly chores began. She spent two hours cleaning the sitting room. "Everything had to be carried into the adjoining room, and there was much china and bric-a-brac," she wrote. The carpet had to be moved, and each slat of the Venetian blinds wiped clean. Twice she had to go to the kitchen to check the bread she was baking (it had risen overnight), and five times she had to answer the doorbell. Lunch required an hour of preparation, and she served her mistress at one. Already she had worked seven hours: "I was thankful for a chance to sit, and dawdled over my lunch for half an hour." By 2:30 P.M. the kitchen and dining room were clean again, and her mistress suggested Godman clean the kitchen floor. Afterwards, she rested in her room from 3:20 to 4:00 P.M.. At 4:00 she had to go downstairs to heat the oven and begin the evening meal. "Dinner was a complex meal," she explained, "and coming at night when I was tired was always something of a worry. To have the different courses ready at just the right moment, to be sure that nothing burned or curdled while I was waiting on the table, to think quickly and act calmly; all this meant weariness."[27]

The alternation of the daily and weekly chores continued during each day. On Friday after breakfast she cleaned the halls, stairs, vestibule, and bathroom: "It was heavy work, for the halls were carpeted with moquette, but I sat on the stairs as I swept them with a whisk broom, thus saving my feet." Before lunch she had gone to the market, then returned and made the midday deal. After cleaning the kitchen and dining room and doing the weekly cleaning of the refrigerator, she wearily climbed to her room. She passed her mistress, who "sat with a flushed face still sewing." She offered to help, and her mistress responded: "I don't know how to rush sewing but I wish to wear this skirt to-morrow, and if you *would* do it I would like to rest." Godman finished it in half an hour. She still had another hour of rest, since she was cooking fish for dinner and would not have to light the oven. She could rest until 4:30. She was rewarded for doing the skirt; her employer gave her Saturday evening off, since she was going out to dinner.[28]

Sunday was filled with daily chores, but Godman was pressed for time because she had to help her mistress dress for church. She rushed and managed to finish by 2:00 P.M. so she could attend a Sunday school class. That night she served a light supper and managed to retire at 8:00 P.M. On Monday morning she cleaned the dining room, polished silver, did the marketing, and baked bread. Since guests were invited to dinner that evening she worked straight through her afternoon break, and did not finish cleaning up until 10:00 P.M. Monday had turned into a sixteen-hour workday, including time for meals. The laundress came on Tuesday, and Godman spent all afternoon plus all day Wednesday and

part of Thursday between her daily chores and ironing. But
Thursday began a new weekly cycle. Wisely her mistress
went out for lunch that first week so Godman could complete
the ironing and clean the sitting room without having to
make lunch and clean up. She finished the ironing at 11:00
A.M. Thursday and then went to the sitting room. She simply rested there for an hour, then cleaned the room in just
twenty minutes. Though she thought it looked clean, she
knew it was not thoroughly done. Each week she failed to
complete the ironing on Wednesday; it was physically impossible for her. The result was that Thursday was "a hard
day, for my lady did not go out to luncheon after that first
week, and with her in the house I could not slight the work
nor stop to rest. Every Thursday night I was ready to
collapse."[29]

Inez Godman's full workdays are typical. Daily chores for
the maid-of-all-work included lighting fires (in stoves, for hot
water, in winter fireplaces or furnaces), preparing and serving meals and cleaning up, making beds, doing light dusting,
sweeping or scrubbing front steps and porch, answering the
doorbell, and running errands. The weekly cycle, dominated
by washing, ironing, and heavy cleaning, was more physically demanding. A typical week would begin with washing
on Monday, ironing on Tuesday, and mending on Wednesday. On Thursday the dining room would be thoroughly
cleaned, including the polishing of silver and glass. On Friday the house would be swept and the windows cleaned.
Saturday would entail major housecleaning—the kitchen, cellar, and rooms not cleaned thoroughly on other days—and
then perhaps breadbaking. Repetition of tasks made the work
monotonous, but the complaint heard most seemed to be that
of physical fatigue and tiredness. Over and over again
women mentioned how they often collapsed in bed at the
end of the day, too tired to read or even take a bath. "If one
of the twelve labors of Hercules had been to solve the servant
girl problem," one servant wrote, "he never would have had
the reputation he has."[30]

Inefficient organization of household work often added to

the domestic's labor. Too often mistresses were concerned only about their personal relationship with the servant. Many employers failed to understand the rhythms of housework; by giving new commands only after a job was finished, they made it impossible for the servant to anticipate the work and pace her energies. Or the domestic equivalent of speed-up on factory assembly lines developed when guests were expected for dinner and inadequate time had been left for preparations. The failure of housewives to set breakfast menus meant cooking a different meal for each individual family member. While this was part of a full-time cook's duties, a general houseworker faced with regular daily and weekly chores would find herself constantly behind. Even with a set schedule many servants found it difficult to complete the work. The tasks might be too much for one servant, as Godman found with the ironing. Or she might be interrupted again and again to tend to her mistress' needs of the moment. "She'd sit in her sitting-room on the second floor," a domestic complained of her mistress, "and ring for me twenty times a day to do little things, and she wanted me up till eleven to answer the bell, for she had a great deal of company." Another counted the number of times she climbed the three flights of stairs to answer the doorbell and and her mistress' summonses: forty times a day! Since the employer furnished the tools of work, the servant was dependent on the judgment and generosity of the mistress. Often the tools of the kitchen and of the house were inadequate and the servant had to make do at the expense of lengthening her workday.[31]

In the South servants had greater control over their work and were less subject to interference. The tradition of black household labor dated back to slavery, so Southern housewives were less likely to take an active interest in the housework or hover over the servants. Left mostly on their own, at least as far as the work was concerned, they tended to set their own pace and develop their own systems. Southern housewives were more likely to defer to the advice of their servants on matters regarding tools and food, and thus

Southern servants had a greater say in how they did the work and what they cooked. Furthermore, because most domestics lived out, the number of hours a servant had to work was finite, and many women—especially the cooks—returned to their own houses during rest time. Nearly all Southern families employing household labor hired a general houseworker, a cook, and a weekly washerwoman, thus easing the burden on the workers. And with black men hired as domestics performing the heavier weekly chores and nearly all the monthly and seasonal labor, the work itself was less demanding. For married black women working as domestics this was hardly a comfort, however, since they still had to work full time and then work in their own homes.

While the patterns and rhythms of domestic work remained constant from the nineteenth century into the twentieth, the actual tasks themselves were changing. In the middle of the nineteenth century household work was labor-intensive. Most work was done with only minimal mechanical assistance, and many of the items consumed or used by the family were produced at home. Meals had to be prepared from scratch; few commercially prepared items were available to shorten the process. Discussions of dough-making and bread-baking took up much space in every household guidebook. Vegetables and fruit had to be canned or made into preserves for the winter months. Candles and soap and other laundry aids were made in the kitchen. A small amount of hot water was available in the water back—a water reservoir attached to the stove—but water for bathing, cleaning, and washing had to be heated on the stove. A stove hot enough to boil large quantities of water was too hot to use for cooking; and while a hot stove did heat the kitchen in winter, it also overheated it in the summer. Nearly all houses were heated by open fires, which had to be tended regularly. Improper chimney flues—a frequent architectural defect—made smoke-filled kitchens and rooms common, while the coal or wood left a residue throughout the house. At mid-century, washing and ironing together constituted "the most trying department of housekeeping." At least four separate

Women washing clothes in turn-of-the-century Queens County, New York. (Photograph by Jeanette Bernard. Culver Pictures.)

washes—white, coarse white, flannels, and colored clothes—and an appropriate number of tubs and amount of heated water were required. Washing and ironing was considered back-breaking labor. Ironing in particular required the constant lifting and replacement of the irons, a strenuous weight-lifting chore.[32]

SEARS, ROEBUCK & CO., Cheapest Supply House on Earth, Chicago. CATALOGUE No. 111. 569

HOUSE FURNISHING HARDWARE DEPARTMENT.

IT IS OUR AIM to illustrate and describe in the following pages, a full and complete line of house furnishing hardware and culinary utensils such as is found only in the highest class hardware stores in large cities.

WE GIVE OUR CUSTOMERS THE BENEFIT of an assortment of all grades of goods, from the cheapest to the most expensive to select from, which has heretofore been enjoyed only by the comparatively few who chanced to reside in large cities, and in many lines we show a greater variety than is carried in stock by any one retail store even in the largest cities.

THERE IS NO MANUFACTURER of high grade kitchen utensils whose goods are not represented in our stock and we illustrate in our catalogue a great variety of labor saving devices,

which tend to make the house work a pleasure instead of drudgery.

OUR LINE OF WASHING MACHINES is the most extensive in America and includes every pattern for which there is any demand. Our refrigerators are made by one of the largest and oldest makers in the country, are of the most approved pattern, and our Seroco porcelain enameled, steel lined refrigerator represents the most advanced ideas in sanitary refrigerator construction. In fact, there is not an article in this line, large or small of any merit, which you will not find listed in the following pages, and at prices which are fixed 20 to 60 per cent lower than it would cost you at home.

WE DO NOT DEAL with middlemen or wholesale dealers; all our goods are bought direct from the manufacturers, and owing to the quantities of goods our enormous trade requires, we are their most desirable customers and buy lower than any wholesale dealer in the country. We sell these goods to you at but a small advance over manufacturers' cost, and at a lower price than the ordinary retail dealer can buy them from his wholesaler.

GREATEST VALUES EVER KNOWN IN WASHING MACHINES.

We Ask Your Orders for These Well Known and Highest Grade Machines Made, Because We Offer the Best and Can Save You Money.

INSTRUCTIONS FOR USING COMBINATION WASHERS. Fill machine from one-half to two-thirds full of hot strong soap suds, and put in six or seven sheets or the equivalent of these clothes for one washing. Work the machine from ten to twelve minutes, wring out and rinse through clear water, blue and hang on the line. Always keep nuts and bolts on machine tight. A wrench is provided with each machine for this purpose. All bearings should be kept slightly lubricated. Do not allow water to stand in machine. Dry out well after using and keep lid open.

HOW TO USE the Fulton American, Scott's Western, Desplaines American, Chicago American or Continental Washers. Soak your clothes the evening before washday, soaping the dirty spots well with good hard soap. When thoroughly soaked, pass them through wringer and place them in the machine. Do not put over six to eight shirts and about half-dozen towels or handkerchiefs in the machine, then fill the machine with hot, strong soap suds until the clothes are well covered, work the lever about ten minutes, wring, rinse and blue your clothes, and they are ready for the line. If accustomed to it, boil the clothes before rinsing; it is not absolutely necessary when good soap is used.

DIRECTIONS FOR USING the Quick and Easy and Sears Washers. Soak the clothes and soap the dirty parts well before washing. Put in the necessary amount of clothes to be washed and add a wash boiler full of hot soapy water, or enough to cover the clothes thoroughly. Operate the machine about ten minutes. Take off the dirty water and fill the machine with clear water. Operate the machine about two or three minutes and the clothes will be rinsed. When through washing, rinse the machine with cold water, hang up lower cylinder on the upper one. Allow the machine to stand open until thoroughly dry.

WE SHIP OUR No. 23R100 to No. 23R138 WASHING MACHINES from Ft. Wayne, Ind., and St. Louis, Mo., and our Nos. 23R140 and 23R143 from Richmond, Va., where we can save our customers any freight by doing so, otherwise we ship from Chicago.

Fulton American No. 1 Washer.

$4.44

Illustration showing inside crate removed.

No. 23R100 This machine is our old standby improved, with our patent malleable iron enameled pinwheel. The crate inside is independent of the tub and can be removed after the washing is done. The machine is made out of white pine, painted and grained an ash color and finished in every respect first class. It will wash five shirts at a time clean, without the use of a washboard, and is fully warranted in every respect. Size, 23x11 inches. Weight, 54 pounds. Price, each.............$4.44

The Chicago American Washer, No. 22.

$2.75

Interior view of No. 22.

No. 23R102 This machine is of the same size and capacity as the No. 1 Fulton American but instead of the loose crate the staves and bottom of it are corrugated. It is made and finished the same as the No. 1, and warranted to do good work. Parties wanting a cheaper machine will do well to try this before buying any other. Inside dimensions, 23x11 inches. Weight, 47 pounds.
Price, each..............................$2.75

The Desplaines American Washer No. 5.

$2.72

No. 23R104 This machine was gotten up at the special request of some of our customers. It is of the same make and finish as our No. 22 Chicago American. Staves and bottom are corrugated; in fact it is the No. 22 Chicago American reversed. Inside dimensions, 23x11 inches. Weight, 47 pounds.
Price, each......$2.72

The Sears Washer.

$5.66

No. 23R110 This machine is made on the rubber principle, the same as used in the Quick and Easy but has two cylinders working in opposite directions at the same motion of the crank shaft, thus cleaning the clothes quicker and more thoroughly than the former machine. It will not tear the clothes and on account of the balance wheel, the machine will work so easy that a child can work it without being fatigued. We have found that the yellow cottonwood grown in the low lands of Arkansas and Mississippi is the best lumber for washing machines, and we have adopted the same in all the box machines. Well made, well painted and varnished, and all the iron parts coming in contact with the water are heavily tinned or galvanized. Weight, 93 pounds.
Price, each, wringer not included............$5.66

The Acme Combination Washer.

This Machine is Warranted not to Leak.

$4.25

In Use — Open

The latest and as we believe the best invention in Washing Machines yet made. This machine combines the reciprocal pinwheel motion with an oscillating movement of the whole suds box. The main advantage that we claim for this machine is that **it works fully one-third easier than any other machine** that operates with a pinwheel agitator, that it takes less water (only four pails), and that it is more simple in construction than any other machine now on the market. The machine when open, locks itself, so that a wringer can be attached on the wringer board without tilting it; a small key inserted in the gear will keep it from tilting when full, thereby preventing accidents of any kind. The machine is well made out of the best yellow cottonwood, finished in superior and excellent style, and we can recommend it and will warrant the same as **the best family washer** that we know of. A 30 days' guarantee goes with every machine sold.

No. 23R114 Family Size Acme Combination Washer No. 11. Size, 15¼x25½x10¼ inches. Weight, 67 pounds. Price, each........................$4.25

No. 23R116 Family Size Ball Bearing Acme Combination Washer No. 6. Weight, 73 pounds.
Price, each..............................$4.90

No. 23R118 Large Size Acme Combination Washer No. 12. Size, 17¾x25¼x12¾ inches. Weight, 71 pounds. Price, each........................$5.00

No. 23R120 Large Size Ball Bearing Acme Combination Washer No. 7. Weight, 77 pounds.
Price, each..............................$5.65

The Genuine Improved Scott's Western Washer.

$2.85

The Standard family machine. The make up and finish of our Scott's Western will be the same as heretofore, and will not be excelled by any other make. All of the bolts, washers, nuts, nails, in fact all iron parts that come in contact with the clothing are heavily tinned, absolutely no danger of rust spots on the clothes. Fitted up with our patented round post, and malleable iron enameled pinwheel, the greatest invention of the age in washing machines. Made in two sizes—No. 2 and No. 3. The former is the family size.

No. 23R124 Scott's Western Washing Machine, size No. 2. Inside dimensions, 17¾x23¼x10¼ inches. Weight, 62 pounds. Price, each..............$2.85

No. 23R126 Scott's Western Washing Machine, size No. 3. Inside dimensions, 19¼x25¼x11½ inches. Weight, 65 pounds. Price, each................$3.10

ABOUT FREIGHT AND EXPRESS. It is seldom necessary to write us to ask what the freight or express will amount to. The weight of almost every item is given under the description. If you will refer to pages 7 to 10 you can get the rate of freight or express to a point near you in your state which will be almost, if not exactly, the same rate as to your nearest railroad station. **From this you can calculate almost exactly what the freight or express will amount to on any shipment to your town and you** will find it will amount to next to nothing as compared to what you will save in price. By noting the weight and the express or freight rates you can tell almost exactly what the cost of the transportation will be and save the trouble and delay of writing us for this information.

Turn-of-the-century washing machines from Sears, Roebuck & Co. catalogue, 1902.

By the end of the century, optimists predicted that technology would end the drudgery of household work and shorten tremendously the time household tasks took each day. "There is no household operation capable of being mechanically performed," A. E. Kennelly wrote in 1890, "of which, through the motor, electricity cannot become the drudge and willing slave." Electricity made possible non-polluting processes, thus making unnecessary much household cleaning. Electric light and heat left no carbon deposits. The dirt and labor of making and maintaining fires were eliminated by means of electric stoves and thermostatically controlled furnaces. Electrically driven water pumps, sewing machines, carpet sweepers, shoe polishers, coffee heaters, and lawn mowers reduced the amount of physical labor called for in doing certain tasks and shortened daily work time. Electricity had even been used to replace table service. "A miniature railroad track runs around the table within the easy reach of each guest," Kennelly described the innovation. "The dishes, as electrically signalled for by the hostess, are laid on little trucks filled with tiny motors, and are started out from the pantry to the dinner-table. They stop automatically before each guest, who, after assisting himself, presses a button at his side and so gives the car the impetus and right of way to his next neighbor."[33]

Turn-of-the-century household guides and domestic-science tracts revealed the extent to which technology had changed many household tasks. Urban apartments and smaller homes meant fewer chores. Indeed, middle-class apartments had central heat, hot water, and modern appliances. Linoleum floors, porcelain and copper sinks, tiled lavatories, and washable wallpaper reduced the physical labor in cleaning. Washing machines and gas and electric irons simplified washing and ironing. Among the most dramatic of changes occurred in the kitchen, where gas stoves began to replace the old coal or wood-burning ones. The gas range is lit by "the touch of the lit taper to the gas jet." Making a hard-coal fire in a stove, however, required great skill and was a job dreaded by household workers:

The first thing to do is to close the draughts. Then we remove the top of the range, and brush all cinders and ashes that have collected at the sides into the grate, and replace the covers. The grate is then dumped, and, after a couple of minutes' waiting to allow the ashes to settle, the covers again taken off. On a newspaper unfolded and lightly crumpled in the bottom of the grate are piled loosely the small blocks of wood sold for kindling, or the sticks from the woodshed. There must be airspace left between the bits of wood. . . . The draughts are then opened, the paper lighted, and the covers replaced on the stove.

When the wood is well ignited a shovel or two of coal, enough to cover the wood, is put on. After this kindles, more is added. One should never turn on half a scuttle at a time. When the fire is fairly burning, the draughts must be closed.

With the gas stove, the gas is turned off after each use and then relit when needed again. A coal fire, however, "must be on the cook's mind during the day. It must not be allowed to become so low that it must be coaxed with wood, nor permitted to burn beyond the point where the red coals grow white with heat." Furthermore, when only a coal fire was used, it had to be kept going all night. "At bedtime," the guide advised, "the ashes should be raked out, fresh coal put on, and the draughts opened for ten or fifteen minutes, or until the coal is fairly kindled," and then adjusted again. A fire kept alive all night had to be tended first thing in the morning. Required were the opening and closing of vents, removing ashes, and adding coal. Once or twice a week the fire would be allowed to die out so the stove and fire chamber could be thoroughly cleaned out, and then lighting the stove would begin anew.[34]

At the same time that technology was promising to change labor inside the home, innovations outside the house were having an even greater effect. Much work formerly done in the home was now being done by commercial interests outside the home. Developments in the garment and soap-making industries meant readily available ready-made clothing and manufactured soap, while commercial food processing in canning and baking could eliminate much household labor. The baking of bread was the first of these innovations. In

Model kitchen, 1899, residence of Mr. K. B. Conger of Irvington-on-Hudson, New York. (From Anna Leach, "Science in the Model Kitchen," *Cosmopolitan*, XXVII, May 1899.)

1850 less than 10 percent of all bread consumed in the United States had been provided by commercial bakeries; in 1900 bakeries furnished about 25 percent of all bread. Similarly, beginning in the 1870s, biscuits and crackers became widely commercially available. By the turn of the century, commercial bakeries had established horse and wagon delivery routes; fresh bread was delivered to grocery stores and private homes. In cities, caterers and restaurants offered complete meals delivered and served in the home. Steam laundries could eliminate altogether the most burdensome of household tasks from the home.[35]

While nineteenth-century household technology was supposed to bring an industrial revolution into the home, this

promise remained unfulfilled until the 1920s and after. All of
the innovations mentioned above actually appeared during
the nineteenth century, but they were not widely introduced
into homes until World War I. Only 3,000 washing machines
were produced in 1909, and 70,000 in 1916. After World
War I, the production of washing machines soared: 500,000
were made in 1919, 882,000 in 1925. Similarly, not until the
1920s did vacuum-cleaner sales reach one million sold in a
single year. Even the adoption of the gas stove spread slowly.
As late as 1940 over one-third of all American dwelling units
still had coal or wood stoves. And the trends in production of
canned fruit and vegetables, as presented by George Stigler,
reveal that it wasn't until the 1920s that Americans came to
depend on processed food. Stigler estimated the domestic
consumption of commercially canned fruit and vegetables by
adding imports and subtracting exports from the domestic
production. He constructed a ratio of production per
hundred persons at ten-year intervals from 1899 through
1929 and found that canned-vegetable consumption rose
fourfold and canned fruit consumption sevenfold during that
period.[36]

Overall, then, it was not until the 1920s that household
technology became widespread in the United States. This
coincided with both the relative decrease in the number of
servants and the prevalence of day work. Regionally, the development of technology inside and outside the home lagged
significantly in the South, where black women provided the
bulk of domestic labor and where the relative decrease in the
servant population did not occur until World War II. Steam
laundries and commercial bakeries, for instance, were concentrated first in Northern cities and then in Western ones;
only later did they appear in the South in large numbers.

A 1922 Indianapolis study gives data on households with
both servants and laundry appliances. At a time when only a
relatively small number of households had washing machines, 48.9 percent of 523 Indianapolis employers of servants had power washing machines, while 98.4 percent had
electric or gas irons or mangles. This data would seem to

suggest that women with servants, rather than those without, were in the forefront of innovation, and that at least in the North the presence of servants did not retard modernization. But this may not have been the case at all. The investigator failed to discern whether or not the employees were laundresses; indeed, her discussion suggests that they were general houseworkers. If one assumes they were, this would indicate a pattern in which technology permitted the transfer of tasks formerly done by a houseworker *and* a laundress to a single houseworker, or in which technology is used to return to the home work previously sent out, as in the case where families had previously used a commercial laundry. It is most likely that the adoption of washing machines in Indianapolis led to the reduction of servants—in this case from two- to one-servant households.[37]

Whether to invest in the new household technologies or to allocate expenditures for servants became reasonable budgetary alternatives for families at the turn of the century. Three decades earlier, a rise in family income for a servantless family probably would have meant an automatic decision to hire a maid. The only cost factor to consider was the expense of maintaining a domestic servant. In the early twentieth century, a family could choose either to hire servants or to invest in appliances that would permit the housewife to perform the household labor. For those entering a new dwelling the choice was easiest. They could live in a relatively small urban apartment designed to make a servant unnecessary, or they could build their own home, adopting the readily available architectural plans that promised to ease the tasks of household work—blueprints for middle-class homes without servants' quarters. A man with an income of $5,000 a year described in 1912 how his family followed the latter course. "Our house is arranged on all one floor," he wrote, "and all unnecessary rooms and partitions are eliminated. Our efforts are directed towards keeping down the accumulation of 'things,' so that we will not be crowded, and dusting and cleaning will be simplified." The house was filled with electrical appliances: vacuum cleaner, washer and ringer, flat-

Sunshine Tells The Tale

You know how sunlight, streaming through the windows, shows the dust-filled air of a broom-swept room. You know that no matter how thoroughly you sweep and "dust," in a few minutes the flying dust resettles on furniture, floors and fixtures, and floats in the air you breathe.

What a bright contrast is seen in the home "washed with air" by a

Western · Electric
Sturtevant
Vacuum Cleaner

Such a home welcomes sunlight, for all dust and dirt is *drawn out* of each room —banished—by the powerful, steady suction of a miniature strong wind. And the only effort required is to pass the light, handy nozzle over the article or surface to be cleaned. No sweeping. No dusting. No backache. Any near-by electric light socket furnishes the power.

Every home, small or large, can have a Western Electric Cleaner exactly the right size to keep that home "spick-and-span." There are many models, both portable and stationary, priced from $47.50 to $400.

Write for our sunlight book, "The Clean Way to Clean." Full of cheer for every housewife. Ask for book No. 15-AZ. It will be sent free.

There is an opportunity for agents to represent us in some unoccupied territories.

The housewife with a vacuum cleaner replaces the maid with her broom and duster in Western Electric advertisement, 1914. (Western Electric)

iron and heater. Other people also reported using technology to replace their servants. "We used to have a woman come in by the day," a man with a $3,000 a year income wrote. "When she stopped coming, we just purchased a vacuum cleaner for $120, which the woman folks now prefer to outside help. . . . We have also a motor-operated washing-machine, two electric sad-irons, and one gas iron!" A wife of a New England physician with an income between $3,000 and $4,000 recorded how "in the last year I have kept no maid, having discharged my last one after nearly six years of service, and have enjoyed the year more than the previous one. . . . I never hesitate to spend money for any labor-saving device."[38]

In general, the introduction of technology tended to reduce the number of household servants or eliminate them altogether. Conversely, the retention of servants delayed the introduction of new technologies. Thus the housewife, not the servant, was most directly affected by household technological innovation. In perhaps the most insightful and perceptive recent work on technology and the household, Ruth Schwartz Cowan describes the industrial revolution in the middle-class home which occurred in the 1920s—the widespread transfer from hand to mechanical power, the change from traditional to modern habits, and the accompanying rise of new ideologies among housewives. "The significant change in the structure of the household labor force," Cowan concluded, "was the disappearance of paid and unpaid servants (unmarried daughters, maiden aunts, and grandparents . . .) as household workers—and the imposition of the entire job on the housewife herself." She found evidence of this in the popular middle-class women's magazines. Before World War I, when illustrators "depicted women doing housework, the women were very often servants. When the lady of the house was drawn, she was often the person being served, or she was supervising the serving. . . . Nursemaids diapered babies, seamstresses pinned up hems, waitresses served meals, laundresses did the wash, and cooks did the cooking. By the end of the 1920s the servants had disappeared from those illustrations; all those jobs were being done by housewives."[39]

As in any industrial revolution, not every home adapted to the new technology. The retention of servants enabled mistresses and employers to rely on hand power, traditional habits, and old ideologies. Since the employment of servants involved class, status, and leisure as well as household labor, the decision to forgo servants was not solely economic, nor did it merely involve the housewife's assuming her servants' chores, with the assistance of the new mechanical tools. Tradition also played a strong part in resistance. One housewife declared her opposition early, when bakeries and laundries first appeared. "Who desires their petition for daily bread answered in the form of the chippy, alumy stuff furnished by two-thirds of the bakers in the country?" she asked. For her, only home-baked bread would do. Moreover, she would not put up with the "outrageous prices" of outside laundries. Many Northern and Western housewives resisted the changes, refusing to adopt the new ideologies and assume the work themselves. In the South, where the hiring of black servants was an integral part of the class and caste system, the household industrial revolution would be delayed until after World War II, when black emigration from the South began to have a cumulative effect. Ironically, then, the new technologically oriented work force, which was transformed by the industrial revolution in the home, consisted of housewives. Servants working in middle-class homes were not greatly affected. Indeed, it is likely that while middle-class employers were beginning to adopt new mechanical devices for use by their day workers, these same innovations were probably being introduced into the servants' own homes. In any case, the households in which servants worked did not provide a training ground for acquiring new industrial skills or for learning about the most recent mechanical domestic innovations.[40]

Nonetheless, domestic service did serve as a modernizing agent as the work disciplines associated with industrialization entered the household. In homes where mistresses systematized the work—defined and ordered the tasks—modern work rules and habits permeated daily life. Before the Civil War, Catherine Beecher had argued that since the household was controlled by women, they ought to be prepared and trained to assume that responsibility. Housewives would be domestic engineers. Slowly, the education of females was expanded to meet Beecher's demands. Girls had long been taught handiwork, with an emphasis on sewing and needlework, but in the early 1880s in Boston a group of women sponsored a household-arts program which led to the introduction of similar programs in the Boston public schools and other urban systems. The program was not vocational; it was not intended to train domestic servants. Instead, it was part of general female education, responding to Beecher's earlier call for domestic education and serving as a forerunner of the growth of domestic science as part of women's college curriculum during the 1890s and 1900s.[41]

Concurrently, women began to call for schools for training mistresses. Writing in *Good Housekeeping* in 1891, Ellen Batelle Diettrick argued that schools for employers would rationalize the work and introduce a sense of professionalism into the running of the household. Kate Hamlin agreed. Those who wished to return to "the simple methods of our grandmothers" were unrealistic, she declared, because it was impossible to go backwards. Education of the mistress was the answer.[42]

The cult of efficiency then so prevalent in American industry found its way into the household as well. Efficiency was the banner carried by employers who sought to adopt industrial or commercial models of employer/employee relations, and the movement contributed to the development of an appropriate academic field, domestic science. The image of the shop and factory, and later of the office, remained in the back of the mistresses' minds. Anna McMahan defined a good mistress in 1886 as "a woman whose domestic business is well managed in all its departments, just as a good merchant is a man whose mercantile affairs are well conducted." In 1892 Josephine Martin analyzed the problem of "the proper management of servants." Managers required proper knowledge: "the people who accomplish most in any department of work, be it in shop or household, are those who know how to conduct the business in every detail; who know how to direct the work that others will do, and to get the best service out of those who are in their employ." Management was the harder task because "it requires a great deal more ability to control and direct a number of employees than it does to do the share of any one of them." Those with "executive ability" would get the best results from their employees. Martin recognized that not all housewives had servants, so she extended the image to fit these cases: "If one's business is too small to require the service of more than one person, one must, of course, do the work himself; and in the case of the housekeeper, if her capital is small and her manner of living so simple that the work would not occupy two persons, it would be much better for her to do the work herself than to spend her time in idleness." The secret to "domestic prosperity" was placing "relations to . . . their servants upon business principles." Dealing mostly with employer/employee relations, Martin stressed the adoption of a detached professional attitude in managing servants.[43]

Whether or not mistresses actually introduced factory and shop discipline into the home, most servants worked within systems designed to promote order and efficiency. As in the factory, time provided the greatest discipline. Morning rising, meals, rest periods, and afternoons out were all governed by the clock. For nearly all servants, domestic work was their first job, and they had little prior experience with a life controlled by the clock. As most servants were immigrants, blacks, and teenage girls, their own cultural or home environments had not accustomed them to the relatively ordered, systematized household of most middle-class homes. Servants themselves had to adapt to order their own work and leisure. Specifically allotted time had to be given to certain tasks so that other ones could be done next; chores undone could cut into time off. Servants had to learn to respond to written as well as spoken orders. They had to substitute learned patterns for instinctive, intuitive, or traditional ones. They were often expected to use cookbooks, recipe books, and household guides to perform tasks in new ways. Traditional recipes or washing techniques or ways of cleaning might not suit the tastes or style of the employing family. Thus many women in domestic service developed new work habits and learned to order and systematize their chores.[44]

Systematization of household work was the responsibility of the employer. As in the shop, factory, or office, management was responsible for order and efficiency. Moreover, it was understood the only successful training of domestics was done on the job. Formal training for domestic service had not met with much success, and only schools for institutional housekeepers and teachers of domestic science did well. Given the low status of servants, those with access to education would not use it to become domestics. Housewives were educated by the woman's magazines, household guides, and domestic-science courses. The principles of modern science and economics were applied to the household to understand it as a system and process. Domestic science, no less than any other science, sought to examine folk traditions and existing knowledge and develop rational principles to replace custom. Beginning in the 1880s, middle-class women's magazines inundated housewives with domestic science, and through them it filtered down to the servants. Judging from the literature of the time, most employers took seriously their responsibility for on-the-job training of servants.[45]

In the South, customs were more persistent than elsewhere. Despite the race and class differences of mistress and servant, both shared common cultural mores. In general, the Southern housewife assumed less responsibility for the running of her own household than did mistresses in other parts of the country, and was therefore slower to systematize the work. For all their complaints about lazy and disorderly servants, Southern mistresses seemed to do little to solve the problem. Only concern over rising wages and black emigration finally spurred them into changing their fixed ways, and domestic education never became as widespread in the South as in the North. Thus the Southern home was less of a modernizing agent than were homes in the North and West.

Servants were wary of the rationalization of household tasks. On the one hand, it contained the promise of a reduction in hours and more free time as employers realized that a rested employee could work more efficiently. Where newly ordered tasks increased the quality of work, servants acquired new skills to be used both in employers' households and in their own. On the other hand, systematization of the work threatened to give the employer more control over it and to increase the relative powerlessness of servants. It made mistresses bolder in demanding that servants defer to the norms of the household; servants' traditional approaches received less respect. Combined with new technology, it could increase the work of many servants by returning some work to the home, as in the case of washing. Yet it did not remove the stigma of service by placing it on the same basis as shop, factory, or office work; the personalized mistress/servant relationship remained unaltered. The servant's response to such problems, as well as to the low wages, the long hours, and the poor living and work conditions, was to switch employers, or even possibly to stop doing household work.

High job turnover was a basic characteristic of domestic service. Mistresses have always complained of servant "restlessness," and nearly every study of domestic service has stressed the short job tenure of servants. In her national sample drawn between 1889 and 1890, Lucy Maynard Salmon found the "average length of service" to be less than one and a half years. In Philadelphia's Seventh Ward, Isabel Eaton found the longest average tenure recorded to be four years, five months. She distinguished between the long-service women (who had served five years or more), who averaged a tenure of six years, eight months, and the rank and file of servants, who averaged three years, six months with their current employer. In Columbia, Missouri, 33 white families employing 39 black servants at the time of the study in 1901 and 1902 reported that the families had employed 141 different servants during the three previous years. One household had 24 servants in three years, and two other families had had 17 and 12 respectively. In New York City during 1906 through 1908, George Haynes found that the modal period was six to eleven months in a position, while in St. Louis in 1914, William Crossland found the mode to be three to six months. Later studies show that more than 50 percent of servants had served less than one year in their current position (see Table 3–4).[46]

In Springfield, Massachusetts, in 1918, Elizabeth Haynes reported that the state employment office had placed 1,000 women in 4,000 domestic jobs during the course of the year. Extremely short job tenure was achieved by the 10

Table 3–4. Length of Service, Female Domestic Servants, Selected Cities, by Percent Distribution

| Length of service | New York City, 1906–9 (blacks) | Gainesville, Georgia, 1919 (blacks) | Baltimore, 1923 | |
			(whites)	(blacks)
Under 3 months	20	38	18	19
3 months to under 6 months	22	16	16	19
6 months to under 1 year	25	13	16	15
1 year to under 2 years	18	7	16	14
2 years to under 5 years	12	13	19	20
5 years to under 10 years	2	4	9	7
10 years and over	1	9	6	6
	100	100	100	100
Under 1 year	67	67	50	43
	n = 761	n = 69	n = 231	n = 552

Sources: New York City: George Edmund Haynes, *The Negro at Work in New York City* (Original, 1912; reprint, New York, 1968), pp. 84–85. Gainesville: Ruth Reed, "The Negro Woman of Gainesville, Georgia," *Bulletin of the University of Georgia* XXII (December 1921), p. 25. Baltimore: Mary V. Robinson, *Domestic Workers and Their Employment Relation*, U.S. Department of Labor, Women's Bureau, Bulletin No. 39 (Washington, D.C., 1929), pp. 72–73.

women—5 white and 5 black—who were placed in at least 41 positions each by the Springfield office during 1917. Not only did domestics change jobs frequently but there also was a steady flow of women out of service as they got married or went to work in other occupations. In a 1911 study of commercial laundries in Chicago, New York, Brooklyn, and Philadelphia, the case histories of 539 laundry workers and operatives were reported. Of those with work experience prior to entering a laundry, more than half had been domestics. Collectively, the former servants had started to work at an average age of twelve and had worked in service for nearly six years. Six left household work to marry, 27 to enter laundries and one to work in a factory.[47]

For women in domestic service, changing positions was part of a constant search for better working and living conditions. With the demand for servants exceeding the supply, many household workers felt free to move as often as they wished. Thus new positions were often begun with optimism as both employer and employee tended to be on their best behavior. In time, however, the personalized work relationship and employer control would take their toll, and the servant would leave to take another position. Changing jobs was the one great power domestics had, but it was an individual rather than a collective response. In small towns such as Springfield, Massachusetts, the 4,000 positions filled by 1,000 women represented the constant shifting of employees among employers without any discernible effect on working conditions. Not all servants were constantly moving, though. A small percentage of servants tended to have long job tenure (see Table 3–4). Satisfaction with the employing family and the attainment of economic and psychological security and stability were important to many household workers. But not all of those with long service felt satisfied. Despite the high turnover rate among servants, the restraints on changing jobs inhibited complete freedom of movement. While jobs were readily available, the job-finding process could be difficult, as has been previously discussed. Moreover, few servants had adequate resources to remain out of work for long, since most were to some degree supporting their families. Often single women had no place to live other than an employer's household, and whatever savings they had put by would be eaten up by room and board while they were job hunting. Married women ordinarily had their own lodging, but their families were more directly dependent upon their income for support.

Other occupations seemed to offer the only escape from domestic work. The disadvantages and advantages of domestic work were well known by the turn of the century, and a woman could weigh the factors. The consensus of social workers in 1913 was that "the houseworker is cut off from her family; the hours are long and irregular; there is only slight opportunity for recreation, and that unsupervised; holidays are few; the work takes the girl out of the main currents of modern life, and isolates her in a back eddy; she is constantly conscious of a galling lack of freedom, independence, and consideration from others, and of a distinctly lowered social standing; and the danger of moral contamination is even greater than in many other forms of work." Domestics also complained about the dull and repetitive nature of the job and the hard physical labor it involved. Moreover, because a large percentage of their income was received in kind rather than in dollar wages, household workers could not order their budgets to reflect their own priorities, as could women in shops, offices, and factories.

The social workers in 1913 also summarized the advantages of housework: "the girl who chooses housework is likely to be better housed, better clothed, and better fed than she would be at home; secures training in a vocation natural to woman; in proportion to her capacity is relatively more highly paid than in any other form of work; and almost universally establishes a better type of home life when she marries than is possible for the factory or shop girl."[48]

Did other occupations represent a release from the conditions of household work? In 1900, Mary E. Trueblood investigated this question under the sponsorship of the Boston-based Women's Educational and Industrial Union. Her study was the only survey of employees specifically designed to compare and contrast the conditions of factory, shop, restaurant, and household labor. One hundred women filled out the lengthy questionnaire: twenty shop workers in Boston, twenty textile-mill workers in Lowell and Fall River, twenty shoe-factory hands in Haverhill and Lynn, twenty restaurant employees in Boston, and twenty domestics in Boston and that vicinity.[49]

As a group, the domestics tended to be younger than the other women, ranging in age from nineteen to twenty-seven, although textile-factory workers had begun work at an earlier age. Trueblood did not explain how she drew her sample, but the age range among servants was lower than the national distribution. All of Trueblood's twenty domestics lived in; none lived out or were day workers. This would have tended to exclude older, married women who dominated live-out or

Table 3–5. Working Women, Massachusetts, 1900

		Birthplace						
	U.S.	(parents U.S.-born)	England	Canada	Ireland	Scotland	Other	Total
Shop workers	18	(16)	1	1				20
Textile-mill workers	7	(5)	8	3	2			20
Shoe-factory workers	15	(13)	1	1	1		2	20
Restaurant workers	11	(9)		8	1			20
Houseworkers			1	7	11	1		20

Working hours

	Average daily	Estimated days a week	Estimated weekly hours
Shop workers	8.2	5½	45.1
Textile-mill workers	9.6	5½	52.8
Shoe-factory workers			
Restaurant workers	9.5	6	57.0
Houseworkers	11.6	6½	75.4

"Real wages"

	Average weekly cash income	Average cost of food and lodging	"Real wage"
Shop workers	$ 7.52	$4.29	$3.23
Textile-mill workers	8.35	2.36	5.99
Shoe-factory workers	10.45	4.00	6.45
Restaurant workers	5.38	1.56	3.82
Houseworkers	3.99	—	3.99

Source: [Mary E. Trueblood], "Social Statistics of Workingwomen," *Massachusetts Labor Bulletin* No. 18 (May 1901), pp. 34, 37–38, 40.

day work, and indeed, none of Trueblood's household workers were married. Moreover, since none of the servants were American-born, her sample probably did not include any blacks. Nonetheless, there were sharp group differences between the women's backgrounds. Among the houseworkers, all were of foreign birth and had been in the United States only a relatively short time—five or six years in all but one case. Among those in shops, eighteen were native-born, sixteen of whom had native-born parents. Shoe-factory workers followed a similar trend. While native-born workers had a bare majority among the waitresses and were a minority among the textile workers, eight of the former were from Canada and eight of the latter from England. In all cases they had been raised in the United States.

Household workers worked the most hours per day and the greatest number of days per week. All the domestics worked seven days a week; no other women worked every day except for a few waitresses. Subtracting one hour from the reported working day of servants (to allow for time spent at meals) and excluding time on call but not actually busy working, Trueblood calculated the domestic's workday at 10.6 hours, or from one to two hours longer than the other women. Moreover, shop workers worked only a half day on Saturday, and during the summers factory women commonly received Saturday as a half-day holiday. Projecting these hours to a weekly basis, Trueblood estimated that domestics probably averaged about two complete days of work per week more than other women.

In comparing wages, Trueblood attempted to estimate "real wages," using a standard of expendable income remaining after food and lodging expenditures. Household workers, she concluded, were marginally better off than restaurant waitresses and significantly better off than shopgirls, but were at a disadvantage when compared to factory hands. The shoe-factory worker's income was inflated, however, by her failure to consider the irregularity of employment during the year. Only restaurant and household workers reported no time lost involuntarily.[50]

There were significant differences in social relations and leisure time between servants and their sisters working elsewhere. The variety of amusements enjoyed by women excluding domestics was as varied as their personal interests. A few servants reported little or no free time, and nearly all found time for recreation limited. On the other hand, factory girls were often too tired after work to participate in social life.

The greatest contrast between domestics and other work-

ing women lay in the area of satisfaction and contentment.
"In the shoe factories, shops and restaurants many of the
girls seemed to enjoy their work," Trueblood observed. "No
doubt the excitement of a crowd and the association with
others doing the same work accounted for it in part. They
knew, too, that their work was definite and would end at a
fixed time. It was particularly noticeable in these three occupations that the girls respected themselves, their work and
their employers. They seemed to feel themselves a part of
the commercial world and they were helping to do a large
thing." Of servants, Trueblood noted that "it was impossible
to detect any feeling that their work was important." Trueblood concluded that "very few seemed satisfied with their
employment, but in no case was objection made to the work
itself. Those receiving the best pay were often the most dissatisfied. Truly no amount of money can compensate a self-
respecting person for the loss of a reasonable amount of free
time and independence." Indeed, in explaining their satisfaction with their present jobs, factory and shop workers compared them favorably to housework. They enjoyed the freedom they felt they had found in factory, shop, or restaurant
work, and they contrasted it with the lack of free time and
the subjugation in household labor, where servants were at
"everybody's beck and call" or were "bossed around."

Most of those who had the opportunity left domestic service, resulting in a relative statistical decline in domestic
work within the female occupational structure and a constant
shortage of available servants. Some women, however, could
not leave domestic service; as relatively unskilled and uneducated immigrant and black women, they had limited job opportunities outside of it. As factory, office, and shop opportunities increased for native-born women, less desirable jobs
opened up to immigrants and blacks. In order to retain single
women in service, mistresses reluctantly had to end one of
the most onerous features of household work—living in.
World War I accelerated this process, as better jobs became
available elsewhere, and working women became more mobile and independent. Moreover, as the percentage of women

in domestic service declined, as immigration halted during the war, and as factory jobs became available, mistresses became more dependent upon married women for servants. Only day work, as Southern housewives knew, permitted large numbers of married women to do household work. By the 1920s, then, the twentieth-century pattern of domestic service had become set: the "cleaning woman" had replaced the "servant girl."

❦ IV ❧

MISTRESS AND SERVANT

HOUSEHOLD WORK WAS BASICALLY A NONINDUSTRIAL OCCUPA-
tion, rooted in servitude and not far removed from slavery.
What set domestic service apart from other occupations was
the mistress/servant relationship, a highly personalized one in
which the worker herself was hired rather than just her
labor. In some cases, the work done by the servant was less
important than the fact that she satisfied the employer's personal or status needs. Moreover, the high degree of personalization of the work, the retention of the home as workplace,
and the relatively little job specialization was maintained in a
society moving toward impersonal economic and work relationships. Household work remained outside of the trend in
a modernizing society that was separating workplace and
home.

Domestic service, however, was not static: work tasks and
conditions, the groups from which employees were drawn,
and the employer/employee relationship changed greatly between the Civil War and World War I. Household work was
an arena of intense cultural, racial, religious, and class conflict because most often mistress and servant were drawn
from different worlds. As job opportunities for women outside of domestic work arose, more and more women left or
did not go into service. This in turn aggravated the seem-

ingly eternal servant shortage and acted as a restraint on the power and control of the mistress. Of equal significance to the mistress/servant relationship was the shift from live-in to live-out work, part of the process of increased depersonalization of domestic work. At the same time, the mistress/servant relationship did not become any less intimate. Although some housewives and reformers urged that mistresses adopt the work relationships found in factories, offices and shops, the mistress/servant relationship remained close.

As Barbara Welter, Kathryn Kish Sklar, and other historians have demonstrated, during the nineteenth century sharper lines were drawn between male roles and responsibilities and female ones. Men specialized in the world outside of the home and were the primary wage earners. In middle-class families, women came to dominate—and to be dominated by—the domestic sphere. The household, child-rearing, education, and religion were the areas that women controlled. As Sklar has pointed out, Catherine Beecher's household guidebooks helped shape this woman's world for the middle class. The training and education of females was increasingly designed to enable them to fulfill this domestic role. Through their writings, Beecher and other reformers altered women's education to allow middle-class women to properly and successfully assume these tasks.[1]

The domestic world of women, however, was very different from the world into which men ventured. Between the home and the rest of society was an imaginary shield protecting the middle-class family from the evils and ugliness of the outside world—the male sphere—and serving to create a private sector within which intimacies were confined and shielded from public view. Increasingly during the Victorian age of the nineteenth century, the home came to represent privacy and intimacy. In the privacy of one's home, one was permitted to do many things that were taboo or could not be expressed in public. The entry of outsiders into the sheltered world of the home could bridge the carefully constructed chasm between public and private spheres. Yet most middle-class American families brought into their private world outsiders, women without ties of kin, to work in the household. Domestic servants, then, occupied a unique place in American society. They alone worked within the most private space within the female sphere; they alone entered the world designed to be insulated from the world of work; and they alone were thrust across the imaginary barrier into a family's private world.

As the middle-class family became more and more private and sheltered from the outside world, it increasingly became dependent on intrusion from the outside into its world for its physical comforts. The inequities in American capitalism that left working-class men unable to support themselves and their families on what they made, and that forced workers' daughters and wives into domestic service, also produced a growing upper and middle class who brought hired servants into their homes. By the end of the nineteenth century, the American millionaires whose mansions lined New York City's Fifth Avenue and Newport's cliffs had become dependent on large retinues of workers and servants to maintain their palaces and homes. Demanding to be treated like royalty and ignoring the problems of servants within a supposedly egalitarian society, they tended to import their staffs of servants directly from Europe. Neither they nor their wives and mistresses ran their households; trained butlers and housekeepers managed the house and supervised the staff.[2]

Middle-class women, however, occupied the world as idealized by Catherine Beecher. In the late nineteenth century they lived in homes too large to run alone. Laundering, ironing, and baking still took place mostly in the home, and basic cleaning had to be done mainly by hand. Ideally, an urban middle-class home would have had two servants, but most families managed with but one, most likely an immigrant or black "girl" who served as cook, baker, chambermaid, cleaning woman, silver polisher, and if she was unlucky, washerwoman and ironer. In most cases, however, the last two chores would be done by a woman who came one or two days a week to do the wash. In areas other than the South hired servants were rare in ranks below the middle class, but petty shopkeepers and skilled artisans might take in a country girl who would exchange household duties for room and board. A woman with a large family found it hard to manage even a respectable working-class dwelling by herself.

It was not just the physical demands of the work that dictated the hiring of servants among the middle class. During the late nineteenth century, medical authorities cautioned women against demanding and enduring physical labor. According to medical guidebooks, adolescent middle-class girls should be excused from such hard physical labor as strenuous domestic chores. More mature women were advised against physical activity during menstruation, and it was widely thought that regular work schedules were injurious to a woman's health. That this advice was not applied to domestic servants simply underscored the difference between mistresses and servants. Employing a servant also represented the attainment of middle-class status in a community, not just for the woman of the house but for the man as well. For the woman it might symbolize the achievement of a more leisurely life-style; for the man it might signify his success as a provider for his family. In the South it was universally accepted that a middle-class woman did not perform household duties herself. The Southern middle-class white felt that should be done only by blacks. In the Middle West and along the Pacific Coast, servants were rarer because those areas lacked the constant influx of immigrants or the presence of large numbers of blacks, but this only increased the differences in status between families with servants and those without them. Throughout the United States, then, middle-class life-style required servants, whether for the comforts servants provided or as an indication of the family's status to the community.

For whatever reasons families hired servants, the world of service was a woman's world in which the work relationship was highly personalized. The worker, and not the work itself, was under constant scrutiny. This was part of the process in which the servant herself, not just her labor, was hired. Because in domestic service work relationships could not be separated from personal relationships, roles could only be loosely defined, which meant in essence that the employer/employee relationship was subject to whatever individual interpretation the employer wished to give it. In the words of an employer, "My servant is hired to do whatever she is told to do and to be at any time subject to my command."[3]

The system of references used in hiring servants tended to further personalize the relationship. References were rarely actually used, but when they were, there were no objective standards by which to evaluate the performance of workers. Evaluations and recommendations tended to be highly personal, indicating the likes and dislikes of the employer more than any objective evaluation of the work done. Consistent with the idea that a worker was hired rather than just the labor of the worker, the evaluations were mostly about the personality of the worker. An examination of the files of the Domestic Efficiency Association of Baltimore in 1923 by Mary V. Robinson revealed this pattern:

Colored woman——Reference 1. Splendid—good, dependable, fine woman.
                 Reference 2. Did not like her.
Colored woman——Reference 1. Honest, clean, very good cook, very nice person.
                 Reference 2. Not satisfactory.

Other references that pertained specifically to the work still depended upon subjective evaluation:

Colored woman——Reference 1. Is not a good cook.
                 Reference 2. Very good cook. Efficient, clean, honest.

The contradictory nature of these references themselves revealed the personalized relationships that dominated the work.[4]

To many mistresses and some servants personalization was

a desired characteristic of domestic service. This was especially true among those who viewed service as a form of apprenticeship, the girl receiving practical training in household skills. In this vein, rural families traditionally placed
their young daughters in farm or town homes. Their leaving
home would ease the burden in their own homes, and they
would perform household chores in return for room and
board (and sometimes clothing) in their new houses. The
girl's family was assured she would live in a moral, religious
home with people who would both train their daughter and
preserve parental values. Often the household heads would
see themselves as surrogate parents, and the girl was accepted into the family not as a servant but as "help." As
Lucy Maynard Salmon has described this pattern, it was free
of the degrading and distinguishing marks of service and cap-
tured the "democratic industrial spirit" dominant in the
United States from the American Revolution until the 1850s.
There was no social chasm between employer and employee,
according to Salmon, and "there was a hearty spirit of willingness with which service was performed."[5]

Salmon saw this as a historical trend; in areas outside the
South domestic service as "help" rather than as a form of ser-
vitude was predominant until the large-scale migration from
Ireland, Germany, Scandinavia, and China brought in
hundreds of thousands of servants. Then, according to
Salmon, service began to change in the 1850s, except in the
West, where the older pattern of "help" and young native-
born farm girls still persisted.

The situation was more complex than Salmon realized,
however. Domestic service as servitude and as a "problem"
does predate Salmon's 1850 demarcation. The annual reports
in the 1820s of the Society for the Encouragement of Faithful
Domestic Servants in New-York include the complaints of
mistresses dealing with a servant class. Indeed, as the first
report states, the society was organized "to excite the ambition of servants by the distribution of prizes for long and
faithful services, to teach them that the way to become *respectable* is by respecting *themselves*, and by acting well the

parts which Providence has assigned to them." At the very
least, the servants whom these benevolent New Yorkers were
trying to reach were neither Salmon's "help" nor apprentice
housekeepers off the farm. Moreover, although in his study
of servants Blaine McKinley agrees with Salmon, he offers
much evidence of the chasm between mistress and servant
during the pre–Civil War era. Where the pattern of "help"
existed, it was generally in rural areas and small towns. Although this kind of domestic service still exists in the United
States, it has little significance in the overall pattern of domestic servants, and nearly none on the market from the
point of view of employer or employee.[6]

Even though the idea of domestic service as a form of apprenticeship was not widely retained, many individual employers still saw their role along those lines. They argued
that domestic service offered a girl a home environment in
which to live as well as a trade. In 1870 the Massachusetts
Bureau of Statistics of Labor offered the mistresses' view that
some positions in service provided more comforts than a
woman would find in any other job, or possibly more than
those found in her own home. In some families she would be
part of the family. Forty years later, in 1910, the Maine labor
bureau echoed the Massachusetts report: "The parents who
realize the value of a wholesome environment, prefer that
their daughters enter homes rather than factories." According to the bureau, even an employer's home was preferable to
the barren existence of the unfortunate woman who lodged
or boarded. "The girl who does housework," the report concluded, "is never obliged to think about her room or her
meals. They are always provided, and generally both room
and meals are of much better quality than her sisters pay
money for."[7]

The protective-guardian role of an employer toward an
employee/servant generally has been viewed as paternalism.
Blaine McKinley has described the paternalistic relationship
between servant and master, and as an example cited Frank
and Marian Stockton's "thought that the mistress should extend 'the same surveillance and authority' over the servant

that she would over the visiting daughter of a friend." The Maine labor bureau reprinted the letter of a man who described his own stewardship over his servant/wards. He employed one servant for six months and helped her graduate from a nearby academy. Of another, he wrote that she "was given to understand when she came into the home that she was helping me in the work of building up the moral and spiritual life of the community" by making his home comfortable. When she did well, she received appreciation. While many men displayed similar caring attitudes toward domestics in their households, paternalism within domestic service was rare, because basically the employer/employee relationship was one of woman to woman.[8]

In nearly all cases in domestic service both employer and employee were women. This was in sharp contrast to the work relations normally found in American society between the Civil War and World War I. The benevolent role which some employers assumed toward their servants during this period could rightfully be termed "maternalism." And indeed many of the salient characteristics of mistress/servant relationships flowed from their roles as women.

In general, women were never taught how to hire and supervise workers. Although Catherine Beecher and other authors of household guidebooks included principles on governing a servant, and although reformers who during the 1890s helped make household concerns a science offered "professional" advice, few women received any formal training in this area. Instead, women tended to follow their own personal experience or intuitive judgments. Many employers had been raised in households with domestics, and their memories of their mothers' relationships with servants served as a guide. Some merely imitated the way in which their mother had dealt with her help; others reacted against that model. Maud Nathan remembered the lack of consideration shown to maids in her mother's home and consciously sought to provide a kinder, more humane environment. For many women, however, experience provided insufficient guidance for dealing with servants. Many women had been brought up in households without servants. Others who had been raised in homes with maids received no better training. In homes where the service was so ideal as to be virtually invisible, children were unlikely to become involved in the dynamics of mistress/servant relationships except during times of crisis when a maid left or was fired. Most women, then, relied on their own intuitive judgment to filter their observations about servants in other households and their reading on the servant problem.

The atomization of the workplace—typically one servant per middle-class household—also tended to promote intuitive principles of management and personalization. There was no structure to bring women together to discuss the problem, study its aspects, and change customary practices. The Massachusetts Bureau of Statistics of Labor concluded, for instance, that the personal note prevailed when mistresses discussed service. "There is no suggestion of a desire to promote the welfare of sister employers or employees; but, as a rule, each housekeeper is absorbed in the aspect presented by her own problem." Household service thus resembled the hundreds of thousands of individual enterpreneurs who hired one or two employees to work in their businesses alongside the employers. Women's magazines and more generalized periodicals attempted to educate mistresses and introduce management principles from commerce, industry, and shops into the home, but the diversity of advice offered by housewives and reformers did nothing but support the existing atomization. If a woman read enough about the possible solutions to the servant problem, she could find support for whatever principles governed her own behavior toward her employee.[9]

Many women adopted a maternal role toward their servants. This role was consistent with the pattern of farm girls entering homes similar to their parental homes. But it was not limited to that special case. Some women naturally felt close and intimate with a servant; after all, the servant entered the domestic sphere, an area in which all relationships were intimate. Age differences between a middle-aged mistress and a young servant made the maternal role the most natural one. In a good home, according to the Maine bureau report, "servant girls are hedged about with every safeguard they could have in their own homes. Their relations with men are regulated with much the same eye to their best interests as are those of the daughter of the family. They go to church more regularly." Mistresses constantly compared their behavior toward servants to their treatment of their own daughters. Whether employers were defending their restrictions on hours or visitors, or explaining privileges and benefits—medical care, eating with the family, sharing the family sitting room—kin relations rather than employer/employee ones served as yardsticks. And most often it was a daughter who provided the model.[10]

Mistresses sometimes saw their servants as children, in both a complimentary and a disparaging sense. Viewed as childlike, especially by those who held stereotyped prejudicial views about blacks and immigrants, servants required greater supervision than other workers. This was appropriate in one sense because many servants were children. In the middle part of the century, most servants probably were teenagers, but childlike treatment of servants also resulted from the maternal instincts of the employers. Women felt responsibility for taking into their homes other women's daughters, especially if those children were of the same religion and race as the employer. And as service was something of a way station between the household of a girl's parents and her own home with a husband, maternal responsibility was clearly called for. A California report asserted that girls in domestic service were "treated like members of the family." A Massachusetts employer declared her own sense of obligation to servants: "The mistress must watch over, care for, and *feel* a personal interest in the girls in her kitchen." The best relationship would be reciprocal: "The girls must feel as much interest in their work and their mistress as if it were their own home. . . . They *must* live together." For those who followed these rules, the rewards were that of any mother. From Maine a man reported that a former servant "regarded my wife as a sort of godmother."

An employer told Frances Kellor during her investigation of employment agencies that "my servants only leave to marry." Another reported: "Three of my maids are married and have called to show me their babies, and one says she feeds her children as I taught her."[11]

Mistresses who played the maternal role with their servants felt obligated to educate them, to prepare them for life, and to provide them with a Christian environment in which to live. Some saw this socialization process as the most important aspect because of the class or religious differences between mistress and servant. Thus a servant could be treated as a wayward or uneducated kin who would become cultured and refined through her contact with her new family. "They live with people of higher refinement and education than themselves," a mistress wrote, "and feel that influence. . . . They are given a chance to learn order, system and economy, patience and forebearance, and thus better fitted to be themselves thrifty housekeepers." Religion was equally important. In discussing service, women frequently took a "Christian stand-point." Others argued that mistresses had a fundamental responsibility to provide a Christian atmosphere and education, and employers often cited church attendance as one of the privileges granted.[12]

Benevolent maternalism was an approach adopted by Helen Mar and described by her in *Good Housekeeping*. With three adults in moderate circumstances in her household, she was "compelled to manage with the help of one servant." She dealt forthrightly with her servant: "sudden company, the non-arrival of provisions, a larger wash than usual—none of these things affects us seriously, for when my maid is troubled she and I talk over the difficulty and together smooth things out." Moreover, she treated her maid as she would a daughter. Since her family tended to spend their evenings at home,

my maid is free to go out whatever evenings I am at home . . . provided she is in at a reasonable hour. I never set a special hour, but make it felt that at "closing-up-time" I like my maid to be in.

Then she has her regular days out, with which I seldom, if ever, let anything interfere. If a special entertainment promises late hours, she tells us freely that she cannot be home early, and goes away with a light heart, knowing that I trust her to come into my house with her key, but knowing too that I shall be wakeful until I hear her step on the stairs—as when a member of my family keeps late hours.

She also taught some of her maids: for months she spent a half-hour every night teaching a colored maid to read; another time she helped a Swedish girl learn English.[13]

Maternal benevolence not only served to order the employer/employee relationship within a personalized and intimate environment, but was also fulfilling for its own sake. Just as the employment of a servant could serve many social purposes, so too could it be psychologically rewarding. Lillian Pettengill discovered this aspect of service when she entered Mrs. Kinderlieber's home as a general houseworker.

"I seemed to take to her from the first, she is so nice and refined-looking and delicate," Mrs. Kinderlieber told Eliza's (Pettengill's) reference on the telephone. "She makes me think of my little Milly, my little girl I buried a week ago Thursday." The day Pettengill began work Mrs. Kinderlieber gave her her orders but did not leave, although she mentioned she had work to do. Pettengill went down to the kitchen to do the dishes left for her from the previous day, the day before she was hired. She began to work while her mistress sat down opposite her and began to talk: "I guess you've never done very much hard work, have you, now? . . . Your hands are so white, just like a lady's. My Milly's hands were that way, too." Later on she said, "You're just like my little Milly."[14]

Not all girls could replace Milly; the black who Mrs. Kinderlieber had hired the previous week had proved unsatisfactory. She had worked two days, "but I let her go," said Eliza's employer. "I couldn't have her around, she was so dirty and slack-looking. . . . I couldn't have her around in the kitchen where my Milly had been." Pettengill, however, was special. "I think I'll have you eat with us when I don't have company," Kinderlieber told her, "like one of the family. . . . None of my girls were ever allowed to do it before, but you're so ladylike and refined; besides, it's lonesome with just my husband and myself, without Milly."[15]

Mrs. Kinderlieber was also a hypochondriac, and she used her loneliness and hypochondria to retain Eliza, enlisting her neighbor to reinforce the situation. The neighbor came to Eliza and said, "I was just down on the porch with Mrs. Kinderlieber, and she is so worried for fear you won't like it with her and are planning to leave! . . . I told her 'Eliza is a nice, sensible girl. She knows you aren't well, and she expects to stay until you get better, or longer.' Isn't it so, Eliza?" Time and again her mistress needed to be reassured that Pettengill would stay.[16]

Mrs. Kinderlieber, who did not work outside her home and was not involved in any voluntary benevolent or social agencies or associations, found herself totally isolated when her daughter Milly died. In hiring a servant she sought womanly companionship from a surrogate daughter. The black servant could not fulfill that requirement; racial prejudice ("dirty and slack-looking,") prevented that. Eliza—young, "nice and refined-looking," with "hands . . . so white"—could easily substitute. Thus at times her mistress followed her around to engage her in conversation and compare her with Milly. She even changed the position of the servant in the household by inviting her to join the family meals. Eliza tried to keep her distance from her mistress—she had hired on to work, not to acquire a mother—and could not fulfill Mrs. Kinderlieber's needs.

Not all mistress/servant love in domestic service was maternal; an occasional glimpse of sisterly or womanly love made its way into the literature as well. It could take a number of forms. It might have entailed the concern of one woman for another within the bonds of womanhood. Or a lonely woman searching for platonic companionship. On the Colorado frontier, Anne Ellis was hired as a companion by her employer. They played and shared the daylight hours together, doing "anything except cleaning house." Another domestic recounted to Lucy Maynard Salmon that "real love exists between my employer and myself," yet as a servant she felt "desperate from the sense of being cut off from those pleasures to which I had always been accustomed." Given the subordinate role of a domestic within the household, within any mistress/servant relationship, it is not surprising that a genuine love between mistress and servant was rare. In 1869, a writer in *Lippincott's Magazine* bemoaned the absence of love. "Our domestics ought to be faithful," she wrote, "and their fidelity ought to awaken love and regard as a rule, and not as a once-in-a-while exception. That they are not generally faithful, nor we especially loving, is a fact that nobody will deny. And perhaps the fault is with us, for it is love that challenges and holds prompt and pleasant service, far oftener than service begets abounding love."[17]

In seeking love in the mistress/servant relationship, a mistress would have had a greater chance of satisfaction than her servant. Womanly love—"the long-lived, intimate, loving friendship between two women," the close emotional relationships which Carroll Smith-Rosenberg has described—required the sharing of common experiences even on a mother/daughter level. For domestic servants, the class, religious, cultural, and racial differences were too great to develop such a relationship with their mistresses. Maternal benevolence was no more successful; for most servants, the gap between mistress and servant was too wide to bridge.[18]

Even when the employer was extremely benevolent, class still profoundly separated mistress and servant. Ideally, most mistresses expected that their own lives would be radically different from those of their servants. For all the discussion of familial relations between household members and servant, nothing was more prized than a servant who remained loyally with one family for twenty, thirty, or more years, while parents encouraged their daughters to leave the nest. Time and again mistresses bewailed their ill fate in losing good servants to marriage. Mistresses expected servants to dedicate themselves to the families they served rather than to their own lives, their own interests, their own families. As domestic service changed and live-out maids and day workers became more common than live-in servants, mistresses opposed the change because it allowed employees to grow and change as independent people, free to pursue their own interests. Employers feared losing control over the servant's environment because then the whole range of human problems and emotions would compete with the employer's needs for the maid's attention.

In the North and West, class differences generally were thought not to be so great as to have been crystallized immutably. A lower-class native-born girl could be taught cleanliness and refinement within her employer's home. Not only would this serve to uplift the girl—possibly ensuring her loyalty by separating her from her background—but it would also guarantee that the standards of the refined household would prevail and be maintained. Ethnic distinctions were thought to be less malleable, and while mistresses thought they could distinguish between class and ethnicity, they did so only rarely. In the South, however, where black women provided nearly all of the general household help, racial differences were viewed as more permanent and biologically fixed than class and ethnic differences, although the latter were also often discussed in racial terms. In the South, many mistresses preferred the live-out system because they thought live-in service would bring into their homes the worst types of Negroes and that would corrupt their households. Many Southerners believed that there were limits beyond which blacks could not be educated or trained. The live-out and day-work systems also enabled married black women to participate in domestic service. While during the late nineteenth and early twentieth centuries less than 10 percent of urban married white women worked outside their own homes, nearly a majority of urban black married women were gainfully employed. Live-out and day work permitted more black women both to work as household help and to run their own households and families; thus a large surplus pool of black female workers was maintained. Not incidentally, the low wages paid Southern black males also served to maintain the large supply of black female workers. In both cases—class and ethnicity in the North, race in the South—the ties of womanhood and sisterhood were hardly noticeable.

One expression of the differences between mistress and servant was the employees' feeling that a servant's household was, in most cases, not a home. "Home is the place where the loved ones live," one servant said, "a place of freedom, with the companionship of equals on equal terms. Home is not the kitchen and back bedroom of a house belonging to another." Another told Lucy Maynard Salmon: "Ladies wonder how their girls can complain of loneliness in a house full of people, but Oh! it is the worst kind of loneliness; their share is but the work of the house, they do not share in the pleasures and delights of a home. One must remember that there is a difference between a *house*, a place of shelter, and a *home*, a place where all your affections are centered." This was the girl who, while expressing love for her employer, felt "desperate from the sense of being cut off from those pleasures to which I had always been accustomed." During the 1880s Almira told Helen Campbell of the social distance between herself and her employers. "From the time I entered the house till I left it," she recalled, "there was never a word for me beyond an order, any more than if I had n't been a human being. . . . That house shone from top to bottom; but a dog would have got far more kindness than they gave me." Jane Addams described the servant as "alien, one who is neither loved nor loving." [19]

Servants, after all, were not family; a domestic was not a daughter. No matter what maternal pangs moved a mistress to "adopt" a servant and treat her as kin, the independent growth experiences and often conflicting cultural, racial, ethnic, and religious backgrounds worked to plant seeds of suspicion and distrust. Even more overriding, of course, was the basic work relationship—employer and employee. While all parents at times feel distrust, resentment, and anger toward their children, the shared experiences of kin and the intertwining of lives and futures will often compensate for hostility in the short run. Servants had none of these things to share with their mistresses. Propinquity was not enough.

If the testimony of domestic servants on their exclusion from home amenities might be considered biased and self-serving, employers readily described the conditions they provided for their servants, and it reflected their attitudes toward domestics. In Minnesota, for example, mistresses expressed their consciousness of class differences:

"I think that many women would be more kind and friendly, but it spoils the girls, gives them false notions about their place."

"Do not think it necessary to give a hired girl as good a room as that used by members of the family. She should sleep near the kitchen and not go up the front stairs or through the front hall to reach her room."

"Do not think a girl ought to be allowed to use the front door."

"I can't give a girl time for church on Sunday morning because she has to get dinner."

"Servants are too independent, want to receive their company in the parlor and eat at the same table with the family. Don't think it proper to allow them to do so."[20]

Employers were acutely aware of the differences between maid and mistress. The 1866 *Annual Report* of the New York Association for Improving the Condition of the Poor broadcast the general reputation of New York domestic servants. The report noted that domestics in the city were chiefly immigrants, mostly Irish and German, and "they occupy the places for which they are best fitted." The respectability and status of that place might be inferred from the statement in the report that servants' "untrustiness and incompetence have long been matters of public agitation and private complaint." Within six years the complaint had become public in New York City. *Scribner's Monthly* took notice of the " 'Young Family Man,' who wails out in newspapers . . . how unspeakably atrocious the Hibernian maid-of-all-work; how unutterably preferable would be an American maid-of-all-work, but she will not come."[21]

As the predominant immigrant service group, the Irish attracted the greatest attention. Most were Roman Catholic and from rural Ireland, so their religion and outlook contrasted sharply with those of their employers. Before the Civil War, Irish servants in Boston and New York had faced widespread prejudice. "Potential employers disliked and even feared their religion," Robert Ernst wrote in describing New York Irish domestics during the 1850s, "shuddered at 'Irish impulsiveness' and turbulence, and were disgusted and morally shocked at the Irish propensity for strong drink." Newspaper advertisements with "No Irish need apply" became common, although the expanding city was dependent upon Irish immigrants as servants. Anti-Catholicism was at the heart of antipathy toward the Irish. Ernst found that French, German, and Swiss Catholic immigrants were also discriminated against. In Boston, Oscar Handlin found the fear of a strong and militant church extreme. "Though Boston could not do without the Irish servant girl," he wrote, "distrust of her mounted steadily; natives began to regard her as a spy of the Pope who revealed their secrets regularly to priests at confession."[22]

The difference between the religion of the kitchen and that of the parlor was a major concern of mistresses. Many employers did not interfere with the beliefs of their servants. Others, however, worked hard to introduce a Calvinistic or evangelical Protestant mood in their household. Reverend And. Ambaven, the author of *Suggestions to Girls at Service*, made an ambitious effort to bridge the gap between servant and employer. Published in 1889, his book was 3 by 4½ inches, apparently designed for a handbag, perhaps to be read and reread as inspirational literature. But if it was meant to inspire servants, it was designed to benefit their mistresses most. Dedicated to "our Catholic servant girls," it offered a Calvinistic view of work while attempting to promote a subservience to one's mistress that few housekeepers would have dared to demand. Failing to distinguish between the master of the next world and the masters of this one, Ambaven used biblical verse—"Servants, obey in all things your masters"— to teach obedience. "Christ the Lord," Ambaven claimed, "knew full well that a girl at service would have a good deal to suffer and a good deal to put up with." Of course, she must endure and elevate herself "by raising her service to the dignity and greatness of a service done to Himself." Servants must have patience and confidence, "suffer and complain not," and never despair. A servant must never complain about insufficient wages; she should be satisfied with whatever wages she had agreed to work at because "a bargain is a bargain." It is difficult to imagine literate servants buying this slight book for themselves, but from the employers' point of view it probably would have made an ideal gift from a mistress to a servant.[23]

In Jersey City at mid-century, Douglas Shaw found that "native-born citizens worked to change the Irish: to make them temperate, respectful of the Sabbath, and if possible even Protestant." Evangelical Protestants stressed the sanctity of the Sabbath and criticized Catholics for violating it. Apparently, however, Protestants tempered their own Sabbath custom when it came to household labor. While Protestants railed against Catholic use of the Sabbath and tried to bring Catholics into conformity with Protestant custom, there is no evidence that Sunday was a widespread day of rest for servants. The biblical injunction against servants working on the Sabbath was apparently overlooked when it suited employers. By the turn of the century, religion was no longer a major concern of mistresses. Whether this reflected the decrease in number of Irish servants, shifting patterns of xenophobia or an acceptance of Catholics can not be determined; in any case, Catholic servants were free to attend their own church and religious differences between mistress and servant had disappeared as a theme of servant literature.[24]

The stories about ignorant domestic servants were legion. They demonstrated the difference in breeding between the cultured mistress and the working-class servant, and seemed to affirm, at least for the mistress, why one woman was in a position of authority over the other. Maud Nathan related a number of such stories, conveyed without malice. When questioned about mock turtle soup, one cook who was being interviewed for a position in the Nathan home in New York City replied that she prepared the stock and before serving, "I gets the little mock turtles and throws them in!" Another servant thought that the thermometer in the dining room to measure room temperature and the one in Mr. Nathan's dressing room were identical. That same maid asked whether she should slice an orange into two or four halves. The cook who was interviewed probably was desperate for employment, and an admission of ignorance might have jeopardized her employment. Most servants believed that they could learn whatever was necessary on the job. For some, it might have been a measure of their self-confidence, as they assured themselves that they could quickly acquire the knowledge or skills involved. But to the mistresses it indicated the ignorance of a servant class destined not to rise.[25]

Mistresses were also aware that the gap was not just between different classes, religious groups, races, and ethnic groups, but between women different in nature as well. Underscoring the differences between servant and mistress was the apparent nineteenth-century assumption, judging from practice, that the bodies of employers worked differently from those of employees. Carroll Smith-Rosenberg has done much research on the life cycle of nineteenth-century women and lucidly details the contemporary medicinal and biological attitudes concerning women's physiological processes. For example, according to the medical writings of the day, puberty not only brought womanhood but also brought weakness, dependency, and fragility. To boys, Smith-Rosenberg noted, it brought "strength, vigor, and muscular development . . . ; to woman it brought increased bodily weakness, a new-found and biologically rooted timidity and modesty, and 'illness' of menstruation." Often the passage to adolescence was traumatic, accompanied by stormy periods: "Girls would suddenly become moody, depressed, petulant, capricious, even sexually promiscuous." Nineteenth-century health guidebooks outline these symptoms.[26]

At puberty young girls had to begin to pay close attention

to their health so as not to impair their ovarian development. Contemporary literature advised that at puberty "a girl should curtail all activity." One doctor, Smith-Rosenberg found, "advised the young woman to take to her bed from the first signs of a discharge until menstruation was firmly established months or perhaps years later." Others suggested avoiding "the display of any strong emotions. . . . They should spend much of their time in the fresh air, enjoy moderate exercise, avoid down beds, corsets, liquor and other stimulating beverages." The activities frequently suggested for young women were light housekeeping chores "such as bed-making, cooking, cleaning and child-tending." While this advice tended to support the restriction of women to the domestic sphere, it had a different effect within the household.[27]

The advice was intended for middle- and upper-class mistresses, not for their servants. Indeed, it justified the hiring of servants, since women were medically required to abstain, during certain periods, from strenuous and prolonged physical labor. Unfortunately for the servant, these prescriptions were not consistent with most of the demands of household work. Domestics did perform the therapeutic light housework enumerated by physicians, and fortunately they could easily avoid "down beds, corsets, liquor and other stimulating beverages," but they could not subscribe to the other regimens. There was no chance for a twelve- or thirteen-year-old domestic to "curtail all activity." And frequently the required domestic chores called for far more than the physical effort involved in light housekeeping, requiring severe physical strain both in lifting and carrying for ten to twelve or more hours a day.

The physiological and biological distinctions between women of different classes was not limited to menarche and puberty. Middle-class women frequently found themselves incapacitated by their monthly periods, while servants' descriptions of the cyclical moodiness, depression, and other symptoms testify to the mistresses' hormonal cycle. But servants were not supposed to express their moods and feelings;

they were not supposed to suffer the same physical "infirmities," whether cyclical or viral, as their mistresses. There is no evidence to suggest that mistresses made any allowances for the menstrual periods of their women domestics, nor for the normal range of sicknesses and infirmities common in the late nineteenth and early twentieth centuries. In reality, however, servants were not biologically different creatures from their mistresses, and the common complaints of employers indicated that servants were also subject to hormones and viruses, even if the mistress found such equality intolerable and unforgivable.

Elizabeth Kilham described these mistress/servant differences in the South in 1869. Kilham told how her servant "announced at breakfast-time, that we should be obliged to dispense with her services for the rest of the day, for she had a 'misery.'" The servant's illness, however, was the employer's misery, in Kilham's view; it placed her in a predicament. "We had dedicated this particular day to house-cleaning. Uncle Phil had been engaged to do the whitewashing, and if we put him off, there was no telling when he could come again." Kilham thought that the whole problem was one peculiar to colored people. "They have the 'misery in their head,' or the 'misery in their back,'" she wrote, "and any bad feeling which they cannot locate, is simply 'a misery.' Their ideas on the subject of health are somewhat peculiar. I never knew one own to being 'very well.'" Servants suffered from the shifting moods of mistresses not only because of propinquity, but also because of the privacy of the home. Servants "get the benefit of uncontrolled tempers and bad dispositions," Frances Kellor noticed, "while a girl in a store, by the publicity of her position, is often spared the worst." From the servant's point of view, Lillian Pettengill found that her mistresses experienced fluctuating emotions and moods, but rarely if ever was any consideration given to the physical or psychological state of the servant.[28]

This difference between the concern for the physical well-being of employer women and that of employee women could be manifested in other ways as well. Maud Nathan recalled an incident from her childhood in New York City in the late 1860s. Her father objected to her mother walking alone at night, and he offered to leave his whist game to escort his wife. She refused his offer, but reassured him by saying that "she would take one of the maids with her, and let her call for her again." Maud Nathan asked her mother why she needed an escort, and "she explained that some rude man might insult her if she walked at night." The daughter, however, could not quite understand how the problem had been solved satisfactorily. "The maid who escorted my mother was young and pretty. Why was there no danger of *her* being insulted?" she asked. "She was permitted to return alone and go out alone at a later hour to call for my mother."[29]

Mistresses were also aware of the cultural differences between people belonging to different classes. Katherine S. Bissell's personal copy of *The Expert Waitress*, a popular household guide, reflected her concern for uplifting the personal habits of her servant. From Philadelphia, she must have acquired the book soon after its publication because she wrote "April 10, 1894" under her name. She underlined or put a line in the margin next to sentences, which probably indicated that she felt these sections particularly important. While some of the marked passages could be of use to anyone—housewife or servant—many related specifically to the duties and person of a servant. It is possible that the book so underlined was given to her presumed succession of servants to guide them in her household.[30]

Bissell, to judge from the underlined sections, was concerned that the servant learn the proper style of table setting and service: "The sharp edge of knives must be turned towards the plate; bowls of spoons and tines of forks must be turned up." Bissell also stressed proper cleaning up after meals: "soiled plates and dishes should be removed from the right; in clearing the table, food must be first removed, then soiled china, glass, silver, and cutlery, the clean china." Moreover nearly the entire detailed chapter on correct washing of dishes was underlined, as was the chapter on the correct care of the pantry, including instructions on proper cleaning.[31]

Bissell consistently underlined advice relating to the servant personally, or to the manner of service. "Work in pantry must be as nearly noiseless as possible," and the servant should stay in the dining room "until she is sure that there is nothing more for her to do." And receiving double stress—both underlined and marked in the margin—was "To dress neatly. To keep tidy hair, clean teeth, and clean finger nails. To close a door without noise. . . . To handle dishes and silver in a quiet manner." Silence was invaluable: "Except in case of an accident which she cannot remedy, she should not speak to the hostess, who should be left perfectly free to entertain her guests without a care about the food." Of course, "listening to what is said at table, instead of concentrating attention upon the waiting," was forbidden. Finally, personal cleanliness was reemphasized. The servant's room should be aired every morning. Clothing was important, both for cleanliness and style. The servant should have adequate underclothing, fresh print dresses for morning work, and a dark costume for the afternoon.[32]

Katherine Bissell was highlighting what was stressed in the guidebooks on home service. The obligation to serve quietly and be unobtrusive, to wear appropriate service dress—"livery"—and to be clean were mentioned in nearly all guides. Another guide counseled that

the up-to-date waitress will no more think of omitting her full morning bath than of sending the butter to the table on an unwashed dish. . . . She comes in close contact with people who are ultra-fastidious. . . . She needs to maintain her own self-respect and claim that of those whom she serves. To do this, she can ill afford to neglect any of the personal niceties classed as "minor moralities." The daily bath and immaculate undergarments are at the foundation of these moralities. Cleanliness is next to godliness, and opportunity for cleanliness should be freely given and freely accepted.[33]

Why the stress on cleanliness? Why the comparison with "ultra-fastidious" people? Why the emphasis on clothes, even

Servant in afternoon dress. A model presented to mistresses in Janet McKenzie Hill's *The Up-to-Date Waitress* (Boston: Little, Brown, and Company, 1910).

undergarments? Why did Bissell respond affirmatively to such advice? These factors highlighted the class and socialization differences between mistress and servant. Urban servants, drawn from immigrant and black stock, presumably were from the unwashed, diseased, and ignorant classes. In bringing them into the middle-class homes, mistresses had to assume the responsibilities of teaching them the basic "moralities" of the higher classes. The guidebooks served to remind those unused to hiring or employing help that these matters required the attention of the mistress.

Mistresses tended to view this process of socialization as an important benevolent aspect of service. In her study of domestic service in industrializing France and England, Theresa McBride focused on paid household work as a modernizing agent. McBride described the process by which country girls entered middle- and upper-class homes and were exposed to a more modern culture. In effect, young girls moved through both space and time, from the backward agrarian countryside into the modern urban industrial society.[34]

In the United States, many servants had experiences similar to those of French and English domestics. This was especially true among native-born servants from country districts and small towns who entered homes in larger communities and thus were entering a more modernized and industrialized sector of the country. These servants began to work as young girls; their employers introduced them to new work disciplines and middle-class norms and values. Moreover, service allowed them to save most of their earnings if they wished, and it might have provided them with an ample dowry.

Immigrant domestic servants' experiences were like those of native-born household workers. The prevalent custom of live-in service most often removed them from their ethnic culture and threw them into direct contact with a more Americanized, more modernized environment. The highly personalized mistress/servant relationship and the close contact with middle-class family life to which servants by duty had to conform served to accelerate the process of acculturation. For immigrant women, this was an important opportunity for upward mobility within the larger society, and the dramatic contrast between propensity to work in service displayed by first-generation immigrants and that shown by second-generation immigrants testified to the intergenerational mobility achieved by immigrant servants (see Tables 2–9 and 2–10).

Yet there were distinct differences between the experiences of servants in Europe and those of white servants in the United States. Opportunities for mobility in station (occupa-

tion) or class (through marriage) were more limited for servants in the United States. In Europe, becoming a servant
was in itself an upwardly mobile step; in the United States
there was no European-type peasantry to inflate the status of
domestics. Moreover, there is no evidence that service provided a vehicle for women to marry men of the household or
local tradesmen. Barriers of ethnicity and religion were
added to divisions of class in the United States and served to
keep servants and members of the employer's family apart.
Mobility for immigrant servants was intergenerational; their
daughters and not they themselves would experience mobility. Black women of course did not experience the same mobility white women did, and their experiences as servants
were significantly different from those of white women (see
Chapter 5).

The significant differences between American and European servants lay in the attitudes of servants toward their
work and their mistresses. In the United States, household
workers seemed to be aware of the promises of mobility.
Rose Cohen's mother expressed this when she cried, "Is this
what I have come to America for, that my children should
become servants." Rose Cohen came to agree with her
mother, as she was stung by her lack of freedom as a servant,
her feelings of inequality, and her lack of opportunities. In
the United States, servants were less satisfied with their position because domestic work offered less upward mobility
than it did in Europe. And American servants expected more
upward mobility than did European domestics. Servants in
the United States tried to get out of household work as soon
as they could. They knew that they performed tasks that
were of low value in American society. After all, it was work
disdained by their employers, and servants faced daily reminders of that situation. Of equal importance was that for a
large number of American women, service was not a temporary way station between parental supervision and the au-
tonomy of their own households. The United States did develop a permanent service class, but unlike the situation in
Europe, where the permanent service class prided themselves

on their work and had a strong positive self-image, the American servant class had the lowest occupational status. They were confined to household labor either because as black and immigrant women they found no other jobs open to them, or because as working mothers they could not find other work compatible with their own family and household duties.[35]

If service offered opportunity for mobility through adaptation to middle-class values, it was solely within the control of the mistress. Servants had no free time other than that granted by the employer, and the question of free time was one of the great struggles between mistress and servant. Unlike the shop and factory girls, whose free time was their own and none of their employer's concern, domestics felt their personel independence restricted. "We are bossed eternally," one servant complained to Frances Kellor. "They ask us where we are going, where we have been, and what we did, and who our friends are." Another wrote: "Our employer feels, somehow, that she is our guardian and has the right to supervise all incomings and outgoings, to question us about what we do in our leisure, and to be 'mistress' as well as employer. All this meddling is usually kindly meant, but none the less it reduced us from the status of a free employee to that of a vassal." One employer fired her servant for lying to her about what she did in her free time.[36]

Restrictions on the servant's free time were not always benevolently motivated. Antoinette Hervey envied her mother's position of having one servant for sixty years; Molly stayed with her mistress and never married. Hervey's own experience was quite different from that of her mother; she had many servants, most of whom left her to get married. She complained that they married "right early—too early for my comfort and satisfaction." Under these circumstances, a mistress might bar her servant from entertaining visitors and limit her time off—as many did. The loss of freedom was deeply felt in the household. Servants had no choice as to what they wore or ate, where they slept, or under what conditions they worked. Restrictions might be levied because a servant wasn't doing her job well. This contrasted with the servants' sisters in the mills or shops, who regulated their own lives.[37]

The testimony of servants, as presented in the first chapter, shows how many of them came to dislike their work, the conditions of work, and the power of the mistress. Fear was one of the dominant feelings of most servants. If anything happened in a servant's presence—from an accident to an act of God—she feared being blamed for it. On her first job, upon learning that the family pet had died the past winter, Lillian Pettengill thought: "If the pet poll parrot had to die after being twenty years as a member of the family, I was glad it happened before my advent." Young women worked briefly as domestics and swore never to enter service again. Often they took jobs that didn't pay as well as domestic service but at least allowed them to assume control over and independence of action in their own lives. While many servants received better shelter and ate better than factory and shop girls, they could not decide to shift their priorities and thus be able to contribute more money to their family or to skimp on shelter in order to save money for a vacation or clothes or some other special treat. The mistress decided the basic allocation of the servant's income, since wages only comprised about half of the total compensation.[38]

The mistresses themselves also claimed to be powerless. One of the recurring themes in employer literature was the tyranny of the servant. A brief note in *Putnam's Magazine* in 1869 offered a solution to counter "The Princess Biddy, who rules so roughly in many an American kitchen." Liberation was possible only for the mistress who could say, "Go; I can do the work myself." "Otherwise," the author declared, "it is the servant who employs the mistress. Know housework and cooking, Madam. Then you can issue your Declaration of Independence."[39]

Another generation of mistresses expressed the same feeling of victimization in the pages of *Good Housekeeping*. Soon after its birth in 1885, *Good Housekeeping* sponsored a contest with a prize of $200 for the best articles on "the Vexed Servant Girl Question." Mrs. E. J. Gurley, a housewife from Waco, Texas, won first prize, and her six articles entitled "Mistress Work and Maid Work. Which Is Mistress and Which Is the Servant?" appeared serially in the journal from April through June 1886. One of her goals was to free the housekeeper from her enslavement at the hands of the servant(s) so mistresses could "regain the ascendancy and disenthrall themselves from the opposition of domestics." The secret lay in housekeepers exerting proper control and restricting servants to their subordinate sphere. Five years later Ellen Battelle Dietrick summed up the power of servants in *Good Housekeeping:* "So long as any Bridget just landed (even before she has learned to walk comfortably in American shoes) can be sure of four dollars a week and her board and prequisites, it is the Bridgets who are really mistress of the situation." [40]

Even European travelers picked up the complaints of mistresses. Paul Blouët, writing under the pseudonym of Max O'Rell, conveyed their viewpoint satirically. In commenting on the egalitarian nature of American domestics, O'Rell claimed that he accepted the notion of servants as equals but wished servants would also accept it; he reported that they felt superior. Servants' wages were so high that he had to write out one salary in words so that the reader would not mistake it for a printer's error. And he found the "servant problem" so bad that Americans were "driven from their homes and obliged to take refuge in hotels and apartment-houses." [41]

O'Rell also reported the tall tales and folklore he heard concerning how servants oppressed their mistresses and masters:

Servant-maids will often refuse to enter your service if there is not a piano in the basement.

Others will demand folding-beds. They will give you to understand that, when they receive their "gentlemen" friends, it is not proper and becoming to entertain them in a room where the bed on which they repose their charms at night is spread out.

A lady, out of patience with her housemaid, said to her: "I expect my servants to do so and so."

"Your what?" cried the indignant damsel. "I'll just tell you what I think of you. You ain't no lady, that's certain."[42]

The complaints of mistresses highlighted one of the peculiarities of domestic service: that it rarely was discussed in economic terms. When observers discussed conflict between mistress/master and servant, it was in terms far different from those used in contemporary discussions of conflicts of capital and labor, of bosses and workers. In 1886, for instance, Edwin P. Whipple described the inherent conflict in household work between employer and employee. The conflict, as Whipple described it, was a struggle over power and authority, divorced from economic questions. The struggle, of course, was not an equal one. "The nominal master and mistress" had to face "the mortifying fact that the object of their help is to render them helpless." "Despotism" would come to their household in the form of hired servants as "tyrants."[43]

Beneath the amenities of the mistress/servant relationship was a struggle between the two. Employers exercised as much power as they could, while domestics attempted to control their own labor and lives and retain their personal dignity. Mistresses maximized their control by requiring servants to live in, thus isolating them from outside influences and making the world of the mistress the exclusive domain of the servant. Employers could also use the intimacy of the mistress/servant relationship to exploit the affection and sympathy which a servant developed for her mistress. Mrs. Kinderlieber was an expert at this stratagem, as Lillian Pettengill discovered. Mistresses could withhold wages as fines or penalties, and the servant was powerless to do anything about it. Finally, the threat of summary dismissal hung heavy over servants. Although they generally experienced little difficulty in finding another position, the fear of unemployment was great because servants were of the class of women who were forced to work because their parents' or husbands' income was inadequate to support them.[44]

By the turn of the century, changes had occurred in domestic service that in effect tempered the nearly absolute power mistresses had exercised for generations. Live-out servants and day workers were becoming more prevalent than live-in maids, and by World War I, the transformation was almost completed. This shift had resulted from the growing dependence on black and married women who preferred live-out or day work. The servant shortage became more and more severe in the late nineteenth and early twentieth centuries as the number of servants failed to expand proportionately with the increase in women working or in the number of families. At the same time, the demand for servants grew as more and more American families could afford servants while the demand for live-in help was somewhat reduced by the increasing urbanization of the population. City living—smaller space, more conveniences, and the transfer of such home services as laundry, baking, and so forth to the marketplace—served to reduce demand. Moreover, the severe labor shortage that resulted from World War I forced mistresses to employ women who would only work as live-out servants or day workers. While some urban housekeepers preferred the employment of live-out help, most did not, and the shift was brought about by the women working in domestic service themselves. This was a rare case in which the workers in domestic service themselves had a great impact on the work conditions.

By and large, mistresses opposed the shift from live-in to live-out service. In 1901–1902, the Boston-based Domestic Reform League surveyed mistresses on their attitude toward supplemental household workers (day workers). Of those who responded, 76 percent said they could arrange to have some work done by outside helpers coming in and 24 percent said they couldn't. Nevertheless, only a minority were willing to even try the hiring of "outside" help, while 58 percent opposed shifting from "inside" to "outside" help, even if it saved money.

Why were mistresses so opposed to live-out service? Basically, employers objected to the loss of control over their servants. "I think outside help upsets the regularity of one's household," one housewife said. "They are more independent and are inclined to make the girls think they are doing too much; in short, cause a restlessness." Others recognized that live-in service permitted them to isolate and control their servants. "I should not be happy if people whose life and principal interests were elsewhere were coming into my house to work," reported a mistress. "I don't think humanity, as a whole, is naturally honest enough to bear the temptations, and besides, I want the love as well as respect of my help." Another said she was unwilling to accept day workers because they "have their own home interests, which take their strength, and they come to work tired." A mistress objected to "the carrying of filth and disease" by live-out servants and day workers. "You can make a girl who lives in your house keep fairly clean and you don't feed her on onions. Girls whom I have tried for 'outside help' need baths and different food." The sheer inconvenience annoyed still another housewife. "I desire servants in the house to answer the bell in the hours when an employee by the day would have left, and for numberless conveniences." Overall, then, live-out or day work was a demoralizing arrangement to many mistresses. "It would go far toward breaking up the *entente cordiale*," thought a mistress, "which should exist between masters and servants. In my opinion the family bond which does exist, in greater or lesser degree, between the two classes is worth maintaining. The mistress of a household would become much more exacting, the servant far less interested in the service of her employer." Finally, it would attract older, married women to service, and not all mistresses appreciated such an enlarged labor pool. Younger girls without extensive experience were doubtless more malleable to the mistresses' norms and desires. Older women, who were likely to be more experienced, more self-confident, and more self-assured than teenage girls, would be more independent.[45]

This relúctance of mistresses to shift from live-in help to outside help or even day workers revealed much about the employers' attitudes toward service and their servants. Clearly, many saw such a shift as threatening their control not only over the work but also over the servants. Outside women were the subject of loyalties, influences, and ideas uncensored by their employers. Live-in servants had little time or opportunity to develop interests outside of their mistresses' homes, and they could not choose between taking care of their employers' needs and wants and their own, as could live-out servants. Also, the shift from live-in to live-out workers would increase the centrality of the economic relationship and diminish the personal dynamics involved. While reformers advocated that depersonalization would make domestic service more attractive, at least some housekeepers felt this was untrue. They found the personal relationships gratifying and used such terms as "love" and "affection" in describing their relationships with servants.

Reformers had long advocated adopting the impersonal economic boss/worker relationship of the factory, office, or shop as a replacement for the intimate mistress/servant relationship of the home. And on the surface, live-out and day work seemed to bring about this change. Many reformers pinpointed the personalized mistress/servant relationship as the underlying cause of nearly all problems within household service. They were listening to the complaints of servants who reported that they suffered at the whims of their employers. A commonly offered solution was the introduction into domestic service of the contractual relationship of the world of work outside the home. One such elaborate proposal, typical of the genre, was Mary Ripley's guidelines for putting "household service on a more systematic and dignified basis." Endorsed by the Women's Educational and Industrial Union of Buffalo, her treatise on domestic service included a model contract prepared by the counsel for the Women's Union and wage receipts for use by servants.[46]

After the turn of the twentieth century, advocates of the rationalization of household work and the introduction of business organization into domestic service began to look to "scientific management" as a model. Writing in the *Outlook* in

1912, John B. Guernsey proposed studying the essential operations in the home, standardizing the work, initiating time studies, and then applying management principles to improve household efficiency. The goal seemed to be Taylorism in the kitchen, as illustrated by Guernsey's citation of "a typical time study covering the task of Mixing and baking ordinary soda biscuit":

Time Study

Materials—Flour, salt, soda or baking powder, milk, water.

Tools—Mixing pan, mixing board, measures, large spoon, large knife, cutter, baking tins.

Operations—Assembling materials, mixing dry ingredients, mixing and kneading dough, beating, cutting, placing in tins, placing tins in oven.

Item	Details of Operations	Actual Time Seconds
1	Goes to cupboard, gets mixing pan, cup, knife	65
2	Goes to storeroom, brings in sack of flour	32
3	Stands gazing out of window	102
4	Gets cook-book and finds recipe	16
5	Measures flour and puts it into mixing pan	34
6	Adds salt and baking powder or soda	10
7	Stirs and mixes dry ingredients	62
8	Time lost in getting milk from refrigerator	116
9	Goes to stove and regulates dampers	40
10	Stirs milk into the flour and makes dough	220
11	Adds more flour and kneads	30
12	Goes to sink, washes hands, goes to pantry for towel	38
13	Brings in mixing board and covers with flour	32
14	Spreads dough on board, beats and kneads	45
15	Gets biscuit tins, butters them, places on table	90
16	Cuts dough into biscuits and places in tins	78

17	Places tins in oven	10
	Total mixing time...(17 minutes)	1,020
18	Baking time........(24 minutes)	

By a better arrangement of facilities and a little planning, time could be saved in items 2, 3, 8, 9, 11, 12, 13, 15.[47]

In outlining four principles for the introduction of scientific management into the household—"realization of the essential operations" and elimination of waste; "scientific selection of the workers"; education and development of the employees; and "intimate, friendly co-operation between the management and the workers"—Guernsey seemed to violate his own goals in the last axiom. He explained "friendly cooperation" as defining tasks for the worker, rewarding "timely performances by a share in the saving," and preserving the workers' own time outside of work for their own use. But nowhere is the "intimate" aspect defined. Indeed, if the intimate relationship overrode the principles of scientific management, the whole scientific system would collapse. But intimacy had to be preserved within the system because it was household work; the worker came into contact with the most private and intimate area of American society—the middle-class home. Developing intimacy with the employee was one way of adapting to the presence of an unrelated individual within the household. It also served to meet the personal needs of at least some mistresses, as discussed earlier. Thus even the advocates of Taylorism within the household did not feel completely free to abandon altogether the domestic model of work and substitute an industrial or commercial one.[48]

The shift from live-in to live-out help and day workers did not altogether remove the intimate and personalized relationship. It served to remove some of the worst abuses—the limitations on servants' freedom and their subjection to the unchecked control of the mistress even in their off-hours. It did not, however, alter the basic tenor of the mistress/servant relationship.

Some servants did wish to retain a degree of mutual intimacy. An anonymous servant writing in the *American Magazine* in 1909 stressed the close contact involved. The servant, she wrote, "broods over her employer's faults . . . ; even kindnesses are slighted as being less than her due." Exposed to the disparity between what she had and did and the comforts of the family she served—indeed, comforts which she provided—a servant often grew envious. Jealousy also arose when servants were excluded from family events. In reality, of course, servants had no right to expect to be included in family events—picnics, outings, treats, successes. Genuine family members could expect to share in these things by right; for the servant it was a favor. But that the servant was sensitive to these distinctions and felt excluded was a sign of the degree to which domestics believed in their role within the family. Moreover, while nearly all servants complained about their powerlessness, isolation, degrading servant status, and overbearing closeness to the family, they seemed to prefer the ideal of maternal benevolence to that of impersonalization of the work. Although it cannot be proven, probably most though not all of the new young domestics preferred an environment in which they felt like a daughter of the house instead of an employee. The ideal they strove for, as they went from job to job, was a mother—someone who would guide and nurture them, whose warmth and comfort would remove isolation and loneliness. Most white servants were hardly out of adolescence, and benevolent mistresses could provide motherly supervision to smooth their way in the world. Ironically, this occurred so infrequently that it was an illusory hope.[49]

Servants, then, tended to feel ambiguous about depersonalizing household work. Many would have preferred a familial relationship in service if it was genuine and reciprocal. Domestics such as the author of the *American Magazine* article accepted the argument that the household was a more desirable and natural place for women to work than elsewhere, and seemed to desire closeness among equals. Like hundreds of thousands of other domestics, however, this author's experience taught her that it was not possible, and she therefore sought the more impersonalized and specialized work roles of the industrial and commercial worlds.[50]

While removing some of the intimacy of the mistress/servant relationship, the shift to day work and live-out service did not radically alter the conditions of work, the low wages, the low status, and the lack of mobility. As an occupation of women who could not find other work, service placed little power in the hands of the servants. The disparity between mistress and servant remained as great as ever after World War I. Collectively, servants remained incapable of countering the power of the mistresses. Numerous attempts were made at unionization, but with servants isolated, each working alone, problems involved in organizing them were insurmountable.[51]

To the servant, however, one power always remained: to quit. While servants frequently left individual employers, it was difficult to get out of the work altogether. Some women could find jobs in factories, a smaller number in shops and offices. Most girls knew, however, that only marriage would release them from this kind of work. It was of course more difficult for servants to meet eligible men because of the restrictions commonly placed on visitors. Nonetheless, most white domestics could expect that by their twenties they would marry and no longer be servants. As a group, black women servants, did not share in that release from servitude.

V

WHITE MISTRESS AND BLACK SERVANT

"I AM THE NEGRO, SERVANT TO YOU ALL," LANGSTON HUGHES wrote in 1936. As live-in servants, day workers, and laundresses, black women comprised a permanent service caste in nineteenth- and twentieth-century America. In the South, of course, there were not many white servants. "When a Southerner speaks of servants," Orra Langhorne, a Virginian, noted, "negroes are always understood. Irish biddy, English Mary Ann, German Gretchen, and Scandinavian maids are as yet unknown factors in our problem. Black Dinah holds the fort." After the Civil War, however, the number of black servants in other sections of the country grew steadily. In 1869, *Lippincott's Magazine* discussed the "Aunt Chloe," "Aunt Hannah," and "Dinah" in the South, and observed that in the North, with the native-born shunning service, "Airs from Erin or Africa or the 'Faderland' invade . . . the parlor." By the turn of the century, black servants had become so common that in some communities no white servants could be found. Helen Santmyer recalled how when she left Xenia, Ohio, to attend college in the East, "it made me uncomfortable at table to see a white hand beside my plate, putting down a cup of coffee; it was out of the order of things for white people to wait on other white people." Wherever one found a household with a white mistress and a black servant, the relationship between them was different from that between other women.[1]

Especially in the South, but throughout the United States, race relations and domestic service were intertwined. Orra Langhorne reported in 1890 that "among the white people of the South, difficulties about servants are generally spoken of as 'trouble with Negroes,'—Negroes and servants being synonomous terms in the average white Southerner's vocabulary." In his study of Athens, Georgia, in 1913, T. J. Woofter, Jr., concluded that "the broadest and most intimate point of contact between the races in the South is through domestic service, and the attitude of the servant to the housewife, and the housewife to the servant had much to do with the attitude of the races in general." Nearly a half a century later sociologists C. Arnold Anderson and Mary Jean Bowman, in studying the post–World War II changes in an industrializing South, concluded that "the servant has played a key role in the South in both class and race systems."[2]

Subordination within the household mirrored the white/black relationship prevalent in the South. "No white person, not even the little children just learning to talk, no white person at the South ever thinks of addressing any negro man or woman as *Mr.*, or *Mrs.*, or *Miss*," a black servant wrote in 1912. "In many cases our white employers refer to us, and in our presence, too, as their 'niggers.' No matter what they teach their children to call us—we must tamely submit, and answer when we are called." Barred from the front doors of Southern white homes, all blacks regardless of calling used the back- or side-door servant's entrance.[3]

In the South, domestic service was a complex system that was part of the racial caste structure. In the North and West, servants were rarely found in homes of lower-middle-class or working-class families. In the former slave states, black servants were equally common in households headed by wage earners as in those headed by white-collar workers. Anderson and Bowman called the South a "housewife utopia," where even low-income families could hire help. Reformers noted this pattern and cited cases of ill-fed and ill-housed servants in the homes of families financially unable to afford hiring servants who nonetheless employed a cook or a nanny or a maid. Many Southerners defended this exploitation by claiming that the employment of black servants was a benevolent duty of the white race. Blacks were incapable of independently governing their own lives, whites argued in justifying everything from social ostracism to denial of suffrage to employment as servants; only white benevolence could insure a respectable and responsible existence for blacks.[4]

Racial stereotypes buttressed and justified the subordination of black women in the South. Blacks, according to popular views, were childlike, lazy, irresponsible, and larcenous.

Walter L. Fleming, a Southern historian who firmly believed in the inferiority of blacks, studied the servant problem in Auburn, Alabama, during the first decade of the century. He concluded that except for "several families of poorer people" all classes of whites were "absolutely dependent upon the African for all servant's work." In turn, according to Fleming, the black community depended upon the earnings of women servants: "many a one of them supports herself and a husband or lover and several children who live in idleness."[5]

In studying Southern urban race relations, Howard Rabinowitz found the incompetence of servants a theme of white newspapers in Richmond, Virginia, Montgomery, Alabama, and Macon, Georgia. The *Macon Journal* concluded that "it is the experience, we believe, of every housekeeper in Macon that colored servants are hard to obtain, and in nine cases out of ten, worthless." In Athens, Georgia, mistresses concur-

Nearly every traveler in the American South reported the ubiquity of the black childnurse. *Opposite page*, Negro childnurse, New Orleans; *this page*, negro childnurse, Mobile, Alabama. J. Wells Champney's drawings of black servants illustrated Edwin King's *The Great South: A Record of Journeys* (Hartford, Conn., 1879).

red. One employer had a high turnover of servants, discharging servants for "worthlessness, untidiness and stealing." "I find them all more or less dishonest, unreliable, dirty and incompetent," another mistress declared. Many bemoaned the inefficiency of black servants and agreed that "they do not want to work." Others were convinced that the problem lay in black childishness: "I think that a negro cook is like a child, more liberty you give her the more she takes," said one employer, while another added: "Negroes have intellects of the type of children's and the only way to get along with negro servants is to humour them and command them just as you would children."⁶

If images of black docility and childishness supported white subjugation of blacks and burdened white mistresses, it also fit the needs of employers as well. One peculiar and most degrading aspect of domestic service was the requisite of invisibility. The ideal servant as servant (as opposed to servant as a status symbol for the employer) would be invisible and silent, responsive to demands but deaf to gossip, household chatter, and conflicts, attentive to the needs of mistress and master but blind to their faults, sensitive to the moods and whims of those around them but undemanding of family warmth, love, or security. Only blacks could be invisible people in white homes. It was even common for whites to discuss the inferiority of blacks in front of their black servants. A Northern woman found this a universal Southern trait. Indeed, she found discussion of black inferiority "peculiarly inspired by a dining-room atmosphere" in which black servants worked. Black household workers could enter a South forbidden to other blacks or even to them when they were not working. Some Southern parks displayed such signs as "No negroes allowed on these grounds except as servants." A black child nurse recalled taking her charges on streetcars and railroad trains: "So long as I was in charge of the children, I could sit anywhere I desired, front or back."⁷

These seemingly contradictory attitudes reflected a basic duality in the Southern white's attitude concerning blacks. White Southerners broadcast their ideas about the inferiority and dependency of blacks, yet they recognized white dependence upon black labor and service. Negro women were called childish and incompetent, yet they reared Southern white children. Southerners were capable of hating blacks so passionately that lynchings and riotous slaughter were condoned, yet they could sing psalms in praise of faithful family retainers. Emancipation did not change this duality experienced by many whites. Eugene Genovese has focused attention on this Southern trait in his provocative discussion of the black "Mammy" of the pre–Civil War era, the slave woman who raised the children of the big house, giving and receiving love and affection in an anomalous relationship within chattel slavery.[8]

Time and again, Southern women spoke of their dependence upon black servants. Orra Langhorne reported that Southern women "would not trust their babies to white nurses." Walter Fleming recalled in 1905 that "this past summer nearly every woman in town who has a cook was shivering with fear lest she would 'quit.'" T. J. Woofter, Jr., reported that Athens housewives feared losing their servants. Some came to believe that the dependent caste had become all-powerful. Mistresses in Athens were afraid that "a blacklist is kept by the negro lodges, and that the servants keep 'tabs' in this way on their employers."[9]

Some mistresses only realized their dependence when servants left. World War I accelerated the late-nineteenth- and early-twentieth-century migration of black domestics to the North, and led to higher wages for both men and women. One result was the greater difficulty housewives faced in finding or holding servants. In Clarke County, Georgia, many black washerwomen retired because their husbands or sons, for the first time, had regular and adequate incomes. Wives and/or mothers received family allotments from their men in the army, so many of the women stopped working outside of their homes. White housewives were resentful. "Negro washerwomen during the war were the most independent I have ever seen," a family head told an investigator. "When negroes draw government money, it is a hard

"An Old Mammy Nurse." (Julian Dimock)

matter to get them to work. Never in my life have I seen such conditions in getting the family wash done."[10]

While some employers felt uncomfortably dependent on their domestic servants, others perpetuated the image of the faithful old black servant. In part a carry-over from the days of slavery of the idea of the faithful house servant, it was expressed toward servants who stayed on with their masters and mistresses after emancipation. For instance, the wife of a prominent Alabama planter reported that her domestics had remained with her after the Civil War and that they were kind and attentive. Although as Peter Kolchin and Joel Williamson have demonstrated for Alabama and North Carolina, respectively, this pattern of loyal servitude was the exception rather than the rule, it happened frequently enough so that images of "Sambo" and "Mammy" appeared in freedom as well as in slavery. Southerners expressed an obligation to continue to employ those who had seen long service with their family. Others claimed that they had maintained servants long after they had use for their services or beyond their productive years out of a sense of paternal obligation toward the servants. The Southern white's condescending benevolence toward a faithful old retainer most commonly reached public notice upon the servant's death. Thomas Hughes, who had been Robert E. Lee's personal servant, served thirty years at Washington and Lee University. "Chesterfieldian in manner," and "beloved by officials, faculty and students," read an 1896 obituary, Hughes had been known since the war as "Uncle Tom." [11]

More commonly, emanicpated slaves who had been servants throughout the South demonstrated their newly acquired freedom by leaving their mistresses and masters. "The frequency with which domestics deserted their masters," Joel Williamson concluded in his study of the Reconstruction period in South Carolina, "discredits the myth of the 'faithful old family servant' (the ex-slave) loyally cleaving to his master through the pinching years of Reconstruction." Those who stayed tended to be the very old, the very young, or the infirm. As Patience Johnson responded to her mistress' request that she remain at work: "No, Miss, I must go, if I stay here I'll never know I am free." Domestics—even those with the closest of contact with white families—tended to depart at the first opportunity. In South Carolina in May 1865, "Old Mary," a child nurse, learned of her freedom on Saturday night and left without notice before dawn on Monday. This pattern repeated itself throughout the South. A Nashville, Tennessee, physician lamented the sudden disappearance of Fanny, who had been born and raised in a neighbor's home. Howard Rabinowitz found similar cases in the urban South, as did Peter Kolchin in both rural and urban Alabama. [12]

The testimony of white Southerners before the United States Senate Committee on Education and Labor in 1883 revealed the difficulty they'd had in adjusting to hiring free labor within a market system, even though their own power made it less than an openly competitive market. An Alabama mill owner thought it a "difficult matter to get house servants at any price." For his wife, the Civil War was most regrettable because of its effect on domestic labor: "My wife says she would not have felt so bad about the results of the war if it had only left her her negro servants." Mrs. Ward, a Southern housewife, recalled that during the days of slavery "there was very little trouble with servants in the households." She testified that among town families, socialization of blacks as servants had begun as early as possible. "It was a common practice in old times,"she said, "when negro children were born, to give them to the white children of the family . . . ; every child in the family had some servant assigned as his or her especial property." The war changed all of that; the servants "that we depended most upon and trusted and believed they would stay with us through it all," she recounted, "were the first to go."[13]

As time passed, Southerners began to romanticize the days of slavery and to recall only the faithfulness, loyalty, and competence of the slave and slave-bred servant. "The old household servant of slavery days," Oswald Garrison Villard told the National Negro Business League in 1905, ". . . is now at most deified. He is not only celebrated in song and story, but he is used to justify the whole institution of slavery. To hear people talk in Georgia or Virginia we might easily think that every slave was a Chesterfieldian butler or a mistress of the art of old-time cooking."[14]

Experiencing less control over free blacks than they had over slaves, whites came to compare the younger generation of servants unfavorably with the old slave-bred servants. "By the time I was fourteen years of age," a Southern white woman wrote in 1904, "the first set of free-born negroes were getting old enough to interpret life for themselves, and without the well disciplined experiences of their parents, who had not only been slaves, but had passed through the very drastic training of the Ku Klux Klans after the war." In describing domestic service in Auburn, Alabama, Walter Fleming observed that the old women were best; unlike the younger generation of blacks they were loyal and tended not to change positions. Marion Harland also felt "that the middle-aged mother or aunt of the smart colored damsel furnishes us with the best 'help' to be had in this, or any other country." Orra Langhorne agreed when she summarized the Southern housewives' plaint that agents had lured to the North the best servants. "Those who are left are mostly what are called the 'new issue,'—negroes who have grown up in freedom, utterly untrained as cooks, housemaids or nurses." [15]

Whites denigrated blacks in part because what a white Southerner might tolerate among whites became reprehensible when practiced by Negroes. In 1883 Mrs. Ward complained to the Senate committee about "one of the greatest annoyances that we have now under the present system of service": excursions. They began in the spring when a train would be chartered for a day's outing. Pleasure was combined with fund-raising; the outing was designed to raise money for churches or societies. Every black went, "regardless of the consequence." "No matter how much they may be needed in the house, no matter how important the occasion may be, or how urgent the need for their services," Mrs. Ward testified, "they will just leave the cooking-stove and the housework . . . and go off." Were these excursions, Mrs. Ward was asked, "as bad as white men on the 4th of July?" "Worse," she replied. "In the first place, the excursions of the white men do not interfere with the business of other white men, but on these occasions we know that everybody is interfered with and annoyed. Our household affairs are, of course, utterly neglected." The result: "In the mean time you have got to go and cook your own dinner, and another housekeeper has to go and wait on her own table, and so on." For the Southern housewife, life had become hard and dangerous. "It is such a makeshift kind of life," Ward concluded, "that it is actually dangerous to invite company three days

ahead, because you cannot depend upon your servants stay-
ing with you so long or doing what you want them to do if
they do stay." "I have known them to leave when they knew
that invitations were out for a dining in the house." She
found that "it is very hard to get along with them," but
didn't realize what her testimony had shown—that it was impossible to get along without them.[16]

Nonetheless, the larger Southern social structure—the
dominance of whites and the subordination of blacks—
provided the authority that ensured the subservient role of
the servant. Two hundred years of domination by Southern
whites set a pattern from which both whites and blacks
found it difficult to vary. Northern mistresses, for instance,
struggled with the dilemma of defining the relationship between employer and servant, not only in an economic but
also in a social sense. Mistresses asked themselves whether or
not the maid should eat with the family or use the parlor or
entertain friends in the house. Guidebooks, neighbors, or
family members might offer advice, but however a housewife
resolved these issues she was free to do whatever she thought
best. If she felt pressured by norms within her social circle,
they were pressures she chose to pay attention to. The constant debate over these questions in late-nineteenth-century
American women's magazines testified to the serious consideration these issues were given.

In contrast, Southern housewives, while equally concerned about the "servant problem," focused on wages, quality of work, and the growing migration of black domestics to
the North. They seemed untroubled by issues relating to
their role as mistresses or their relationships with their servants. Probably they felt more secure in dealing with their
servants, since the Southern racial code defined clearly their
role.

It is important to stress that Southern racial etiquette con-
strained mistress and servant alike. Southerners would cite
the experiences in the South of Northern white women who
would attempt to treat black servants as they had their servants in the North. The "new notions" brought by these

women included the ideas "that the native whites do not know how to manage, that the wages are too low, and that the servants are not treated as free American citizens should be." According to Southerners, this approach was doomed to fail; it could only result in the mistress "becoming a philosophical and perhaps an extreme Southerner on the negro problem," or the employer dispensing with servants and doing the work herself. While Walter Fleming and others saw in this some proof of Negro inferiority, they failed to understand the degree to which both mistress and servant were confined by community mores. Reform, especially by an outsider, was difficult because it threatened not only domestic service but also the caste system, an integral part of Southern culture. The black subordinate role was maintained by the community, regardless of any one family's actions.[17]

Given these circumstances, blacks responded in familiar ways. Laziness, poor work performance, and absenteeism, given the Southern belief in Negro inferiority, were acceptable black responses. In the process, however, they exerted control and power over their work conditions. Fleming concluded that "an incipient strike is going on nearly all the time except in the winter when food is scarce." While he used this to justify white dependence on inferior blacks, it also described the continual conflict between mistress and servant for control over work tasks and conditions. While this conflict was similar to mistress/servant tension elsewhere in the United States, the nature of the conflict was more rigidly defined in the South. No black could demand to use the front door or eat with the family; Southern racial etiquette ruled these out as areas of legitimate conflict.

At the same time, any effort by black servant women to organize and strike would have been interpreted as a black challenge to white superiority; the white response would thus transcend the economic issues involved. The Knights of Labor had a number of assemblies consisting of black domestics—in Washington, D.C., Norfolk, Virginia, Wilmington, North Carolina, and Philadelphia—in the 1880s, but there is no record of any economic activity. Black newspapers occasionally reported strike action by domestics, but their failure to record any results from the action suggests the strikes petered out. In 1886, servants at Greenville, Pennsylvania, formed a labor association and sought a fifty-cent weekly raise. Three years later, Bibb City, Arkansas, blacks, including domestics, refused to work because of ill treatment.[18]

The one strike about which most is known, the 1881 boycott by Atlanta washerwomen, illustrated the relative powerlessness of servants. In Atlanta, whites successfully mounted private and public power to destroy the organization and deny the washerwomen the wage increase they had demanded. In his work on race relations in the urban South, Howard Rabinowitz has described how in 1880 the Atlanta black washerwomen organized an association "in one of the black churches." A year later they revived the movement and struck for a dollar per dozen pounds of wash. Three thousand washerwomen joined the strike, and cooks, servants, and child nurses requested pay increases as well. The issues went beyond employer/employee relations, and white community power quashed the strike. Landlords threatened to raise the rents of women who were on strike. The *Atlanta Constitution* warned that "if they persist in their exorbitant demands, they will find house rents going up so rapidly they will have to vacate." In the city council a bill was introduced requiring all members of the washerwomen's association to pay license fees of $25.00 annually, the same amount levied against businesses in the city. Many women returned to work, but most remained on strike. Courageously they sent a letter to the mayor warning him that "We mean business this week or no washing." But the police had already intruded into the strike and had broken the movement. Within two days, eight strike leaders had been convicted of "disorderly conduct and quarreling." The recorder's court judge assessed five with five-dollar fines, three with twenty-dollar fines.[19]

Further weakening the bargaining power of blacks was the presence of an excess labor supply in the South. Although some black women did handwork in tobacco factories, few occupations other than domestic service were open to black women. Forced to do household labor to earn a living or to supplement the low wages of their husbands or parents, they formed a large labor pool in which they competed for the low-paying available work. Inadequate educational opportunity ensured that young girls would further enlarge the labor pool of domestics. Strikes inevitably had to fail in the South because, as Walter Fleming succinctly noted, "the country darkies will come in and take the place of some of the strikers."[20]

While Southern black servants were unable to counter the economic, political, and social power of whites, they could still exert influence over the work tasks. Thus the "incipient strikes" were just that—the only economic tool available to the servant. Since holidays were rare and servants were expected to work seven days a week, servants declared their own holidays by not showing up for work, as they did in Mrs. Ward's town. The only way to cut down on the number of demands made by employers was to do the work slowly and poorly, and thus using white-held stereotypes to the blacks' own advantage. Mistresses would accept slower-paced work because they attributed it to the nature of blacks. And of course visiting home during the long day and wishing to return home after a late supper was interpreted as saving time for laziness and theft, though in reality it gave black married women time to care for their families and homes. The time was not given freely, so blacks took it.

Because of the Southern custom of having black servants, domestics did have greater control over household tasks. If Northern housewives felt insecure about hiring servants or having outsiders perform tasks they themselves had once done well, Southern women had no such anxieties. Southern white women tended to leave their servants alone to clean, wash, cook, and nurse the children. As in the days of slavery, servants returning from work in the "big house" would take home for their own use leftover food and discarded clothing. Since black servants ran the kitchen virtually without supervision, only their own judgment limited the amount of the food carried home after work.

The food basket was the custom in every Southern town, and with the migration of black servants to the North, it became common there as well. A Southern servant described this practice, called the "service pan": "every night when the cook starts from her home she takes with her a pan or a plate of cold victuals. The same thing is true on Sunday afternoons. . . ." Many black families depended upon that food; wages were so low that the food was needed to supplement their income, and they viewed the custom as "a part of the oral contract, exprest or implied." Within the racial code, the food basket represented white benevolence toward blacks. From the white point of view, it was something unearned and given benevolently. At the same time, it confirmed the white belief that blacks could not control their tendency to commit petty theft.[21]

At least some Southerners saw in this custom the downfall of blacks. The chief of police of Norfolk, Virginia, claimed that "the 'basket habit' among the Negro women is the direct cause of the great excess of idleness and viciousness among Negro men." By receiving food through the women of the family, the men "become lazy and will soon prefer stealing to working," according to the chief. Northern reformers tended to think that wage-earning women resulted from under- or unemployment among their husbands; the Norfolk police chief was claiming the reverse—that if wives worked, their husbands became idle. Helen Pendleton, an agent of the Baltimore Charity Organization Society, agreed that the Norfolk problem was common in Baltimore.[22]

But more than race set the Northern and Southern patterns of domestic service apart. In the South the live-out system of domestic work had predominated since slavery, whereas in the North it did not become widespread until World War I. For blacks, emancipation and live-out service had become linked. A Mobile, Alabama, industrialist and banker testified in 1883 that black women who worked as household labor "want to live at home, and very few of them, cooks or servants, will consent to sleep on the premises where they work. They seem to think," he observed, "that it is something against their freedom if they sleep where they are employed, and I suppose that nine-tenths of the negro women who are in service in Mobile insist" on sleeping out. When asked how he accounted for the practice, he said blacks "think it is more like being free to have their own home and to go to them after their work is done." Indeed, live-out service did mean that at least for part of a day a black servant was beyond the direct control of her mistress.[23]

Although some black married women worked as live-in domestics, only a live-out system enabled large numbers of black married women to work as servants. Black women servants as a group were older and more likely to be married than white servants, whether native or foreign-born. The inadequacy of the wages received by black men forced their wives to work while raising families and running their own households, and black married women in 1900 were at least ten times more likely to be gainfully employed than white married women. Residential patterns also facilitated live-out work. In the North, the great physical distance between most white dwellings and black ghettos encouraged live-in service. In the South, however, the former slave pattern of black housing adjacent to white dwellings meant that blacks could work a sixteen-hour day or be on call twenty-four hours a day, yet live at home. Finally, within the South, there was nothing comparable to the "hired girl" system in which the employer provided a surrogate family and home for a young girl in the period between her parents' home and that of her husband. While Southern whites might assume that blacks were childlike and required a firm parental hand to guide them, they believed that this was a genetic trait rather than simply a stage of life; they did not believe that blacks would ever grow up or mature. Overall, in the South the live-out system seemed to serve both mistress and servant best.

On the surface, the conditions of domestic service in the South, unlike the conditions in the East and West, seemed to remedy some of the worst features of service. In some ways it seemed to resemble an industrial occupation. With most

Southern servants living apart from their employers, work-place and home were separate. White/black relations, with their set caste roles, could cool the intensely personal atmosphere that characterized mistress/servant contact elsewhere. Moreover, the abundance of servants in the South led to highly specialized work tasks—cook, laundress, child nurse, maid, and so forth—which seemed to mirror developments in commerce and industry.

In practice, however, domestic service in the South was no less personalized nor was it more similar to industrial or commercial occupations than it was in the North. Rather than creating greater social distance, the Southern racial etiquette served to ensure highly intimate relationships between black and white. For Southerners, the presence of black servants did not represent an intrusion into the privacy of the family.

For all the differences between black and white in the South, they had in common Southern cultural traditions. The cultural differences between whites and blacks in the South were far fewer than the dissimilarities between native-born white mistresses in the North and their immigrant or black servants. And given the degree to which black servants were an "invisible" presence in white company, whites did not experience any discomfort or anxiety at the presence of "strangers within the gates." Nevertheless, social distance was maintained by the Southern caste system. Since individual white action would not affect the subordinate role of blacks—Southern racial etiquette ensured this—whites could develop a far greater intimacy with their black servants than could mistresses in the North with their servants. Northern mistresses were faced with the problem that their own actions determined the nature of their relationship with their servants.

Ironically, the intimacy of the mistress/servant interaction in the South was one-dimensional. Few whites knew much about their black servants except for the stereotyped views which they held about the nature of all blacks. Many black servants spent most of their lives in white homes, while mistresses never entered their servants' homes. Blacks acquired encyclopedic knowledge of white communities and knew the intimate details of white lives, while whites remained ignorant of black lives. This increased the extent to which personalized white mistress/black servant relationships could exist within the South because it in no way implied reciprocity, which in turn might have implied equality.

Similarly, Southern caste etiquette worked against the impersonalization that could have arisen from the development of specialized work tasks within the household. While the abundance of servants in the South fostered specialization, the workers themselves did not become specialists. In white eyes, the work tasks of blacks were interchangeable. A woman could be hired one day to cook, another day to wash, and a third day to clean house. The hiring conditions were controlled by white employers; the terms of hire or work might be altered by whites in response to black actions, but the situation could not result from negotiations between equals. The Southern racial etiquette dictated that it could not appear that blacks controlled their own work.

The constraints of Southern racial etiquette on both white mistresses and black servants were such, then, that while the work performed by servants in the South resembled the work done elsewhere in the country, the employer/servant relationship differed significantly. The thread of woman-to-woman interaction that interwove the pattern of service in the North and West was almost nonexistent in the South. While Genovese has suggested that close white/black relationships were a significant aspect in the lives of female slaves in the plantation "big house," there is no evidence that it was widespread after the slaves were freed. Race divided mistress and servant, suppressing nearly every interest they might have shared as women. At one extreme, even shared roles of motherhood could be denied. A black child nurse discovered that her white mistress demanded all her time to the neglect of her own children. The nurse was allowed to go home to her own children "only once in two weeks, every other Sunday afternoon—even then I'm not permitted to stay all night." Periods with her own children were brief: "I see my own children," she wrote, "only when they happen to see me on the streets when I am out with the children [of her mistress], or when my children come to the 'yard' to see me, which isn't often, because my white folks don't like to see their servants' children hanging around their premises." While this was an extreme case of a married women with children working as a live-in servant, it did illustrate the divisions of race.[24]

Overall, black servants were less subject to the psychological needs and whims of the mistress. The Southern caste system kept the mistress from turning to her black servant to fulfill maternal or affectionate feelings. Blacks could neither benefit nor suffer from the situation in which Lillian Pettengill found herself when her mistress sought a substitute daughter in her servant. Similarly, blacks were less often the object of employer campaigns to reform or uplift their servants. Because most whites believed that Negro traits were fixed and inherited, they focused on rules for servants to follow. Probably few white mistresses ever assumed the role of surrogate mother for their black servants. Nonetheless, black servants as well as white ones were subjected to the rule of mistresses, which far exceeded the ordinary province of work relationships in industrializing America.

As a group, Southern blacks were less affected by the atomization of domestic service than white servants or Northern blacks. W. E. B. DuBois's study of the Farmville, Virginia, black community illustrated the greater integration of Southern black servants into the life of the community. Nearly three-quarters of the women servants in Farmville (143 of 202 sixteen years or over) lived out, returning to their own homes after their daily chores. The increased independence of the servant explained the worker's preference for this system. Moreover, the 59 live-in domestics were less completely isolated from their community than servants were elsewhere. A majority of Afro-Americans lived in Southern towns or villages comparable to or smaller than Farmville (1890 population: 9,924 blacks, 4,770 whites) or in rural areas. As in Farmville, black servants in small towns or rural

Black servant in a Turkish bath reposing room, 1904. (Photograph by Byron. The Byron Collection, Museum of the City of New York.)

rate and "their willingness to work made former slaves especially desirable." A similar program brought 350 freedwomen from Kentucky to work as servants in Springfield, Ohio.[28]

When the ex-slaves arrived by steamer in Boston, they were sent either to Cambridge Industrial School or to a Boston home. Three teachers trained the women as servants. From 1866 through 1868, about 100 orphans and young mothers with children were sent to the Cambridge school alone. "Rumors of exploitation by unscrupulous Northerners, the slackening demand for black labor in the North, and perhaps the wavering participation of Southern blacks" led to a diminishing migration that soon halted. Elizabeth Pleck discovered that altogether, 325 women had been sent to New England from Fort Monroe, Virginia, and the District of Columbia. In the long run, this sponsored migration failed to leave its mark on domestic service in Boston. Pleck traced the migrants in Boston, and in 1870 she identified 56 men and women living there, less than one-tenth of the 621 sent to Boston. Twenty-three of the 56 were domestics, 20 of them live in. By 1880 only 12 still remained in Boston—9 men and 3 women. The 3 "freedwomen—all married in Boston soon after their arrival—did not work outside their homes." Thus, none of the women remained domestics in Boston.[29]

Hampton Institute, a pioneering industrial training school in the South from which Booker T. Washington had graduated and after which he modeled his own Tuskegee, also attempted to sponsor the migration of blacks to work as domestics in the North. An open letter "To Northern Employers and Southern Workers" in the institute's monthly newspaper, *Southern Workman*, noted the growing shortage of servants in the North. At the same time, the South was "filled with half-paid suffering freedmen, anxious to work." The *Southern Workman* would bring the two together, communicating with Northern employers who would sponsor black migrants and providing blacks with references. A separate notice declared that "advertisements from colored people wishing situations at the North, will be inserted in the 'Southern Workman' free of charge, if accompanied by references from responsible persons," while "advertisements from Northern employers for colored servants will be received at our usual charge of ten cents a line." The monthly also offered to act as a mail exchange. By January 1873, situations-wanted advertisements began to appear. Julia Banks, for instance, requested cooking and washing work in the North, while Mary Harris advertised to become a chambermaid or waitress. Neither one listed their home communities; their addresses were care of the *Southern Workman*.[30]

For young black women, the North acted as a powerful magnet. At about the same time that the Exoduster movement led blacks from the South to Kansas, Orra Langhorne reported a migration of 700 blacks to Iowa. The women kept boardinghouses, washed and cooked for miners, or became live-in servants in Iowa. Black newspapers reported the unceasing demand for black servants, their welcome reception, and the high wages. In 1892 the *Wisconsin Afro-American* boosted settlement in Milwaukee by describing the great demand for servants under the heading NOTICE TO OUR SOUTHERN READERS. A few months later the newspaper followed up its campaign with a report of its success: "We can count twenty-one colored women in our city who have lately been employed by white families as domestics, and everyone has the reputation of being superior to the white servant." On the West Coast, where Orientals provided the bulk of California servants, the San Francisco *Elevator* broadcast the apparently unlimited demand for colored servants. "We have constantly applications for colored servants," A. W. Brevett advertised, "which we cannot supply." The correspondent from Stockton reported the great need there for black women, while the *Elevator* editorialized on the "great demand in California for colored domestic servants" and the need for migration of Southern blacks to the West Coast. Correspondents from cities in the South, writing in Northern black newspapers with a Southern readership, described in endless repetition the migration of black women to the North and the higher wages paid in the North. The Danville, Virginia, reporter for the Indianapolis *Freeman*, for instance, mixed her social news with details on higher wages in New York City and elsewhere and information about the women who had left in search of that higher pay.[31]

Intelligence offices or employment agencies assisted in boosting the migration to the North. Agents appealing for colored servants advertised regularly in black newspapers. In San Francisco, A. W. Brevett, M. A. Jackson, and Kennedy and Jackson announced their inability to meet the employer demand. By the 1880s the connection between employment agencies and migration had become bolder. New York City agencies placing "colored help" in positions offered to store trunks and baggage and provide lodging at "reasonable terms." In 1886 the *New York Freeman* correspondent in Louisville, Kentucky, reported that an employment agent from the North had visited the city. The agent talked with domestics and informed them of the scarcity of servants in

the North. By the turn of the century the abuses of employment agencies had become so notorious that many cities and
states sponsored their own labor bureaus, and reformers became concerned about black domestics victimized by unscrupulous agents. Frances A. Kellor investigated the situation
and found two types of agencies: Southern employment
agencies dealing directly with Northern employers, and
Northern ones who directly brought young servant girls to
the North from the South. Because many Southern domestics were unable to finance their way to the North, they
turned to these agencies, who readily paid their passage.[32]

The steady stream of black servants who left the South for
work in the North and West were not lured solely by recruiters or by the boosterism of the Northern black press;
conditions in the South also sent them northward. The only
effective way most blacks had to counter the power of Southern white mistresses was to leave the South. And they did so
in increasingly large numbers. In his study of Georgia Sea
Islanders who migrated to the North, Clyde Vernon Kiser
recorded the varying personal reasons for the original decision, ranging from natural disaster to family death to the
desire for greater opportunity. But two reasons appeared in
nearly all of the case histories: the Southern caste system and
the perception of greater opportunity in the North. The cy-
clone of 1893 and the hurricane of 1911, for example, had
severe effects on the economically marginal Sea Island way
of life. For island women, migration to the mainland offered
job openings, but within the Southern caste system, only escape through migration to the North offered reasonable opportunities. For many, as Kiser related, it was a movement
from farm to Southern city and then to the North. No labor
recruiter had to come to the Sea Islands; women knew they
had to leave. Similarly, when in 1886 the *New York Freeman*
reported the presence of an agent in Louisville, the newspaper's correspondent made it clear that out-migration was
caused by the poor working conditions. A Louisville domestic told the paper that "she had been working for a lady on
Third Avenue about two years at $3 per week and sleeping

outside . . . , paying $4 per month for room rent." She asked rhetorically: "how can we working women who have to do that way, clothe ourselves comfortably or save a cent to take care of us when we are sick? And if we lose a place we haven't sufficient funds laid up to buy food."[33]

A relatively small number of black servants managed to escape the Southern caste system by working in black households. In Farmville, Virginia, DuBois recorded that ten black families regularly hired one servant each, while several others occasionally hired day workers. "This system is, however," he concluded, "very different from the hiring of Negroes by whites." It was an anachronism similar to the old New England system of the "hired girl." Servants were neighbors' children. Moreover, since many of the employers themselves had been domestics, they had an unusual respect for the work performed.[34]

In the North, too, there were black families with servants. In 1883 the *New York Globe* reprinted an item from the *Hartford* (Connecticut) *Courant* in which a reporter had visited the home of "an accomplished colored lady." "Instead of telling me of her travels and distinguished acquaintances as I hoped she would do," the reporter found that the hostess "turned the conversation upon the difficulty of obtaining competent domestics." A few years later, Mrs. N. F. Mossell explored the "servant girl question" in her column in the *Globe*, "Our Woman's Department." Her column was aimed at black employers, and she discussed the problems of granting servants independence and freedom and of providing a good home environment for them. These few articles aimed at black employers revealed a rare sensitivity to servant needs and an enlightened progressive attitude concerning the treatment of servants. Inevitably, however, what they offered was maternal benevolence with its familiar advantages and disadvantages.[35]

The most common escape from Southern white mistresses was migration to the North. While wages and race relations in the North seemed enviable to Southern blacks, the adjustment to life in the North was not an easy one. A 1913 study of thirty-five blacks, ten of whom were women, compared their experiences in the South with their lives in their new environment, New York City's Harlem. Nine of the ten women had come to the North after the turn of the century, and from October 1912 through February 1913, three worked as cooks, two each as dressmakers, laundresses, and domestics, and one as a duster. In the South two had worked as domestics, and one each as dressmaker, cook, and laundress.[36]

In the South the "church was the center of social life." All had belonged to a church, which had housed the communal social events. All liked music, and most had had instruments in their homes. Social visiting had been an important part of their world; thirty-three of the thirty-five had spent at least one evening a week visiting friends, listening to music, singing, or conversing. Christmas and Thanksgiving had been their central home festivals. "Great preparations were made and even the poorest family had his kitchen white washed," Benjamin H. Locke wrote in describing the Southern custom. " 'Company was sure to come and everything must look good,' " one of the group told Locke. "Stores of provisions were laid in and cooked in order that all might have. . . . Friends visited the homes of each other at this time, who visited at no other time during the year." In their ordinary diet, they preferred fish and fowl. Most had raised their own poultry; fish had been bought from hucksters. Fruit was a great luxury, but vegetables had been plentiful.[37]

In the North, the church was of less importance to them. Some found other institutions more rewarding. While none, for instance, had attended movies in the South, thirty-two did so in the North. Twenty-seven attended the cinema at least once a month, and they went to theaters catering to blacks. Visiting as a social custom was much reduced in the North, and they had fewer friends. They were more suspicious of their environment and of their neighbors in the North. In the South, for example, they had responded to a doorbell with "Come in"; in the North, their response was likely to be "Who's there?" Overall, their social life was greatly diminished. Food remained important, and Locke concluded that lower-class blacks had "better and more abundant food than is eaten, perhaps, by any other race of people of the same economic status." Locke's conclusion was that as a group they found better wages in the North, which in turn increased their needs and led to a higher standard of living. At the same time, they faced competition from immigrants, a factor not present in the South.[38]

While Locke did not discuss the effect of the uprooting from South to North on the women, information on the experiences of other domestics revealed the effects. In exchanging the intimacy of small Southern black community life for the impersonal relations of urban life or the overpersonalized mistress/servant relationship, black women paid a heavy price. In the North any live-in domestic servant would have found herself cut off from her family as well as from the social world of her Southern community. As DuBois reported for Farmville, Virginia, in going to the cities married couples and widows left their children with grandparents, splitting up their families. For the unmarried or childless, going North meant severing ties with the fabric of their everyday life. Limited free time would cut them off from the church; lack of a home in which to entertain would bar the domestic from reestablishing a visiting circle. Servants were in special demand on Christmas and Thanksgiving, and only rarely was a domestic released from work on these holidays. Although Locke indicated that the Harlem group of Southern blacks attempted to maintain their standards in diet, adhering to a Southern diet was difficult in the North. Fish were plentiful in New York, but nearly all were salt-water species. There were fewer kinds of vegetables, and what vegetables were available were much more expensive than in the South. And a live-in domestic would have to eat the meals provided by her mistress. Thus like the immigrants who came to the United States from abroad, these internal migrants from another section of the country faced difficult adjustments.[39]

Black domestic servants in the North shared with white

domestics the impact of the migration experience on their lives. As a group they were movers; uprooted from their original homes, they tended to keep on moving. Vernon Kiser recounted the peripatetic career of Beatrice Bingham. Born on St. Helena Island in 1896, she was taken by a relative to Philadelphia in 1900. A year later her mother brought her to Boston. She graduated from Hampton Institute in 1911 and taught school in Virginia for one year. She returned to Boston and after three months found a job as a domestic in Connecticut. She traveled to California and New York with her mistress, but became dissatisfied with her job. Moving from Bronxville to Manhattan, she found more satisfactory housework. Two years later she returned to California to work for three sisters she had met on her earlier trip there. "Her loneliness was unbearable in her new place," Kiser reported, so she moved to Chicago to become a hairdresser. Three years later she was back in New York. While Bingham's experiences were probably an extreme example of mobility, servants as a group tended to be highly mobile workers.[40]

Since all servants, white or black, had very little economic power, only a change of mistress could alter their working conditions. Constant change became the hallmark of servants, as mistresses complained, because in general it was the structure of the work relationship that was at the heart of servants' dissatisfaction. Domestic servants, however, were also part of the general pattern in nineteenth-century American society by which men and women without real estate or savings were more geographically mobile than people of means. Elizabeth Pleck found a relatively high rate of turnover among black women in nineteenth-century Boston. Eliminating those who had died in the interim, Pleck could find only 24 percent of black women enumerated in the 1870 census in Boston in the census ten years later. Black women had dropped out of the population of Boston even faster than black men in the city. There was an especially high rate of turnover among Canadian-born black women, and Pleck attributed this to Nova Scotian domestics returning to their home island. In some cases women migrated out with family or friends, while others left "alone to find domestic work." Finally, wage earning black women were more likely to leave Boston than housewives.[41]

The serious shortage of domestic servants throughout the latter part of the nineteenth century allowed black women relatively independent geographic mobility. A woman could at least anticipate little difficulty in finding a job in a household wherever she went. At the same time, the relatively difficult conditions under which domestics worked produced a large job turnover, which in some cases produced a voluntary out-migration from a city and in others, where a worker's reputation might have been besmirched by a dissatisfied employer, might have produced involuntary out-migration. Only a minor role would be played by recruiters in this process. A black woman might have come to Boston or have left the city for another town lured by the promise of higher wages. Once there, separated from family and familiar surroundings, she might have chosen to return to her original home or to follow a more promising lead elsewhere. All of these factors would have tended to increase the geographic mobility of domestic servants, aside from the normally high population turnover that Pleck and Thernstrom and Knights and others have reported among the lower classes.[42]

Migration exposed young black and white women to the misfortunes associated with domestic service. Reformers, scandalized by cases of immigrant girls lured into prostitution, crusaded against this "white slavery." Young black women found themselves trapped in the same circumstances by recruiters or employment agents. Blacks commonly comprised the servant class in houses of prostitution throughout the North, and Frances Kellor revealed that the worst employment agencies were notorious for sending black servants to work for prostitutes. Presumably the agencies were paid more to send the women to work in houses of prostitution, and the women were forced to accept these assignments because they were in debt to the agencies. When a Southern agent paid for the servant's transportation North, the office in the city controlled the domestic until the debt was repaid. Kellor claimed that it was a frequent practice not to place a girl with money until her resources had run out and she became indebted to the agency. Generally the agent held the girl's trunk or baggage until the debt was liquidated. "These dangers are not exaggerated," Kellor wrote. "They are really underestimated. From one Georgia town this year some three hundred Negro women have been sent North."[43]

The perils faced by women in the South were no less severe. Agents in Richmond, Norfolk, and Lynchburg, Virginia, made no inquiries of a man when he approached them requesting "good-looking girls of no particular ability, for employment in a clubhouse on the east side of New York City." The only guarantee of the employer's good faith they required was the payment of the office fee. The intelligence offices "have freely offered to supply girls who will sign a contract to work out their transportation." In Virginia and the Carolinas there were reports "of men who offer all sorts of inducements to girls who will go North," some men to get women for legitimate employment, others to lure girls unexpectedly into vice.[44]

While domestic servants had to contend with other women on a day-to-day basis, the problem of labor agents shows that men were not altogether absent from a domestic's world. In theory women governed the household, but men often played an active role or established a framework within which the mistress pursued her duties and obligations. The initial decision to employ a servant, for instance, might emanate from the husband. A man might want to release his wife from what he perceived as household burdens or might wish to hire servants to announce his status in the community. Or the idea might originate with the mistress, with the actual decision being made by the man in his role as financial decision maker in the family. Moreover, the wages of live-in servants and the hours of day workers might be set by the man.

Men had political and economic power outside the household as well, and some servants depended upon them for guidance and help. In the South, black servants sometimes asked their employers' husbands to intercede on their behalf, since blacks were powerless within the white commercial and governmental structure. A Shelby Country, Alabama, planter and lawyer responded to his servant's request and bailed her husband out of jail. While this might have been part of the paternal benevolence Northern white families could assume toward their servants, it was an ordinary occurrence in the South, where blacks needed white assistance to deal with Southern institutions outside the black community. In the North, men performed a similar paternal role—finding jobs for husbands, children, or siblings, giving financial advice, and so forth.[45]

Within the household the man also might become involved, although in a more passive way than the woman, in the day-to-day dealings with the servant. His own personal needs—such as, for example, a breakfast before the rest of the family—might place him in direct contact with the servant. This intrusion into domesticity could cause serious role conflict for a servant. Lillian Pettengill found herself invited to eat at the breakfast table by the man of the house, which was contrary to the rules laid down by the mistress. She sat down only after being ordered to do so, and it produced great self-consciousness and anxiety. "Suppose Miss Arleen, into whose place I had dropped," she thought, "should appear and be wrath." Although it turned out that Miss Arleen would not have objected, situations such as this one involving a conflict over authority put the servant in a position in which she could become an innocent victim, caught between mistress and master. In most accounts of domestic service written by servants, the male figures were generally distant, shadowy figures. They seemed to intrude into the household rather than to be an actual part of it. Or they seemed to be relatively powerless in the household. Pettengill related an incident told to her by another servant about a husband who was fed up with his wife changing servants every two months. "I'm tired of it—you never get absolute perfection," he told his wife. "I can't in my business and it's unreasonable to expect it. This one is all right, and I say she must stay."

The woman's supremacy over domestic matters in this household was preserved, however, when she "began to cry, and he gave in. She always cried when she couldn't get her way."[46]

Some servants preferred a master to a mistress. In her *Good Housekeeping* "Woman's Work and Wages" section, Helen Campbell quoted servants who preferred male employers. Both women stressed that "a man knows what he wants." "A woman," the daughter of an Irish cook declared, "never knows what she wants, and sort of bosses you everlastingly." Probably Campbell used these statements to emphasize that mistresses ought to have been more businesslike in running their households. Nevertheless, not all women found women employers satisfactory, nor did they appreciate the dynamics of a woman-run enclave. But few servants had any alternatives to female employers.[47]

The one area of great power of men over servants was in sexual contact. The sexual exploitation of servants by masters—the initiation of boys and young men into sexual relations—was an important theme of Victorian literature. The success of the master or of other men of the household in using a maid as a sexual object reflected the powerlessness of servant girls. Afraid of dismissal, some submitted to private indignities. On the other hand, servant women who were lonely and cut off from normal social contacts also needed warmth and passion. Working within a private home and having intimate contact with the men of the household, a servant had opportunities for sexual play with them as well as for mutual sharing of love. But given the sharp social, ethnic, religious, and racial divisions between servants and their employer families, U.S. domestics rarely married a member of the employer's family.

For Southern blacks, white sexual exploitation was a major problem. Blacks were outspoken in declaring this to be one of the major abuses of the Southern caste system. Domestic service seemed to compound white male sexual exploitation because it placed young girls even more directly under white power within a system that condoned white male/black female relations. From slave days when slaveholders had liaisons with their female slaves this sexual contact had been tolerated by whites, whereas relations between black males and white females was taboo in the South. Moreover, the practice of black nurses bringing up white children made exchanges of affection between black women and white children acceptable. With affectionate contact legitimized from the white point of view, black women often found themselves harassed by whites who expected no resistance from blacks. A child nurse recalled that she "lost my [last] place because I refused to let the madam's husband kiss me." Apparently he had been accustomed to intimacies with servants, she thought, because without preliminaries "he walked up to me, threw his arms around me, and was in the act of kissing me, when I demanded to know what he meant, and shoved him away." Her husband was arrested and fined twenty-five dollars after he filed a complaint against the white employer. The nurse observed that from her experience this was common in the South. DuBois believed that blacks were "coming to regard the work [service] as a relic of slavery and as degrading, and only enter it from sheer necessity, and then as a temporary makeshift. Parents hate to expose . . . their daughters to the ever-possible fate of concubinage." A middle-class black woman who had been spared the experience of working as a servant pledged that "there is no sacrifice I would not make, no hardship I would not undergo rather than allow my daughters to go in service where they would be thrown constantly in contact with Southern white men for they consider the colored girl their special prey." Southern black women servants could resist at their own peril or submit, but no outside force could or would provide support.[48]

White servants were also the prey of unscrupulous employers. In 1908–1909, the labor bureau secured the case histories "of 100 women living habitually immoral lives in Boston." In a number of cases an employer had seduced and abandoned an employee, and this had led, according to the bureau, to a life of prostitution. The victims included a waitress, a saleswomen, a stenographer, and two domestic servants. Initiation into sexual intercourse by an employer was not limited to servants, but they were particularly vulnerable. "If the men of her employer's family have any desire to mislead her," the report on women and child wage earners concluded, "her position makes it peculiarly easy to do so." In the case of the two former domestics, both were "young girls seduced by employers' husbands." One had been fifteen years old, the other sixteen, when they had been "seduced and deserted in such cold-blooded fashion." The Chicago Vice Commission reported similar cases among servants.[49]

Men also openly sought domestic servants for purposes other than household work. One of Frances Kellor's investigators examining employment agencies reported that a well-dressed woman entered a prominent Chicago office and asked, "Have you the girl you promised?"

"Yes" was the reply.

"You are sure you understand—his wife is dead, and he wants a girl who can play the piano and is entertaining—and—you know the rest."

The agency sent out a young, fresh, good-looking girl with her. Interestingly, the woman-to-woman character of domestic service was preserved by having a woman relative or friend of the male employer do the actual hiring. Kellor observed that "offices continually send young girls to homes where they know there are unscrupulous husbands and sons and say: 'If they don't stay, that's another fee; if they do, that's not our look-out.' "[50]

Reformers—white and black middle-class women—were concerned with the exploitation faced by single women migrants in the North. As migration to the North increased during the late nineteenth century, a few white institutions opened their doors to migrant black women. In 1888 the New York Working Women's Industrial League opened its home for working girls to blacks, and in 1897 the Philadelphia Young Women's Association established a bureau to help black working women. By the first decade of the twentieth century when the stream of black domestics migrating

North had become a flood, black women had established working-class homes in cities throughout the North, including the Pittsburgh Working Girls' Home and the Detroit Refugee and Rescue Home. In Philadelphia in 1905 black women organized an Association for the Protection of Colored Women "to protect women coming from the South." Frances Kellor's exposé of unscrupulous employment agency practices publicized the abuses of the private agents, but the reforms—working girls' homes and public and charity-run employment agencies—did not affect any of the conditions of domestic work. Instead, these reforms were aimed at alleviating the exploitation of domestics who naively came to New York and other large cities without friends or means, dependent upon the agent who sponsored them or the men who met the boats in the East and the trains throughout the North and West.[51]

The experiences of black domestic servants in the North were different from the experiences of other domestics. Although the tensions between white mistress and black servant in the North were similar to the mistress/servant tensions in the cases of other domestic workers, caste still was present. Black women had few job opportunities outside of household labor. In 1900 in New York City, for example, 84 percent of all black women wage earners were servants or laundresses; among whites, only 30 percent were. Black servants tended to be older and were more likely to be married than white servants. Among black married women in New York City in 1900, 31.4 percent held gainful employment, compared to 4.2 percent of white women. Among women forty-five and over, 53 percent of black women worked, but only 13.5 percent of whites. Urban black women worked most of their lives. While marriage and childbearing gave many urban black women a respite from wage-earning, probably a majority would work after marriage at some point.[52]

The differences between white servants and black ones must have affected their attitudes toward service and their relations with their mistresses. Married black women, with their own homes and families, must have found it difficult to submit unquestioningly to the judgment of a housewife who was sometimes younger and less experienced than they themselves were. Among other things, marriage offered an escape for white women, since so few worked after marriage; in general, no such escape was available to black women as a group. Indeed, black women probably took with them to their employers' households concerns about the responsibilities for their own homes, which they had just left. Although an occasional nursery for children of working mothers appeared in Northern cities, most mothers who could not take their children to work with them had to make arrangements to leave them with family or friends.

Cultural as well as racial differences separated North and South, and both mistress and servant could find the adjustment difficult. Antoinette Hervey told the story about "big black Katherine" and her recipe for her best cookies. Hervey asked Katherine for her recipe:

"Wal, I takes a yaller bowl, and the yaller bowl mustn't have no spout. In that yaller bowl I dumps a hunk of butter. Then frow in a good mess of sugar, so they'll be nice and crusp. Mux 'em up thorough. Then comes aigs. Ef they's cheap, I takes four. Ef I feels a leetle close, I takes three. Ef they's dear, I takes two. One'll do rat well. An ef they's very dear, I discharge aigs and don't use no aigs at all. Then I mux in the aigs or no aigs, dump in flour, bakin'-powder, milk, an seasoning. For seas'ning I use my jedgmunt. Sometimes it's one, sometimes it's another. Then mux, roll out, cut, and bake."

Even though the recipe was hard for someone else to follow, Katherine knew it well enough to turn out delicious cookies every time. The recipe came from experience, not from any cooking manual. Perhaps it had been handed down from her mother or a close relative. In any case, food played an important role in black culture in the South, and creativity in cooking was part of a folk tradition shared by many black women. And cooking was part of an oral or practical tradition, not a written one. Recipes were transmitted orally or learned by working with other cooks, mostly within a family setting. Rather than reflecting ignorance—the point of Hervey's retelling the story—the ancecdote revealed Katherine's mastery of the kitchen arts. She was not unsettled by the scarcity or lack of eggs, for due to her knowledge of cooking, she could use substitutes to provide the required results. But her Northern mistress had little understanding of this Southern folk system.[53]

Overall, mistresses in the North and West probably adapted more to their black servants than the servants adjusted to their mistresses. Although it is impossible to precisely weigh the variables influencing the shift in domestic service outside the South from live-in to live-out work, the growing importance of blacks in Northern service was probably the most important. As a group in which married servants predominated, black servants probably forced white housewives to reluctantly accept live-out workers. As in the South, blacks could use the racial prejudices of white mistresses to exert greater control of the work. Although not with unanimity, many Northern whites viewed blacks as stereotypically as Southerners did.

What black servants could not do was to elevate the status of service in any way. Ethnic stereotyping was the stock in trade of all employers of servants, and it is difficult at times to figure out whether blacks and immigrants were held in contempt because they were servants or whether urban service was denigrated because most of the servants were blacks and immigrants. When Californians, for example, sung the praises of Chinese men as domestics, they ascribed to them racial characteristics that had been long associated with domestic servants of any race or ethnicity. The Chinese promised to relieve California housewives from the tyranny of female servants. Chinese men were "economical": they paid for their own food and clothing, and for ten dollars a month they did the work of a thirty-dollar servant. A room was not required; they would sleep on the kitchen floor or in a shed. But they were also wily; they used the Christian Sunday school merely to learn English. Conversion led them to assume "sanctified airs" and shirk their work and neglect their duties "so as to hurry away to evening school." Still, they made good, quiet servants: they worked harder than Bridget and didn't bring company into the kitchen. As the Chinese adjusted to the American environment, they began to demand higher wages and better conditions. Mistresses reacted as they had to the independence of blacks and immigrants, interpreting their requests for adequate housing in the home as a license for theft. Moreover, they were considered disloyal or irresponsible for leaving positions. A mistress complained that no matter how badly their service might be needed, they left without any advance notice. Despite these faults, "as has so often been said, in many respects they are the best servants that we ever had." [54]

What is most interesting about this discussion—and about similar ones concerning Irish, black, Scandinavian, and other servants—was that aspects of the employer/employee relationship came to be touted as racial characteristics of the servant group itself. Employer suspicion and employee theft were translated into a racial characteristic: all Chinese or blacks or Irish were thieves. Quitting a position, the only way to improve conditions that was available to a servant, became a racial trait of disloyalty, and so on. It is remarkable how interchangeable were the employers' descriptions of the hereditary behavior of their servants. Indeed, while these descriptions provide us with very little information about race, they reveal a great deal about the uniformity of conditions and relationships in domestic service.

With other women shunning domestic service, if possible, blacks also sought to get out of it. They sought escape not only from white male domination and exploitation but also from work connoting caste. In describing the disinclination of Maine-bred women to enter domestic service, the Maine labor bureau concluded that the feeling had become "as strong, almost, as the Southern pride which asks: " 'Do you think I am a nigger to wait on you?' " As soon as industrial opportunities began to open to black women during World War I, they left service as rapidly as possible. Not enough opportunities elsewhere were open to all black women, and they still remained the single largest group in service. [55]

❧ VI ❧

THE SERVANT PROBLEM

THE SERVANT PROBLEM WAS THE BREAD AND BUTTER OF women's magazines between the Civil War and World War I, and it filled volumes of general-circulation weeklies and monthlies as well as the earliest issues of social-science journals. The servant-girl problem, to one housewife, was that "thoroughly competent girls for general housework are not to be had 'for love of money' in some places. Girls rush into stores and shops as 'salesladies' and go half-starved, half-clothed, and half-housed, and wear themselves out in soul and body rather than 'degrade themselves' by going out as servants." In the form most commonly discussed, the servant question was the housewives' problem of an insufficient supply of workers; even as wages and working and living conditions improved, the status of the job remained too low to attract or retain adequate numbers of workers.[1]

If mistresses were to be believed, since the Industrial Revolution nothing had approached an eternal verity more than the ever-present shortage of servants. The servant problem was a middle-class one, since the upper class could always command the hire of whatever servants they needed. The expansion of the middle class—accompanying modernization, urbanization, and industrialization in Western society—apparently occurred more rapidly than the growth of the servant pool, and complaints of a servant shortage followed the widespread hiring of servants. From the start, commentary on servants noted the general shortage, the inefficiency of those employed, and the constant turnover among household workers. Eighteenth-century English employers no less than early-twentieth-century American ones were plagued by the servant problem. The servant problem appeared early in U.S. history as well.[2]

During the colonial period the demand for servants was filled mostly by indentured servants, black slaves, or transported convicts. The word "servant" itself was used imprecisely, and among servants during this period, household workers could not always be differentiated from farm laborers. Probably the number of families who required or could afford to hire a household servant was relatively small. If unfree labor solved the problem of servant shortage, mistresses were no more satisfied than their progeny would be centuries later. In his study of Plymouth Colony John Demos described servants as integrated into the basic day-to-day life of the household, and from his examination of wills, he deduced mutual kindness, loyalty, and affection between master and servant. Lucy Maynard Salmon, however, discovered more substantial evidence of unsatisfactory service. John Winter of Richmond Island, Maine, wrote to Trelawny on July 10, 1639: "You write me of some yll reports is given of my Wyfe for beatinge the maid; yf a faire waye will not do yt, beatinge must, sometimes. . . . Yf you think yt fitte for my wyfe to do all the worke & the maide sitt still, she must forbeare her hands to strike, for then the worke will ly vndonn." In 1636, Mary Winthrop Dudley of Boston wrote her mother about "what a great affliction I have me withal by my maide servant, and how I am like through God his mercie to be freed from it. . . . she hath got such a head and is growen soe insolent that her carriage towards vu, especially myselfe is vnsufferable." Two generations later, in 1717, a Winthrop of New London, Connecticut, complained of "the trouble and plague we have had with this Irish creature the year past." And this was the golden age for mistresses and masters, when white or black servants could be purchased rather than bargained with and hired.[3]

After the American Revolution, in areas other than the slave South free labor replaced indentured servants as the source of workers. By the 1820s, American cities had reached the stage of urbanization and modernization where they became fertile ground for organized efforts to deal with the servant problem. The speeding up of American development with the accompanying expansion of the middle class made the shortage and quality of servants a public issue. In 1825 a group of New Yorkers formed the Society for the Encouragement of Faithful Domestic Servants in New-York, modeled after a similarly named London society. They sought to attract greater numbers of and more respectable girls and women to service, to promote longer tenure of servants, and to uplift morally the city's domestics. They intended to fulfill these goals by instituting a respectable employment agency to attract more and better servants and act as a conduit between servant and mistress by distributing money premiums and Bibles to servants who stayed longer than a year with one employer. To upgrade the status of their agency, they required references from applicants seeking positions, and they offered to place "nurses of the sick" as well. To build a broad base of job applicants, they charged servants no fee for registration or placement.[4]

The concerns of the New York society and its discussion of the servant problem spanned the discussions of servants from Daniel Defoe in the early eighteenth century to commentaries in the late twentieth century. "That the number of faithful and respectable servants in our city, has, latterly, been quite inadequate to our wants," the society's first report stated, "is a fact as notorious as it is lamentable." They blamed the government, rapid city growth, higher earnings in other occupations, "the vitiated character of the Intelligence Offices," the low status of servants—"as a kind of Paria caste"—and the restlessness and love of "incessant change" of young servants, who comprised the majority of domestics. The society's members were equally concerned

about the decrease in the number of white American-born
servants, the "extravagance in dress, and general improvidence" among servants, and the "species of *kidnapping*" in
which one employer hired another's servant away, in viola-
tion of the biblical injunction, "Thou shalt not covet. . . ."
The report acknowledged that the society's subscribers were
dependent on servants "for a large share of our daily comforts," and the present conditions impaired their domestic
comfort.[5]

Thereafter, the servant problem became a staple of housewives' discussions of servants, housekeeping, and the family,
regardless of section. In 1910 a New England housekeeper
from Cumberland Mills, Maine, described her personal
plight. The paper mill offered seven dollars weekly for work
from 7:00 A.M. to 5:00 P.M., with the opportunity to live at
home; housewives could not compete with those inducements. Instead of working in households, French girls from
Canada worked in the nearby Westbrook mills. The electric
interurban took local girls to Portland, five miles away. Even
Irish servants proved difficult to attract: the local Catholic
church was French, "and the Irish girls do not care to attend
it." The New England housekeeper had five children, which
of course made it more difficult to hire a servant. New England girls were widely thought to make the best houseworkers, but housekeepers were unable to hire enough daughters
of New England to satisfy the demand. "They have imbibed
the foolish idea," Mrs. John Sherwood wrote in her etiquette
book in 1884, "that the position of a girl who does housework is inferior in gentility to that of one who works in a factory, or a printing-office, or a milliner's shop." New England
industrialists knew from their experience in recruiting
women for mills that young women from that section preferred factory work to housework. Thomas Livermore, agent
for the Manchester, New Hampshire, Amoskeag Manufacturing Company, pinpointed the independence of factory
work and the "menial character" of service as the major factors. Factories offered "fixed hours of labor, outside of which
she is her own mistress."[6]

Elsewhere in the nation, mistresses complained that available servants were scarce, especially white native-born domestics. In 1912, the branches of the Michigan state employment bureaus reported the continuing short supply of servants. The Kalamazoo office worked "to overcome the prejudice which seems to prevail with girls in general concerning domestic work." Forty years earlier, the servant question had so troubled the *Cleveland Leader* that it saw opportunity amidst the tragedy of the Great Chicago Fire. To solve the servant shortage in Cleveland, the paper editorialized, "it might pay the housekeepers in Cleveland to send a committee to Chicago to collect and forward a still more numerous delegation of help than will come in the natural course of things." On the West Coast, supply and demand were also unbalanced. The California labor bureau in 1888 reported an "especial scarcity of young and strong girls who wish to take positions as house servants."[7]

Southern housewives, despite the plethora of servants, also complained about the servant problem. The Louisville correspondent of the *New York Freeman* reported on the Southern servant shortage in 1885. During the same period, Robert Kyle, a Gadsen, Alabama, mill owner, told a Senate committee that "it is a very difficult matter to get house servants at any price." Orra Langhorne reported that the Southern "weary housekeeper" would say, "We all employ negroes, but it is rare to find a good and satisfactory servant." But it was not just a question of quality, for the Southern housewife believed that "the agents from the North and West are offering high wages and taking away all the well-trained, reliable colored people." Thus the shortage in the North was creating scarcity in the South. "So great is the demand for general houseworkers and so small their supply," Frances A. Kellor reported in 1905, "that Northern housewives are willing to let unknown, unseen, untrained and unvouched-for workers enter their homes." Even that, however, according to a YWCA committee in 1915, would not provide a cure, because there appeared to be a "boycott of household employment on the part of wage-earning young women" throughout the United States.[8]

While there was no actual measure of servant demand, all

evidence pointed to an increasing imbalance between supply and demand. In 1930 the number of families was four times larger than it had been in 1870, while the number of household workers had doubled in that period (see Table 2–1). In 1870 there were 127 household workers per thousand families; in 1930, 67 per thousand. Between 1890 and 1930, the number of nonfarm families grew more rapidly than the number of all families, thus widening the gap further between supply and demand, as reflected in the decrease of household workers per thousand families in major cities (see Table 2–6). Accompanying the family and population expansion was a significant increase in the number of middle-class families who could afford servants. The general upward mobility of the entire society, as reflected in the occupational structure, suggested a growing middle class, as did the outward expansion of cities with middle-class rings around the central-city districts. At the same time, the growth of apartment living, the construction of smaller houses, the introduction of machine power into the household, and the transfer of household tasks to agencies outside the home all tended to decrease the demand for domestics. On balance, however, the testimony of housewives and reformers and state labor reports indicated an growing disequilibrium between supply and demand.

Nothing seemed to frustrate housewives more than that every year a smaller proportion of young wage-earning women entered household work. From the housewives' point of view, the declining number of servants per thousand families occurred while the total number of women wage earners was growing more rapidly than the number of families. In other words, more and more women held gainful employment while fewer and fewer entered paid household service. In 1870 a majority of employed women worked in households; in 1930, less than a fifth (see Table 2–2). It was clear that given a choice, women preferred factory, shop, or office work over domestic labor, and when job opportunities in fields other than domestic service increased in the rapidly industrializing and urbanizing society of the late nineteenth and early twentieth centuries, women took them.

Domestic service was thoroughly examined around the turn of the century as reformers sought to uncover, understand, and improve or remedy the condition of household labor. Elaborate inventories of the advantages and disadvantages of domestic service appeared; housewives and reformers hoped to use these to attract more servants. The economic attraction of service often received primary stress. The annual wages of live-in servants were competitive with or better than the wages of those in other unskilled and semiskilled occupations. Most importantly, for a young girl who wished to save money—for a wedding trousseau, for instance—live-in household work could be most attractive. The employer provided room and board, and servants, with limited time off and protected from what employers described as the competitive conspicuous consumption common among other working women, could bank their entire wages. If any single inducement was widely cited, it was this one. "The life of the domestic servant may be one to be envied by working women in other fields," a space filler in *Good Housekeeping* announced. "A New York housekeeper writes that she has a maid-servant now working for $14 a month, and who has several thousand dollars in railroad stock which she has accumulated." Fillers such as that one were common in magazines and newspapers, although this kind of experience was rare among servants. More realistically, however, single domestic servants who did not have to support their own families could save money.[9]

The other commonly cited benefits of service related to the servants as women. Service offered physical work conducive to good health, "at least the externals of a home," knowledge and education in household affairs, and employment congenial with women's work—housework. Servants told Lucy Maynard Salmon that they chose household service because "it was healthy work" or "there is no healthier work for women." Women's magazines quoted physicians recommending housework, saying they could think of "no exercise more beneficial in result." "One year of such muscular effort within doors," the *Medical Record* advised, "together with regular exercise in open air, will do more for a woman's complexion than all the lotions and pomades that were ever invented." Domestic work was clearly considered healthier than women's work in stores, factories, and laundries. In the latter, according to the Missouri labor bureau, women were "being kept standing all day long, confined in hot and illy ventilated rooms, being compelled to eat their meals hastily and prevented from observing the ordinary physical laws," with the result that "their health is undermined and they are physical wrecks early in life." The salubrious environment of a home would cure that.[10]

Women also were attracted to service because it was women's work in the home. Some women liked it and others did not, but it had a special appeal for some. "I like it best, was used to it at home," a houseworker told Lucy Marynard Salmon, "and it seems more natural-like." "I have a natural love for cooking," explained another, "and would rather do it than anything else in the world." Others considered the home environment important. "I came to a strange city and chose housework," reported a servant, "because it afforded me a home." "I am well treated by the family I am with, feel at home and under their protection," responded a second domestic, while a third added, "Housework gives me a better home than I could make for myself in any other way." And for their future roles as wives and mothers, women felt domestic service most appropriate. "I choose housework as my regular employment," explained a houseworker, "for the simple reason that young women look forward to the time when they will have housework of their own to do. I consider that I or anyone in domestic employment will make a better housekeeper than any young woman who works in a factory."[11]

Household labor was so strongly identified with women, and entry into it was so easy, that not all servants had chosen to become domestics. At the turn of the twentieth century, long past the end of slavery and the pre–Civil War custom of apprenticing young girls as servants, some domestics came to household work without having made a conscious choice. In the late 1890s, a young Irish girl and her siblings "were put out in families for their keep" after the death of their father. She received six dollars a month plus board, and worked for the family for eight years. In the 1880s an English American-born girl was sent to a workhouse at age five after her parents had both died. She was given no education, and the workhouse sent her out when she was twelve years old to work as a child nurse. She "was sent from one family to another until she was 16 with no pay for her work except scant clothing and what she ate." In the 1880s another girl whose parents—of Irish extraction—had died also began work before she was ten. She "was taken in by neighbors, and worked for her board and clothes until she ran away from them" when she was fifteen.[12]

Lack of education forced many women into service and barred them from moving into other work. Literacy was an advantage in household work, but was in no way a requisite. Many immigrants, though literate in their native tongue, could not read or write English. Moreover, Ireland had offered little educational opportunity to the women who had migrated to the United States, and many came without the ability to read or write. "I think that most of the illiterates are Irish," a Minneapolis employment agent observed in 1887. "In fact they are the only class I know of that cannot read or write," she continued. In an 1892 Maine study, nine houseworkers born in Ireland had been questioned. Three had received no formal education, and only one had more than four years of schooling. American-born Irish, on the other hand, were all educated, the Minneapolis agent reported, and shunned housework. The difference between the proportions of first- and second-generation Irish working women who were servants confirmed her observations. In the middle of the nineteenth century, young native-born girls who were placed out in households to work had little or no opportunity for education, and they had little chance to find other work. The generation of Southern black servants immediately after emancipation had received no formal education either. Thereafter, most Southern blacks received little schooling beyond the basic rudiments, and what education

they did receive, especially in the rural districts, was of very
poor quality. Whatever the average educational level of any
given community, domestics were probably far below it.
Thus even if prejudice and discrimination had not barred
domestics from entering women's jobs in shops and offices,
their lack of education was a nearly insurmountable barrier.[13]

Many women chose domestic service because they felt
they had no alternative. One of the most difficult problems
for urban working women was finding respectable but inex-
pensive lodgings. In the nation's largest cities, men had a
wide variety of choices, but women did not, according to
Dorothy Richardson. In smaller cities and towns a woman had
even more difficulty living outside a family setting—whether
that of her own family or that of an employer's family. A
reporter of the *Topeka Commonwealth* accompanied the assistant commissioner of the Kansas labor bureau on an investigation of this problem, and they found in Topeka placards
such as BOARDING FOR GENTS ONLY and FURNISHED ROOMS FOR
RENT. GENTS ONLY. They interviewed a young working
women who complained: "A man, provided he wears good
clothes, or isn't a manual laborer, can get a room anywhere
in this city, and no questions asked. . . . He will be asked
no questions, but my antecedents will be the subject of inquiry, and if I say I am a working girl, the door will be shut
against me." Live-in domestic service offered the path of least
resistance in solving this problem. Similarly, other women
just drifted into household labor. "I don't know how to do
anything but wash dishes, etc.," a Maine domestic declared,
"if I did I should not be at housework." "My mother was a
housekeeper and did most of her own work and taught me
how to help her," recounted a houseworker. "When my father and mother died, and it became necessary for me to earn
my own living, the question was, 'What can I do?' The answer was plain—housework."[14]

The disadvantages of domestic service were numerous,
and many working women, including domestics, shared intensely negative feelings about being servants. The work it-

self was not objectionable to most women. While some women disliked the repetitiveness and ephemeral quality of housework, more seemed to enjoy it. Indeed, many women who stayed out of domestic service testified they did not mind the work itself. "I object to doing housework for others," a Minnesota servant said, although "have no object to doing it at home." A Massachusetts shoe-factory worker expressed similar feelings to Mary Trueblood in 1900. Her sister was a servant, and she said "that she would like housework itself, if there were limited hours and business-like methods." A teacher wrote Lucy Salmon: "I am fond of children, and should like nothing better than to be a nurse-girl, but I will not wear livery."[15]

Much of the literature on the servant problem—both by servants and by mistresses—focused on the treatment of workers and the quality of their living environment. The long, irregular hours, the meanness, unpleasantness, disorganization, or arbitrariness of mistresses, the inadequacy of diet and paucity of amenities—all were troubling and serious to servants who experienced them, but they reflected the individual employer's characteristics. None were particularly inherent in domestic service itself, and as many mistresses learned, the alleviation of these complaints never contributed to solving the servant problem. It might enable an employer to retain a servant longer than normal, but that advantage was lost if, for example, all mistresses went to an eight-hour day, as happened in the 1920s.

One characteristic of domestic service from which many problems flowed was the atomization of work. Working without the company of fellow workers, many servants felt alone and isolated on the job; in the case of live-in servants, this feeling persisted around the clock. Lillian Pettengill experienced it immediately in her first position. "I felt my isolation," she wrote, "alone in a big house full of people." In four weeks she didn't have a single visitor. The opportunities for live-in servants both to receive friends and to meet new people were severely restricted. Pettengill missed the contact with other women and began to look forward to coffee and tea with other servants on Mondays and Tuesdays—laundry days—"more for the sake of the sisterhood than from any physical need for refreshment." As Jane Addams observed, young urban girls, especially immigrants and the children of immigrants, were used to contact with their peers; they mixed with them in school and in large families. In service, "she is isolated from the people with whom she has been reared, with whom she has gone to school, and among whom she expects to live when she marries." Moreover, many young women were very attached to their parents and siblings, and were more responsive than men "to the needs of the aged parents and helpless members of the family." Yet live-in service kept them from fulfilling family obligations.[16]

Atomization and isolation also made organization and collective action by domestics difficult, if not impossible. Moreover, as unmarried women who expected to work only temporarily as servants before marriage, many lacked the consciousness to devote a good part of their time to radical action, even if they had had the energy, which they often didn't. Ironically, the lack of collective action among domestics was a contributory factor to the high turnover among servants. Unable to organize and collectively influence work conditions, they resorted to short job tenure. The failure of domestics to organize during the late nineteenth and early twentieth century occurred during a period of intense labor struggles. Nationally, trade-union membership rose from 440,000 in 1897 to nearly 3,000,000 in 1917. I have not uncovered any efforts to unionize servants during this period, unlike during the earlier period of the 1880s, when the Knights of Labor had included household workers' assemblies and probably had acted as a catalyst for the organization of unaffiliated locals and for spontaneous strikes. World War I was a period of union expansion, spurred on by the federal government, and union membership surpassed five million in 1920, a total not to be attained again by organized labor until 1937. Among those who temporarily swelled the tide of union membership were domestic workers. In 1919, household workers' locals existed in Mobile,

Alabama; Fort Worth, Texas; and Richmond, Tulsa, and Lawton, Oklahoma. In 1920 there were ten locals affiliated with the American Federation of Labor, including three in Texas, two each in California and Illinois, and one each in Pennsylvania, Louisiana, and Georgia. In 1923 there were none.[17]

Changes in domestic service as well as the growing national influence of organized labor and the support of the federal government made many domestics more receptive to collective action, but the problem of atomization was truly insurmountable. Live-out or day work eliminated the isolation experienced by live-in servants, and at the least, live-out work made it easier for workers to get together and share experiences. The atomization of the workplace, however, still made it difficult to meet and contact servants. Jane Street, an Industrial Workers of the World organizer in Denver, did a remarkable job of organizing domestics in 1917, but found the atomization of work the major roadblock. Street worked in service, collecting names, and when she was between jobs, she would advertise for workers and for situations, placing some workers. In three months she had collected the names of 300 servants. She organized a local with 13 initial members, and began an employment exchange—the only exchange actually run by houseworkers that I have uncovered. In the first year Street claimed that "we have interviewed personally in our office about 1500 or 2000 girls, telling them about the I.W.W. and making them more rebellious, and placing probably over 1000 in jobs." The local had 155 members, but only 83 "we can actually call members. A great many leave town and some of them in town drift away and we are unable to locate them." Moreover, she found attendance at meetings difficult to obtain. Overall, her success in manipulating the system to increase wages and shorten hours was real, but it probably had but a limited effect on the Denver servant market. The 1,500 to 2,000 girls interviewed were probably not all domestics, and the 1,000 jobs placed probably represented jobs, not women. The 1920 census recorded 3,638 household workers (servants and washerwomen) in Denver, and given the high turnover in and out of service, Street had only contacted a relative handful of servants.[18]

Working alone in the home of a strange family served to intensify the personal rather than the work relationships within household service. The live-in servant was on alien ground, dependent upon the family that employed her for the basic necessities of life. Whatever the relationship she established with her mistress, the servant had no one in the household who would provide supportive encouragement; her basic resource would have to be her own sense of self and security. In most cases, from the start the relationship was highly personal, since the worker herself and not merely her labor had been hired. "The essential quality of service," Helen Campbell perceptively argued in the 1890s, "is that it is done under the direction of some one person, for the further expression of that person's will." The servant was an extension of her mistress' personality. Contrasting servant and laborer, Campbell might have been describing a medieval vassal and a modern industrial worker. "The difference between the servant and the laborer," Campbell wrote, "is the difference between obedience and agreement, the difference between submission and acquiescence." Servants had to obey; they were subservient to another's will. Servants were hired not to follow a given pursuit or reach a given industrial goal, but to serve people and cater to their whims. Hence the common complaint of insubordination—disobedience, lack of submissiveness. Moreover, this was an important element in the servile role expected of household workers; whether the servant lived in or lived out mattered little.[19]

At every stage of domestic service, a servant faced reminders of her subservient role and the distinction between mistress and servant. Employment agents kept two waiting rooms—one for ladies, the other for servants. Potential employers were treated as ladies while the workers received discourteous treatment and were even subdued with physical force. Nothing made Frances Kellor's investigators feel more like servants than to be addressed by their given names,

whether looking for a job or while working. "Why should every mistress do it before she even engages us," a servant asked, "and why should it be done in such a way that the iceman and grocer's boy and every Tom, Dick and Harry always call us that?" "I am Mary to every guest in the house," she complained, "and every stranger who appears at the kitchen door; in fact, how can I respect myself when no one else shows me any!"[20]

Most mistresses attempted to maintain the social distance between themselves and their servants. Forcing a servant to wear livery, designating the back door as the service entry, excluding servants from the family living space, and failing to even exchange greetings with a servant in public were ways in which an employer maintained social distance. Increasingly around and after the turn of the twentieth century, housewives complained of the tendency of servants, especially the American-born, to behave as though they were the social equals of their employers. Mistresses grew resentful. "I believe that the ready-made shops have done more to hurt the servant problem than you can imagine," an employer wrote the Maine labor bureau in 1910. "A maid can buy, nowadays, a cheap replica of anything which her mistresses wears, or, as if often the case, having her board and expenses paid and good money in hand every week, actually has more money and better things than the mistress who has hundreds of ways to spend her money, and usually puts it first into house and literary and club matters." The answer to this presumptuousness was the requirement that a servant wear livery—a badge of servility.[21]

Nothing seemed to go against the American grain more than the wearing of livery. The servant's cap and apron could have been practical—defenders of the practice argued that they were "conducive to neatness and economy. . . . No costume in itself could be more desirable or better adapted to the work of the wearers." Yet it was widely accepted that livery was often required to "indicate the rise of the employer in the social scale." "The wider the separation in any community between employer and employee," Lucy

Maynard Salmon concluded, "the greater is the tendency to insist on the cap and apron." Nearly every household manual stressed the wearing of cap and apron, while servants objected to wearing a cap, dress, or apron identified as servant attire. Many who were neither master/mistress nor servant felt it conflicted with the democratic, egalitarian ideals upon which the nation had been founded or with the equality of opportunity many claimed America offered. In Article I, Section 9, the Constitution specifically prohibits the bestowal of titles of nobility within the United States, and some considered servants in livery a similar alien importation from monarchical Europe. In 1884, Mrs. John Sherwood in her etiquette guidebook discussed the deep-seated American prejudice against livery. She told the story "only seven years ago of a gentleman of the most aristocratic circle of aristocratic Philadelphia who declared that he refrained from having a liveried servant behind his carriage from fear of shocking public opinion." An 1887 labor newspaper described livery as "a sign of the loss of self-respect among poor people condemned to a wretched struggle for the privilege of earning a living. It is also a sign of the growth of an un-American spirit among the rich; of a desire to perpetuate and mark caste difference." Livery, then, could serve not only to announce the status of an employing family but also to mark the subordinate status of servants, for both the community and themselves.[22]

The word "servant" itself seemed to conflict with the democratic spirit. The word "help," with its connotation of a past age when employer and employee were on the same social level, seemed to be preferred. A servant told Lucy Maynard Salmon, "I know many nice girls who would do housework, but they prefer doing almost anything else rather than be called 'servants.'" A servant who in 1902 wrote an unsolicited letter to the *Independent* felt the change in name from "servant" to "household worker" would be an important step in elevating service. "What's in a name?" she asked. "Ask Shakespeare. A good deal sometimes." In the Scharff household, Lillian Pettengill thought she had improved on the ac-

Maid with baby, Rutland, Vermont. (W. C. Bosford)

cented English of the German cook Frieda when she referred to Mrs. Scharff as "mistress."

"Vhat *fur* you call she mistress?" demanded Frieda, irate. "She iss no great lady over me to say to me *was* I do. I my own mistress. I do so I vant."

"But you call Mr. Scharff 'boss,' " I argued.

"*Ach—er ist* head *von sein* familie, *das iss* different. I only work *hier fur* money. I cook *fur* my business, *und* I take orders *fur* my business like girl in store. *Dies iss* Amerika. Cook so *gut wie* anybody was vorks for a living *hier.*"

Pettengill came to share Frieda's prejudice against the word "servant." "I will be a servant no more," she wrote. "A domestic tradeswoman I am, a chambermaid, a waitress, an employee with an employer, but a servant with a mistress—never. I am an American."[23]

Similarly, houseworkers found employer demands for a servile attitude, including deference and obedience, objectionable. To many young women, the subordinate role of servant—one which extended around the clock among live-in servants—was incompatible with the egalitarianism of American life. "In a country whose battle cry is equality," a Maine employer wrote in 1910, "there is no such thing as a good servant class." This view was widespread among Maine housewives, and seemed to reflect the trend in Maine. Mistresses thought American girls more independent than immigrants, and maintained that they "appear to feel they are conferring a great favor upon those they work for rather than receiving favors for themselves." "American born girls breathe in at their birth a desire to be independent," another mistress declared, "to be every women's equal, and they cannot be blamed for not wishing to spend their lives in the kitchen. . . . Servants are born, not made, and America does not furnish the environment conducive to such birth."[24]

What seemed so un-American was the loss of individual freedom experienced by servants. For a live-in domestic, her entire life while in another's home was determined by the will of the employer. In a society that revered individualism—the personal responsibility of an individual for his or her life and future—nothing could have more radically excluded a worker from the ideals of that society. Mistresses defended their maternal benevolence by claiming that many servants were better cared for than other working women. Lillian Pettengill dismissed this argument as a source of harmful results: she felt it could destroy the employee's individualism. "She is too completely cared for," Pettengill declared, "she should be caring for herself." Another aspect of loss of freedom was the lack of opportunity offered in household labor. For the overwhelming majority of servants, promotion had no meaning. A servant could not rise within her profession to run her own business; indeed, success only came by leaving service. Moreover, there were no significant rewards given an efficient servant, since personal relations and not work performance determined work tenure—the basic influence on wages.[25]

The objections to domestic service were frequently expressed. Many women who had a choice entered factories, offices, or shops rather than domestic service, and as opportunities for women increased, especially in offices and shops, a rapidly diminishing percentage of all women workers entered service (see Table 2–2). Sometimes women were willing to accept lower wages simply to avoid service. For most women, however, the decision was not an economic one. They worked from necessity, but probably most women would have avoided doing paid household work if they could have. Some women even pledged to themselves that they or their children would never be domestics. In the 1880s an Irish American girl who was the daughter of a cook but would never herself work as a domestic warned every girl she met: "Whatever you do, don't go into service. You'll always be prisoners and always be looked down upon." In 1904 a black woman in the South declared that "I have the same feeling my parents had. There is no sacrifice I would not make, no hardship I would not undergo rather than allow my daughters to go in service. . . ." A black migrant who in 1919 went from Lexington, Georgia, to Chicago had worked as a cook in the South. At fourteen she had entered household service as an assistant to her mother, who had been a cook. After her mother's death, the daughter continued to work for the family until she was twenty, when she went northward. In Chicago she became a factory hand. "I'll never work in nobody's kitchen but my own anymore," she vowed. "No, indeed! That's the one thing that makes me stick to this job."[26]

What caused these and other women to shun paid household work? Why did they feel so intensely about not becoming servants? An inventory of the disadvantages of domestic service was a long one: the lack of opportunity for advancement, the monotony, the unsystematized approach of employers, the length and irregularity of hours, the limited freedom, the isolation and loneliness, the role of subordinate and servant, and the employer's demand for deference and servility. All these contributed to the dislike of domestic service expressed by many servants and factory, office, and shop workers. Others held it in low regard because of those who performed the work—immigrants in cities, blacks in the South, women everywhere. Many women considered it degrading because it was women's work, done by unskilled, poorly educated women who couldn't find other work. After all, who in the United States aspired to be a servant? Moreover, the work relationship—the intensely personal mistress/servant relationship—and place—within the private family—gave it a medieval character at odds with the general trend of employer/employee interaction in modern, industrializing American society. Finally, the work itself—personal service for another individual within her home— seemed to be degrading within the context of all the other disadvantages. All of these factors combined to give domestic service the lowest status of any widespread occupation in American society. And it was this stigma of servitude, of servile status, that women sought to escape. For a woman in service, according to Lucy Maynard Salmon, a "badge of social inferiority is put upon her in characters as unchangeable as are the spots of a leopard."27

Nearly all studies of household labor and servants' memoirs agreed that in the urban United States white servants had very low status. The California labor bureau reported that "society taboos servants." Other working women were accepted in "genteel" society, but not household workers. "I do not like to do housework," a Minnesota factory worker said, "because people look down upon you." A Maine study observed that "girls who are forced to give up high school or academy courses and turn their hands to housework find they are no longer welcome among their former companions." "Social caste" separated the "house girl from other female workers." A Maine housewife illustrated this by noting that "my husband has a servant who acts as his stenographer. She is welcome anywhere in any society." On the

other hand, "I have a servant who does my work," she declared. "She is a graduate from Robinson's seminary in Exe-
ter. She cannot even look inside anybody's house." A Chicago domestic thought that Northern servants shared caste
status with blacks. "The negroes in the South," she wrote,
"have as much chance of social recognition as have those who
do domestic service in the North. Between them and society
there is a great gulf fixed." For many, being a servant involved personal shame. Rose Cohen's mother wept and cried,
"Is this what I have come to America for, that my children
should become servants." In the 1880s, Leander, a young
man from New Hampshire, laid dying in a New York City
tenement; the thought of his wife working as a domestic dis-
turbed his last days. "You'd never believe how the thought o'
that weighed on him," his widow Almira told Helen Campbell. "He'd wake me up in the night to say, 'Now, Almiry,
jest give up that thought an' promise me you'll try something
else. I think I'd turn in my grave if I had to know you was
slavin' in anybody's kitchen.' " Almira wasn't convinced it
would be "a bad change," but she "promised him I wouldn't
do it unless I had to."[28]

Books and articles of advice and guidance for middle-class
women underscored the low status and lack of respect-
ableness of paid household labor. Hundreds of articles and
little books advised young girls of the vocational opportunities awaiting them in late-nineteenth-century America.
They were written for middle-class girls or for those who
aspired to the middle class. George J. Manson's *Work for
Women*, a sequel to his series of articles under that title in a
New York newspaper, described the respectable occupations
for women—industrial designing, shorthand, telegraphy,
feather curling, photography, professional nursing, proof-
reading, bookbinding, lecturing, teaching, millinery, and so
forth. Conspicuously absent was the single largest employment for women: domestic service. Presumably service
lacked the respectability that was at the heart of Manson's
advice. At the same time, Ella Church advised housewives
on how to earn money in respectable occupations. Sugges-

tions ranged from sewing to gardening and beekeeping, and even included a "refined" boardinghouse, but not day work, cooking, or general housekeeping. A quarter of a century later, Josephine Bacon discussed "our daughters" and their future expectations and roles, whether as housewives or as workers. The only mention of domestic servants was as employees, not as daughters. The daughters of readers would hire servants, not work as domestics.[29]

The movement to raise the status of unpaid household labor—housewives—and to professionalize allied household work that arose during the 1890s was careful to separate itself from concern about servants. Though college and industrial-school women received instruction in domestic economy or science, they certainly did not intend to become servants. Domestic education was primarily aimed at preparing women to be better housekeepers in their own homes. In higher education where programs were designed to train women for careers, such as at the School of Household Science and Arts, Pratt Institute, New York City, women trained to become teachers of domestic science or dieticians or industrial housekeepers. Like the newly trained business managers—who were not expected to work in factories themselves—these women were professional managers. When Marie Francke outlined some of the professional roles in domestic science for the Association of Collegiate Alumnae in 1916, she stressed the "professional opportunities." Her book *Opportunities for Women in Domestic Service* was mistitled, since it made no mention of servants, maids, cooks, or other domestic workers. In secondary education, the rumor that courses in home economics were training students for domestic service could kill a program, as the School of Domestic Science and Domestic Art in Rochester, New York, found out during its first year in 1909. When such a rumor arose, the students rebelled and other schools sent their "undesirable pupils" to the domestic-science institution, which was under the joint sponsorship of the city's board of education and the state division of trade schools. After one year the school had to change the curriculum, stressing dressmaking and millinery to save the school.[30]

Vocational training for black women followed a direction different from that of schools for whites. Although black secondary schools provided training for future housewives as well as programs in dressmaking and millinery, they also had courses specifically designed to train girls for domestic service. At the Armstrong Manual Training School in the District of Columbia, the domestic-science course prepared its students for both home duties and service, and the commissioner of labor reported that "a number of the girls go into domestic service upon graduation." Every Southern black industrial school also included practical training courses in laundry work. Armstrong sent young women out to work in private homes, and they received school credit for the weeks spent working. These programs reflected a pragmatic approach to industrial training, to offering programs that would lead to jobs after graduation. Since few jobs other than domestic or personal service were open to black women, training them for office work, for instance, would have made little sense. This was also the path of least resistance for black schools, for black educators received the support of whites by preparing their graduates to live within the caste system rather than challenging it. By emphasizing programs in domestic arts, educators appeared to be accommodating themselves to the role society had assigned to black women.[31]

That black schools trained at least some of their women students for domestic service while white schools did not suggests differences in the status of domestic servants within black and white communities. Household labor declined in importance among white working women, so by 1920 only 9 percent of native-born and 23 percent of foreign-born women in nonagricultural occupations worked as servants and washerwomen (see Table A–11). Among all white women less than 2 percent of native-born and 4 percent of immigrants worked as household workers. This obviously permitted the kind of social differentiation that left service work with very low respectability. Among blacks, however, such a large percentage of women held gainful employment and did service work that it could not have been held in such low regard. In 1920, 71 percent of all employed black women

Tuskegee Institute class in domestic science. (Library of Congress)

were domestics or laundresses, and nationally, 20 percent of all black women were paid houseworkers. In urban areas in 1920, among women ten and over, as many as four out of ten black women in some Southern cities worked as servants and washerwomen (see Table A–12). Economic necessity forced black women to work, and of those who worked more than a majority were domestics.

If black women servants maintained reputable status and acceptance within the general black community, they were not among the middle class or the upper-class elite. With but one notable exception, black domestic servants in the South and the North were part of the working class. Peter Kolchin describes the group that constitutes the exception as "the house Negroes on the large plantations and the personal servants of rich whites"; this was a relatively small, mostly male group who tended to be set off from the black community. The men were not an elite group *within* the black community; they lived mostly outside the community. And while they were sometimes considered by other blacks "to be a notch above the mass of freedmen," this was not always true. They thought of themselves as superior to other blacks and developed a consciousness of themselves as separate from the mass of blacks. They often had privileges denied other freed men and women, and "identified more closely with their white masters . . . and sometimes felt real affection for [them]." Within a generation this group would disappear, so that by the turn of the century there was not even a self-appointed elite among black servants.[32]

All other empirical and contemporary evidence indicated the exclusion of servants from the black middle class and elite. There is nothing to support the assumption that within their own community black domestics attained high prestige by virtue of the social standing of their employing family. An early discussion of the black middle class—Joseph Willson's 1841 essay—gave no indication that servants were found among the members of Philadelphia's black society or were involved in the artistic or literary associations. In 1860, a letter from a black working woman to the weekly *Anglo-African* asked "why persons who labor are so generally neglected by others more fortunate?" She had been taught that "it is honorable to work," yet "many a young lady at service is made to feel most keenly the unnatural distinction made between them and those who were blessed with trades." The " 'Lions of society,' " however, were "raised in idleness, kept in ignorance and luxury" and "do nothing but dress and promenade."[33]

After the Civil War, black class lines were defined even more clearly. In Detroit from the Civil War to World War I, there is no evidence to indicate the inclusion of servants in any of the institutions—church, clubs, and societies—of the middle class or elite. Indeed, few elite women held gainful employment, and many families hired servants. A study of "Brown Brahmins" found domestics excluded from elite black society in Boston. Elizabeth Ross Haynes examined the occupations of Negro graduates of Sumner High School.

St. Louis, from 1895–1911; of the high school in Gainesville, Georgia, 1917–1919; and of Miner Normal School, Washington, D.C., 1913–1922. Of the 911 graduates, none were servants, 5 were recorded as "housekeepers," and 32 were listed as being in "miscellaneous" occupations. Even with limited occupational opportunities, educated black women did not enter domestic service, although some taught domestic science. At the same time, of 7,975 black women who applied to the U.S. Employment Service for domestic work in Washington, D.C., from 1920 to 1922 and of 387 black domestics (female and male) using the office in Indianapolis in 1922, not a single one had completed more than eight grades of school. Howard Woolston's early sociological study of a New York City neighborhood noted that "the negroes on 130th and 131st Streets are at the bottom in this community." Heads of families worked as laborers, drivers, and servants; wives were day workers. After the Civil War black women complained of the low status of service, as had the writer to the *Anglo-African* in 1860. The White Sulphur Springs, West Virginia, correspondent of the *Cleveland Gazette*, for example, complained that blacks "despised" household labor. In an attempt to counter the low status of servants, the reporter argued that "a good domestic is as essential in her sphere as the teacher is in his." In 1895, Katherine Tillman complained of the fashion of "our younger women to scorn a life of service" and to look down upon women in service. In trying to raise the prestige of the large group of black domestics, they revealed the relatively low status of this occupation within the black community.[34]

Unable to attract the kind of servants they wanted and faced with an inadequate supply of servants and constant turnover among them, mistresses, feminists, reformers, and utopians all offered an endless stream of solutions to the "servant problem." In the early and middle part of the nineteenth century, reform focused on benevolent Christian solutions, emphasizing the good will of the mistress qua surrogate parent. By the turn of the century, with the rise of domestic science, the introduction of professional and businesslike demeanor into the household was stressed, with an emphasis on efficiency and contractual relations. Some proposals even suggested abolition or modification of the private household. What all the proposals shared, however, was a disregard of the interests of servants as women and workers; none of the reformers dealt with the persistence of the personalized work relationship, which survived the shift from live-in to live-out service and day work.

In the 1820s, the Society for the Encouragement of Faithful Domestic Servants had addressed itself to the three major goals of employers interested in the servant problem: (1) to increase the supply of servants, (2) to raise the level of competency, and (3) to ensure long tenure of service. To attract more and better servants, it opened its own free employment exchange to provide a respectable instrument for native-born women to find jobs. To increase the average length of service and to promote loyalty among servants, the society awarded cash prizes and Bibles to servants of one or more years' tenure, upon the recommendation of their employers. Moreover, it distributed proverbs from Benjamin Franklin's *Poor Richard's Almanack* "to counteract that extravagance in dress, and general improvidence, which are too common among servants." This approach, which accepted as given the social distance between mistress and servant and emphasized Christian benevolence as the solution to working women's dislike of service, persisted as the major thrust of reform until after the Civil War. Catherine Beecher, for instance, while stressing domestic education, associated servants with a fall in status and counseled mistresses to adopt a Christian attitude of enlightened benevolence toward their servants.[35]

During the 1860s and 1870s, housewives and others concerned with the servant problem continued to offer similar advice. In 1869, M.E.M., writing in *Lippincott's Magazine*, bemoaned the disappearance of the faithful family retainer and the absence of faithfulness and love between mistress and servant. "Perhaps the fault is with us," she suggested, "for it is love that challenges and holds prompt and pleasant service." She suggested that mistresses should apply their feminine social skills—"the arts of pleasing"—in winning "the admiration of the untutored peasant-girl." Regardless of her own feelings, the housekeeper should be solicitous toward her servant—sympathize with her concerning her position away from her own home, inquire gently about her family, and refrain from giving vent to anger. Impertinence should be pardoned, even though it was irritating "from a subordinate." The Bible provided the proper Christian approach. Finally, "servants should be considered a part of the family, under the control of the heads thereof, and having a right to due consideration and care."[36]

Essentially this article invoked the benevolent Christian and maternal roles to which mistresses aspired. It took for granted the existing structure of domestic service and emphasized the role of the employer in ameliorating the conditions about which servants complained. Reflecting the close personal relationship and the intimacy of the private household that was also the workplace, it stressed a kinder, more benevolent interaction. It accepted the essential women-to-women relationship and urged women to use their perceived social skills to advantage, to win the affection of their employees by using the same skills they employed to gain the loyalty of men. Overall, the approach was individualistic and emotional; as the resources most needed in maintaining a good mistress/servant relationship, it cited experience, sensitivity, and expressions of personal feelings. It found little wanting in the essential conditions of work.

By the turn of the century, however, most advice offered to housekeepers had an entirely different tone. Principles of impersonal professional management took the place of the Christian maternal benevolent ideals of an earlier generation; efficiency replaced satisfaction, and democratic ideals were substituted for demands for servility. The cult of efficiency so prevalent in American industry had entered the household. Theoretically, the work relationships of the factory and shop should be introduced into the home. Then the principles of scientific management—at its extreme, Taylorism— should be adopted within the household. At the same time the movement for women's education and the scientific study of domestic economy resulted in the development of household management—domestic science—and its inclusion in the curricula of colleges and universities throughout the United States. Science and education would attack not only the inertia and medievalism of the household but also tradition and folklore. Custom would give way to principles founded on general laws derived from study and investigation. It was expected that the end result would be the disappearance of the servant problem; progress would triumph.

In the 1890s the analogy of business firms became as firmly entrenched as any proposed reform. In 1892, Josephine E. Martin used the vocabulary of business, manufacturing, and commerce to describe the ideal structure of the household. The major question, according to Martin, was "that of the proper management of servants." Whether in a business or in the household, such management involved getting "the best service out of those who are in their employ"; success followed "executive ability." In the "business of housekeeping," every woman who dealt with servants "has an opportunity to show her executive ability, or her lack of it." They should "base their relations to their servants upon business principles" to achieve "domestic prosperity." Martin also suggested that mistresses adopt a detached professional stance toward their servants. After all, as another advocate of the business model had pointed out, Andrew Carnegie did not discuss with his workers "the private affairs of his family; nor make envious and damaging statements to them regarding other business houses." These reformers thought that incorporation of systems and relations found in other work—factory or shop—would attract more women into household service.[37]

A similar approach emphasizing the need for systematic management principles was to treat the servant question as part of the general question of capital and labor. "We must admit the commercial spirit of our people," Flora Thompson wrote in 1900, "and accept the fact that the relation between mistress and maid is before anything else a money relation, and that not poetic sentiment, not Christian charity, but straight business principles are to govern." The problem with service, Thompson implied, was that it was not considered as work. Domestic labor was not viewed as productive; no one placed any value on it. She recalled visiting a school of domestic science in Boston, where she observed a class preparing a twenty-five-cent dinner: "They had marketed for it all the morning before; they had spent the most of a morning cooking it, and heaven knows how many nights they had lain awake planning it, and it cost only twenty-five cents. . . ." In valuing it at twenty-five cents, however, they added not one penny for the women's labor—"that was not worth a penny." Thompson argued that if the same principles utilized in business were applied to household work—whether paid or unpaid labor, whether housewives themselves, their children and kin, or hired servants—it would have altered radically the structure of the work and relationships.[38]

One aspect of focusing on the adoption of business practices was the emphasis on the contractual relationship between employer and employee. An early proposed improvement had been the introduction of a written contract that would define the work conditions—duration of service, wages, and character of employment. It would also spell out responsibility for events such as breakage, illness, and termination of contract. In spite of serious efforts to create model contracts and the support of organizations such as the Women's Education and Industrial Union of Buffalo in the 1880s and the Legal Aid Society of New York in the 1900s, there is no evidence of the widespread adoption of the practice of using such contracts. Nonetheless, some reformers thought that better understanding of the unwritten contractual relationship would further the systematization of household work and work relationships. Writing in the *Atlantic Monthly* in 1913, Annie Winsor Allen sought to define the legal responsibilities of mistress and maid. They were employer and employee, as their oral contract specified; they were principal and agent, a relationship of trust in which the servant acted for the mistress; they were bailor and bailee, the maid possessing the instruments of the housekeeper; and they were host and boarder, where the domestic lived in her employer's household. Additionally, Allen identified two more mutual ties not "legally" held toward one another, but nonetheless present: guardian and ward and confidential adviser and confidential agent. By specifying the mutual obligations Allen sought to reduce the personalization involved and to answer charges that service inevitably required ambiguous conditions.[39]

The extreme cases of invocation of the business or factory metaphor were presented by those who were influenced by Frederick W. Taylor. They attempted to introduce the time studies and scientific management associated with Taylorism, and standardize the work and procedures. Bertha Terrill, a professor of home economics at the University of Vermont, described the worker as she would a machine in her textbook *Household Management*. "Simply from the selfish standpoint," she wrote, "that of getting the best work from the machine, reasonable forethought should be given, not only for the comfort, but [also] for the personal freedom of the employee." "This means that if the best work is expected from the worker," she pointed out, "an endeavor should be made to keep her in the best physical condition for the work." Continuing the analogy, she concluded that "there is far too frequently an utter disregard of the actual condition of what may be termed the rolling stock of this business. It is economy to keep the machine well oiled, well repaired and well housed."[40]

The movement to introduce management principles into the home was inseparable from the development of the science of domestic economy and educational programs in that area. Important ideals in scientific management, for instance, were the scientific investigation of the work in all its aspects, the control and improvement of the work environment, and the training of managers and workers in the appropriate and most efficient skills and organization of the work. Scientific study—domestic science—approached the problem as would any other science; it dealt with both the theory and practice of life in the household—for example, the chemical and physical principles of heat and diet and the applied aspects of cleaning and cooking. At the University of Chicago in 1900 the elective "Sanitary Science" dealt with "house structure and furnishing, ventilation, sewerage, economy of labor in the household, the value and chemistry of foods, the principles of the effect of the application of heat, etc." Similar courses in domestic science were offered at universities throughout the nation, and scholars investigated the science and economy of the household.[41]

The domestic-economy movement and its goal of professionalizing the role of housekeeper stimulated the research and publication of articles and books on women's work as well as on the household, the family, and domestic servants. It represented the flowering of Catherine Beecher's emphasis on women's education of a half century before, but it was more significantly influenced by recognition of the spread of women's education, an increase in the number of women who worked, and the growth in the natural and social sciences at the end of the century. From the 1890s through World War I, more investigations of domestic service were undertaken than had ever been before or have ever been since, and more publications on household labor were put out than had been or would ever be printed again. The basic investigations of domestic service—those of Lucy Maynard Salmon, Isabel Eaton, Gail Laughlin, Lillian Pettengill, Frances Kellor, I. M. Rubinow, and the Women's Educational and Industrial Union, and state labor reports—were all undertaken during this era.

While domestic education was an essential element in the move to modernize and systematize household work, there was no consensus on how best to carry it out. The pressing question was whether the education of servants or the training of mistresses would be most effective. Those who favored training schools for domestics argued that it would have the effect of upgrading the status of household labor by professionalizing it and by raising the educational levels of those who performed it. In 1892, Kate Hamlin cited the examples of nursing and teaching, fields in which training schools certified the entrants into the occupations. "Nursing by means of the systematic training given in these schools," Hamlin argued, "has risen from a position as low down in the social scale as many departments of domestic service, to a position and standing second only to that of the physician." Essentially the problem within the household was that of ignorance on the part of both mistress and servant. The logical conclusion was that education would remedy the situation, and Hamlin thought that "education of the servant will be more easily accomplished than the education of the mistress." Reformers such as Ellen Dietrick argued that schools for mistresses were the solution to the servant problem. Training for servants would not work: "they have neither the ambition, foresight, nor the capital," Dietrick contended, "to lead them to make a sacrifice of present gain for a possible future good." A school for employers, on the other hand, would attract mistresses and provide them with the necessary management skills. Furthermore, it would help shift control from the servant to the mistress, who could rely on her educated judgment rather than deferring to the servant's ideas. It would also introduce a sense of professionalization in housework.[42]

The emphasis on education took many forms. In 1903, *The Child Housekeeper*, with music and illustrations, appeared. Part of the domestic-science movement, the exercises not only introduced children into the routines of household care—setting the table, washing dishes, making beds, cleaning, and doing laundry, for example—but also told them about the chemistry of preparations and their history. In the introduction, Jacob Riis called the approach "a great thing to do." "Whoever helps make it better and brighter by putting cheer into the things which were slavery before," he went on, "why, that one is a real Santa Claus of all the seasons." But teaching housekeeping in the elementary grades was part of the domestic-science movement, part of a larger scheme to elevate household labor and train females in household economy. The authors stressed that "our object is to teach young

girls to work neatly and intelligently at home with the utensils and materials there provided, and not to train them to
become servants." After all, domestic science had a higher
purpose than training respectable girls to be domestic servants.[43]

Concern with modernization and rationalization of the
home and household tasks led others to look to technology to
solve the servant problem by making servants unnecessary.
Writing in *Outlook*, Martha Bruère predicted that domestic
technology and industrial advances would make it possible to
forgo servants. "We used to have a woman come in by the
day," a man wrote her. "When she stopped coming, we just
purchased a vacuum cleaner for $120, which the woman
folks now prefer to outside help. . . . We have also a motor-
operated washing-machine, two electric sad-irons, and one
gas iron." A wife of a New England physician reported her
pleasure in living for a year without a maid after discharging
her servant, who had been with her for six years. "I use a gas
range, a fireless cooker, have an excellent vacuum cleaner,
and an adequate supply of all kitchen utensils and conveniences," she wrote. "My household expenses have been cut
down about five hundred dollars a year, and I know of no
easier way of saving that amount than by being free from the
care and annoyance of a maid." Others agreed that labor-saving appliances were less expensive and freed housekeepers
from their responsibilities toward servants. Bruère also predicted that household chores would be transferred to agencies outside the home, citing as examples the assumption by
industry of such chores as dressmaking, baking, and laundry.[44]

Such utopians as Edward Bellamy and William Dean
Howells solved the servant problem by depicting servantless
societies. In his romance "A Traveler from Altruria" Howells portrayed a Christian cooperative commonwealth without servants; the dignity of labor and cooperative efforts had
eliminated service and servants from the mythical island of
Altruria. This theme was a significant one in the romance,
which first appeared serially in *Cosmopolitan* during 1892 and

1893, as the opening scene described the Altrurian's failure to treat American servants as subordinates, to the embarrassment of his host—a scene with variations which would be repeated throughout the novel. Edward Bellamy, the leading utopian novelist of nineteenth-century America, addressed himself directly to solving the servant problem when he offered his futuristic visions in *Good Housekeeping* in 1889. Dividing household tasks into three categories—laundry; cooking; waiting and kitchen work and cleaning—Bellamy proposed cooperative laundries and kitchens as the means by which to eliminate household washing and meal tasks and reduce demand for servants. Other innovations based on cooperation, such as central distribution of heat from cooperative societies, would make even more servants redundant. Where household labor was still thought essential, Bellamy outlined the organization of a cooperative agency that would hire out household workers by the hour. The laborers would be employees, not servants, and they would work for the agency, not for the individual household. "Household service under such conditions," Bellamy predicted, "would wholly lose the flavor of feudal dependence in the relation of employed and employer . . . and cease to be what it now is—an anachronism."[45]

Another utopian solution to the servant problem was to uncover an untapped reservoir of servants. Northern housewives sung the praises in turn of the Irish, Southern blacks, Eastern Europeans, and West Indians. None proved wholly satisfactory in relieving the inevitable tensions between mistress and servant, and many left housework at the first chance for marriage or another job. Northern housewives looked enviously at the large pool of black servants in the South, and they supported programs to recruit servants in the South—whether by the Freedmen's Bureau in 1865 and 1866 or by employment agents around the turn of the century. Some housekeepers looked enviously at the Chinese servants to be found on the West Coast. Woman's magazines praised the Chinese as servants, but alas, they were "growing extinct" as the older generation died off and restrictions on immigration prevented a large-scale immigration. If Southern housewives were envied by their Northern counterparts, they did not feel blessed, and they too looked for new sources of servants. A South Carolinian reported in 1866 that Irish women were replacing blacks in Charleston, but they proved even less satisfactory. Efforts in the 1870s to settle Chinese in the Mississippi Valley proved no more successful.[46]

Mistresses also tried to lure into service the great number of women who they thought traditionally shunned service—the native-born middle-class educated women, the very women who under other financial conditions would be hiring servants themselves. According to Lida McCabe in 1904, "gentlewomen forced to earn a living" should "secure positions in good families as housekeepers, caretakers, parlor maids, housemaids." To demonstrate the great rewards of such jobs, McCabe related the story of a gentlewoman who was forced to earn a living. She went to New York and assumed a position as caretaker of a Fifth Avenue mansion. After the sixteen servants had left for the summer country house, she engaged a maid to cook for her and help in "putting the house in its summer dress." She found the house disorganized, and under her management it was put into efficient order. " 'What do I receive for my services?' " the gentlewoman said. " 'Seventy-five dollars a month, my living and these quarters.' She touched a button, and an electric elevator slowly rose to the sixth floor." Satin-covered walls and carpeted floors were everywhere. In her apartment, "the double bed was brass. . . . The dressing room and bath were tiled in white and perfect as any room in the house." " 'Every day or so,' said the caretaker, in closing, 'the maid says to me: 'Madame, you should be the mistress of this house.' But I feel more like the curator of a museum, so personal is the appeal of all these beautiful pictures and works of art with which I'm entrusted.' " Though of an entirely different genre, the odyssey of McCabe's gentlewoman served functions similar to the Horatio Alger stories so popular at the time. Pluck, luck, and good breeding were rewarded in the long run, even in the most menial of careers. One needed only the courage to enter the fray. And in the process, if more entered, they would solve the servant problem.[47]

Other suggested solutions to the servant problem ranged from fantasy to serious thoughts. Some people, for instance, credited Mormonism with providing a divinely inspired solution to the servant problem. "Joseph Smith introduced polygamy into his religious system," Francis Walker of the census bureau wrote in relating a popular delusion, "merely as an indirect solution of the problem of domestic service; a shrewd device, at once to keep his handmaidens under discipline, and to defraud them of their rightful wages." Other suggestions included abolishing the public schools above the primary grades and the state licensing of domestics. Lucy Maynard Salmon proposed a profit-sharing system in which the housekeeper would budget a month's household expenses, including food, fuel, breakage, ice, and replacement of kitchen utensils. A prorated sum would be added for each guest. If at the end of the month expenses were below the allotted funds, the servant would share in the surplus.[48]

In 1906 Lucy Maynard Salmon reviewed the changes that had occurred in household labor in the decade since the publication of her path-breaking *Domestic Service*. She found that a new tone had entered the published discussions of the servant question, the "gradual disappearance of the fault-finding, the sentimental, the goody-goody magazine article, and the appearance in its place of genuine contributions to the subject." By "genuine contributions" she meant the studies of service and the suggestions for reform outlined above. Knowledge of the conditions under which servants worked and lived and of the work itself had increased geometrically, yet the conditions themselves had not improved. "The average housekeeper," she thought, "does not yet know the best, the easiest, the most practical, or the most scientific way to manage her household affairs." Why did a gap exist between theory and practice in household employment and management? One easy explanation was that domestic-science training was still in its infancy and had not become

widely disseminated nor universally acquired by mistresses.
It is more likely, however, that mistresses were exposed to
the arguments for rationalizing and systematizing household
labor, and most rejected them or were opposed to changing
their own methods.[49]

The greatest obstacle facing reformers was the resistance
of housewives themselves. Missing from the debate over restructuring housekeeping and employer/employee relations
were the voices of ordinary mistresses. Instead, reformers
argued among themselves, suggesting this or that reform or
change in service without noticing that most employers did
not wish to alter significantly the traditional personalized
relationship. Essentially, the reformers were modernizers,
women and men attempting to rationalize the organization of
the home by introducing contemporary principles of science
and management. They looked to developments in manufacturing, commerce, and education and noted the sharp contrast with the medievalism of the home. Not surprisingly,
the inhabitants of the traditional environment
—housewives—resisted the modernizers. But they could
not compete successfully with the rational, logical arguments of the reformers and simply withdrew from public
discussion. By the turn of the century there was no debate. In most homes, housekeepers continued using their
traditionally based methods, modified but traditional, while
modernizers argued among themselves. Moreover, in an age
that idolized progress and efficiency, it was difficult to argue
for tradition, and rarely did magazines or journals give the
traditionalists a platform.

Apparently housekeepers found tradition more comfortable than the reforms of the modernizers. Reformers defined
tradition in negative terms: "inertia," "their inability to assume an impersonal attitude toward any subject under discussion," lack of planning, and so forth. But traditional
methods had worked in these women's mothers' homes and
kitchens—that is, the households in which most housewives
of the day had been raised—and most of these women probably had positive if not somewhat nostalgic feelings about

their mothers' homes. Tradition was familiar, in harmony with the way they lived; reform represented alien methods that went against their instincts. Undoubtedly the unceasing attacks of the modernizers strengthened the housewives' defense of their traditional ways.[50]

Housekeepers probably recognized that reformers did not understand many of the fundamental aspects of household service. Many employers wanted to be mistresses or desired the companionship of another woman in the household. While business methods might increase the efficiency of work performance, this was not a major goal of a significant number of employers. They wanted a personal relationship; they didn't want to hire just the labor of a servant, but consciously chose to hire the person. Many families liked the comforts provided by a servant waiting on them; they were accustomed to having a servant on call twenty-four hours a day. They also understood that some servants did not want to fill impersonal roles; some had entered service because it represented an alternative to the impersonal world of factory, store, or office. Enough servants had voluntarily chose service to reinforce the defenses of mistresses. In addition, not all servants were ambitious for promotion or even marriage, and live-in housework offered them a sought-after environment.[51]

Mistresses probably also saw the weakness or irrelevancy of many of the proposed reforms. The atomization of workplace meant that no single employer would have any effect on the structure of the occupation or work. Under these conditions, the traditional methods of retaining a servant—benevolent maternalism—would probably have been most successful for an individual housekeeper. The employer probably perceived herself as being in competition with other housekeepers for servants, rather than seeing herself and all other housekeepers as competing with factories or shops or offices for servants, which was the reformers' frame of reference. Moreover, the utopians who called for cooperative institutions were not only threatening the intimacy of the private family but also suggesting social and economic changes that had not been widely adopted in the United States. And because the period was one of strife between labor and capital throughout American industry and because exposés of business corruption and exploitation of workers had been widely publicized, the rationalized, systematized methods of manufacturing and business could hardly have been considered exemplary by many housewives. Mistresses recognized, even if reformers didn't, that social distinctions existed in factories, shops, and offices no less than in households. If the banker or merchant treated clerks or bookkeepers as social equals, it was because they "are the future proprietors and the sons of present ones." But janitors, porters, draymen, and laborers were not treated as equals. Some housewives also probably interpreted reformers as advocating "masculine lines" or "imitating men" in urging the adoption of business and industrial principles. This would have appeared as a negation of the sexual roles traditionalists upheld.[52]

Even more damaging to the reformers was that the implementation of their proposals did not significantly affect the servant problem. The YWCA commission had astutely summarized the problem of domestic service: "as long as a person must have all her living conditions, her social life, her entertaining, her educational and spiritual development at the sufferance of her employer, there will be abundant occasion for servile treatment and the social stigma." When it would become possible for young women in service to sell their labor alone, reserving "equal opportunity for self-direction and self-development with the office, store and factory worker," then the " 'servant problem' will have disappeared." The only problem with this thoughtful, clear remedy was that it didn't prove true. By the 1920s, when live-out and day work came to dominate, the eight-hour day had become widespread and technological innovation inside and outside of the home had altered the work tasks. Yet service still attracted a smaller and smaller percentage of working women, demand still far outstripped the supply, and the disappearance of the servant began to replace the servant problem as a topic of discussion.[53]

Why did reform fail? Basically, the shift from live-in service to live-out or day work did not significantly affect the low status of household labor. The work itself retained its objectionable features as unskilled black and immigrant women's work with a personalized employer/employee relationship. Housekeepers proved extremely resilient in maintaining an intimate relationship with their servants even though most workers now lived away from their place of work. Moreover, service lost its relatively favorable position in wages. Since a significant part of annual earnings had been paid in kind, in the form of room and board, the shift to liveout work meant a sharp reduction in earnings when compared to other occupations, for there was only a slight differential, if any, in wages between live-in and live-out servants. All the while, employers continued to demand servility and deference and retained their enormous power over the workers.

For all their humanitarian impulses, most reformers were more interested in easing the servant shortage than in radically improving the lot of domestics. Indeed, the major motivation for better wages, hours, and working conditions in households was that they would make the work more attractive and increase its status, thereby luring more girls and women into service. No doubt self-interest played a part in motivating some reformers, because middle-class female reformers—progressives—depended upon servants to free them from their household duties so that they could enter the reform arena. What reform did not suggest was transferring control of the work to the employees. This is in part what workers in other industries were battling for—and successfully so in the building trades. To reformers this was probably anathema, because most agreed that housewives were superior to servants and that control of the work should remain in the hands of employers.

In nearly all cases, reform represented an employer movement. When Edward Bellamy suggested a cooperative agency to employ household workers and shift their position from servant to employer, it was a housewives', not a workers', cooperative. When the Baltimore Domestic Efficiency Association demanded references on servants, as had the New York society of the 1820s, no files were kept on employers. The president of the Baltimore association recognized that collecting references on employers would be equitable, but she thought that "any association which professed to record the opinions of employees as to their employers would be doomed at its birth." When domestic training schools were proposed and organized, they were designed to meet employers' needs. "Those schools are not for us," a domestic told Frances Kellor, "no one ever finds out what we want to learn; they start out with a theory and everything must fit that, and we won't fit—that's all."[54]

Two solutions remained—legislative regulation or unionization—and they proved as illusory as had Howells's and Bellamy's utopias. I. M. Rubinow dealt with household labor as he would have any other group of laborers, and suggested either government regulation of service—similar to other Progressive-era labor and factory legislation—or the introduction of collective bargaining. Not only did regulation not come but domestic service was specifically excluded from labor legislation and the social-welfare umbrella of the federal government and most state governments. No matter how weak mistresses might have been, their employees were even weaker. The atomization of the workplace was the greatest obstacle to unionization, and would continue to be so.[55]

In suggesting unionization, Rubinow proposed an instrument for employee control of the work. In citing unionization and collective bargaining together, he probably was stressing more employee input into and influence over working conditions, yet it could have led to employee control over the hiring and organization of the work in the same way that the building-trades or longshore unions operated as a hiring hall. If workers themselves had been able to control the work assignments—as in the building trades or longshore work—through their union, then the personalized mistress/servant relationship would have faded away. If the workers themselves had been able to gain control over the work and supply their own tools, the stigma of servility and subordination would have disappeared. Given the atomization of the workplace, the power of the middle class and the powerlessness of the mostly black and immigrant servants, the millions of employers and the ease of entry into service, possibly only legislative action giving exclusive hiring control to a workers' (union) hiring hall would have ensured employee control. Yet those conditions are as utopian as Howells's Altruria. For domestic servants and housekeepers in industrial society, then, the servant problem was no closer to solution in the last quarter of the twentieth century (though conditions had changed radically) than it had been during the previous one hundred and fifty years. What reformers and housewives could not grasp was that the real victims of the servant problem were not the mistresses but the servants.

⤀ VII ⤣

DOMESTIC SERVICE IN AN
INDUSTRIALIZING SOCIETY

"A MAN'S WORK IS AS GOOD A CLUE AS ANY," EVERETT C. Hughes wrote in 1958, "to the course of his life, and to his social being and identity." The apparent truth of this maxim buttresses not only economic determinism in historical writing but also much of recent American social history with its concern for social (occupational) mobility. Certain groups, however, are not included in Hughes's axiom. Deviants, people who differ from societal norms, and such social oddities as dwarfs are excluded. Moreover, being a black, Hughes observed, "may be called a master status-determining trait. It tends to overpower, in most crucial situations, any other characteristics which might run counter to it." But where do women fit into this categorization? Should women be considered social deviants, since between the Civil War and World War I only a relatively small minority of women were gainfully employed at any one time? [1]

Is a woman's work, to paraphrase Hughes, as good a clue as any to the course of her life? Or perhaps, is a husband's work as good a clue as any to the course of his wife's life? If the last axiom seems reasonable, then perhaps it could be more accurately reworded as a father's work provides the clue to his daughter's unmarried life until she marries, when her husband's work becomes the indicator. After all, in the

United States before the 1920s most women if they held gainful employment worked only temporarily, as a stage in their life cycle between their parents' home and that of their husband. And if they were unfortunate enough to work for a longer period, it was thought to be not from choice; the ideal environment of the woman in American society had been the home, not the workplace. Nonetheless, women did work, but only rarely for wages. Most did unpaid household labor as wife and mother, maid and cook, teacher and instructor. For many women, unpaid household work and wage-earning represented mutually exclusive stages in their life cycle. For a minority of women—predominately black, secondarily foreign born—they represented simultaneous roles.

If women had two roles—home and work—which was a truer indication of the course of their lives? Patricia Branca has suggested that "working-class women as a group never chose to make employment a primary means of identification in their lives." Instead, work was thought to fill the period between childhood and their own maternal role. When it became necessary for them to be wage earners, they welcomed the work if it was compatible with their family roles and helped them grow personally; but if it conflicted with family-centered goals, they rejected it or accepted it with extreme reluctance. In this regard, women's lives were significantly different than those of men in late-nineteenth- and early-twentieth-century America. Yet in choosing not to work, working-class women were not assuming lives of leisure or merging themselves completely into their husbands' identities. Instead, they preferred another kind of work—providing a home environment, having and raising children, caring, nurturing, and teaching. Not all women necessarily preferred the maternal roles nor did they all have a greater aptitude for it than they did for a career, but it was the ideal to which most working-class women aspired. And given that many would have to be wage earners while still performing the unpaid family and home roles, this probably reinforced their aspiration to attain the ideal of the women's role—not to work outside of their own household.[2]

For working-class women, domestic service was as compatible with women's roles as any occupation. For young girls, an important element in service until the turn of the century, it provided something of a home environment. It was seen as an environment intermediary between their past and future lives, less restrictive than the parental home but more structured than the lodging houses independent working women lived in. The home as workplace provided shelter from the outside world, with all its temptations and possibilities of exploitation. Service was women's work—work appropriate to women—and it provided a form of apprenticeship in the skills and arts to be employed in their own homes after marriage. For women from rural districts or for immigrants, it was an introduction to a more urban and modern environment. They were exposed to new work habits and a more refined cultural and social environment. If married servants found live-in service in conflict with their own home roles, live-out or day work was relatively easily matched with their own home obligations. Indeed, married women concentrated in an early form of day work—hand laundry—and as washerwomen disappeared, they helped transform service from primarily live-in to primarily live-out work. Day work was conducive to part-time work and limited working hours, thus allowing a married woman greater freedom in reconciling her own home duties with wage-earning.

Yet in spite of these benefits and others, when given a choice, most women chose shop, office, or factory work over household labor. Domestic service was clearly considered undesirable by most working women. The extremely low status, the personalized mistress/servant relationship, the atomization of work, the designation "servant," and the servility and deference required led nearly all who could to avoid it. Added to these disadvantages were the restricted personal freedom, the indefinite and long hours, and the inability to control their own living environment experienced by those who lived in. If most women did not draw their identity from their work, they at least looked for labor that would impinge less on their personal lives than household labor did. Service, judging from the intensely negative reactions to it expressed by factory and "white-blouse" workers as well as by domestics themselves, left servants scarred socially and psychologically. Within society, paid household labor carried a stigma that separated household workers from other laborers. Internally, it left a mark of inferiority and servility. Though nearly all servants resisted in one way or another, they must have internalized some of the constant tensions between mistress and servant and some of the treatment they received day after day at the hands of their mistresses or masters. Lillian Pettengill, a college-educated woman, began to feel uncomfortable eating at a mistress' table or spending time in the parlor, and she developed a sensitivity to the shifting moods of her employers.

Indeed, the all-encompassing environment of the mistress' home may have been one of the most pernicious elements in live-in service. Living in broke down the separation of work and family that allowed young single women to avoid close identification with work and maintain expectations of marriage. It served to limit contact with other servants, families, and peers, and thus forced a servant to become more work-oriented. Moreover, because her personal freedom was restricted, she had fewer chances to meet men and thus less of a chance to get married. If family interests were to be maintained by servants, many mistresses encouraged servants to express their nurturing and loving instincts on the employing family. In exploiting the emotional needs of the domestic, the employer might be winning a faithful and loyal servant, one who lost her own vision of an independent life and instead adopted the family she worked for as a substitute for her own.

The woman-to-woman relationship was a peculiar characteristic of domestic work. Middle-class women, the employers, gained freedom from family roles and household chores and assumed or confirmed social status by the employment of a servant. Having a servant might have freed them to combine professional careers with family roles or to engage in benevolent work or to indulge in leisure activities. The greater liberty of these middle-class women, however, was achieved at the expense of working-class women, who, forced to work, assumed the tasks beneath, distasteful to, or too demanding for the family members. As employers, mistresses assumed a role that was unusual for an American woman in the late nineteenth or early twentieth century to play—the part of a female "boss." It was an unfamiliar role, and most housewives probably increased the personalization of the mistress/servant relationship in compensation for their own insecurities. Equally important was that many mistresses hired servants to fulfill psychological needs independent of the work involved. Mistresses might seek companionship, a loving relationship, or a surrogate daughter in a young girl or women who, more often than not, sought fulfillment in work rather than in an intimate relationship with a stranger. Whatever the relationship, it was not an equal one, and mistresses rarely offered chances for mutual fulfillment.

In search of better living conditions and to avoid being shackled to her mistress' home—to secure, in a sense, her own freedom just as black women had done at emancipation—a servant had to change employers constantly. Thus, high turnover was an important characteristic of household labor. Rather than indicating worker instability, it represented the attainment of basic security and stability in the servant's own work life. Powerless to control most of the work and living conditions, a domestic only had one defense: to change employers. Within a household a servant was on alien ground without supportive friends. Moreover, a servant was more sensitive to relationships with others within the household, since the home filled more of her life than it did for anyone else in the house. On the other hand, because the servant was confined mostly to the home, external forces affected her less than they did her employers. The members of her employer's family, however, brought back into the home the tensions and pressures from the external world, and expressed feelings toward the servant generated not by their relationship but by those outside pressures. A mistress' black day could spell disaster for an unsuspecting maid. Public exposure and presence generally sheltered a factory, shop, or office worker against an employer's emotionalism; nothing except the conscience of an employer and her self-control protected a servant against her mistress's wrath. Furthermore, no allowances were made for the biological rhythms of servants, who had to contend with the shifting moods of mistresses.

If they could, women avoided household work. Increasingly urbanization and modernization brought new opportunities for women in stores and offices, and the increase in the number of jobs in these areas was responsible for the declining importance of household labor within the women's occupational structure. In 1870, half of all gainfully employed women had worked as servants and washerwomen; by 1920, only 16 percent were paid household workers. Domestic service drew less from women who chose service and more from those who due to race, ethnicity, lack of education, or marital condition had no choice. Very young servants began to disappear by the turn of the twentieth century as compulsory education and then child-labor laws forced them out of the employment market. Native-born white women were drawn first to factory employment, then to the expanding opportunities in retail stores and offices, and then to professional work as teachers and trained nurses. In the major urban areas, immigrants and black women filled the expanding middle class's ever-increasing demand for servants. As the source of immigration shifted in the 1890s, the proportion of immigrants in service declined. Black women then began to replace immigrants as domestics in Northern cities, and this process accelerated when World War I created many new jobs for women and virtually halted immigration. In the South, where the pace of urbanization, industrialization, and modernization lagged far behind the North, domestic service remained at levels comparable to the late-nineteenth-century North.

Black, Irish, and Scandinavian women were closely identified with domestic service. Historically, each group had formed a servant class. Blacks more than any other group of women were wage earners. They had worked in slavery, and the low wages paid black males guaranteed that they would work in freedom as well. With office and shop work closed to them, except in the case of black employers, and with only menial factory work available—tobacco sorting, for instance—black women had to work in kitchens and parlors. Women in Ireland also tended to work and to work as servants. Familiar with service, mostly uneducated and tending to marry late, Irish women comprised the most important source of immigrant household workers, and a greater proportion of them than of any other significant group of immigrants worked in household labor at any one time.

Italian and Jewish women were the least likely to find employment in private families. If they worked—and relatively few did—they tried to hold jobs that would not take them outside their own homes and away from their families. Instead, when they worked, they formed an important source of piecework home-sewing labor, but not servants. In addition, they seemed to share a cultural dislike of service.

For white women, regardless of birth, work could be expected to be but a temporary period in their life cycle, which in turn reinforced the separation between work and identity. Among black women, however, work would form an essential element throughout their lives. More than 40 percent of black women of any age were wage earners; there was no significant decline as women reached marrying or childbearing age. For white women, then, a clear distinction existed between single, divorced, or widowed women on the one hand and those who were married on the other. Among blacks, the differences were blurred. Since most black women outside rural areas were confined to domestic service, the black response was to shape household labor to be compatible with their family roles. Live-out service and day work were the norms in the South long before they played a significant role in the urban North and West. Most commonly, black servants lived at home and returned home sometime during the

day. As blacks became the dominant group in service in the
urban North after 1900, they played an essential role in shifting service to live-out and day work there.
Black women formed a permanent pool of servants. In the
South, race and service were inseparable, and blacks formed
a service caste. By virtue of caste and work, blacks were a
servile, subordinate stratum socially removed from white society. As migration brought black women to Northern cities,
they replaced white and immigrant women who were leaving, although the white decrease exceeded the increase in
black household workers. The total number of black servants
nationally remained virtually the same, but migration
reduced their concentration in the South and served to
redistribute black domestics. By 1920 blacks had become
the primary servant group in Northern cities, and their appearance there served to cushion the effects of the departure
of whites.

What is most ironic about the caste lines confining blacks
to domestic service and the discrimination pushing some immigrants into household labor is that they were being pushed
into an occupation with earnings higher than most other
comparable occupations. In other words, domestic servants
tended to receive a higher annual income, including the value
of board and room, then laborers in other unskilled and
semi-skilled occupations. This factor more than any other
underscores the degree to which domestic service must be
examined primarily within the social, not the economic,
structure. Once women met their basic goal of achieving a
subsistence income—which varied in individual cases—they
could use other criteria in selecting one occupation over another if they had any choice. Overwhelmingly those who
had a choice—native-born white women—rejected domestic
service. The higher earnings could not compensate for the
social disabilities accompanying service.

Servants were also in an enviable position because of the
control they had over their work tasks. Unlike the general
trend of work in the industrializing economy, where factory
workers and others were losing the control they once had had

over their individual work tasks, most servants retained this power. In cooking, in cleaning, and in laundry servants were free to use their own judgment in performing the tasks. This was especially true in the South, where white mistresses were accustomed to leaving the rearing of children and the running of the household to black workers. Servants were limited by having to work with tools and materials supplied by the employer, but most often they could complete the job as they saw fit, generally at their own pace. The major problem was that this great power was exercised within a larger system in which they had less control than other workers over their own personal lives. Whatever work advantage was gained from their control over individual tasks could not balance their larger loss in personal power.

The issue of control over work tasks and the presence of the workplace within the household highlights the degree to which domestic service was, and still is, a nonindustrial occupation. Although live-in service represented a medieval anachronism in which workplace and home were one and the worker personally was hired and not her labor alone, it was essentially nonindustrial in the sense that it was non-product-oriented work in which often the status of having a servant was as important to the employer as the work performance. Yet domestic servants in the United States from the Civil War through the 1920s labored at a time when the nation was being transformed by industrialization, urbanization, and modernization.

As in Europe, domestic service was a modernizing agent for many domestics. Theresa McBride and Patricia Branca have described this as the most important characteristic of service in England and France. For immigrants, it was often their first encounter with the city, and for live-in servants the work experience was as vital as any other factor in that encounter. They learned new work habits based on the clock and a systematized approach to work. For immigrant women especially, this first exposure and contact could provide an essential integrating mechanism. Immigrants who entered live-in service would be isolated from their ethnic communi-

ties and thus would be more likely to experience acculturation. Moreover, the employer required conformity to the
standards and overt values of the family; whether or not the
servant accepted these, she would have to live by the standards and rhythms of the middle-class employers.[3]

Yet it is far too easy to exaggerate domestic service as a
modernizing agent. The private home and family were
organized as conservators of tradition, and especially in
homes with servants they proved remarkably resistant to
modernization. There is no evidence to suggest, for instance,
that women actually adopted the widely advocated systematized work organization urged by reformers. The presence
of servants permitted continued reliance on hand labor instead of machine power, and allowed the home to retain
processes—baking, laundry, canning—which could have
been transferred outside of the household. In the South,
where in 1920 Southern families had as many servants available as had Northern housewives two generations earlier, the
growth of commercial bakeries and laundries lagged far behind such developments in the North and West. More importantly, as Ruth Cowan has shown, when the industrial
revolution entered the home during the 1920s, it replaced
servants rather than modernizing them. The presence of servants probably retarded modernization in the household, and
domestics would benefit little from its belated appearance in
the home.[4]

There is also the strong possibility that the selection process among women workers left as servants the groups most
resistant to modernization. Those among the native-born
who chose service work did so in the face of the stigma attached. The selection of traditional women's work within the
household probably indicated their desire for work least associated with the tide of modernization and industrialization.
In addition, while servants in Europe tended to be better
educated than other working-class women, in the United
States they were less well educated than other women and
were more likely to be illiterate. Indeed, blacks and immigrants in the United States had less exposure to formal

schooling than did native-born women, and schools were probably more of a modernizing agent than service. Furthermore, servants in Europe were probably more open to change than those in the United States because domestic service offered greater rewards. "Young women," McBride concluded, "found servanthood a useful and respectable occupation before marriage." It offered access to other occupations as well as opportunities for education, and servants in France found upward mobility through marriage relatively easy. In the United States, on the other hand, domestic service represented an occupational dead end, and mobility through marriage opportunities emanating from household labor was blocked by the status, racial, cultural, and religious differences between servants on one side and petty merchants, skilled tradesmen, and the employing family on the other.[5]

Finally, the low status of domestic service raises serious questions about the valuation of women's work in America between the Civil War and World War I. Theresa McBride has argued that women chose household labor because "it stresses human contacts, although tension was as probable as a close relationship. But this need for personal contact has been preserved in much of what women seek from very modern jobs." Or as Patricia Branca framed the point: "in female work choices both old and new, an extraordinary personal element seems to predominate, a desire for a warm human relationship at work. This obviously fits the preference for a home or shop industry, where familial or friendly contacts can be assumed. It serves as at least partial explanation for the preference for servanthood over factory work." However true these generalizations may be for France and England, the experiences of American women seriously challenge their application to the United States. In America the salient feature of the formation of an immigrant and black servant class was the absence of choice or preference. Thus if human contacts and a "warm human relationship at work" were characteristics of domestic service—and possibly they were—these were elements that were valued at a low level in industrializing American society. That a selection process existed in which native-born white women preferred other work to household labor and left the occupation to immigrants and black suggests that not only men but also women considered household labor undesirable and base. That white women's work careers were only temporary should have made them more willing to enter service, where they could find the personal contact that was an inherent part of the mistress/servant relationship within a family. Instead, they chose other work. Perhaps the subordinate role required of servants was a greater detriment than the personal contact was an enticement. Whatever the case, domestic service had much lower status in the United States, a society stressing egalitarianism and individualism, than it did in Europe.[6]

The radical changes in service and the restructuring of the work did little to remove the stigma attached to it. Although the shift to live-out and day work eradicated many of the prominent objections to household labor—loss of personal freedom, indefinite and unlimited hours, unity of work and home environment—the new work structure proved no more popular to most working women than the old. The decrease in the number of single women in service accelerated as modernization in education and commerce and bureaucratization in the business firm created more and more "white blouse" jobs. As the proportion of married women working inched higher, and washerwomen virtually disappeared outside of the South, more married women entered live-out service and day work, replacing many single females. As the ratio of servants per thousand families continued to decline in the 1920s, innovation and technology entered Northern and Western households, but it left servants unaffected. Indeed, the existence of servantless homes stimulated the home industrial revolution. With outside hand power not available to many households, machine power became a necessity. This same process would be repeated in the South during the 1940s and 50s when World War II would spur further black out-migration and expanded work opportunities for black women. As the difference in servants per thousand families between the South and the rest of the nation began to disappear, the industrial revolution began to appear in Southern homes.

Domestic service continued, then, as day work, with relatively few housewives commanding a servant more than one or two days a week. As woman's work, as personal work, as servile work, as service, women continued to avoid it if possible, and it was left to a small group of lower-class uneducated and unskilled women, mostly black and foreign-born, largely married and part-time workers. Ironically, housewives had become liberated from their dependence upon servants only to become chained to performing the tasks themselves. Whether the work was performed by paid labor or by housewives themselves, the low status and stigma remained unchanged.

No one better summed up the experiences of domestic work for many young women than a factory worker who had formerly worked in service. In response to the inquiry, "Why do girls dislike domestic service?" she wrote:

In the first place, I don't like the idea of only one evening a week and every other Sunday. I like to feel that I have just so many hours' work to do and do them, and come home and dress up and go out or sit down and sew if I feel like it, and when a girl is in service she has very little time for herself, she is a servant. In the second place, a shop or factory girl knows just what she has to do and can go ahead and do it. I also think going out makes a girl stupid in time. She gets out of style, so to speak. She never reads and does not know what is going on in the world. I don't mean to say they all get stupid, but it makes gossips of girls that if they worked in shops or factories would be smart girls. Then I think shop or factory girls make the best wives. Now I don't mean all, but the biggest part of them, and the cleanest housekeepers. The domestic after she gets married gets careless. She don't take the pride in her home that the shop-girl does. She has lived in such fine houses that her small tenement has no beauty for her after the first glow of married life is over. She don't try either to make her home attractive or herself, and gets discouraged, and is apt to make a man disheartened with her, and then I think she is extravagant. She has so much to do with before she is married and so little to do with after she don't know how to manage. She can't have tenderloin steak for her breakfast and rump roast for her dinner, and pay the rent and all other bills out of $12 a week—and that is the average man's pay, the kind of man we girls that work for a living get. Of course I don't mean to say the domestics don't have a good time, they do; some of them have lovely places and lay up money, but after all, what is life if a body is always trying to see just how much money he or she can save?[7]

1

APPENDIX

TABLES

Regions and Divisions of the United States

The North *New England:* Maine, New Hampshire, Vermont, Massachusetts, Rhode Island, Connecticut.
Mid-Atlantic: New York, New Jersey, Pennsylvania.
Eastern North Central: Ohio, Indiana, Illinois, Michigan, Wisconsin.
Western North Central: Minnesota, Iowa, Missouri, North Dakota, South Dakota, Nebraska, Kansas.

The South *Northern South Atlantic:* Delaware, Maryland, District of Columbia, Virginia, West Virginia.
Southern South Atlantic: North Carolina, South Carolina, Georgia, Florida.
Eastern South Central: Kentucky, Tennessee, Alabama, Mississippi.
Western South Central: Louisiana, Arkansas, Oklahoma, Texas.

The West *Mountain, Basin, and Plateau:* Montana, Idaho, Wyoming, Colorado, New Mexico, Arizona, Utah, Nevada.
Pacific: Washington, Oregon, California.

Table A–1. Female Domestic and Personal Service Wage Earners, 1870–1930 (10 Yrs. and Over)

Occupation (1930 classification)	1870	1880	1890	1900	1910	1920	1930
Domestic and personal service	982,307	1,118,105	1,610,068	1,962,035	2,530,403	2,186,682	3,180,251
Barbers, hairdressers, and manicurists	1,548	3,463	3,691	7,284	22,298	33,246	113,194
Boarding and lodging housekeepers	7,123	12,313	32,593	59,455	142,400	114,740	127,278
Hotel keepers and managers	883	2,136	5,276	8,533	14,235	14,134	17,310
Janitors and sextons	154	713	2,808	8,033	21,452	29,038	35,820
Elevator tenders					25	7,337	12,359
Laborers, domestic and personal service	1,154	1,340	1,930	2,352	3,215	1,669	4,350
Laundresses (not in laundry)	58,102	108,198	216,631	335,282	520,004	385,874	356,468
Laundry owners, managers, and officials					986	1,453	2,063
Laundry operatives					76,355	80,747	160,475
Midwives and nurses (not trained)	10,592	12,948	37,190	97,645	117,117	137,431	143,142
Restaurant, café, and lunchroom keepers	648	846	2,416	4,845	10,516	15,644	40,008
Housekeepers and stewards			86,089	146,929	173,333	204,350	263,363
Cooks					333,436	268,618	371,095
Other servants	901,954	970,257	1,216,615	1,283,727	976,113	743,515	1,263,864
Waitresses					85,798	116,921	231,973
Charwomen					26,839	24,955	40,989
Porters, domestic and personal service					52	279	13
Porters, professional service							16
All other occupations	149	5,891	4,829	7,950	6,229	6,731	23,471

Source: *Sixteenth Census: 1940, Population*, Alba Edwards, *Comparative Occupation Statistics for the United States, 1870 to 1940*, p. 129.

Table A–2. Male Domestic and Personal Service Wage Earners, 1870–1930 (Selected Occupations) (10 Yrs. and Over)

Occupation (1930 classification)	1870	1880	1890	1900	1910	1920	1930
Domestic and personal service	270,408	405,620	623,890	857,408	1,225,395	1,193,313	1,772,200
Launderers (not in laundry)					13,693	10,882	4,565
Laundry owners, managers, and officials	5,953	15,207	35,309	56,858	17,057	12,239	22,482
Laundry operatives					35,909	39,968	80,229
Housekeepers and stewards			5,947	3,224	15,940	17,262	20,383
Cooks					117,004	129,857	194,297
Other servants	130,702	182,965	234,982	272,203	145,672	128,956	169,877
Waiters					102,495	112,064	161,315
Cleaners					7,195	11,848	20,943
Porters, domestic and personal service					54,560	42,929	57,599
Porters, professional service							7,750

Source: *Sixteenth Census: 1940, Population*, Alba Edwards, *Comparative Occupation Statistics for the United States, 1870 to 1940*, p. 121.

Table A–3. Female Wage Earners by Industry, 1870–1930 (Including Selected Occupations) (10 Yrs. and Over)

	1870	1880	1890	1900	1910	1920	1930
All industries	1,917,446	2,647,157	4,005,532	5,319,397	7,444,787	8,636,512	10,752,116
All nonagricultural industries	1,462,502	2,021,308	3,209,553	4,311,032	6,269,148	7,466,365	9,842,177
Agriculture	454,944	625,849	795,979	1,008,365	1,175,639	1,170,147	909,939
Selected manufacturing and mechanical industries	364,097	657,762	1,047,968	1,380,469	1,820,847	1,930,352	1,886,307
Cigar and tobacco factories	4,290	10,868	27,991	43,497	76,801	97,822	74,435
Clothing industries	197,367	352,360	596,655	699,487	865,086	613,259	575,484
Food industries	2,436	4,458	10,068	19,518	47,762	93,140	114,630
Textile industries	108,637	168,515	234,695	293,134	402,640	471,463	452,301
Transportation and communication	1,050	3,676	17,605	42,181	115,347	224,470	281,204
Telephone operators					88,262	178,379	235,259
Trade	18,735	57,032	141,593	247,966	472,703	671,983	962,680
Saleswomen (stores)	8,995	31,466	98,209	215,864	250,487	356,321	542,646
"Clerks" in stores					111,594	170,397	163,147
Public service	145	672	1,643	3,198	4,836	10,586	17,583
Professional service	94,166	176,824	312,747	436,174	734,752	1,017,030	1,526,234
Teachers*	85,548	153,372	244,467	335,485	478,027	639,241	860,278
Trained nurses	1,154	1,464	4,206	11,046	76,508	143,664	288,737
Domestic and personal service	982,307	1,118,105	1,610,068	1,962,035	2,530,403	2,186,682	3,180,251
Clerical occupations	1,910	7,040	77,060	187,053	588,609	1,421,925	1,986,830
Bookkeepers, cashiers, and accountants	884	4,252	27,772	74,153	187,155	359,124	482,711
Clerks (except in stores)	923	315	24,283	18,332	122,665	472,163	706,553
Stenographers and typists	7	2,000	21,270	86,118	263,315	564,744	775,140

*Includes college presidents and professors 1870–1900.

Source: *Sixteenth Census: 1940, Population*, Alba Edwards, *Comparative Occupation Statistics for the United States, 1870 to 1940*, pp. 122–129.

Table A–4. Female Wage Earners in Selected Industries and Occupations
Formerly Performed in the Household, 1870–1930 (10 Yrs. and Over)

	1870	1880	1890	1900	1910	1920	1930
Food industries	2,436	4,458	10,068	19,518	47,762	93,140	114,630
Restaurant, café, and Lunchroom keepers	648	846	2,416	4,845	10,516	15,644	40,008
Waitresses				42,839	85,798	116,921	231,973
Laundry operatives				9,933	76,355	80,747	160,475
Laundry owners, managers, and officials					986	1,453	2,063
Cleaning, dyeing, and pressing shop workers					2,645	4,573	21,603
Total (two occupations)	3,084	5,304	12,484				
Total				77,135	224,062	312,478	570,752

Sources: See tables 2–1, A–1, and A–3.

Table A–5. Ratio of Female Servants and Laundresses per 1,000 Families, 1880–1920, for Selected Cities and States (10 Yrs. and Over)

	1880		1900		1920	
	Servants	Laun-dresses	Servants	Laun-dresses	Servants	Laun-dresses
Boston	219	20	167	25	79	8
Rest of Massachusetts	109		104	12	46	4
Buffalo	145	12	118	15	47	8
New York City*	188	29	141	22	66	8
Rest of New York	113		87	11	43	8
Detroit	147	14	115	17	35	6
Rest of Michigan	74		70	6	28	6
Denver	109	18	101	20	50	8
Rest of Colorado	34		42	11	23	7
Baltimore	212	65	159	74	91	48
Rest of Maryland	152		115	20	60	27
Atlanta	331	233	214	238	136	113
Rest of Georgia	85		67	60	53	54
New Orleans	206	80	157	101	121	86
Rest of Louisiana	65		59	34	56	32

*1880 includes Brooklyn and New York City.

Source: *Tenth Census: 1880, Population*, vol. I, passim. *Twelfth Census: 1900, Population*, vol. II, pt II, pp. clx–clxiv; *Occupations*, passim. *Fourteenth Census: 1920, Population*, vol. III, pp. 34–46; *Occupations*, passim.

Table A–6. Percentage of Women Wage Earners in
Household Labor (Servants and Laundresses), 1880–1920,
Selected Cities (10 Yrs. or Over)

	1880	*1900*	*1920*
Boston	44.8	31.9	12.9
Hartford	45.3	34.9	11.3
Buffalo	84.5	34.2	12.9
New York	43.1	32.7	13.8
Philadelphia	36.7	27.8	15.2
Rochester	28.8	20.1	7.5
Chicago	41.6	28.0	10.5
Cincinnati	40.8	32.0	19.3
Cleveland	45.2	29.9	11.8
Detroit	46.6	29.2	10.5
Indianapolis	54.0	34.4	16.1
Kansas City, Missouri	59.4	40.5	16.1
Minneapolis	50.7	35.3	12.6
St. Louis	56.7	36.1	17.9
Atlanta	73.8	62.3	36.2
Baltimore	55.1	40.3	25.1
Richmond	71.7	52.8	30.6
Washington, D.C.	65.1	54.5	22.3
Wilmington, Delaware	48.6	36.5	21.2
Louisville	64.7	46.9	24.5
Nashville	73.7	62.7	38.3
New Orleans	67.8	56.3	35.3
Denver	44.9	30.8	12.5
Los Angeles		24.5	11.6
San Francisco	41.7	26.2	9.6

Source: *Tenth Census: 1880, Population,* vol. I, passim. *Twelfth Census: 1900, Occupations,*
passim. *Fourteenth Census: 1920, Occupations,* passim.

Table A–7. Laundresses, 1900–1920, by Regions (16 Yrs. and Over)

	1900	*1920*
United States	328,935	383,622
The North	119,712	121,688
New England	15,004	9,203
Mid-Atlantic	43,671	43,072
Eastern North Central	36,572	43,276
Western North Central	24,465	26,137
The South	200,410	252,128
Northern South Atlantic	38,942	41,935
Southern South Atlantic	62,232	82,674
Eastern South Central	60,618	71,500
Western South Central	38,618	56,019
The West	8,813	9,806
Mountain and Basin	4,514	5,569
Pacific	4,299	4,237

Sources: U.S. Bureau of the Census, *Statistics of Women at Work* (Washington, D.C., 1907), p. 185. Joseph Hill, *Women in Gainful Occupations 1870 to 1920*, Census Monograph IX (Washington, D.C., 1929), pp. 186–199.

Table A–8. Percentage Distribution of Female Servants in Large Cities and Other Areas by Nativity and Race, 1900 (16 Yrs. and Over)

	Native-born white	Foreign-born white	Negro, Indian, and Oriental
United States			
Cities of 50,000 or more	31.8	45.3	22.9
Smaller cities and country districts	53.5	17.2	29.4
North Atlantic			
Cities of 50,000 or more	27.4	60.7	11.7
Smaller cities and country districts	58.0	33.2	8.9
North Central			
Cities of 50,000 or more	49.9	38.0	12.0
Smaller cities and country districts	77.3	17.4	5.2
South Atlantic			
Cities of 50,000 or more	10.8	6.7	82.5
Smaller cities and country districts	22.3	0.9	76.8
South Central			
Cities of 50,000 or more	18.8	5.5	75.7
Smaller cities and country districts	22.6	2.0	75.4
The West			
Cities of 50,000 or more	46.8	47.1	6.2
Smaller cities and country districts	67.6	27.3	5.1

Source: U.S. Bureau of the Census, *Statistics of Women at Work* (Washington, D.C., 1907), p. 44.

Table A–9. Percentage Distribution of Female Servants in Large Cities and Other Areas by Nativity and Race, 1920 (10 Yrs. and Over)

	Native-born white	Foreign-born white	Negro
United States			
Cities of 100,000 or more	27.0	33.4	39.4
Smaller cities and country districts	46.8	13.1	39.8
North Atlantic			
Cities of 100,000 or more	24.3	50.0	25.6
Smaller cities and country districts	57.0	29.0	13.9
North Central			
Cities of 100,000 or more	42.7	29.2	28.1
Smaller cities and country districts	77.8	12.4	9.6
South Atlantic			
Cities of 100,000 or more	8.5	4.4	87.1
Smaller cities and country districts	15.4	1.0	83.6
South Central			
Cities of 100,000 or more	11.0	2.9	85.8
Smaller cities and country districts	18.9	3.1	78.0
The West			
Cities of 100,000 or more	45.6	37.8	14.0
Smaller cities and country districts	65.7	24.6	5.9

Source: Based on *Twelfth Census: 1920, Occupations*, passim.

Table A–10. Percentage of Native-born White Women Wage Earners in Domestic Service, Selected Cities and States, 1900 and 1920 (10 Yrs. and Over)

| | *1900* | | | *1920* | | |
| | *White* | | *Ratio all servants per 1,000 families* | *White* | | *Ratio all servants per 1,000 families* |
	Number	*Percent all servants*		*Number*	*Percent all servants*	
New York City	22,616	21.7	141	15,097	17.8	66
Rest of New York	50,662	63.2	92	30,631	60.5	44
Chicago	12,714	36.0	98	6,963	26.6	57
Rest of Illinois	37,012	78.0	71	22,682	72.9	34
Indianapolis	2,274	54.8	104	1,366	44.0	49
Rest of Indiana	25,532	87.4	55	13,186	80.3	25
Detroit	3,407	48.8	115	3,155	41.5	35
Rest of Michigan	22,125	73.0	70	13,673	77.0	28
Baltimore	2,951	17.6	159	1,930	12.8	91
Rest of Maryland	5,546	35.8	115	2,619	27.4	60
Atlanta	135	3.1	214	289	4.3	136
Rest of Georgia	2,430	8.5	67	1,481	4.8	53

Sources: *Twelfth Census: 1900, Population*, vol. II, pt. II, pp. clx–clxiv; *Occupations*, passim. *Fourteenth Census: 1920, Population*, vol. III, pp. 34–46; *Occupations*, passim.

Table A–11. Percentage of Women Wage Earners in Service and Laundry Work, by Nativity and Race, 1890–1920 (16 Yrs. and Over).

	*1890**	*1900*	*1910*	*1920*
Servants				
Native-born white	24	18	11	7
Foreign-born white	48	38	28	19
Negro	31	28	22	27
Laundresses				
Native-born white	2	2	2	1
Foreign-born white	4	5	4	3
Negro	17	19	20	19
Servants and laundresses				
Native-born white	26	20	13	8
Foreign-born white	52	43	32	22
Negro	48	47	42	46
Servants and laundresses as a percentage of nonagricultural workers				
Native-born white	29	24	15	9
Foreign-born white	55	46	34	23
Negro	82	77	80	71

* 1890: 15 years and over.

Sources: U.S. Bureau of the Census, *Statistics of Women at Work* (Washington, D.C., 1907), pp. 158–159, 185. Joseph Hill, *Women in Gainful Occupations 1870 to 1920*, Census Monograph IX (Washington, D.C. 1929), pp. 59, 90, 96, 105, 117.

Table A–12. Percentage of Black Women in Population, Among Wage Earners, Servants, and Laundresses, Selected Cities, 1920 (10 Yrs. and Over).

			Percentage			
	Black women	*Wage-earning black women*	*Black servants*	*Black laundresses*	*Wage-earning black women servants and laundresses*	*Black women servants and laundresses*
Boston	2	3	11	29	54	25
Hartford	3	5	16	51	45	22
Buffalo	1	1	6	4	57	21
New York	3	6	22	40	58	33
Philadelphia	8	13	54	78	68	33
Rochester	.5	1	6	15	64	30
Chicago	4	7	24	43	44	19
Cincinnati	7	12	32	68	70	32
Cleveland	4	7	30	45	58	22
Detroit	4	6	23	54	49	16
Indianapolis	11	16	61	86	67	27
Kansas City, Missouri	9	16	60	90	69	32
Minneapolis	1	1	6	10	55	22
St. Louis	9	14	33	80	64	29
Atlanta	33	52	95	99	71	41
Baltimore	15	29	81	96	75	43
Richmond	33	49	93	99	59	31
Washington, D.C.	25	31	87	98	65	37
Wilmington, Delaware	10	21	69	92	74	42
Louisville	18	33	49	93	61	37
Nashville	32	51	94	98	73	39
New Orleans	28	45	86	96	71	35
Denver		4	20	38	69	31
Los Angeles	3	5	27	53	69	31
San Francisco	.5	1	5	4	55	29

Source: *Fourteenth Census: 1920, Occupations*, passim.

Table A–13. Percentage of Women Employed, by Race, Nativity, and Age, 1890 and 1900

Age (yrs.)	Native-born White		Foreign-born White		Negro	
	1890	*1900*	*1890*	*1900*	*1890*	*1900*
All ages	15.3	17.4	19.8	19.4	39.9	43.2
15–24	23.1	25.3	50.4	48.9	45.3	47.4
25–34	13.6	16.7	19.8	19.8	37.4	41.8
35–44	9.7	12.6	12.0	13.0	37.0	41.6
45–54	10.0	11.7	10.5	11.7	37.8	42.2
55–64	10.0	11.2	9.4	9.8	37.2	41.0
65 and over	6.7	7.8	6.1	6.2	26.2	28.5

Source: U.S. Bureau of the Census, *Statistics of Women at Work* (Washington, D.C., 1907), p. 21.

Table A–14. Percentage of Women Employed, by Race, Nativity, and Age, 1900 and 1920.

Age (yrs.)	Native-born White		Foreign-born White		Negro	
	1900	*1920*	*1900*	*1920*	*1900*	*1920*
All ages	17.4	22.6	19.1	18.8	43.2	43.7
16–24	26.4	36.2	48.8	43.9	47.9	42.7
25–44	15.0	20.2	16.7	18.6	41.6	45.2
45–64	11.5	15.1	13.9	10.9	41.8	45.7
65 and over	7.8	7.0	5.9	6.2	28.5	27.1

Sources: U.S. Bureau of the Census, *Statistics of Women at Work* (Washington, D.C., 1907), p. 12. Joseph Hill, *Women in Gainful Occupations 1870 to 1920*, Census Monograph IX (Washington, D.C., 1929), pp. 260–261, 265–266. *Fourteenth Census: 1920, Occupations*, p. 694.

Table A–15. Percentage of Women Employed, by Race, Nativity, and Age, in Large Cities and Other Areas, 1900.

	Native-born white		Foreign-born white		Negro	
Age (yrs.)	Cities of 50,000 or more	Smaller cities and country districts	Cities of 50,000 or more	Smaller cities and country districts	Cities of 50,000 or more	Smaller cities and country districts
All ages	28.5	14.5	23.6	15.0	54.7	41.5
16–24	44.9	21.3	56.5	40.3	58.0	46.6
25–34	26.7	13.5	23.5	15.7	53.7	39.5
35–44	19.2	10.7	16.2	10.1	54.4	39.2
45–54	15.7	10.8	13.8	9.9	57.0	39.9
55–64	12.3	11.0	10.8	9.0	52.6	39.3
65 and over	6.2	8.1	6.4	6.1	32.9	27.9

Source: U.S. Bureau of the Census, *Statistics of Women at Work* (Washington, D.C., 1907), p. 19.

Table A–16. Servant Girls, 1880–1920 (10 to 15 Yrs. Old).

Number and Percentage All Female Servants			
	1880	1900	1920
Percent	9.9	9.4	3.0
Number	93,211	117,963	30,576

Percentage Distribution by Nativity and Race			
	Native-born white	Foreign-born white	Negro
1900*†	63.3 (74,952)	9.1 (10,815)	27.3 (32,295)
1920†	55.1 (16,837)	5.2 (1,582)	39.6 (12,105)

As a Percentage of All Women in Service in Nativity or Racial Class			
	Native-born white	Foreign-born white	Negro
1900*	12.4	3.2	9.4
1920	4.2	.8	3.0

*Includes servants and waitresses.
†Less than 100 percent because of small percentage of Oriental and Indian servants.

Sources: 1880: *Tenth Census: 1880, Population*, p. 729. 1900: U.S. Bureau of the Census, *Statistics of Women at Work* (Washington, D.C., 1907), p. 40. *Twelfth Census: 1900, Occupations*, pp. clxii, 20–39. 1920: *Fourteenth Census: 1920, Occupations*, pp. 493–505.

Table A–17. Female Servants in Eleven Selected Cities, 1920 (16 Yrs. and Over).

A. *Servants by Race and Residence*

City	Number of servants	Percentage black (10 yrs. and over)	Number living with employer	Percentage living with employer
Fall River	438	6.0	345	78.8
Providence	3,009	14.0	2,075	69.0
Rochester	2,412	6.4	1,572	65.2
Paterson	744	27.3	477	64.1
Cincinnati	6,750	32.0	3,322	49.2
Indianapolis	3,941	60.9	1,154	29.3
St. Paul	2,628	6.7	1,710	65.1
Kansas City, Missouri	4,668	60.4	1,758	37.7
Atlanta	6,501	95.5	1,143	17.6
Louisville	4,309	48.7	1,111	25.8
New Orleans	9,967	86.1	1,722	17.3

B. *Servants by Marital Status and Residence*

City	Single	Percentage living with employer	Married	Percentage living with employer	Widowed or divorced	Percentage living with employer
Fall River	438	78.8	92	25.0	123	40.7
Providence	2,075	84.1	371	24.8	563	42.1
Rochester	1,498	81.7	409	26.9	505	47.1
Paterson	410	79.5	165	39.4	169	50.9
Cincinnati	3,907	69.2	1,441	15.8	1,402	28.0
Indianapolis	1,548	49.5	1,217	10.4	1,176	22.2
St. Paul	1,848	82.2	367	14.7	413	33.2
Kansas City, Missouri	2,000	55.3	1,399	19.6	1,269	29.9
Atlanta	1,880	22.2	2,687	14.4	1,934	17.5
Louisville	1,805	41.7	1,259	7.9	1,245	20.7
New Orleans	4,011	26.5	3,413	7.9	2,543	15.3

Sources: Joseph Hill, *Women in Gainful Occupations 1870 to 1920*, Census Monograph IX (Washington, D.C., 1929), pp. 299–345. *Fourteenth Census: 1920, Occupations*, passim.

Table A–18. Laundresses in Eleven Selected Cities, 1920 (16 Yrs. and Over).

City	Number of laundresses	Percentage black (10 yrs. and over)	Number living with employer	Percentage living with employer
Fall River*	64		4	6.3
Providence	436	58.3	43	9.8
Rochester	390	14.8	21	5.4
Paterson	149	24.7	3	2.0
Cincinnati	2,935	67.8	86	2.9
Indianapolis	1,794	86.2	55	3.1
St. Paul	442	11.1	53	12.0
Kansas City, Missouri	1,744	89.8	18	1.0
Atlanta	5,549	99.0	21	.4
Louisville	3,978	93.3	24	.6
New Orleans	7,282	95.7	46	.6

*Census did not give laundresses by race for Fall River in 1900.

Source: See Table A–17.

Table A–19. Percentage of Female Servants and Waitresses Living at Home in Eleven Selected Cities, 1900 and 1920 (16 Yrs. and Over).

City	1900	1920
Fall River	15.6	35.7
Providence	15.2	25.8
Rochester	14.2	28.9
Paterson	14.6	30.4
Cincinnati	27.4	43.7
Indianapolis	30.2	54.7
St. Paul	14.5	27.5
Kansas City, Missouri	22.2	41.5
Atlanta	63.1	68.5
Louisville	41.6	59.4
New Orleans	54.9	62.3

Source: Joseph Hill, *Women in Gainful Occupations 1870 to 1920*, Census Monograph IX (Washington, D.C., 1929), pp. 139–140.

2

APPENDIX

QUALITY OF DATA
ON SERVANTS

THE PROBLEMS IN THE VARYING QUALITIES OF CENSUS, especially in regard to statistics of women at work, are notorious. Edith Abbott and Sophonisba P. Breckinridge reviewed the statistics of women's employment for the 1900 census and noted the ambiguities in the enumeration. "Gainful occupation" was never directly defined for the enumerators; instead they were instructed:

If a married woman has a gainful occupation, return the occupation accordingly, whether she does the work at her home or goes regularly to a place of employment, and whether she is regularly or only occasionally so employed.

Did "gainful occupation," for instance, include children or wives of farmers laboring in the fields without receiving any wages? Did it include young girls in service who worked for room and board without any other wages?[1]

In 1910 the Bureau of the Census attempted to remove the ambiguities in the 1900 instructions. Specifically, the instructions emphasized returning an occupation for every women and child working:

Column 18. *Trade or profession.*—An entry should be made in this column for *every* person enumerated. The occupation, if any, followed by a child, of any age, or by a woman is just as important,

ous occupational classifications then in use. It is also possible that many of these women were returned on the census as domestic servants. A majority of Jersey City's working women were servants, and more than 80 percent of servants were Irish. Not sharing native-born women's distaste for domestic service, some Irish women might have given their occupation as servant instead of factory worker.[7]

Another problem is that there is almost no comparative base between data on female domestic service and data on males. Laundresses and male laundry workers before 1910 cannot be compared because nearly all of the men, except for Chinese hand launderers, were operatives in commercial laundries. Similarly, male waiters and cooks tended to work in commercial or institutional establishments and cannot be compared with women in these occupations, who were generally household workers. While porters were insignificant within the general female servant classification, they formed a large portion of the male classification. The result was that before 1910 most men within the servant category worked outside of private households, while nearly all women in the servant classification worked in families. Thus any direct statistical comparison would be spurious.

Finally, the total number of servants recorded in various tables in Chapter 2 and Appendix 1 vary. Alba Edwards's data could not be used for state- and city-level analysis, since his work revised only the national data. The number of servants reported in a given table reflects the sources used. Moreover, the census changed age categories over time, and this has resulted in tables with different age bases. The important factor here was my attempt to simplify time series as well as supply the most meaningful information. In evaluating servant patterns, for instance, I have tried to include all servants ten years and over, while in discussing patterns among married servants, sixteen years and over was most appropriate. But similar age data was not always available; the base age of fifteen in the 1890 census was the most notable exception.

dresses before 1900 was not significant. In 1900, only 10,000 of the 335,000 laundresses worked in laundries. The greatest growth in women employment in commercial laundries occurred after the census began to segregate the categories. While waitresses and laundry operatives are excluded from the total number of servants in 1900 (see Table 2–1), they were included in all data at state and city levels as well as those of nativity and race.

The 1920 census also reported that the data on cooks was inaccurate. "In the occupation returns, especially the returns for the colored females of the South, a careful distinction was not made," the bureau stated, "between cooks and general servants." Thus I have not attempted to analyze the statistics on cooks. Similar problems emerged in the enumeration of untrained nurses. This category was intended to encompass practical nurses, but "it is believed," the bureau reported, "that a large number of nurse maids and children's nurses were included with the practical or untrained nurses." To the degree that this was the case, my estimate of servants would be low, and the proportion of black servants would be understated.[6]

Errors due to inaccurate enumerations and false responses are difficult to estimate. Given the social stigma of domestic service work and the low status of servants among particular ethnic groups, it is possible that some women might not have responded truthfully to being a domestic or working at all. Or a husband might not give an enumerator a correct response, being unwilling to admit that his wife worked. On the other hand, Douglas Shaw's Jersey City study suggested that at least among the Irish in Jersey City the number of servants might have been inflated by their disinclination to accurately report factory work. Shaw reported that in Jersey City in 1860 one factory reported eighty female workers, yet only five women responded to census enumerators that they did factory work. Although Shaw attributed this to the possibility that married women were hesitant to report gainful employment, it is also possible that the women were properly enumerated but could not be identified by the ambigu-

3

APPENDIX

SERVANT WAGES

HOUSEHOLD WORK WAS UNIQUE IN AMERICAN SOCIETY IN THE degree to which it was most often discussed in noneconomic terms. The work and living environment, the mistress/servant relationship, and the shortage of domestics were the dominant themes of the "servant problem." These considerations stemmed from the highly personalized relationship in which the worker herself and not just her labor was hired.

In discussing wages, this appendix is intended to suggest the general trends in domestic service. The raw data on women's wages, including household employment, in federal and state reports, newspapers, and household account books is so numerous that it is beyond the scope of this study. Moreover, the quality of the extant data presented serious problems. Little is known about the sampling techniques used and their biases. Even the range of weekly wages is suspect. Although other evidence suggested that some girls worked only for room and board without receiving any additional money wage, not a single statistical survey of domestic servants reported such a case. And before the wages or earnings of domestics and other women workers can be compared, the effect of unemployment and the value of room and board must be weighed. Even then, other factors must be considered—race, ethnicity, skills and education of servants, urban and rural differences, and geographic variations. Under these conditions I will use the data presented here to illustrate my impressionistic views of domestic wages; it does not represent a comprehensive statistical analysis.[1]

Nearly all studies of women's wages indicated that annual earnings in household work (annual wages plus the equivalent cost of room and board) was competitive with earnings in other female unskilled and semiskilled occupations, and below wages in professional, clerical, and skilled work. During the late nineteenth century servants' wages remained relatively constant, fluctuating narrowly within a range of two to four dollars depending on the region, size of community, length of service, race of employee, and specific job function. Increases in average wages occurred in small increments, and during depressions wages fell. After the depression of the 1890s, weekly wages rose steadily, except during periods of deflation and recession, as opportunities for women in other occupations expanded. The steady increase in wages, however, did not attract larger numbers of women into household work. Even where domestic earnings were significantly higher than most other women's occupations, more women did not enter service because they shunned it for noneconomic reasons—the lack of freedom, the mistress/servant relationship, the long hours, and the low status. But low wages did not reduce the supply of available workers nationally. Most women in domestic service had no other work open to them.[2]

Blacks, immigrants, married women, and teenage girls already working in service could not go into other occupations; discrimination, ignorance of English, poor education, and the necessity to work at home in the case of married laundresses forced them to do household labor. This tended to depress wage levels. Since higher wages would not attract more workers, and lower wages would not diminish the supply, the lowest possible wage could be paid by employers. Indeed, the greatest factor affecting demand probably was the household income of the employing family, which was unaffected by the supply of servants. The active hiring market was maintained by the constant turnover in servants, which resulted from personal dissatisfaction rather than from low wages. While there was an overall excess of demand over supply, the high turnover rate guaranteed that there were always servants to be hired. While employers did not bid up wages of domestics within a given market, they used higher wages in New York, for instance, to hire servants from the South, from the rural hinterland, or from Europe. Higher wages were a factor between markets and served to promote urban migration to fill some of the demand. Within their own markets, mistresses used noneconomic inducements to attract workers. Thus offers of a "good home," better working conditions, specified time off, and fewer hours were offered to hire servants. There was a theoretical point to which wages might have risen that would have induced women to shift to household work from other labor, but this level was never even approached. Instead, mistresses kept wages relatively low and turned to the hiring of one another's servants.

Within a household there were significant variations in servants' wages. Nearly all studies reported that cooks were the highest paid and general household workers the lowest. This confirmed the general tendency that the greater the skill or specialization involved in work, the higher the wage (see Table A–20). At the same time, however, it reflected that rarely was a cook hired as a single household employee, and that outside of the South, higher wages were paid in homes with a staff of employees rather than in middle-class households. The same was true for other specialized household workers. Young girls, those below sixteen, generally received lower wages than did older workers. In Pennsylvania in the 1870s adult women received a $2.00 weekly wage, while adolescents were paid $0.50. The California labor bureau reported in 1887–1888 that servant girls aged twelve to sixteen received $8.00 to $12.00 monthly, while women's wages ranged from $12.00 to $25.00. A 1911 federal study of laundresses recorded four cases of women who had started out working as domestics and had received no wages other than

Table A–20. Average Weekly Wages, Household Work by Occupations: Selected Studies, 1872–1899.

| Occupation | Massachusetts, 1872 | U.S., 1889–1890 | | Maine, 1892 | Philadelphia (blacks), 1897 | U.S., 1899 |
		Employer	Employee			
Cooks	$7.53	$3.80	$3.64	$3.75	$4.02	$3.81
Parlormaids	4.33					
Cooks and laundresses		3.50	3.27		4.00	
Chambermaids	4.27	3.31	3.47		3.17	
Waitress	4.43	3.23	3.15		3.31	3.34
Second Girls		3.04	3.27			
Chambermaids and waitresses		2.99	3.21		3.17	
Child nurses	4.09			2.38	3.35	
Kitchen workers				2.86		
General house- work	3.48	2.94	2.88	2.67	3.24	3.28
Laundresses					4.04	

Sources: Massachusetts, 1872: Massachusetts Bureau of Statistics of Labor, *Annual Report 1872* (Boston, 1872), p. 66. U.S., 1889–1890: Lucy Maynard Salmon, *Domestic Service* (New York, 1897), p. 90. Maine, 1892: Maine Bureau of Industrial and Labor Statistics, *Annual Report 1892* (Augusta, 1893), pp. 118–123. Philadelphia, 1897: Isabel Eaton, "Special Report on Negro Domestic Service in the Seventh Ward, Philadelphia," in W. E. B. DuBois, *The Philadelphia Negro: A Social Study* (original, 1899; reprint, New York, 1967), p. 447. U.S., 1899: Gail Laughlin, "Domestic Service," *Report [and Testimony] of the Industrial Commission* . . . , vol. XIV (19 vols.; Washington, D.C., 1901), p. 754.

room and board. In all four instances the death of one or both parents had led to the placement of these girls in families who provided for them and relieved their own families from having to support them. Blacks as a class received lower wages than did white women. William Crossland's study of St. Louis blacks, for instance, recorded a dual wage structure. Only Isabel Eaton's study of domestic workers in Philadelphia reported no significant differences in servant salary according to race. Limiting herself only to Philadelphia's Seventh War and not recording statistics on white workers, Eaton probably underestimated the white wage scale. Finally, continued tenure of service in an employer's household was rewarded with a higher wage. In Philadelphia, Eaton reported that the average weekly wage of women with five or more years of tenure was 9 percent higher than the average weekly wage of those who had worked a shorter period of time with the same employer. In Gainesville, Georgia, Ruth Reed found that servants earning weekly wages of $3.00 to $4.00 had averaged 3.1 months of service in their employer's household, those earning in the range of $4.00 to $5.00 had served an average of one year, while those above $5.00 weekly had been employed an average of four years.[3]

Within the United States, wages also varied by region. Lucy Salmon's 1899–1890 investigation reported the following average weekly wages for servants:

Pacific section	$4.57
Eastern section	3.60
Middle section	3.21
Western section	3.00
Border section	2.55
Southern section	2.22

Except for the highest rate of wages on the Pacific Coast, Salmon concluded that the variation in wages conformed to regional differences in pay scales. She attributed the higher Pacific pay rates to the small sample drawn from that region. The Southern and Border states, with nearly exclusively black labor in service, ranked at the bottom, with the industrialized East near the top. It is possible that the Pacific Coast's wage ranking was not in error. California appeared to have the severest shortage of household workers; because of the distance from populous rural areas in the South, Midwest, and East and from the ports of entry of newly arrived immigrants, the Western states had general labor shortages in nondepression years. Chinese men provided the bulk of West Coast immigrant servants, but there were not enough of them to meet the demand. Thus the higher West Coast wage acted to draw some servants westward (although not an adequate supply given the distance). "Nowhere in the world," the California Bureau of Statistics of Labor bragged in 1887–1888, "are they [servants] paid such good wages." Studies in 1874, 1886, and 1887–1888 indicated California domestic wages were significantly above those paid in other sections. The overall effect of the regional variations, then, was to stimulate migration from the Southern and Border sections to higher-paying regions.[4]

Rural domestic help received the lowest wage. A Michigan investigation of rural domestics, the only one I found, revealed the trends in the remnants of the old "hired girl" pattern of before the Civil War. Of the 2,300 women surveyed in rural Michigan during the depression of the 1890s, 1,431 were American-born. Only 19 women were day workers; the remaining 99 percent lived in. As a group they were particularly hard hit by the depression: 25 percent had lost work time during the year through lack of work. Including work lost due to unemployment and illness, they averaged only 39.2 weeks of work during the year, the lowest total reported in any study. They also suffered from deflation: of those responding, 33 percent reported a cut in wages from the previous year, 13 percent an increase, and 54 percent no change. Over the prior five years, 42 percent reported a decrease in wages and 20 percent an increase; 38 percent reported that their wages had remained constant. The average weekly wage was $1.85, with average annual earnings of $73.24. Because they lived in rural districts, there were probably relatively few temptations on which to spend money during their limited time out, and 45 percent reported saving money during the year, averaging $34.80 for those who saved. Fifty-nine percent considered the wage sufficient to support themselves. Interestingly, a significant percentage—38 percent—reported that they had no scheduled payday; they were paid only on demand. This was a clear indicator of the traditional pattern of rural domestic work.[5]

A study of working women in Kansas done at about the same time as the Michigan study suggests that urban domestics in a rural state did not fare significantly better in wages. The 241 servants responding reported a weekly average wage of $2.40, with the average wage ranging from $1.50 to $3.50 in fifteen cities. Yearly earnings averaged $119.00 plus room and board. Only 30 percent reported saving money during the year, averaging $24.00 per saver. Of the eleven female occupations studied, only hotel and restaurant employees and bookbinders were in the same range of annual earnings, although women in both occupations earned about one more month's salary on an annual basis (see Table A–21). Hotel and restaurant work was an occupation allied to household service, while bookbinders were the only manufacturing occupation surveyed. This study suggests that domestic annual earnings (including room and board) tended to be at the bottom of the wage scale, and that women in allied fields and manufacturing were only marginally better off.[6]

Table A–21. Annual Income of Female Wage Earners, Kansas, 1894 (Selected Occupations).

Occupation	Annual earnings	Annual expense for subsistence	Annual wages after room and board
Bookkeepers	$327.22	$138.88	$188.34
Bookbinders	254.85	126.28	128.57
Clerks (dry goods)	326.80	124.67	202.13
Clerks (office)	330.09	126.59	203.50
Domestics	119.00	0.00	119.00
Dressmakers	328.28	128.58	199.70
Hotel and restaurant employees	128.58	0.00	128.58
Laundresses	316.40	133.00	183.40
Milliners	398.37	127.62	270.75
Printers (compositors)	314.12	137.65	176.47
Stenographers and typewriters	368.33	142.08	226.25

Source: Bureau of Labor and Industry, *Annual Report 1894* (Topeka, 1895), pp. 198–203.

The wages of servants in the great metropolitan centers were probably the highest. Alice Hanson and Paul Douglas investigated the wages of Chicago domestic labor and produced a time series of average weekly wages (see Table A–22). Drawn from newspaper advertisements for general housework, it excluded specialized work roles (for example, cooks, laundresses) and those ads specifying colored help. No attempt was made to value room and board or distinguish between live-in and day-work positions. When compared with the fragmented data on servants in other states and cities, their study suggested that domestic wages in large cities were significantly higher than those in rural districts, and wages in smaller towns and Northern cities were higher than those in Southern cities. The higher cost of living was not a particularly significant factor among live-in servants, since the employer provided the room and board. The wage differentials were most likely attributable to the generally higher urban wage levels and the need to attract women to urban household work from rural areas, smaller towns, and other sections.[7]

Table A–22. Average Daily Wage Rates, Selected Cities and States and Nationally, 1889–1923

Year	Average weekly wage in Chicago	Other places	Average weekly wage
1889		U.S.	$3.23
1890	$3.82		
1891	4.15		
1892	4.23	Indiana	2.64
		Maine	2.78
1893	4.50	Baltimore	2.41
		Chicago	4.60
		New York	3.84
		Kansas	2.40
1894	3.99	Michigan	1.85
1895	4.16		
1896	3.83		
1897	3.60	Philadelphia (blacks)	3.67 (5 or more years service)
			3.26 (under 5 years service)
1898	4.12		
1899	4.08	United States	3.42 (mistress reporting)
			4.06 (servants reporting)
1900	4.28		
1901	4.40		
1902	4.57		
1903	4.93		
1904	5.10		
1905	5.08		
1906	5.36		
1907	5.77		
1908	5.60		
1909	5.68	Maine	4.04
1910	6.16		

Nearly all studies tended to show that household workers' annual earnings, including room and board, were equal to or even higher than other occupations. Three studies showed domestic earnings at very low levels compared to other occupations: the Michigan study of rural domestics, the 1894 Kansas report, and Mary E. Trueblood's comparative study of one hundred Massachusetts working women in five industries. All other studies presented evidence to indicate that domestics earned more than factory and shop workers. Lucy Maynard Salmon's national survey concluded that domestics received higher earnings than most other working women. Gail Laughlin concurred, observing that "wages paid in shops and factories . . . would range considerably lower"

Year	Average weekly wage in Chicago	Other places	Average weekly wage
1911	6.41		
1912	6.64	St. Louis (blacks)	6.18
1913	6.68		
1914	7.03		
1915	6.14		
1916	7.08		
1917	7.63		
1918	8.40		
1919	10.50		
1920	14.05		
1921	14.83		
1922	12.77		
1923	14.84		
1924	15.00		
1925	14.06		

Sources: Chicago: Alice C. Hanson and Paul H. Douglas, "The Wages of Domestic Labor in Chicago, 1890–1929," *Journal of the American Statistical Association*, new series, XXV (March 1930), p. 48. 1889, U.S.: Lucy Maynard Salmon, *Domestic Service* (New York, 1897), p. 88. 1892, Indiana: Gail Laughlin, "Domestic Service," *Report [and Testimony] of the Industrial Commission . . .* , vol. XIV (19 vols.; Washington, D.C., 1901), 750. 1892, Maine: Maine Bureau of Industrial and Labor Statistics, *Annual Report 1892* (Augusta, 1893), pp. 118–123. 1893, Baltimore, Chicago, New York: U.S. Commissioner of Labor, *Special Report 1894: The Slums of Baltimore, Chicago, New York and Philadelphia* (Washington, D.C., 1894), pp. 220–221, 271–274, 341–343. 1893, Kansas: Kansas Bureau of Labor and Industry, *Annual Report 1894* (Topeka, 1895), p. 178. 1894, Michigan: Michigan Bureau of Labor and Industrial Statistics, *Annual Report 1895* (Lansing, 1895), p. 335. 1897, Philadelphia: Isabel Eaton, "Special Report on Negro Domestic Service in the Seventh Ward Philadelphia," in W. E. B. DuBois, *The Philadelphia Negro: A Social Study* (original, 1899; reprint, New York, 1967), p. 479. 1899, U.S.: Laughlin, "Domestic Service," p. 748. 1909, Maine: Maine Bureau of Industrial and Labor Statistics, *Annual Report 1910* (Augusta, 1910), p. 334. 1912–1913, St. Louis: William August Crossland, *Industrial Conditions Among Negroes in St. Louis*, Washington University Studies in Social Economics, I (St. Louis, 1914), p. 20.

Table A–23. Annual Earnings in Selected Women's Occupations Massachusetts, 1872.

Industry or occupation	Women surveyed	Average weekly wage	Average number of weeks worked	Average annual earnings	Average weekly cost of board
Domestics	1,220	$4.76	52	$247.52	$0.00
Men's clothing					
Wholesale	12,507	6.53	34	222.02	4.50
Custom	2,003	8.05	24	193.20	4.50
Dresses and cloaks					
Wholesale	1,945	7.77	24	186.48	4.50
Custom	1,257	9.93	24	238.32	4.50
Bed manufacturing	1,369	4.33	24	103.92	4.50
Shirts	1,297	5.96	32	190.72	4.50
Store and saloon	1,270	5.27	44½	234.51	4.35
Hotel and restaurant	337	5.28	52	274.56	0.00
Miscellaneous manufacturing					
Apron makers	124	9.00	30	270.00	4.50
Bookbinders	101	6.75	40	270.00	4.50
Bonnet frames	141	4.25	16	68.00	4.50
Boot heels	81	6.00	30	180.00	4.50
Envelopes	121	5.12	30	153.60	4.50
Mattress makers	120	6.75	24	162.00	4.50
Paper bags	126	4.00	24	96.00	4.50
Paper boxes	314	3.50	24	89.00	4.50

Source: Massachusetts Bureau of Statistics of Labor, *Annual Report 1872* (Boston, 1872), pp. 66–67, 71–72, 74, 80, 85–89.

than in household work. The 1910 Maine study of domestic service agreed, although it was somewhat self-serving in the sense that it was intended to promote an increased supply of servants. Those studies that tended to study the question statistically came to the same conclusions. The first detailed study of women's wages, the 1872 report of the Massachusetts Bureau of Statistics of Labor, presented data indicating that household work was equal to or better paying than many factory occupations. While domestics received the lowest weekly wages (average $4.76 for all servants, $4.27 for general houseworkers), the highly seasonal nature of Massachusetts factory work meant that the annual wages of domestics exceeded those of workers in many other industries and occupations (see Table A–23). Indeed, according to the report, few women were able to earn sufficient income to cover ordinary costs of board. The problem was that many of the women in other occupations worked in more than one industry during the year. Workers in bonnet-frame manufacturing, for instance, the industry with the shortest manufacturing season, worked as saleswomen, in saloons, or at other work when not in the factories. If it is assumed that women worked about forty weeks of the year, and that the cost of board given in the report (c. $4.50) per week was accurate, then earnings in the industries listed in Table A–23 and domestic service were about equal. Later Massachusetts studies indicated that unemployment was a very important factor in weighing service against other occupations; domestic servants consistently reported the lowest rates of unemployment of any occupation (see Table A–24).[8]

Other studies confirmed this pattern; when the equivalent cost of room and board are added to the annual earnings of domestic servants, their wages were at the same level or exceeded those of women in shops and in un- or semiskilled factory jobs. The data from a study of women workers in Minnesota in 1887–1888 confirmed this trend. The obvious discrepancy between low wages in factory work and higher earnings in domestic service led the Minnesota bureau to explore the noneconomic factors which led working women to prefer nonhousehold labor. In Chicago, in 1919, wages in household work were in the same range as industrial work open to black women. In St. Louis, a border-state city with a service pattern somewhat similar to the South, the pattern was repeated. Although St. Louis was more of an industrial city than Southern cities, in 1900 92 percent of black women worked in service, and day work predominated, rather than live in. Daily wages in St. Louis among day workers averaged from $1.00 to $1.50 per day, with a majority of black women working from three to four days a week (a common pattern among married women). The average weekly wage among full-time domestic workers was $6.18, which was higher than the $5.00 average among black women in factories. In St. Louis only two manufacturing industries were open to black women: nut cracking and tobacco sorting

Table A–24. Unemployment Among Women Wage Earners, Massachusetts and Boston, 1887 (Selected Occupations)

Industry or occupation	Female work force	Percentage unemployed during the year	Average number of months unemployed out of work
Massachusetts			
All Massachusetts	212,623	29.6	3.91
Servants (in families)	48,687	6.8	4.57
Cotton-mill operatives	31,747	43.6	3.36
Boot and shoe makers	14,420	71.1	3.80
Dressmakers	13,290	24.0	4.35
Teachers	9,979	49.6	3.43
Woolen-mill operatives	9,176	45.0	3.85
Bookkeepers and clerks	5,374	9.2	4.65
Housekeepers	5,069	3.7	4.75
Laundry workers	4,862	24.0	5.16
Tailoresses	4,466	33.0	3.91
Hotel employees*	1,865	6.0	4.64
Merchants and dealers*	1,358	3.6	5.47
Boston			
All Boston	48,107	16.0	4.25
Servants (in families)	14,445	8.6	4.43
Dressmakers	4,168	23.5	3.88
Saleswomen	2,189	11.6	4.75
Laundry work	2,159	19.1	4.54
Seamstresses	1,743	25.4	4.39
Tailoresses	1,625	29.7	3.98
Bookkeepers and clerks	1,614	6.4	4.80

*Occupations with lower percentages unemployed than domestics.

Source: Massachusetts Bureau of Statistics of Labor, *Annual Report 1887* (Boston, 1887), pp. 205–206, 218–219.

and stemming. The abundance of white female labor, Crossland reported, kept blacks out of better-paying factory work.[9]

The overall pattern, then, suggested that women in unskilled and semiskilled work received no higher earnings than domestics, and when widespread unemployment occurred during hard times, probably they earned significantly less. Yet whatever economic advantage household employment offered, it was not sufficient to attract women from other occupations to any great degree.

NOTES

CHAPTER 1

1. Lucy Maynard Salmon, *Domestic Service* (New York, 1897), p. 113n.
2. Ibid., p. 132n.
3. Young Woman's Christian Association, Commission on Household Employment, *Report 1915* (n.p., n.d.), p. 8.
4. Salmon, *Domestic Service*, p. 132n.
5. Ibid., p. 133n.
6. Ibid., p. 137n.
7. Lillian Pettengill, *Toilers of the Home: The Record of a College Woman's Experience as a Domestic Servant* (New York, 1903); Inez A. Godman, "Ten Weeks in a Kitchen," *Independent* LIII (October 17, 1901), 2459–2464.
8. See "A Washerwoman," *Independent* LVII (November 10, 1904), 1073–1076; "The Story of an Irish Cook," ibid., LVIII (March 30, 1905), 715–717; "More Slavery at the South. By a Negro Nurse," ibid., LXXII (January 25, 1912), 196–200.
9. Helen Campbell, *Prisoners of Poverty: Women Wage-Workers, Their Trades and Their Lives* (Boston, 1887).
10. Isabel Eaton, "Special Report on Negro Domestic Service in the Seventh Ward, Philadelphia," in W. E. B. DuBois, *The Philadelphia Negro: A Social Study* (original, 1899; reprint, New York, 1967), p. 465.
11. Salmon, *Domestic Service*, pp. 141–142n, 145n–146n.
12. Young Woman's Christian Association, Commission on Household Employment, *Report 1915*, p. 10.
13. Ibid., pp. 10–11.
14. U.S. Senate, 61st Congress, 2nd Session, Document No. 645, *Report*

on *Condition of Woman and Child Wage-Earners in the United States*, vol. XII, *Employment of Women in Laundries* (19 vols.; Washington, D.C., 1911), 39, 53, 60, 72, 74, 85, 87, 108.

15. Ibid., pp. 48, 73–74, 104, 107.

16. Helen Campbell, "Why Is There Objection to Domestic Service? II," *Good Housekeeping* XI (September 27, 1890), 255. Campbell also related these stories in *Prisoners of Poverty*, pp. 228–229.

17. Campbell, *Prisoners of Poverty*, pp. 229–231.

18. Ibid., pp. 224–225.

19. Rose Cohen, *Out of the Shadow* (original, 1918; reprint, New York, 1971), pp. 158–159, 171–172, 180–182.

20. Salmon, *Domestic Service*, p. 157n; Frances A. Kellor, *Out of Work: A Study of Employment Agencies . . .* (New York, 1904). p. 10.

21. Salmon, *Domestic Service*, p. 155n.

22. Ibid., p. 157n.

23. Mary E. Trueblood, "Housework versus Shop and Factories," *Independent* LVI (November 13, 1902), 2693.

24. Edward A. Filene, "The Betterment of the Conditions of Working Women," *Annals* XXVII (June 1906), 158–159.

25. Campbell, *Prisoners of Poverty*, p. 226; Kellor, *Out of Work*, p. 146.

26. Salmon, *Domestic Service*, p. 151n.

27. Godman, "Ten Weeks in a Kitchen," p. 2462.

28. Pettengill, *Toilers of the Home*, p. 273.

29. Kellor, *Out of Work*, p. 147.

30. Pettengill, *Toilers of the Home*, pp. 128–129.

31. Ibid., pp. 214–216.

32. Campbell, *Prisoners of Poverty*, pp. 139–149. Although it appears certain that Campbell embellished the stories, and possibly added dialogue, the stories have a ring of fact rather than fiction about them. They originally appeared in the Sunday editions of the *New York Tribune*.

33. "A Washerwoman," pp. 1073–1076.

34. Pettengill, *Toilers of the Home*, pp. 30–31.

35. Ibid., p. 74.

36. Ibid., p. 84.

37. Ibid., pp. 87–90.

38. Ibid., pp. 92–93.

39. Ibid., pp. 104, 107.

40. "More Slavery at the South . . . ," pp. 196–198. This story has been widely circulated in recent years. Gerda Lerner excerpted it in her documentary on black women, and the Brownlees reprinted it in their reader on women and the economy. "I Live a Treadmill Life," in Gerda Lerner (ed.), *Black Women in White America: A Documentary History* (New York, 1972), pp. 227–229; W. Elliot and Mary M. Brownlee (eds.), *Women in the American Economy: A Documentary Historyl 1675 to 1929* (New Haven, 1976), pp. 244–249.

41. A Southern Colored Woman, "The Race Problem—An Autobiography," *Independent* LVI (March 17, 1904), 587.

42. *New York Freeman*, September 26, 1885, p. 1.

43. Maine Bureau of Industrial and Labor Statistics, *Annual Report 1892* (Augusta, Maine, 1892), p. 156.

44. Seymour Paul, "A Group of Virginia Negroes in New York City" (M.A. thesis, Columbia University, 1912), pp. 26, 43.

45. Kansas Department of Labor and Industry, *Annual Report 1914* (Topeka, Kansas, 1915), pp. 26–27.

46. Minnesota Bureau of Labor Statistics, *Biennial Report 1887–8* (n.p., 1887), pp. 149–153.

47. Godman, "Ten Weeks in a Kitchen," pp. 2459–2462.

48. "A Servant Girl's Letter," *Independent* LIV (January 2, 1902), 36–37.

49. Kellor, *Out of Work*, pp. v–vi, 4.

50. Ibid., pp. 7–9.

51. Ibid., pp. 13–14.

52. Pettengill, *Toilers of the Home*, pp. 162–164.

53. Anne Ellis, *The Life of an Ordinary Woman* (Boston and New York, 1929), pp. 58–59.

54. "The Story of an Irish Cook," pp. 715–716.

55. "The Household Servant Problem in Maine," Maine Bureau of Industrial and Labor Statistics, *Annual Report 1910* (Augusta, Maine, 1910), pp. 311–312.

56. Kellor, *Out of Work*, p. 130.

57. Campbell, "Why Is There Objection to Domestic Service?" *Good Housekeeping* XI (September 13, 1890), 232.

58. "Why Is There Objection to Domestic Service? II," *Good Housekeeping* XI (September 27, 1890), 255.

59. Minnesota Bureau of Labor Statistics, *Biennial Report 1887–8*, pp. 153–154.

60. Gail Laughlin, "Domestic Service," *Report [and Testimony] of the Industrial Commission . . .* , vol. XIV (19 vols.; Washington, D.C., 1901), 761.

61. "The Experience of a 'Hired Girl,' " *Outlook* 100 (April 6, 1912), 778–780.

62. Young Women's Christian Association, Commission on Household Employment, *Report 1915*, pp. 12–14.

CHAPTER 2

1. For a discussion of the census categories and the quality of the data, see Appendix 2.

2. Lucy Maynard Salmon's *Domestic Service* (New York, 1897) had been motivated by a desire to "solve" the servant problem.

3. Joseph A. Hill, *Women in Gainful Occupations 1870 to 1920*, Census Monograph IX (Washington, D.C., 1929), p. 24; U.S. Bureau of the Census, *Historical Statistics of the United States, 1789–1945* (Washington, D.C., 1949), pp. 35, 36, 37–38; U.S. Senate, 61st Congress, 2nd Session, Document No. 282, *Reports of the Immigration Commission, Occupations of the First and Second Generations of Immigrants in the United States* (Washington, D.C., 1911), pp. 71–79. Further supporting the argument that the 1920 decline was real and not a census error was the data on servants from the Canadian dicennial census. In 1901, the Canadian census recorded 81,000 female servants; in 1911, 98,000; and in 1921, 89,000. The trend was similar to that found in the United States. Genevieve Leslie, "Domestic Service in Canada, 1880–1920," in Janice Acton, *et al.* (eds.), *Women at Work: Ontario, 1850–1930 (Toronto*, 1974), p. 75.

4. *Sixteenth Census: 1940, Population*, Alba M. Edwards, *Comparative Occupation Statistics for the United States, 1870 to 1940*, pp. 122–129.

5. The importance of suburban homes as employers of domestic servants was reflected in the high ratio of servants per 1,000 families in towns on the periphery of large cities. In 1920, New Rochelle, New York, and Evanston, Illinois, were both suburban bedroom communities and independent cities. Their ratios of servants and laundresses per 1,000 families were 213 and 215. Brookline, Massachusetts, was less of an independent town and served more as a commuting suburb for Boston. The ratio there was 415.

6. *Twelfth Census: 1900, Occupations*, passim; *Tenth Census: 1880, Population*, I, 860–909; Blaine Edward McKinley, " 'The Stranger in the Gates': Employer Reactions Toward Domestic Servants in America 1825–1875" (Ph.D. dissertation, Michigan State University, 1969), p. x; Arnold Schrier, *Ireland and the American Emigration 1850–1900* (Minneapolis, 1958), p. 159.

7. U.S. Senate, *Reports of the Immigration Commission*, pp. 71–79.

8. Virginia Yans McLaughlin, "Like the Fingers of the Hand: The Family and Community Life of First-Generation Italian-Americans in Buffalo, New York, 1880–1930" (Ph.D. dissertation, State University of New York at Buffalo, 1970), pp. 346–350; Rose Cohen, *Out of the Shadow* (original, 1918; reprint, New York, 1971), pp. 158–159, 171–172; *London Times* and *Tuam Herald* quoted in Schrier, *Ireland and the American Emigration*, p. 75. In 1881, 49.4 percent of all female wage earners and 22 percent of all women fifteen years of age and older in Ireland worked as domestics. Charles Booth, *Occupations of the People: England, Scotland, Ireland, 1841–1881* (London, 1886).

9. Maine Bureau of Industrial and Labor Statistics, *Annual Report 1910* (Augusta, Maine, 1910), p. 340; Minnesota Bureau of Labor Statistics, *Biennial Report 1887–1888* (n.p., 1887), p. 154.

10. U.S. Senate, *Reports of the Immigration Commission*, pp. 71–79, 352–371.
11. 1880 manuscript census; David M. Katzman, *Before the Ghetto: Black Detroit in the Nineteenth Century* (Urbana, Illinois, 1973), pp. 61–64.
12. Isabel Eaton, "Special Report on Negro Domestic Service in the Seventh Ward, Philadelphia," in W. E. B. DuBois, *The Philadelphia Negro: A Social Study* (original, 1899; reprint, New York, 1967), p. 434. Eaton's data included both servants and washerwomen.
13. Michael B. Katz, *The People of Hamilton, Canada West: Family and Class in a Mid-Nineteenth-Century City* (Cambridge, Massachusetts, 1975), pp. 256–257. Katz also showed that women began to leave home later in 1861 than they had in 1851. Ibid., p. 288; Lawrence Admiral Glasco, "Ethnicity and Social Structure: Irish, Germans and Native-Born of Buffalo, New York, 1850–1860" (Ph.D. dissertation, State University of New York at Buffalo, 1973), pp. 224–225, 205, 208, 201; Susan J. Kleinberg, "Technology's Stepdaughter: The Impact of Industrialization Upon Working Women, Pittsburgh, 1865–1890" (Ph.D. dissertation, University of Pittsburgh, 1973), pp. 207–211.
14. U.S. Bureau of the Census, *Statistics of Women at Work* (Washington D.C., 1907), p. 22; *Fourteenth Census: 1920, Population*, II, 694.
15. Hill, *Women in Gainful Occupations . . .* , passim.
16. Herbert George Gutman, "Social and Economic Structure and Depression: American Labor in 1873 and 1874" (Ph.D. dissertation, University of Wisconsin, 1959), pp. 290–292; Gwendolyn Salisbury Hughes, *Mothers in Industry: Wage-Earning by Mothers in Philadelphia* (New York, 1925), pp. x, 22; William Henry Chafe, *The American Woman: Her Changing Social, Economic and Political Roles, 1920–1970* (New York, 1972), p. 63; DuBois, *The Philadelphia Negro*, pp. 193–194; Mary White Ovington, *Half A Man: The Status of the Negro in New York* (reprint, New York, 1969), p. 77.
17. Elizabeth Hafkin Pleck, "Black Migration to Boston in the Late Nineteenth Century" (Ph.D. dissertation, Brandeis University, 1973), pp. 145–148.
18. Elizabeth H. Pleck, "The Two-Parent Household: Black Family Structure in Late Nineteenth-Century Boston," *Journal of Social History* 6 (Fall 1972), 9, 11; John Blassingame, *Black New Orleans, 1860–1880* (Chicago, 1973), pp. 87–88; Katherine Davis Tillman, "Afro-American Women and Their Work," *A.M.E. Church Review* XI (1895), 485, 487; E. Azalia Hackley, *The Colored Girl Beautiful* (Kansas City, Missouri, 1916), pp. 151, 181–206. For a general discussion of single as well as married working women see Barbara Klaczynska, "Why Women Work: A Comparison of Various Groups—Philadelphia, 1910–1930," *Labor History* 17 (Winter 1976), 73–87.
19. "A Washerwoman," *Independent* LVII (November 10, 1904),

1073–1076; Mary White Ovington, "The Negro Home in New York," *Charities* XV (October 7, 1905), 25–30; Inez A. Godman, "Ten Weeks in a Kitchen," *Independent* LIII (October 17, 1901), p. 2459.

20. *Twelfth Census: 1900, Occupations,* passim; *Fourteenth Census: 1920, Occupations,* passim.
21. Hill, *Women in Gainful Occupations . . .* , pp. 138–140.
22. *Twelfth Census: 1900, Occupations,* pp. 218–305.
23. Mary V. Robinson, *Domestic Workers and Their Employment Relations,* U.S. Department of Labor, Woman's Bureau, Bulletin No. 39, (Washington, D.C., 1924), pp. 15–16, 24, 67, 69–71; Lillian Pettengill, *Toilers of the Home: The Record of a College Woman's Experience as a Domestic Servant* (New York, 1903), p. 27.
24. *The Family Status of Breadwinning Women,* U.S. Department of Labor, Women's Bureau, Bulletin No. 23 (Washington, D.C., 1923), pp. 10–11, 25, 29, 31–34.

CHAPTER 3

1. *Coast Seamen's Journal* VIII (March 13, 1895), 10; Chicago Commission on Race Relations, *The Negro in Chicago* (Chicago, 1922), pp. 371–372.
2. Lucy Maynard Salmon, *Domestic Service* (New York, 1897), pp. 54–60. Salmon described the "help" system as the dominant form of service among free household labor from the Revolution to 1850, but studies since—namely, Handlin's work on Boston and Ernst's on New York City—have shown conclusively the immigrant base to domestic service in cities even before the great famine in Ireland. Oscar Handlin, *Boston's Immigrants: A Study in Acculturation* rev. ed. (New York, 1975), passim; Robert Ernst, *Immigrant Life in New York City 1825–1863* (New York, 1944), pp. 66–68.
3. Frances A. Kellor, *Out of Work: A Study of Employment Agencies . . .* (New York, 1904), p. 70.
4. "Servant-Girls Advertising for Situations," *Frank Leslie's Illustrated Newspaper* XXXIX (December 19, 1874), 247–248.
5. "A Washerwoman," *Independent* LVII (November 10, 1904), 1073; Kellor, *Out of Work,* pp. 68–69, 98.
6. Kellor, *Out of Work,* pp. 68–69.
7. Ibid., pp. 17, 33, 53, 118; New York Bureau of Statistics of Labor, *Annual Report 1896* (Albany, 1897), pp. 920–923; Maryland Bureau of Industrial Statistics, *Annual Report 1896* (Baltimore, 1897), pp. 69–77.
8. Kellor, *Out of Work,* pp. 6–9, 28–29; Lillian Pettengill, *Toilers of the*

Home: The Record of a College Woman's Experiences as a Domestic Servant (New York, 1903), pp. 35–42.

9. Lou Murray, *How to Get a Situation and How to Keep It* (Philadelphia, 1887), pp. 11–12; New York Bureau of Statistics of Labor, *Annual Report 1896*, pp. 919–924; Kellor, *Out of Work*, pp. 44, 47, 53, 72, 78, 87, 89.

10. Kellor, *Out of Work;* New York Association for Improving the Condition of the Poor, *Annual Report 1866* (New York, 1866), p. 58; Society for the Encouragement of Faithful Domestic Servants in New-York, *Annual Report 1826* (New York, 1826), pp. 5, 27. A Boston imitation of the New York society appeared one year later, calling itself the [Boston] Society for the Mutual Benefit of Female Domestics and Their Employers, *Constitution* (Boston, 1827). Blaine Edward McKinley has more fully described these reforms in his chapter on "Charitable Activities Relating to Servants" in " 'The Stranger in the Gates': Employer Reactions Toward Domestic Servants in America 1825–1875" (Ph.D. dissertation, Michigan State University, 1969), pp. 99–147. He saw them in a much more benign light than I have.

11. Society for the Encouragement of Faithful Domestic Servants in New-York, *Annual Report 1826*, pp. 4–5, 7; *Annual Report 1827* (New York, 1827), pp. 12–13. The licensing of employment offices proved no more successful in controlling abuses, and government-sponsored offices later in the century excluded domestics either because they were incapable of dealing with such an atomized market or they could not attract sufficient employers to meet the demand. Gail Laughlin, "Domestic Service," *Report [and Testimony] of the Industrial Commission . . .* , vol. XIV (19 vols.; Washington, D.C., 1901), 755; Maryland Bureau of Industrial Statistics, *Annual Report 1896*, p. 65.

12. Helen Campbell, *Prisoners of Poverty: Women Wage-Workers, Their Trades and Their Lives* (Boston, 1887), p. 145.

13. For descriptions of experiences during probationary weeks, see Pettengill, *Toilers of the Home*, passim. For examples of model contracts, see Mary A. Ripley, *An Essay on Household Service . . .* (Buffalo, 1889), pp. 44–45, and Legal Aid Society, New York, *Domestic Employment: A Handbook* (New York, 1908).

14. Kellor, *Out of Work*, p. 110; I. M. Rubinow, "The Problem of Domestic Service," *Journal of Political Economy* XIV (October 1906), 512; Campbell, *Prisoners of Poverty*, pp. 145–146.

15. Pettengill, *Toilers of the Home*, passim; Zenas Dane, "Our Hetty," *Good Housekeeping* IV (February 19, 1887), 186–187; Kellor, *Out of Work*, p. 110; Laughlin, "Domestic Service," p. 757; William Paul Gerhard, "Domestic Sanitary Appliances," III, "In the Servants' Quarters . . . ," *Good Housekeeping* I (May 2, 1885), 3–4; Campbell, *Prisoners of Poverty*, pp. 145–146.

16. Pettengill, *Toilers of the Home*, p. 56; "A Washerwoman," *Independent* LVII (November 10, 1904), 1074.

17. Pettengill, *Toilers of the Home*, pp. 92–93; New York Bureau of Labor Statistics, *Annual Report 1896*, p. 923; Campbell, *Prisoners of Poverty*, p. 147.

18. Minnesota Bureau of Labor Statistics, *Biennial Report 1887–8* (n.p., 1887), p. 153; Kansas Department of Labor and Industry, *Annual Report 1914* (Topeka, 1915), p. 26; Orra Langhorne, *Southern Workman* (October 1890), in Charles E. Wynes (ed.), *Southern Sketches from Virginia 1881–1901* (Charlottesville, Virginia, 1964), p. 110.

19. [T. J. Woofter, Jr.], "The Negroes of Athens, Georgia," Phelps-Stokes Fellowship Studies No. 1, *Bulletin of the University of Georgia* XIV (December 1913), 47–48; Josephine C. Goldmark, "Working-women and the Laws: A Record of Neglect," *Annals* XXVIII (September 1906), 70–71; Lucille Eaves, *A History of California Labor Legislation*, University of California Publications in Economics II (Berkeley, 1910), 204–205.

20. "Hours of Labor in Domestic Service," *Massachusetts Labor Bulletin* No. 8 (October 1898), pp. 6–7, 22. In the South, where it was customary for day workers to have some time off in the middle of the day to return to their own homes, rest periods were thus institutionalized and call time lessened. In Gainesville, Georgia, in 1919 only 27 of 73 servants (excluding the 72 washerwomen, who worked in their own home) were away from home all day. Ruth Reed, "The Negro Women of Gainesville, Georgia," Phelps-Stokes Fellowship Studies No. 6, *Bulletin of the University of Georgia* XXII (December 1921), p. 17.

21. "Saturday Half-Holiday," *Good Housekeeping* III (July 10, 1886), 129; McKinley, " 'The Stranger in the Gates,' " p. 31; Maud Nathan, *Once Upon a Time and Today* (New York, 1933), p. 81; [Mary E. Trueblood], "Social Statistics of Workingwomen," *Massachusetts Labor Bulletin* No. 18 (May 1901), p. 38; Salmon, *Domestic Service*, p. 134; Pettengill, *Toilers of the Home*, pp. 162–164.

22. "Hours of Labor in Domestic Service," pp. 14–17; Salmon, *Domestic Service*, p. 146n.

23. "Social Conditions in Domestic Service," *Massachusetts Labor Bulletin* No. 13 (February 1900), 10–12; Inez A. Godman, "Ten Weeks in a Kitchen," *Independent* LIII (October 17, 1901), 2462; Salmon, *Domestic Service*, p. 152n; Antoinette B. Hervey, "The Saints in My Kitchen," *Outlook* 100 (February 17, 1912), 370.

24. I. M. Rubinow and Daniel Durant, "The Depth and Breadth of the Servant Problem," *McClure's Magazine* XXXIV (March 1910), 578; "Social Conditions in Domestic Service," pp. 1–2.

25. Laughlin, "Domestic Service," p. 749; Gilson Willets, *Workers of the Nation*, vol. II (2 vols.; New York, 1903), 1035.

26. Godman, "Ten Weeks in a Kitchen," p. 2459.

27. Ibid., p. 2460.

28. Ibid.

29. Ibid., p. 2461.

30. Catherine Owen, *Progressive Housekeeping* . . . (Boston and New York, 1896), p. 14; "A Servant Girl's Letter," *Independent* LIV (January 2, 1902), 37.

31. Campbell, *Prisoners of Poverty*, p. 229; "A Servant Girl's Letter," p. 36. See also "The Experiences of a 'Hired Girl,' " *Outlook* 100 (April 6, 1912), 778–779.

32. Catherine Beecher, *Miss Beecher's Housekeeper and Healthkeeper* . . . (New York, 1873), passim.

33. A. E. Kennelly, "Electricity in the Household," *Scribner's Magazine* VII (January 1890), 103, 107, 110–111, 113. See also Anna Leach, "Science in the Model Kitchen, *Cosmopolitan* XXVII (May 1899), 95–104.

34. Carlotta Norton Smith, *The Homemaker: Her Science* (New York, 1905), pp. 41, 45, 46, 54–55, 168, 256–257.

35. William G. Panschar, *Baking in America*, vol. 1, *Economic Development*, (2 vols.; Evanston, Illinois, 1956), 34, 47–48, 53, 71, 74; Laughlin, "Domestic Service," p. 750.

36. George J. Stigler, *Domestic Servants in the United States 1900–1940*, National Bureau of Economic Research Occasional Paper 24 (New York, 1946), pp. 24, 28.

37. Elizabeth Ross Haynes, "Negroes in Domestic Service," *Journal of Negro History* VIII (October 1923), 430–431.

38. Martha Bensley Bruère, "The New Home-Making," *Outlook* 100 (March 16, 1912), 592.

39. Ruth Schwartz Cowan, "The 'Industrial Revolution' in the Home: Household Technology and Social Change in the Twentieth Century," *Technology and Culture* 17 (January 1976), 8–10.

40. "Biddy Dethroned," *Putnam's Monthly Magazine*, new series, V (January 1870), 115.

41. William D. and Deborah C. Andrews, "Technology and the Housewife in Nineteenth-Century America," *Women's Studies* 2 (1974), 317–319; Isabel Bevier and Susannah Usher, *The Home Economics Movement*, pt. I (Boston, 1912), 52, 62–67.

42. Ellen Battelle Dietrick, "Once More the Servant Problem," *Good Housekeeping* XII (August 1891), 63–65; Kate Hamlin, "The Domestic Problem, Again," *Good Housekeeping* XIV (May 1892), 219–223.

43. Anna B. McMahan, "Something More About Domestic Service," *Forum* I (June 1886), 399; Josephine E. Martin, "Concerning Servants," *Good Housekeeping* XV (July 1892), 7–8.

44. This modernization of household tasks is a major theme of Theresa M. McBride, *The Domestic Revolution: The Modernisation of Household Ser-*

vice in England and France *1820–1920* (New York, 1976), and she has explored this question at greater length. For the larger industrial and cultural context of modernization, see Herbert G. Gutman, "Work, Culture and Society in Industrializing America, 1815–1919," *American Historical Review* 78 (June 1973), 531–588.

45. For a survey of domestic training at the turn of the century, see Laughlin, "Domestic Service," pp. 761–766.

46. Salmon, *Domestic Service*, pp. 109–110; Isabel Eaton, "Special Report on Negro Domestic Service in the Seventh Ward, Philadelphia," in W. E. B. DuBois, *The Philadelphia Negro: A Social Study* (original, 1899; reprint, New York, 1967), pp. 479–480; William Wilson Elwang, *The Negroes of Columbia, Missouri* ([Columbia], 1904), p. 27; George Edmund Haynes, *The Negro at Work in New York City: A Study in Economic Progress* (original, 1912; reprint, New York, 1968), p. 85; William August Crossland, *Industrial Conditions Among Negroes in St. Louis*, Washington University Studies in Social Economics 1 (St. Louis, 1914), 30.

47. Elizabeth Ross Haynes, "Negroes in Domestic Service," p. 394; U.S. Senate, 61st Congress, 2nd Session, Document No. 645, *Report on Condition of Woman and Child Wage-Earners in the United States*, vol. XII, *Employment of Women in Laundries* (19 vols.; Washington, D.C., 1911), pp. 39–115.

48. Robert A. Woods and Albert J. Kennedy (eds.), *Young Working Girls: A Summary of Evidence from Two Thousand Social Workers* (Boston, 1913), pp. 28–29.

49. This and the following paragraphs are drawn from Trueblood's reports "Social Statistics of Workingwomen," 29–49, and "Housework versus Shop and Factories," *Independent* LVI (November 13, 1902), 2691–2693. Statistical comparisons among women's occupations are very difficult. Few surveys of women wage earners included complete data for domestic service. Typically they gave average weekly wages for all women's occupations except domestic workers and teachers, for whom monthly wages were listed. See, for example, California Bureau of Labor Statistics, *Biennial Report 1885 and 1886* (Sacramento, 1887), pp. 21–33, and *Biennial Report 1887* and *1888* (Sacramento, 1888), pp. 83–84. The Massachusetts study of 1872 permits comparison of wages, since weekly wages were recorded, but as in the California reports, hours had been omitted for servants. Massachusetts Bureau of Statistics of Labor, *Annual Report 1872* (Boston, 1872), p. 66. With the later development of statistical bureaus in the South and their disinterest in black and women's labor, no comparable data exists for Southern states.

50. For a discussion of wages in household service, see Appendix 3.

CHAPTER 4

1. Barbara Welter, "The Cult of True Womanhood: 1820–1860," *American Quarterly* XVIII (Summer 1966), 151–174; Kathryn Kish Sklar, *Catherine Beecher: A Study in American Domesticity* (New Haven, 1973).

2. For a brief discussion of upper-class servant patterns, see E. S. Turner, *What the Butler Saw: Two Hundred and Fifty Years of the Servant Problem* (London, 1962), pp. 270–273.

3. Gail Laughlin, "Domestic Service," *Report [and Testimony] of the Industrial Commission . . .* , vol. XIV (19 vols.); Washington, D.C., 1901), 759.

4. Mary V. Robinson, *Domestic Workers and Their Employment Relations*, U.S. Department of Labor, Women's Bureau, Bulletin No. 39 (Washington, D.C., 1924), pp. 43–44.

5. Lucy Maynard Salmon, *Domestic Service* (New York, 1897), pp. 54, 61.

6. Society for the Encouragement of Faithful Domestic Servants in New-York, *Annual Report 1826* (New York, 1826), p. 4; Salmon, *Domestic Service*, pp. 61–67; Blaine Edward McKinley, " 'The Stranger in the Gates': Employer Reactions Toward Domestic Servants in America 1825–1875" (Ph.D. dissertation, Michigan State University, 1969), pp. 55–61. For an excellent discussion of rural "help," see "Hired Girl," in David E. Schob, *Hired Hands and Plowboys: Farm Labor in the Midwest, 1815–1860* (Urbana, Illinois, 1975), pp. 191–208.

7. Massachusetts Bureau of Statistics of Labor, *Annual Report 1869–1870* (Boston, 1870), p. 198; Maine Bureau of Industrial and Labor Statistics, *Annual Report 1910* (Augusta, 1910), pp. 330–331.

8. McKinley, " 'Stranger in the Gates,' " pp. 56, 65; Maine Bureau of Industrial and Labor Statistics, *Annual Report 1910*, pp. 345–346. The presence of men in households is discussed in Chapter 5.

9. Massachusetts Bureau of Statistics of Labor, *Annual Report 1906* (Boston, 1907), p. 98.

10. Maine Bureau of Industrial and Labor Statistics, *Annual Report 1910*, p. 317.

11. California Bureau of Labor Statistics, *Biennial Report 1887–1888* (Sacramento, 1888), p. 92; Massachusetts Bureau of Statistics of Labor, *Annual Report 1906*, p. 114; Maine Bureau of Industrial and Labor Statistics, *Annual Report 1910*, p. 346; Frances A. Kellor, *Out of Work: A Study of Employment Agencies . . .* (New York, 1904), p. 123.

12. Massachusetts Bureau of Statistics of Labor, *Annual Report 1906*, p. 96; Mary A. Ripley, *An Essay on Household Service . . .* (Buffalo, 1889), p. 18. For Christian approaches toward service, see Rev. Charles M. Sheldon, "Servant and Mistress," *Independent* LII (December 20, 1900), 3018–3020.

13. Helen Mar, "Good Service in General Housework," *Good Housekeeping* XLII (February 1906), 171.

14. Lillian Pettengill, *Toilers of the Home: The Record of a College Woman's Experience as a Domestic Servant* (New York, 1903, pp. 48, 50–52.

15. Ibid., pp. 53–55.

16. Ibid., pp. 59–60, 62.

17. Anne Ellis, *The Life of an Ordinary Woman* (Boston and New York, 1929), pp. 58–59; M.E.M., "Parlor and Kitchen," *Lippincott's Magazine* IV (August 1869), 208.

18. Carroll Smith-Rosenberg, "The Female World of Love and Ritual: Relations Between Women in Nineteenth-Century America," *Signs: Journal of Women in Culture and Society* I (Autumn 1975), 1, 9.

19. I. M. Rubinow and Daniel Durant, "The Depth and Breadth of the Servant Problem," *McClure's Magazine* XXXIV (March 1910), 578; Lucy M. Salmon, "Domestic Service from the Standpoint of the Employee," *Cosmopolitan* XV (July 1893), 350; Helen Campbell, *Prisoners of Poverty: Women Wage-Earners, Their Trades and Their Lives* (Boston, 1887), p. 197; Jane Addams, "A Belated Industry," *American Journal of Sociology* I (March 1896), 538.

20. Minnesota Bureau of Labor Statistics, *Biennial Report 1887–8* (n.p., 1887), pp. 166–168, 170–171.

21. New York Association for Improving the Condition of the Poor, *Annual Report 1866* (New York, 1866), pp. 37, 56–57; "A Small Piece of the Woman Question," *Scribner's Monthly* III (February 1872), 483.

22. Robert Ernst, *Immigrant Life in New York City 1825–1863* (New York, 1944), pp. 66–68; Oscar Handlin, *Boston's Immigrants: A Study in Acculturation*, rev. ed. (New York, 1975), p. 186. For an excellent discussion of mistress–Irish servant conflicts before 1870, see McKinley, " 'Stranger in the Gates,' " pp. 148–190.

23. Rev. And. Ambaven, *Suggestions to Girls at Service* (Dodgeville, Wisconsin, 1889), passim.

24. Douglas V. Shaw, *The Making of an Immigrant City: Ethnic and Cultural Conflict in Jersey City, New Jersey, 1850–1877* (New York, 1976), pp. 2, 119.

25. Maud Nathan, *Once Upon a Time and Today* (New York, 1933), pp. 82–83.

26. Carroll Smith-Rosenberg, "Puberty to Menopause: The Cycle of Femininity in Nineteenth-Century America," *Feminist Studies* I (Winter–Spring 1973), 58–61. See also Carroll Smith-Rosenberg and Charles Rosenberg, "The Female Animal: Medical and Biological Views of Woman and Her Role in Nineteenth-Century America," *Journal of American History* LX (September 1973), 332–356.

27. Smith-Rosenberg, "Puberty to Menopause," pp. 61–62.

28. Elizabeth Kilham, "Sketches in Color," I, *Putnam's Monthly Magazine*,

new series, IV (December 1869), 741; Kellor, *Out of Work,* p. 149; Pettengill, *Toilers of the Home,* p. 48.

29. Nathan, *Once Upon a Time,* pp. 26–27.
30. Anne Frances Springsteed, *The Expert Waitress: A Manual for the Pantry, Kitchen, and Dining-Room* (New York, 1894). The book appeared first as a regular column in *Good Housekeeping* under the authorship of Frances Spalding beginning in January 1892. Katherine Bissell's copy of *The Expert Waitress* is in my possession.
31. Springsteed, *Expert Waitress,* pp. 30–31, 34–35, 49–58.
32. Ibid., pp. 75–76, 83, 92–93, 96–97.
33. Janet McKenzie Hill, *The Up-to-Date Waitress* (Boston, 1910), pp. 5–6.
34. Theresa M. McBride has studied European service within the context of industrializing Europe. See her "Social Mobility for the Lower Classes: Domestic Servants in France," *Journal of Social History* 8 (Fall 1974), 63–78, and *The Domestic Revolution: The Modernisation of Household Service in England and France 1820–1920* (New York, 1976).
35. Rose Cohen, *Out of the Shadow* (Original, 1918; reprint, New York, 1971), pp. 158–159, 171–172.
36. Kellor, *Out of Work,* pp. 147–148.
37. Antoinette B. Hervey, "The Saints in My Kitchen," *Outlook* 100 (February 17, 1912), 367.
38. Pettengill, *Toilers of the Home,* p.14.
39. "The Princess Biddy; or 'Help' and Self-Help," *Putnam's Monthly Magazine,* new series, IV (August 1869), 247.
40. Mrs. E. J. Gurley, "Mistress Work and Maid Work," I, *Good Housekeeping* II (April 3, 1886), 311–312; ibid., III, *Good Housekeeping II* (May 1, 1886), 365; Ellen Battelle Dietrick, "Once More the Servant Problem," *Good Housekeeping* XII (August 1891), 63.
41. Max O'Rell [Paul Blouët], *Jonathan and His Continent: Rambles Through American Society* (Bristol, England, 1889), pp. 262, 264.
42. Ibid., pp. 264–265.
43. Edwin P. Whipple, "Domestic Service," *Forum* I (March 1886), 26, 32–33.
44. Withholding wages was a common complaint. In 1920, two thousand servants applied to the Legal Aid Society, New York, for assistance in collecting wages. The society reported that three-quarters were meritorious claims. Laughlin, "Domestic Service," pp. 757–58.
45. Massachusetts Bureau of Statistics of Labor, *Annual Report 1906,* pp. 102, 104–106.
46. Ripley, *An Essay on Household Service,* passim.
47. John B. Guernsey, "Scientific Management in the Home," *Outlook* 100 (April 13, 1912), 821–825.
48. Ibid., pp. 821, 825.
49. "A Servant on the Servant Problem," *American Magazine* LXVIII

(September 1909), 502–504. In suggesting that some servants were searching for motherly love when they left their parental home, I am not implying that they were seeking to compensate for affection once received. Some might have, but many young servant girls came from large families, and depending on the size of the family, their position in the birth order, the age of their mother, whether or not their mother worked, and so forth, they may or may not have received motherly affection as a matter of course.

50. Ibid., 502–504.
51. For a discussion of domestic service in contemporary American society, see David M. Katzman, "Domestic Service: Woman's Work," in Ann H. Stromberg and Shirley Harkess (eds.), *Women Working: Theories and Facts in Perspective* (Palo Alto, 1978), pp. 377–391.

CHAPTER 5

1. Langston Hughes, "Let America Be America Again," in Langston Hughes and Arna Bontemps (eds.), *The Poetry of the Negro 1746–1949* (Garden City, New York, 1949), p. 107; Orra Langhorne, "Domestic Science in the South," *Journal of Social Science* XXXIX (November 1901), 169; M.E.M., "Parlor and Kitchen," *Lippincott's Magazine* IV (August 1869), 207; Helen Hoover Santmyer, *Ohio Town* ([Columbus, Ohio], 1962), p. 95. Robert Roberts's 1827 *The House Servant's Directory* . . . symbolized the long American connection between domestic service and blacks. Maxwell Whiteman has described Roberts's *Directory* as "the first book by a black American published by a commercial publisher"; appropriately it was a guide to servants, advising them on how to behave and do household work. Maxwell Whiteman, "A Bibliographical Note," in Robert Roberts, *The House Servant's Directory, or A Monitor for Private Families: Comprising Hints on the Arrangement and Performance of Servant's Work* . . . (original, 1827; reprint, Wilmington, Delaware, n.d.).
2. Orra Langhorne, *Southern Workman* (October 1890), in Charles E. Wynes (ed.), *Southern Sketches from Virginia 1881–1901* (Charlottesville, Virginia, 1964), p. 108; [T. J. Woofter, Jr.], "The Negroes of Athens, Georgia," Phelps-Stokes Fellowship Studies No. 1, *Bulletin of the University of Georgia* XIV (December 1913), p. 43; C. Arnold Anderson and Mary Jean Bowman, "The Vanishing Servant and the Contemporary Status System of the American South," *American Journal of Sociology* LIX (November 1953), 215.
3. "More Slavery at the South. By a Negro Nurse," *Independent* LXXII (January 25, 1912), 198.
4. Anderson and Bowman, "Vanishing Servant . . . ," p. 223.

5. Walter L. Fleming, "The Servant Problem in a Black Belt Village," *Sewanee Review* XIII (January 1905), 1, 5.
6. Howard N. Rabinowitz, "The Search for Social Control: Race Relations in the Urban South, 1865–1890" (Ph.D. dissertation, University of Chicago, 1973), I, 64–65; Woofter, "Negroes of Athens, Georgia," pp. 59–61.
7. "Observations of the Southern Race Feeling. By a Northern Woman," *Independent* LVI (March 17, 1904), 595; "More Slavery at the South," pp. 198–199.
8. Eugene D. Genovese, *Roll, Jordan, Roll: The World the Slaves Made* (London, 1975), pp. 343–347, 353–361.
9. Langhorne, *Southern Workman*, February 1884, in *Southern Sketches from Virginia . . .* , p. 37; Fleming, "The Servant Problem . . . , p. 11; Woofter, "Negroes of Athens, Georgia," p. 45.
10. Frances Taylor Long, "The Negroes of Clarke County, Georgia, During the Great War," Phelps-Stokes Fellowship Studies No. 5, *Bulletin of the University of Georgia* XIX (September 1919), 41–42.
11. Peter Kolchin, *First Freedom: The Responses of Alabama's Blacks to Emancipation and Reconstruction* (Westport, Connecticut, 1972), pp. 131–133; Joel Williamson, *After Slavery: The Negro in South Carolina During Reconstruction, 1861–1877* (Chapel Hill, North Carolina, 1965), pp. 105–108, 159–160; *Freeman* (Indianapolis), July 25, 1869, p. 6.
12. Williamson, *After Slavery*, pp. 33–36; Rabinowitz, "Search for Social Control," I, 64–66; Kolchin, *First Freedom*, pp. 131–132.
13. Testimony of Robert B. Kyle, in U.S. Senate Committee on Education and Labor, *Report Upon the Relations Between Labor and Capital*, vol. IV (4 vols.; Washington, 1885), 26; testimony of Mrs. Ward, *ibid.*, 313, 318, 328.
14. Oswald Garrison Villard, "The Negro and the Domestic Problem," *Alexander's Magazine* I (November 15, 1905), 6.
15. "Experiences of the Race Problem. By a Southern White Woman," *Independent* LVI (March 17, 1904), 592; Fleming, "The Servant Problem . . . ," p. 11; Marion Harland, *House and Home: A Complete Housewife's Guide* (Philadelphia, 1889), p. 93; Langhorne, "Domestic Science in the South," pp. 169–170.
16. *Report Upon the Relations Between Labor and Capital*, vol. IV, 328, 343.
17. Fleming, "The Servant Problem . . . ," pp. 11, 15.
18. Sidney H. Kessler, "The Organization of Negroes in the Knights of Labor," *Journal of Negro History* XXXVII (July 1952), 258; Frenise A. Logan, *The Negro in North Carolina 1876–1894* (Chapel Hill, North Carolina, 1964), p. 103; *New York Freeman*, December 18, 1886; *Weekly Pelican* (New Orleans), December 18, 1886; *Freeman* (Indianapolis), October 19, 1889, p. 4.
19. Rabinowitz, "Search for Social Control," I, 194–198.

20. Fleming, "The Servant Problem . . . ," p. 16.
21. Ibid., pp. 6–15; Isabel Eaton, "Special Report on Negro Domestic Service in the Seventh Ward Philadelphia," in W. E. B. DuBois, *The Philadelphia Negro: A Social Study* (original, 1899; reprint, New York, 1967), p. 486; "More Slavery at the South," p. 199.
22. Helen B. Pendleton, "Negro Dependence in Baltimore," *Charities* XV (October 7, 1905), 52.
23. Testimony of Albert C. Danner, *Report Upon the Relations Between Labor and Capital*, Vol. IV, 105.
24. Genovese, *Roll, Jordan, Roll*, p. 343; "More Slavery at the South," pp. 196–197.
25. W. E. Burghardt DuBois, "The Negroes of Farmville, Virginia: A Social Study," *Bulletin of the Department of Labor* III (January 1898), 2, 16.
26. Clyde Vernon Kiser, *Sea Island to City: A Study of St. Helena Islanders in Harlem and Other Urban Centers* (reprint, New York, 1969), pp. 96–97; Elizabeth Ross Haynes, "Negroes in Domestic Service in the United States" (M.A. thesis, Columbia University, 1923), pp. 69–70.
27. David Macrae, *The Americans at Home* (Glasgow, 1874), p. 43; Max O'Rell [Paul Blouët], *Jonathan and His Continent: Rambles Through American Society* (Bristol, England, 1889), p. 264.
28. Elizabeth Hafkin Pleck, "Black Migration to Boston in the Late Nineteenth Century" (Ph.D. dissertation, Brandeis University, 1973), pp. 27–30; David A. Gerber, "Ohio and the Color Line: Racial Discrimination and Negro Responses in a Northern State, 1860–1915" (Ph.D. dissertation, Princeton University, 1971), p. 283.
29. Pleck, "Black Migration to Boston . . . ," pp. 31–38. It should be noted that of the 23 servants in 1870, not all were women.
30. *Southern Workman* I (November 1872), 2, 3; II (January 1873), 3.
31. Langhorne, *Southern Workman* (June 1881), in *Southern Sketches from Virginia* . . . , p. 11; *Wisconsin Afro-American*, October 8, 1892, February, 1893; *Elevator* (San Francisco), January 1, 1869, July 30, 1869, May 6, 1870, May 30, 1874, June 20, 1874, October 23, 1874; *Freeman* (Indianapolis), August 13, 1892, July 1, 1893.
32. *Elevator* (San Francisco), January 1, 1869, July 30, 1869, May 30, 1874; *New York Globe*, January 6, 1883, April 19, 1884; *New York Freeman*, September 11, 1886; Frances A. Kellor, "Assisted Emigration from the South: The Women," *Charities* XV (October 7, 1905), 11–12.
33. Kiser, *Sea Island to City*, passim; *New York Freeman*, September 11, 1886.
34. DuBois, "Negroes of Farmville, Virginia," p. 21.
35. *New York Globe*, November 3, 1883, January 2, 1886.
36. Benjamin H. Locke, "The Community Life of a Harlem Group of

Negroes" (M.A. thesis, Columbia University, 1913), pp. 1–2, 6, 9, 18.

37. Ibid., pp. 10–16.
38. Ibid., pp. 22–32.
39. DuBois, "Negroes of Farmville, Virginia," p. 9.
40. Kiser, *Sea Island to City*, pp. 185–186.
41. Pleck, "Black Migration to Boston . . . ," pp. 66–67, 69.
42. Ibid., pp. 66–67; Stephan Thernstrom and Peter R. Knights, "Men in Motion: Some Data and Speculations on Urban Population Mobility in Nineteenth-Century America," *Journal of Interdisciplinary History* I (Fall 1970), 7–35.
43. Frances A. Kellor, "Opportunities for Southern Negro Women in Northern Cities," *Voice of the Negro* II (1905), 470.
44. "Migration of Colored Girls from Virginia," Hampton Negro Conference, *Annual Report 1905* (Hampton, Virginia, 1905), pp. 75–79. Blacks were more likely to be servants in houses of prostitution than prostitutes in these places. In studying prostitution in the late-nineteenth-century mining frontier, Marion Goldman discovered that "a very small number of blacks were employed as prostitutes' maids, but there is no record of black women being permitted to join the line." In Chicago, the Vice Commission concluded that nearly all servants in houses of prostitution were black. Marion Goldman, "Prostitution and Virtue in Nevada," *Society* X (November/December 1972), 34; Vice Commission of Chicago, *The Social Evil in Chicago* (Chicago, 1911), pp. 38–39. See also George J. Kneeland, *Commercialized Prostitution in New York City* (New York, 1913), pp. 21, 44, 152–153.
45. Testimony of John W. Lapsley, *Report Upon the Relations Between Labor and Capital*, vol. IV, 161.
46. Lillian Pettengill, *Toilers of the Home: The Record of a College Woman's Experience as a Domestic Servant* (New York, 1903), pp. 20–21, 38.
47. Helen Campbell, "Why Is There Objection to Domestic Service? I, II," *Good Housekeeping* XI (September 13, 1890), 232, (September 27, 1890), 255.
48. "More Slavery at the South," pp. 197–198; DuBois, "Negroes of Farmville, Virginia," p. 21; "The Race Problem—An Autobiography. By a Southern Colored Woman," *Independent* LVI (March 17, 1904), 578.
49. U.S. Senate, 61st Congress, 2nd Session, Document No. 645, *Report on Condition of Woman and Child Wage-Earners in the United States*, vol. XV, *Relation Between Occupation and Criminality of Women* (19 vols.; Washington, D.C., 1911), 74, 104–105; Chicago Vice Commission, *Social Evil . . .* , pp. 166–167.
50. Frances A. Kellor, *Out of Work: A Study of Employment Agencies* (New York, 1904), p. 96.

51. *New York Age*, April 21, 1888; "A Women's Exchange," *Outlook* LVI (August 28, 1897), 1063; Helen A. Tucker, "The Negroes of Pittsburgh," *Charities and the Commons* XXI (January 2, 1909), 606; David M. Katzman, *Before the Ghetto: Black Detroit in the Nineteenth Century* (Urbana, Illinois, 1973), p. 156; R. R. Wright, Jr., "Economic Condition of Negroes in the North. Third Paper: Poverty Among Northern Negroes," *Southern Workman* XL (December 1911), 708; Kellor, *Out of Work*.

52. Mary White Ovington, *Half a Man: The Status of the Negro in New York* (reprint, New York, 1969), pp. 79–80.

53. Antoinette B. Hervey, "The Saints in My Kitchen," *Outlook* 100 (February 17, 1910), 368.

54. Di Vernon, "The Chinese as House Servants," *Good Housekeeping* XII (January 1891), 20–22.

55. Maine Bureau of Industrial and Labor Statistics, *Annual Report 1892* (Augusta, 1893), p. 10. For evidence of black women shunning service because of the status, see Katherine Davis Tillman's discussion of service as preferable to an unhappy marriage or a "life of shame." "Afro-American Women and Their Work," *A.M.E. Church Review* XI (1895), 495–496. A South Carolina school principal reported that black women tried to avoid service because they were "treated as in the old slave days . . . ," in E. C. Hobson and C. E. Hopkins, *A Report Concerning the Colored Women of the South*, John F. Slater Fund Occasional Paper No. 9 (Baltimore, 1896), p. 8.

CHAPTER 6

1. Zenas Dane, "Our Hetty," *Good Housekeeping* IV (February 19, 1887), 186; Amy E. Watson, "Domestic Service," *Encyclopaedia of the Social Sciences*, vol. V (New York, 1931), 198.

2. J. Jean Hecht, *The Domestic Servant Class in Eighteenth-Century England* (London, 1956), p. 23.

3. John Demos, *A Little Commonwealth: Family Life in Plymouth Colony* (New York, 1970), pp. 69, 107–117; Lucy Maynard Salmon, *Domestic Service* (New York, 1897), pp. 16–17; Winter, Dudley, and Winthrop quotes in Salmon, *Domestic Service*, pp. 33, 35, 36.

4. Society for the Encouragement of Faithful Domestic Servants in New-York, *Annual Report 1826* (New York, 1826), pp. 25–26.

5. Ibid., pp. 3–5, 13; Society for the Encouragement of Faithful Domestic Servants in New-York, *Annual Report 1827* (New York, 1827), pp. 10, 13.

6. Maine Bureau of Industrial and Labor Statistics, *Annual Report 1910* (Augusta, 1910), pp. 309–310; Mrs. John Sherwood, *Manners and Social Usages* (New York, 1884), pp. 270–271; testimony of Thomas

L. Livermore, in U.S. Senate Committee on Education and Labor, *Report Upon the Relations Between Labor and Capital* . . . , vol. III, (4 vols.; Washington, D.C., 1885), 16.

7. Michigan Department of Labor, *Annual Report 1912* (Lansing, 1912), pp. 39–42; *Cleveland Leader*, October 19, 1871, quoted in Works Progress Administration, Ohio, *Annals of Cleveland 1818–1935*, vol. LIV (59 vols.; Cleveland, 1938), p. 182; Bureau of Labor Statistics, *Biennial Report 1887–1888* (Sacramento, 1888), p. 93.

8. *New York Freeman*, October 17, 1885, p. 2; testimony of Robert B. Kyle, in U.S. Senate Committee on Education and Labor, *Report Upon the Relations Between Labor and Capital* . . . , vol. IV, 26; Orra Langhorne, "Domestic Science in the South," *Journal of Social Science* XXXIX (November 1901), 170; Frances A. Kellor, "Assisted Emigration from the South," *Charities* XV (October 7, 1905), 12; Young Women's Christian Association, Commission on Household Employment, *Report 1915* (n.p., n.d.), p. 6.

9. Salmon, *Domestic Service*, p. 131; *Good Housekeeping* IV (February 5, 1887), 149. For a discussion of earnings, see Appendix 3.

10. Salmon, *Domestic Service*, pp. 131–137; *Medical Record*, quoted in "Housework as an Exercise," *Good Housekeeping* XV (September 1892), 137; M. V. Carroll, "The Domestic Help Problem," in Missouri Bureau of Labor Statistics and Inspection, *Annual Report 1900* (Jefferson City, 1900), p. 148.

11. Salmon, *Domestic Service*, pp. 133n, 137n.

12. U.S. Senate, 61st Congress, 2nd Session, Document No. 645, *Report on Condition of Woman and Child Wage-Earners in the United States*, vol. XII, *Employment of Woman in Laundries* (19 vols.; Washington, D.C., 1911), 44, 63.

13. Minnesota Bureau of Labor Statistics, *Biennial Report 1887–7* (n.p., 1887), p. 155; Maine Bureau of Industrial and Labor Statistics, *Annual Report 1892* (Augusta, 1893), pp. 120–121. For a comparison of level of schooling among women in various occupations of which domestics had the least years of education, see Kansas Bureau of Labor and Industry, *Annual Report 1894* (Topeka, 1895), pp. 198–302.

14. Dorothy Richardson, "The Difficulties and Dangers Confronting the Working Woman," *Annals* XXVII (June 1906), 162–163; *Topeka Commonwealth*, May 12, 1888, p. 4, courtesy of Tom Johnson; Maine Bureau of Industrial and Labor Statistics, *Annual Report 1892*, p. 156; Salmon, *Domestic Service*, p. 137n.

15. Minnesota Bureau of Labor Statistics, *Biennial Report 1887–8*, p. 151; [Mary E. Trueblood], "Social Statistics of Workingwomen," *Massachusetts Labor Bulletin* No. 18 (May 1901), p. 47; Salmon, *Domestic Service*, p. 137n.

16. Lillian Pettengill, *Toilers of the Home: The Record of a College Woman's Ex-*

perience as a Domestic Servant (New York, 1903), pp. 30–31, 273; Jane Addams, "A Belated Industry," *American Journal of Sociology* I (March 1896), 543–544.

17. U.S. Bureau of the Census, *Historical Statistics of the United States 1789–1945* (Washington, D.C., 1949), p. 72; Elizabeth Ross Haynes, "Negroes in Domestic Service in the United States," *Journal of Negro History* VIII (October 1923), 435–436.

18. Daniel T. Hobby (ed.), " 'We Have Got Results': A Document on the Organization of Domestics in the Progressive Era," *Labor History* 17 (Winter 1976), 104–105.

19. Helen Campbell, *Household Economics*, rev. ed. (New York, 1907), pp. 210–213.

20. Frances A. Kellor, *Out of Work: A Study of Employment Agencies . . .* (New York, 1904), pp. 7, 9–10.

21. Maine Bureau of Industrial and Labor Statistics, *Annual Report 1910*, p. 348.

22. Salmon, *Domestic Service*, pp. 157, 209–210; Sherwood, *Manners and Social Usages*, pp. 249–250; "The Livery of Servitude," *Standard* (n.p., n.d.), quoted in *Work and Wages* I (August 1887), 7.

23. Salmon, *Domestic Service*, p. 155n; "A Servant Girl's Letter," *Independent* LIV (January 2, 1902), 36–37; Pettengill, *Toilers of the Home*, pp. 241–242.

24. Maine Bureau of Industrial and Labor Statistics, *Annual Report 1910*, pp. 347, 359–350, 355, 357, 381. Helen Campbell also stressed the incompatibility of service with the American spirit in "Why Is There Objection to Domestic Service?" *Good Housekeeping* XI (September 13, 1890), 231.

25. Pettengill, *Toilers of the Home*, p. 371; Salmon, *Domestic Service*, p. 141. Blaine McKinley has argued that the "loss of personal freedom" was the principal drawback of service. While this was important, it is difficult to agree with his assessment when live-out and day work are compared with live-in service. Since living out removed most of the loss of personal freedom, the predominance of living out after World War I should have removed the basic objections to service. It didn't. Blaine Edward McKinley, " 'The Stranger in the Gates': Employer Reactions Toward Domestic Servants in America 1826–1875" (Ph.D. dissertation, Michigan State University, 1969), p. 26.

26. Helen Campbell, "Why Is There Objection to Domestic Service? II," *Good Housekeeping* XI (September 27, 1890), 255; "The Race Problem—An Autobiography. By a Southern Colored Woman," *Independent* LVI (March 17, 1904), 587; Chicago Commission on Race Relations, *The Negro in Chicago* (Chicago, 1922), p. 387.

27. Salmon, *Domestic Service*, pp. 154–155.

28. California Bureau of Labor Statistics, *Biennial Report 1887–1888*, p. 92; Minnesota Bureau of Labor Statistics, *Biennial Report 1887–8*, p.

149; Maine Bureau of Industrial and Labor Statistics, *Annual Report 1910*, pp. 315–316, 391; "A Servant Girl's Letter," p. 36; Rose Cohen, *Out of the Shadow* (original, 1918; reprint, New York, 1971), p. 159; Helen Campbell, *Prisoners of Poverty: Women Wage-Workers, Their Trades and Their Lives* (Boston, 1887), p. 144.

29. George J. Manson, *Work for Women* (New York, 1883); Ella Rodman Church, *Money-Making for Ladies* (New York, 1882); Josephine Daskam Bacon, "We and Our Daughters," *American Magazine* LXIII (April 1907), 608–615.

30. U.S. Commissioner of Labor, *Annual Report 1910* (Washington, D.C., 1911), pp. 37, 293–297, 307; Marie Francke, *Opportunities for Women in Domestic Service* (Philadelphia, 1916).

31. U.S. Commissioner of Labor, *Annual Report 1910*, pp. 131, 314–336.

32. Peter Kolchin, *First Freedom: The Responses of Alabama's Blacks to Emancipation and Reconstruction* (Westport, Connecticut, 1972), pp. 131–132.

33. [Joseph Willson], *Sketches of the Higher Classes of Colored Society in Philadelphia* (Philadelphia, 1841), pp. 30–31; "One Who Works," in *Weekly Anglo-African* (New York), June 30, 1860.

34. David M. Katzman, *Before the Ghetto: Black Detroit in the Nineteenth Century* (Urbana, Illinois, 1973), pp. 135–174; Adelaide Cromwell Hill, "The Negro Upper Class in Boston—Its Development and Present Social Structure" (Ph.D. dissertation, Radcliffe College, 1952), p. 104; Haynes, "Negroes in Domestic Service . . . ," pp. 400–403; Howard Brown Woolston, *A Study of the Population of Manhattanville*, Columbia University Studies in History, Economics and Public Law XXXV (New York, 1909), 90; *Cleveland Gazette*, September 8, 1883, p. 1; Katherine Davis Tillman, "Afro-American Women and Their Work," *A.M.E. Church Review* XI (1895), 495–496. DuBois cited a case which showed that the status and position of the employer was not transferred to the servant's family: "——, a woman worked long in a family of lawyers; a white lad went into their office as office-boy and came to be a member of the firm; she had a smart, ambitious son and asked for any sort of office work for him—anything in which he could hope for promotion. 'Why don't you make him a waiter?' they asked." W. E. B. DuBois, *The Philadelphia Negro: A Social Study* (original, 1899; reprint, New York, 1967), p. 343.

35. Society for the Encouragement of Faithful Domestic Servants in New-York, *Annual Report 1826*, pp. 4, 25–26; *Annual Report 1827*, p. 10; Catherine E. Beecher, *A Treatise on Domestic Economy for the Use of Young Ladies at Home and at School*, 3rd ed. (New York, 1845), pp. 205–208.

36. M.E.M., "Parlor and Kitchen," *Lippincott's Magazine* IV (August 1869), 208–210.

37. Josephine E. Martin, "Concerning Servants," *Good Housekeeping* XV

(July 1892), 7–9; Mary A. Ripley, *An Essay on Household Service: also Legal Points and Other Matters* . . . (Buffalo, 1889), p. 19.

38. Flora McDonald Thompson, "The Servant Question," *Cosmopolitan* XXVIII (March 1900), 521, 525–526. Isabel Kimball Whiting took the same approach in discussing "household industry" in "The General Housework Employee," *Outlook* 89 (August 15, 1908), 851–855.

39. Ripley, *Essay on Household Service;* Legal Aid Society, New York, *Domestic Employment: A Handbook* (New York, 1908); Annie Winsor Allen, "Both Sides of the Servant Question," *Atlantic Monthly* 111 (April 1913), 496–500.

40. Bertha M. Terrill, *Household Management* (Chicago, 1914), pp. 84–85. See also John B. Guernsey, "Scientific Management in the Home," *Outlook* 100 (April 13, 1912), 821–825.

41. Gail Laughlin, "Domestic Service," *Report [and Testimony] of the Industrial Commission* . . . , vol. XIV (19 vols.; Washington, D.C., 1901), 765–766.

42. Kate S. Hamlin, "The Domestic Problem, Again," *Good Housekeeping* XIV (May 1892), 219–223; Ellen Battelle Dietrick, "Once More the Servant Problem," *Good Housekeeping* XII (August 1891), 63–65. For another debate on the same topic, see Edwin P. Whipple, "Domestic Service," *Forum* I (March 1886), 25–36, and Anna B. McMahan's rebuttal, "Something More About Domestic Service," *Forum* I (June 1886), 399–403.

43. Elizabeth Colson and Anna Gansevoort Chittenden, *The Child Housekeeper. Simple Lessons, with Songs, Stories and Games* (New York, 1903), pp. v, vii.

44. Martha Bensley Bruère, "The New Home-Making," *Outlook* 100 (March 16, 1912), 592–594. See also A. E. Kennelly, "Electricity in the Household," *Scribner's Magazine* VII (January 1890), 102–115.

45. W. D. Howells, "A Traveler from Altruria," reprinted in *The Altrurian Romances* (Bloomington, Indiana, and London, 1968), pp. 8–9, 12, 15, 166–167; Edward Bellamy, "A Vital Domesitc Problem," *Good Housekeeping* X (December 21, 1889), 75–76. Charlotte P. Gilman drew on Bellamy and others to spearhead a major assault on accepted limitations on women's roles in contemporary society. The elimination of household drudgery through communal activity would provide the answer. "As to the kitchen," she wrote in 1913, "that has no place in a model home." "The Model Home," *Forerunner* (1913), quoted in Robert E. Riegel, *American Feminists* (Lawrence, Kansas, 1963), p. 168.

46. Di Vernon, "The Chinese as House Servants," *Good Housekeeping* XII (January 1891), 20–22; Jean Faison, "The Virtues of the Chinese Servant," *Good Housekeeping* XLII (March 1906), 279–280; Joel Williamson, *After Slavery: The Negro in South Carolina During Reconstruction, 1861–1877* (Chapel Hill, North Carolina, 1965), p. 119.

47. Lida Rose McCabe, "Gentlewomen in Domestic Service," *Good House-keeping* XXXIX (October 1904), 405–406.

48. Francis A. Walker, "Our Domestic Service," *Scribner's Monthly* XI (December 1875), 276n; Salmon, *Domestic Service*, pp. 179, 236–242.

49. Lucy Maynard Salmon, *Progress in the Household* (Boston and New York, 1906), pp. 7–9, 69–70.

50. For an attack on tradition in the household, see Salmon, *Progress in the Household*, pp. 95–118. Salmon considered the household the most conservative element in American society.

51. The best source for housekeepers' views was the 1910 Maine report, which published extracts of letters from more than 150 employers. Maine Bureau of Industrial and Labor Statistics, *Annual Report 1910*, pp. 343–393. See also Massachusetts Bureau of Labor Statistics, *Annual Report 1906* (Boston, 1907), 102–115, for the resistance of mistresses to day work.

52. Maine Bureau of Industrial and Labor Statistics, *Annual Report, passim;* Hester Crawford Dorsey, "The Domestic Service Difficulty," *Good Housekeeping* VI (January 21, 1888), 147; New York City House-keeper to Editors, *Good Housekeeping* X (March 1, 1890), 214–215; Daniel Tracy Rodgers, "The Work Ethic in Industrial America, 1865–1917" (Ph.D. dissertation, Yale University, 1973), pp. 220–222. Rodgers described the approach of reformers such as Jane Addams, Lucy Maynard Salmon, Lillian Pettengill, and Charlotte Gilman as a "masculine" approach to the problem. While this probably represented a contemporary view, it seriously distorts the domestic economy movement. Men held no monopoly on efficiency nor science; women could and ought to adopt, the reformers argued, established methods from business and industry. To claim that it was imitative of men distorted these women's beliefs in the capabilities of women and their own commitment to the contemporary progressive movement. Management was not inherently a male sphere, but involved skills which any educated person dedicated to efficiency could acquire.

53. Young Women's Christian Association, Commission on Household Employment, *Report 1915* (n.p., n.d.), p. 33.

54. Bellamy, "Vital Domestic Problem," p. 75; Mary V. Robinson, *Domestic Workers and Their Employment Relations*, U.S. Department of Labor, Women's Bureau, Bulletin No. 39 (Washington, D.C., 1924), pp. 13–14; Kellor, *Out of Work*, pp. 130–131.

55. I. M. Rubinow, "Household Service as a Labor Problem," *Journal of Home Economics* III (April 1911), 137. For a summary of government benefits denied servants in the second half of the twentieth century, see Ethlyn Christensen, "Restructuring the Occupation," *Issues in Industrial Society* 2 (1971), 49.

CHAPTER 7

1. Everett Cherrington Hughes, *Men and Their Work* (Glencoe, Illinois, 1958), pp. 7, 111. Hughes's maxim is not intended to deny or neglect other roles, such as citizen or father, but implies that they are essentially determined by the primary identity and circumstances, which are a function of work roles and identity.

2. Patricia Branca, "A New Perspective on Woman's Work: A Comparative Typology," *Journal of Social History* 9 (Winter 1975), 147. For a discussion of the two roles of women, see Alva Myrdal and Viola Klein, *Woman's Two Roles: Home and Work*, 2nd ed. (London, 1968).

3. Theresa M. McBride, *The Domestic Revolution: The Modernisation of Household Service in England and France 1820–1920* (New York, 1976), pp. 117–121; Branca, "New Perspective . . . ," 136–138.

4. Ruth Schwartz Cowan, "The 'Industrial Revolution' in the Home: Household Technology and Social Change in the Twentieth Century," *Technology and Culture* 17 (January 1976), 1–23.

5. McBride, *Domestic Revolution*, p. 90.

6. Ibid., p. 121; Branca, "New Perspective . . . ," p. 141.

7. Lucy Maynard Salmon, *Domestic Service* (New York, 1897), pp. 149–150.

APPENDIX 2

1. Abott and Breckinridge, "Employment of Women in Industries—Twelfth Census Statistics," *Journal of Political Economy* XIV (January 1906), 17; *Twelfth Census: 1900, Occupations*, p. ccl. Other ambiguities in the 1900 census of occupations were noted by John Cummings, " 'Occupations' in the Twelfth Census," *Journal of Political Economy* XIII (December 1904), 66–76.

2. *Sixteenth Census: 1940, Population*, Alba M. Edwards, *Comparative Occupation Statistics for the United States, 1870 to 1940*, p. 137.

3. *Fourteenth Census: 1920, Occupations*, pp. 13, 23; Edwards, *Comparative Occupation Statistics*, pp. 138–139; George Stigler, *Domestic Servants in the United States 1900–1940*, National Bureau of Economic Research Occasional Paper 24 (New York, 1946), pp. 38–39.

4. Edwards, *Comparative Occupation Statistics*, pp. xi, 88, 194.

5. *Fourteenth Census: 1920, Occupations*, p. 17.

6. *Fourteenth Census: 1920, Occupations*, pp. 16–17.

7. Douglas V. Shaw, *The Making of an Immigrant City: Ethnic and Cultural Conflict in Jersey City, New Jersey, 1850–1877* (New York, 1976), pp. 36, 40–41. I am grateful to David Doyle of University College, Dublin, for suggesting this tie between Irish servants and census enumerations.

APPENDIX 3

1. For a good discussion of the specific problems in servants' wage data, see George Stigler, "Appendix B: Wage Data," *Domestic Servants in the United States 1900–1940*, National Bureau of Economic Research Occasional Paper 24 (New York, 1946), pp. 40–43.

2. The giving of gratuities—tips or fees—to servants in private families was rare in the United States, and tips have been excluded in estimating wages. See "Feeing Servants," *Good Housekeeping* III (August 7, 1886), 178.

3. Susan J. Kleinberg, "Technology's Stepdaughter: The Impact of Industrialization Upon Working Women, Pittsburgh, 1865–1890" (Ph.D. dissertation, University of Pittsburgh, 1973), p. 220; California Bureau of Statistics of Labor, *Biennial Report 1887–1888* (Sacramento, 1888), p. 93; U.S. Senate, 61st Congress, 2nd Session, Document No 645, *Report on Condition of Woman and Child Wage-Earners in the United States*, vol. XII, *Employment of Women in Laundries* (19 vols.; Washington, D.C., 1911), 44, 63, 67, 91; William August Crossland, *Industrial Conditions Among Negroes in St. Louis*, Washington University Studies in Social Economics I (St. Louis, 1914), 94; Isabel Eaton, "Special Report on Negro Domestic Service in the Seventh Ward Philadelphia," in W. E. B. DuBois, *The Philadelphia Negro: A Social Study* (original, 1899; reprint, New York, 1967), p. 449; Ruth Reed, "The Negro Women of Gainesville, Georgia," Phelps-Stokes Fellowship Studies No. 6, *Bulletin of the University of Georgia* XXII (December 1921), 26.

4. Lucy Maynard Salmon, *Domestic Service* (New York, 1897), pp. 88–89; Edward Young, *Labor in Europe and America . . .* , U.S. 44th Congress, 1st session, House of Representatives, Executive Document No. 21 (Washington, D.C. 1876), pp. 783–784; California Bureau of Labor Statistics, *Biennial Report 1885–1886* (Sacramento, 1887), p. 30, *Biennial Report 1887–1888*, p. 83.

5. Michigan Bureau of Labor and Industrial Statistics, *Annual Report 1895* (Lansing, 1895), pp. 334–337.

6. Kansas Bureau of Labor and Industry, *Annual Report 1894* (Topeka, 1895), pp. 198–203.

7. Alice Hanson and Paul H. Douglas, "The Wages of Domestic Labor in Chicago, 1890–1929," *Journal of the American Statistical Association*, new series, XXV (March 1930), 47–50.

8. Michigan Bureau of Labor and Industrial Statistics, *Annual Report 1895*, pp. 334–337; Kansas Bureau of Labor and Industry, *Annual Report 1894*, pp. 198–203; [Mary E. Trueblood], "Social Statistics of Workingwomen," *Massachusetts Labor Bulletin*. No. 18 (May 1901), pp. 38–40; Salmon, *Domestic Work*, pp. 98–105; Gail Laughlin, "Domestic Service," in *Report [and Testimony] of the Industrial Commission*

. . . , vol. XIV (19 vols.; Washington, D.C., 1901), 751; Maine Bureau of Industrial and Labor Statistics, *Annual Report 1910* (Augusta, 1910), pp. 328–329; Massachusetts Bureau of Statistics of Labor, *Annual Report 1872* (Boston, 1872), pp. 66–67, 71–72, 74–75, 80, 85–89, *Annual Report 1887* (Boston, 1887), pp. 205–206, 218–219, *Annual Report 1889* (Boston, 1889), pp. 582–585.

9. Minnesota Bureau of Labor Statistics, *Biennial Report 1887–8* (n.p., 1888), pp. 140, 144, 147, 149; Chicago Commission on Race Relations, *The Negro in Chicago* (Chicago, 1922), pp. 368–369; Crossland, *Industrial Conditions Among Negroes in St. Louis*, pp. 20, 22, 95.

A NOTE ON SOURCES

DOMESTIC SERVICE

THE STARTING POINT FOR ANY STUDY OF DOMESTIC SERVICE IN the United States is Lucy Maynard Salmon, *Domestic Service* (New York, 1897). Based on extensive historical research as well as her own national survey of employers and employees in 1889–1890, it has long been the standard work. Sensitive to the plaints of servants as well as those of mistresses, it is a reasoned consideration of popular attitudes toward service and reform, although she believed, as did her contemporaries, that day work would solve much of the servant problem, which it did not. Most importantly, it shaped nearly all discussions of household service that ensued during the next two decades until the "domestic revolution" in the household made discussions of the "servant problem" an anachronism. The second edition (New York, 1901) included a supplementary chapter on domestic service in Europe; the discussion of American service was not revised. The historical sections of *Domestic Service* appeared in somewhat different form as "Some Historical Aspects of Domestic Service," *New England Magazine*, new series, VIII (April 1893), 176–184. Ten years after *Domestic Service* first appeared, Lucy Maynard Salmon published *Progress in the Household* (Boston and New York,

1906), a collection of essays that dealt primarily with the effect of the domestic-science movement on household labor.

A recent full-length study of domestic service in the United States is Blaine Edward McKinley, " 'The Stranger in the Gates': Employer Reactions Toward Domestic Servants in America 1825–1875" (Ph.D. dissertation, Michigan State University, 1969). It is very good on the nature of service work and mistresses' and reformers' attitudes, but focuses exclusively on live-in servants in the North. For this earlier period of service, McKinley found it "impossible to locate material written by servants themselves. . . ." (p. vii). An excellent and suggestive economic analysis of domestic service in the twentieth century is George J. Stigler, *Domestic Servants in the United States 1900–1940*, National Bureau of Economic Research Occasional Paper 24 (New York, 1946). Part of the NBER investigations of American industries, this was their first venture into services. Stigler thoroughly examined the available statistical data, but did not deal with factors difficult to quantify, such as the mistress-servant relationship, the nature of service work, the change from live-in to live-out and day work, occupational status, and so forth. Somewhat outdated but still useful is Amy E. Watson's overview of domestic service in *Encyclopaedia of the Social Sciences*, vol. V (New York, 1931), 198–206. Her historical discussion depended heavily upon Salmon's work, and writing in the 1920s, Watson failed adequately to appreciate the significance of the shift to live-out and day work. Daniel E. Sutherland, "Americans and Their Servants, 1800–1920: Being an Inquiry into the Origins and Progress of the American Servant Problems" (Ph.D. dissertation, Wayne State University, 1976) became available too late to be consulted.

At the turn of the century I. M. Rubinow of the Departments of Agriculture and Commerce and Labor tried to analyze household labor as he would have treated any other occupation. While recognizing the medievalism and anachronistic employer-employee relations, he placed the question of supply and demand in the forefront. See his

"The Problem of Domestic Service," *Journal of Political Economy* XIV (October 1906), 502–519; "Household Service as a Labor Problem," *Journal of Home Economics* III (April 1911), 131–140; and with Daniel Durant, "The Depth and Breadth of the Servant Problem," *McClure's Magazine* XXXIV (March 1910), 576–585. Jane Addams also stressed that domestic service was a feudal anachronism in modern society in "A Belated Industry," *American Journal of Sociology* I (March 1896), 536–550. Writing from her experiences in Chicago, she perceptively described the difficulties faced by urban tenement girls who entered household labor.

Gail Laughlin's "Domestic Service," in *Report [and Testimony] of the Industrial Commission . . .* , vol. XIV (19 vols.; Washington, D.C., 1901), 743–767, is a good review of contemporary discussions and knowledge of domestic service, although she spent too much time analyzing an inadequate national sample of housekeepers and servants. She also included a survey of existing training schools for servants and domestic economy courses for college women. Earlier, Francis A. Walker of the census bureau had discussed trends in domestic service in the 1870s in "Our Domestic Service," *Scribner's Monthly* XI (December 1875), 275–278. An important local study based on extensive data of applicants for service work to the Domestic Efficiency Association of Baltimore, 1921–1923, is Mary V. Robinson, *Domestic Workers and Their Employment Relations*, U.S. Department of Labor, Women's Bureau, Bulletin No. 39 (Washington, D.C., 1924). The association's files recorded the work histories and work preferences of servants by age, race, and nativity.

More recent studies of domestic servants can be found in monographs by David E. Schob and John Demos. The latter presented a rather idyllic view of colonial domestic service as supremely enlightened benevolent paternalism in *A Little Commonwealth: Family Life in Plymouth Colony* (New York, 1970). One of the best single studies of a group of domestic servants is Schob's description of the "hired girl" in the pre–Civil War Midwest, in *Hired Hands and Plowboys: Farm Labor in the Midwest, 1815–1860* (Urbana, Illinois, 1975). A recent popular history of servants—mostly of men and Europeans, but including chapters on the United States—is E. S. Turner, *What the Butler Saw: Two Hundred and Fifty Years of the Servant Problem* (London, 1962).

VOICES OF DOMESTICS AND MISTRESSES

The most extensive record of a domestic servant's career can be found in Lillian Pettengill, *Toilers of the Home: The Record of a College Woman's Experience as a Domestic Servant* (New York, 1903). Pettengill worked for two years in Philadelphia households and recorded her experiences, observations, and conversations with other domestics. Similar to Pettengill, Inez A. Godman entered domestic service as a participant observer to learn first hand about household labor. Her experiences in ten weeks confirmed those of Pettengill's two-year experiment in "Ten Weeks in a Kitchen," *Independent* LIII (October 17, 1901), 2459–2464. See also her suggestions for reform in "A Nine-Hour Day for Domestic Servants," *Independent* LIV (February 13, 1902), 397–400. "A Servant Girl's Letter," *Independent* LIV (January 2, 1902), 36–37, was a response to Godman's first article, and the servant took a more cynical view about the chances of improving conditions in service.

In the first decade of the twentieth century, the *Independent* published a series of autobiographies of ordinary people. These first-person accounts are a unique source for workers' views on their work and their own experiences, and a selection of these autobiographies will appear in David M. Katzman and William M. Tuttle, Jr. (eds.), *The Life Stories of Undistinguished Americans* (Urbana, Illinois, 1978). Individual essays dealing with domestic service included "The Negro Problem. How It Appears to a Southern Colored Woman," *Independent* LIV (September 18, 1902), 2221–2224; "The Race Problem—An Autobiography. By a Southern Colored Woman," *Independent* LVI (March 17, 1904), 586–589; "A Washerwoman," *Independent* LVII (November 10, 1904) 1073–1076; "The Story of an Irish Cook," *Independent* LVIII

(March 30, 1905), 715–717; "More Slavery at the South. By a Negro Nurse," *Independent* LXXII (January 25, 1912), 196–200.

Helen Campbell, a late-nineteenth-century journalist and reformer concerned about working women, interviewed New York City working girls in the 1880s. Many of the stories were told in the words of the workers themselves, and they included domestic servants. These "photographs from life," as Campbell referred to them, appeared first in the Sunday editions of the *New York Tribune* and were collected and published as *Prisoners of Poverty: Women Wage-Workers, Their Trades and Their Lives* (Boston, 1887). Other memoirs of servants included Anne Ellis's brief record of her first job as a prostitute's servant in a Colorado mining frontier in *The Life of an Ordinary Woman* (Boston and New York, 1929); Rose Cohen's brief venture as a servant in New York City in *Out of the Shadow* (original, 1918; reprint, New York, 1971); and the views of a servant with thirty-three years of household experience expressed in "The Experiences of a 'Hired Girl,' " *Outlook* 100 (April 6, 1912), 778–780.

Among mistresses, Maud Nathan's autobiography recalled domestic servants in her mother's home and her own household in late-nineteenth-century New York City in *Once Upon a Time and Today* (New York, 1933). Helen Hoover Santmyer's reminiscences of turn-of-the-century Xenia, Ohio, and college in the East recalled the days of numerous black servants, *Ohio Town* ([Columbus, Ohio], 1962). Antonette B. Hervey described her own domestics and cooks in "The Saints in My Kitchen," *Outlook* 100 (February 17, 1912), 367–371.

CONDITIONS OF WORK

Frances A. Kellor's investigation of employment agencies in Boston, Chicago, New York, and Philadelphia during 1902–1903 was the most thorough examination of the hiring patterns and experiences of household labor. In the process of studying agencies, she also examined migration, exploitation of workers, conditions of servants, and so forth. See *Out of Work: A Study of Employment Agencies* . . . (New York, 1904). "Migration of Colored Girls from Virginia," Hampton Negro Conference, *Annual Report 1905* (Hampton, Virginia, 1905) dealt with the role of agencies in the migration process and suggested abuses that flowed from that role. The exploitation of black domestics coming to the North were revealed in "Southern Colored Girls in the North," *Charities* XIII (March 18, 1905), 584–585, "Assisted Emigration from the South," *Charities* XV (October 7, 1905), 11–14, and "Opportunities for Southern Negro Women in Northern Cities," *Voice of the Negro* II (1905), 470–473. Reformers often focused on employment agencies as a catalyst for high employee turnover and blamed the agencies for the low repute in which service was held. See, for example, New York Association for Improving the Condition of the Poor, *Annual Report 1866* (New York, 1866). Lou Murray described an employment office as a "swindling trap" in *How to Get a Situation and How to Keep It* (Philadelphia, 1887), while "Servant-Girls Advertising for Situations," *Frank Leslie's Illustrated Newspaper* XXXIX (December 19, 1874), 247–248, poked fun at servants' use of newspapers to find situations.

The working conditions of twenty domestics in Massachusetts were examined by Mary E. Trueblood, and were compared with eighty other working women in four occupations in "Social Statistics of Workingwomen," *Massachusetts Labor Bulletin* No. 18 (May 1901), 29–49. The results were presented in more abbreviated form in "Housework versus Shop and Factories," *Independent* LVI (November 13, 1902), 2691–2693. One of the most valuable studies, because of its time length, was Alice C. Hanson and Paul C. Douglas, "The Wages of Domestic Labor in Chicago, 1890–1929," *Journal of the American Statistical Association*, new series, XXX (March 1930), 47–50. Since the wage data was derived from sampling one Chicago newspaper and the study did not distinguish between live-in and live-out positions, its results must be used with caution. U.S. Commissioner of Labor, *Seventh Special Report: The Slums of Baltimore, Chicago, New*

York and Philadelphia (Washington, 1894), recorded data on women wage earners in selected slum districts. The survey included household workers and washerwomen. Some additional wage data for California in 1869 and 1874 can be found in Edward Young, *Labor in Europe and America . . .* (Washington, D.C., 1876), U.S. House of Representatives, 44th Congress, 1st Session, Executive Document No. 21. "Feeing Servants," *Good Housekeeping* III (August 7, 1886), 178, discussed the absence in the United States of the custom of tipping private household workers.

DOMESTIC SERVICE—BLACKS

The first and still most thorough study of black domestics is Elizabeth Ross Haynes, "Negroes in Domestic Service in the United States" (M.A. thesis, Columbia University, 1923), which appeared in a slightly revised version as "Negroes in Domestic Service in the United States," *Journal of Negro History* VIII (October 1923), 384–442. Based on contemporary literature on domestics and data drawn from federal employment service offices, it was a sociological survey of contemporary patterns of blacks in service. Lorenzo J. Greene and Carter G. Woodson's *The Negro Wage Earner* (Washington, 1930) was a pioneering study that dealt with domestic servants (male and female) within the larger context of the black occupational structure. The authors devoted two chapters to service work and explored the historical ties between blacks and household labor, but they never confronted directly the problem of black women and work. Julian Roebuck's "Domestic Service: With Particular Attention to the Negro Female Servant in the South" (M.A. thesis, Duke University, 1944) was a superficial survey that relied heavily on Salmon's *Domestic Service* and Bertram W. Doyle's *The Etiquette of Race Relations in the South* (Chicago, 1937).

An excellent overview of the changing twentieth-century patterns of black domestic service in the South is provided by C. Arnold Anderson and Mary Jean Bowman, "The Vanishing Servant and the Contemporary Status System of the

American South," *American Journal of Sociology* LIX (November 1953), 215–230. They described and analyzed the decline of black domestic servants in the South beginning with World War II. David Chaplin attempted to analyze the general patterns of blacks and household labor in "Domestic Service and the Negro," in Arthur B. Shostak and William Gomberg (eds.), *Blue-Collar World: Studies of the American Worker* (Englewood Cliffs, New Jersey, 1964), pp. 527–536, but he was severely handicapped by the absence of contemporary research in the area.

The indivisibility of blacks and domestic service in the South made black servants a major theme for observers of black life. Orra Langhorne discussed this aspect in "Domestic Service in the South," *Journal of Social Science* XXXIX (November 1901), 169–175. Many of her columns in the *Southern Workman* related to domestics, and they have been reprinted in Charles E. Wynes (ed.), *Southern Sketches from Virginia 1881–1901* (Charlottesville, Virginia, 1964). Testimony by Southerners about black domestics in slavery and freedom were recorded in U.S. Senate Committee on Education and Labor, *Report Upon the Relations Between Labor and Capital*, vol. IV (4 vols.; Washington, D.C., 1885).

Community surveys are a rich source of information on blacks in service. W. E. B. DuBois pioneered in the study of black communities and specifically focused attention on the role of female servants. Important data on household labor and servants are found in his "The Negroes of Farmville, Virginia: A Social Study," *Bulletin of the Department of Labor* No. 14 (January 1898), 1–38, and *The Philadelphia Negro: A Social Study* (original, 1899; reprint, New York, 1967), which included a separate study by Isabel Eaton, "Special Report on Negro Domestic Service in the Seventh Ward, Philadelphia," pp. 425–509.

Other early community surveys and studies included discussions of black servants. In *The Negroes of Columbia, Missouri* ([Columbia], 1904), William Wilson Elwang investigated a black community in a border state that provided domestics to white families. Howard Brown Woolston, *A Study of the Pop-*

ulation of Manhattanville, Columbia University Studies in History, Economics and Public Law XXXV (New York, 1909), a survey of a New York City neighborhood, included a group of lower-class black families. Walter L. Fleming's "The Servant Problem in a Black Belt Village," *Sewanee Review* XIII (January 1905), 1–17, was a racist polemic within the form of a sociological community study. Oswald Garrison Villard responded to Fleming in "The Negro and the Domestic Problem," *Alexander's Magazine* I (November 15, 1905), 5–11, which originally was a speech given before the National Negro Business League convention.

An important study of black wage earners from the 1900 census, from a special canvas, and from the unpublished schedules of the 1905 New York State census was George Edmund Haynes, *The Negro at Work in New York City: A Study in Economic Progress* (original, 1912; reprint, New York, 1968). Haynes included discussions of women's work, including service. Benjamin Locke, in a brief work, provided data and observations on the migration experiences of thirty-five Southern blacks, including ten women, in New York City: "The Community Life of a Harlem Group of Negroes" (M.A. thesis, Columbia University, 1913). William August Crossland in his social survey of 1912–1913 St. Louis gathered information on domestics among workers surveyed, although his discussion of women is modest in *Industrial Conditions Among Negroes in St. Louis*, Washington University Studies in Social Economics I (St. Louis, 1914).

T. J. Woofter, Jr., examined domestic servants in exploring race relations and women's work in "The Negroes of Athens, Georgia," Phelps-Stokes Fellowship Studies No. 1, *Bulletin of the University of Georgia* XIV (December 1913). World War I's reduction of the pool of servants in one Southern county was explored by Francis Taylor Long in "The Negroes of Clarke County, Georgia, During the Great War," Phelps-Stokes Fellowship Studies No. 5, *Bulletin of the University of Georgia* XIX (September 1919). The resulting change in servant patterns in the North can be seen in the Chicago Commission on Race Relations, *The Negro in Chicago*

(Chicago, 1922), which contains much valuable information on migration and work, including female domestics. Clyde Kiser described the migration experience of Southern women, many of whom were domestic servants, in *Sea Island to City: A Study of St. Helena Islanders in Harlem and Other Urban Centers* (reprint, New York, 1969).

Recent histories of black communities have recognized the ties between black women and service work, although none have explored extensively the relationship between the two or the work itself. Probably the fullest discussion, though inadequate, appeared in David M. Katzman, *Before the Ghetto: Black Detroit in the Nineteenth Century* (Urbana, Illinois, 1973). Those studies which do deal with working women have revealed domestic service as the major employment of black women. Allan H. Spear, *Black Chicago: The Making of a Negro Ghetto, 1890–1920* (Chicago, 1967), and Kenneth L. Kusmer, *A Ghetto Takes Shape: Black Cleveland, 1870–1930* (Urbana, Illinois, 1976), show the importance of service work to black women wage earners and its persistent role over time. John W. Blassingame's *Black New Orleans 1860–1880* (Chicago, 1973) is the best study of a Southern black community, and is especially sensitive to the role of women and family. Among the more important studies of the process from slavery to freedom are Peter Kolchin, *First Freedom: The Responses of Alabama's Blacks to Emancipation and Reconstruction* (Westport, Connecticut, 1972) and Joel Williamson, *After Slavery: The Negro in South Carolina During Reconstruction, 1861–1877* (Chapel Hill, North Carolina, 1965). Both studies discuss the slave servant's road to freedom.

Recent dissertations have begun to open up knowledge about black social history. Elizabeth Hafkin Pleck's "Black Migration to Boston in the Late Nineteenth Century" (Ph.D. dissertation, Brandeis University, 1973), a detailed study of blacks in Boston, is one of the few mobility studies sensitive to the presence and mobility of women. Pleck records the Freedman's Bureau's role in sponsored migration to Boston and the relatively high rate of turnover among black working women. See also her "The Two-Parent Household: Black

Family Structure in Late Nineteenth-Century Boston," *Journal of Social History* 6 (Fall 1972), 3–31. Howard N. Rabinowitz was especially sensitive to black household labor in the South in his "The Search for Social Control: Race Relations in the Urban South, 1865–1890" (2 vols.; Ph.D. dissertation, University of Chicago, 1973). David A. Gerber described an 1866 program that brought freedwomen to Ohio to work as servants in "Ohio and the Color Line: Racial Discrimination and Negro Responses in a Northern State, 1860–1915" (Ph.D. dissertation, Princeton University, 1971).

DOMESTIC SERVICE—IMMIGRANTS

Robert Ernst's *Immigrant Life in New York City 1825–1863* (New York, 1944) reveals the importance of blacks and immigrants in pre–Civil War domestic service. This study documents the presence of Irish servants in the prefamine years and the hostility with which they were greeted. Similarly, Oscar Handlin's *Boston's Immigrants: A Study in Acculturation*, rev. ed. (New York, 1975) details the importance of servants in the occupational structure of Boston Irish women and the prejudice Irish immigrants met in Boston, as does Douglas V. Shaw in *The Making of An Immigrant City: Ethnic and Cultural Conflict in Jersey City, New Jersey, 1850–1877* (New York, 1976), Shaw also explores the cultural conflict between Irish immigrants and Protestants. For an excellent overview of Irish migration to the United States, see Arnold Schrier, *Ireland and the American Emigration 1850–1900* (Minneapolis, 1958). Data from the nineteenth-century Irish census can be found in Charles Booth, *Occupations of the People: England, Scotland, Ireland, 1841–1881* (London, 1886).

An excellent study of Italian women that explains their tendency to avoid paid household employment is Virginia Yans McLaughlin's "Like the Fingers of the Hand: The Family and Community Life of First-Generation Italian-Americans in Buffalo, New York, 1880–1930" (Ph.D. dissertation, State University of New York at Buffalo, 1970). The virtues of Chinese male servants were argued in Di Vernon's "The Chinese as House Servants," *Good Housekeeping* XII (January 1891), 20–22, and in Jean Faison's "The Virtues of the Chinese Servant," *Good Housekeeping* XLII (March 1906), 279–280.

WOMEN AND WORK

The best rethinking and synthesis of women and work is Patricia Branca's "A New Perspective on Women's Work: A Comparative Typology," *Journal of Social History* 9 (Winter 1975), 129–153. Proposing a "two-model construct" for different rates of industrialization, Branca attempts to change the "historical timetable" used in the study of women's work, reorder the problem of exploitation of women, and refocus the discussion away from factory work. Her general discussion provides keen insight on American working women, although her specific discussion on domestic service is drawn too closely from European studies. Branca's difficulty is that research on servants and the female working class in the United States has lagged far behind developments in European history. A suggestive article urging case studies of urban women in their various roles and intended to stimulate the study of women during American industrialization is Susan J. Kleinberg's "The Systematic Study of Urban Women," *Historical Methods Newsletter* 9 (December 1975), 14–25.

The best recent studies of women and work have been drawn from urban social history. Susan J. Kleinberg's examination of working women in late-nineteenth-century Pittsburgh deals with work and life cycle, and notes the sharp differences between the tendency of white and black women to be gainfully employed. She exaggerates, however, the role of technological improvements in providing leisure time for housewives; servants provided that until after World War I. Kleinberg's work is entitled "Technology's Stepdaughter: The Impact of Industrialization Upon Working Class

Women, Pittsburgh, 1865–1890" (Ph.D. dissertation, University of Pittsburgh, 1973). Lawrence Admiral Glasco's study of pre–Civil War Buffalo sheds light on the early-nineteenth-century pattern of domestic service in the life cycle of working-class women: "Ethnicity and Social Structure: Irish, Germans and Native-Born of Buffalo, New York, 1850–860" (Ph.D. dissertation, State University of New York at Buffalo, 1973). Michael B. Katz came to similar conclusions within a much broader study of change in a neighboring city across the border. As had Kleinberg and Glasco, Katz described domestic service as a period of "semi-autonomy" in the lives of working-class women, and he also explored the importance of servants in middle-class life, in *The People of Hamilton, Canada West: Family and Class in a Mid-Nineteenth-Century City* (Cambridge, Massachusetts, 1975).

A general survey of shifting patterns of women's work before and during World War I can be found in U.S. Department of Labor, Women's Bureau, Bulletin No. 27, "The Occupational Progress of Women" (Washington, D.C., 1923). Two census publications provided basic statistical data on the female occupational structure: U.S. Bureau of the Census, *Statistics of Women at Work* (Washington, D.C., 1907), and Joseph A. Hill, *Women in Gainful Occupations 1870 to 1920*, Census Monographs IX (Washington, D.C. 1929). The most recent survey of women in American society, William Henry Chafe's *The American Woman: Her Changing Social, Economic and Political Roles, 1920–1970* (New York, 1972), covers the post–World War I years and only incidentally deals with the earlier period. A valuable documentary collection that includes much material on women and work is Gerda Lerner (ed.), *Black Women in White America: A Documentary History* (New York, 1972). A recent collection of mostly familiar documents is W. Elliot Brownlee and Mary M. Brownlee, *Women in the American Economy: A Documentary History, 1675 to 1929* (New Haven, 1976).

The experiences of married working women were significantly different from those of other women. Gwendolyn Salisbury Hughes studied the experiences of 728 white working mothers in Philadelphia during 1918–1919 and reported her findings in *Mothers in Industry: Wage-Earning By Mothers in Philadelphia* (New York, 1925). An investigation of wage-earning women in Passaic, New Jersey, based on a retabulation of the 1920 census provided valuable information on married wage earners: "The Family Status of Breadwinning Women," U.S. Department of Labor, Women's Bureau, Bulletin No. 23 (Washington, D.C., 1923). More recently, Barbara Klaczynska discussed the patterns among Philadelphia women wage earners in "Why Women Work: A Comparison of Various Groups—Philadelphia, 1910–1930," *Labor History*, 17 (Winter, 1976), 73–87. Black women were more likely to hold gainful employment than white women, and Mary White Ovington's *Half A Man: The Status of the Negro in New York* (reprint, New York, 1969) includes a chapter on "The Colored Woman as a Breadwinner" which inevitably concentrated on married women and domestic servants. Ovington stresses that not all black women were best suited for household labor, that many were "round pegs in square holes." See also her "The Negro Home in New York," *Charities* XV (October 7, 1905), 25–30. In "Afro-American Women and Their Work," *A.M.E. Church Review* XI (1895), 477–499, Katherine Davis Tillman reviewed the progress of black women from slavery to freedom and discussed the role of black working women.

The low status of domestic service as women's work was reflected in the occupational guidebooks and advice columns, which excluded domestic service from lists of respectable jobs for women. Typical of this genre were Ella Rodman Church's *Money-Making for Ladies* (New York, 1882), George J. Manson's *Work for Women* (New York, 1883), and Josephine Daskam Bacon's "We and Our Daughters," *American Magazine* LXIII (April 1907), 608–615. Gilson Willets's survey of occupations at the turn of the twentieth century gave little space to household labor, reflecting the degree to which few women aspired to be domestics: *Workers of the Nation* (2 vols.; New York, 1903). Marie Francke discussed professional opportunities—teaching, institutional housekeeping—

while failing to mention servants or cooks in *Opportunities for Women in Domestic Service* (Philadelphia, 1916). The disadvantages encountered in service by young women were summarized by Robert A. Woods and Albert J. Kennedy (eds.) in *Young Working Girls: A Summary of Evidence from Two Thousand Social Workers* (Boston, 1913), while the exclusion of domestic servants from the legislative protections provided female industrial workers was noted in Josephine C. Goldmark, "Workingwomen and the Laws: A Record of Neglect," *Annals* XXVIII (September 1906), 63–78, and in Lucille Eaves, *A History of California Labor Legislation*, University of California Publications in Economics II (Berkeley, 1910).

Dorothy Richardson discussed the problems faced by working women in "The Difficulties and Dangers Confronting the Working Woman," *Annals* XXVII (June 1906), 162–164. An investigation of 315 commercial laundries in Chicago, New York, Brooklyn, and Philadelphia recorded the case histories of 539 wage-earning women, of whom 36 had been servants, in U.S. Senate 61st Congress, 2nd Session, Document No. 645, *Report on Condition of Woman and Child Wage-Earners in the United States*, vol. XII, *Employment of Women in Laundries* (19 vols., Washington, D.C., 1911).

Barbara Welter and Kathryn Kish Sklar describe and analyze middle-class women's roles in the nineteenth century in Welter, "The Cult of True Womanhood: 1820–1860," *American Quarterly* XVIII (Summer 1966), 151–174, and Sklar, *Catherine Beecher: A Study in American Domesticity* (New Haven, 1973). Carroll Smith-Rosenberg's recent work has contributed greatly to the understanding of women's roles in the late nineteenth century. In "Puberty to Menopause: The Cycle of Femininity in Nineteenth-Century America," *Feminist Studies* I (Winter–Spring 1973), 58–72, she indirectly shows the irrelevancy of contemporary attitudes toward puberty and menopause in the lives of working women. "The Female Animal: Medical and Biological Views of Woman and Her Role in Nineteenth-Century America," co-authored with Charles Rosenberg, *Journal of American History* LX (September 1973), 332–356, suggests the significant class differences between middle-class and working-class women, while Smith-Rosenberg examines the relations among women in "The Female World of Love and Ritual: Relations Between Women in Nineteenth-Century America," *Signs: Journal of Women in Culture and Society* I (Autumn 1975), 1–29.

The writings of Herbert G. Gutman provide a necessary touchstone for any historian dealing with work in the United States in the late nineteenth or early twentieth century. See "Work, Culture and Society in Industrializing America, 1815–1919," *American Historical Review* 78 (June 1973), 531–588, and "Social and Economic Structure and Depression: American Labor in 1873 and 1874" (Ph.D. dissertation, University of Wisconsin, 1959).

TECHNOLOGY AND THE HOME

Any study of technology and the household should begin with Ruth Schwartz Cowan, "The 'Industrial Revolution' in the Home: Household Technology and Social Change in the Twentieth Century," *Technology and Culture* 17 (January 1976), 1–23. In an imaginative and insightful discussion, Cowan examines the Industrial Revolution within the home and focuses on the shift from hand to mechanical power, the changes in the workforce—including housewives as well as paid labor—and the resultant changes in ideologies. Most importantly, she argues that mechanization did not become widespread in American homes until the 1920s. See also her earlier "A Case Study of Technological and Social Change: The Washing Machine And The Working Wife," in Mary S. Hartman and Lois Banner (eds), *Clio's Consciousness Raised: New Perspectives on the History of Women* (New York, 1974), 245–253.

William D. and Deborah C. Andrews have suggested some of the changes in household technology and architecture which occurred in the nineteenth century, as well as attitudinal changes found in guidebooks, in "Technology and the Housewife in Nineteenth-Century America," *Women's Studies* 2(1974), 309–328. Contemporary descriptions of innovations entering the household can be found in guidebooks as well as in A. E. Kennelly, "Electricity in the Household," *Scribner's Magazine* VII (January 1890), 102–115, and Anna Leach, "Science in the Model Kitchen," *Cosmopolitan* XXVII (May 1899), 95–104. Developments in baking and the changeover from home baking to commercial processes are discussed in William G. Panschar, *Baking in America* (2 vols.; Evanston, Illinois, 1956).

DOMESTIC SERVICE REFORM

Most of the literature on domestic service focused on suggestions for solving the eternal "servant problem." This reform-minded literature not only reflected the large trends in American reform movements but also revealed a great deal about domestic service and household labor in the process.

Traditionally, reformers had focused on attracting better-quality servants and reducing turnover, as reflected in Society for the Encouragement of Faithful Domestic Servants in New-York, *Annual Report 1826* and *Annual Report 1827* (New York, 1826–1827). For a Boston society that followed the same scheme, see [Boston] Society for the Mutual Benefit of Female Domestics and Their Employers, *Constitution* (Boston, 1827). After the Civil War, mistresses continued to stress the importance of kindness and Christian charity—maternal benevolence—in winning over the faithfulness of their servants, as did M.E.M., "Parlor and Kitchen," *Lippincott's Magazine* IV (August 1869), 207–210. In the 1880s Zenas Dane described how enlightened benevolence solved the domestic problem in her home in "Our Hetty," *Good Housekeeping* IV (February 19, 1887), 186–187. Increasingly, however, "modernizers" began to drown out the voices of "traditionalists," and only an occasional article stressing maternalism appeared. In 1899, for instance, the views of fifty young women were distilled into "The Ideal and Practical

Organization of a Home," *Cosmopolitan* XXVII (June 1899), 166–171, yet no mention was made of business methods; the emphasis was on enlightened benevolence. Similarly, Hester Crawford Dorsey and an anonymous New York City housekeeper opposed modernization in favor of benevolent maternalism in Dorsey, "The Domestic Service Difficulty," *Good Housekeeping* VI (January 21, 1888), 147, and New York City Housekeeper to the Editors, *Good Housekeeping* X (March 1, 1890), 214–215.

By the 1890s modernization had become the major focus of reform. Domestic education was an important component of the move to modernize and systematize household work. Whether the primary goal should have been mistress or servant education, however, was widely debated. For advocates of mistress training, see Edwin P. Whipple, "Domestic Service," *Forum* I (March 1886), 25–36, and Ellen Battelle Dietrick, "Once More the Servant Problem," *Good Housekeeping* XII (August 1890), 63–65. For proponents of servant education, see Anna B. McMahan, "Something More About Domestic Service," *Forum* I (June 1886), 399–403, and Kate S. Hamlin, "The Domestic Problem, Again," *Good Housekeeping* XIV (May 1892), 219–223. In *The Home Economics Movement*, (Boston, 1912), Isabel Bevier and Susannah Usher described the introduction of household arts into the public school curricula, while U.S. Commissioner of Labor, *Annual Report 1910* (Washington, D.C., 1911), surveyed schools and colleges providing domestic education. A curriculum for children can be found in Elizabeth Colson and Anna Gansevoort Chittenden's *The Child Housekeeper. Simple Lessons with Songs, Stories and Games* (New York, 1903).

The introduction of business methods into the household was another basic element of reform. Josephine E. Martin used the metaphor of business management in proposing the introduction of new relationships in the household in "Concerning Servants," *Good Housekeeping* XV (July 1892), 7–9. Winner of *Cosmopolitan*'s prize of $150 for the best paper on the "servant question" in 1900 was Flora McDonald Thompson, "The Servant Question," *Cosmopolitan* XXVIII (March

1900), 521–528. She stressed the need for examining the question within the context of labor and capital, and attacked the failure to place a value on household labor, whether performed by servants or housewives. A clear, mature statement of the depersonalization of the mistress/servant relationship and the introduction of business methods into the household is Isabel Kimball Whiting, "The General Housework Employee," *Outlook* 89 (August 15, 1908), 851–855. The contractual relationship between servant and employer was explored in Mary A. Ripley, *An Essay on Household Service: also Legal Points and Other Matters Concerning Domestic Service . . .* (Buffalo, 1889); Legal Aid Society, New York, *Domestic Employment: A Handbook* (New York, 1908); and Annie Winsor Allen, "Both Sides of the Servant Question," *Atlantic Monthly* 111 (April 1913), 496–506. The Young Women's Christian Association emphasized systematizing the work and defining the contractual relationship in Commission on Household Employment, *Report 1915* (n.p., n.d.). The extreme systematizers followed Frederick W. Taylor; in 1912 an "efficiency engineer" examined household labor using the principles of time and motion study and scientific management and concluded that Taylorism could solve the servant problem, in John B. Guernsey, "Scientific Management in the Home," *Outlook* 100 (April 13, 1912), 821–825.

More utopian were those who sought to eliminate household tasks through cooperative methods, as did W. D. Howells in *The Altrurian Romances* (Bloomington, Indiana, and London, 1968) and Edward Bellamy in "A Vital Domestic Problem," *Good Housekeeping* X (December 21, 1889), 74–77. More realistically, Martha Bensley Bruère predicted that technology would solve the servant problem by making servants unnecessary in "The New Home-Making," *Outlook* 100 (March 16, 1912), 591–595.

STATE LABOR REPORTS

The annual reports of state labor bureaus in the late nineteenth and early twentieth centuries provide the best collection of data on domestic servants and their work between the Civil War and the 1920s. Although their primary interest in factory labor and the difficulty in surveying such atomized workplaces led the bureaus to omit service from their regular reporting on occupations and industries, special investigations of women's work occasionally included household labor; some states, in response to the clamor of housewives, issued special surveys of domestic work.

The Massachusetts Bureau of Statistics of Labor, the first state bureau, exhibited a greater and more sustained interest in women's work and domestic labor than any bureau in any other state. The *Annual Report 1872* (Boston, 1872) included domestic servants among women wage earners surveyed. Similarly, analyses of data on women's employment in the 1880s included domestic labor in *Annual Report 1887* (Boston, 1887) and *Annual Report 1889* (Boston, 1889). In 1906, the bureau published "Trained and Supplemental Employees for Domestic Service," *Annual Report 1906* (Boston, 1907), pp. 89–123, an invaluable study of employers' attitudes toward the training of servants and the use of day workers.

The *Massachusetts Labor Bulletin* published the studies of domestic service sponsored by the Boston-based Women's Educational and Industrial Union. One of the most thorough and detailed investigations of hours in household labor was "Hours of Labor in Domestic Service," *Massachusetts Labor Bulletin* No. 8 (October 1898), 1–27. [Mary W. Dewson], "Social Conditions in Domestic Service," ibid., No. 13 (February 1900), 1–16, is an excellent study of living conditions among a sample of live-in servants, while [Mary E. Trueblood], "Social Statistics of Workingwomen," ibid., No. 18 (May 1901), 29–49, is a well-designed investigation comparing the conditions of women in five occupations in Massachusetts in 1900. It was specifically intended to compare and contrast household labor with other women's work.

Among the more valuable state investigations is the Minnesota investigation of "wage-working women," which gave prominent coverage to domestic service: Minnesota Bureau of Labor Statistics, *Biennial Report 1887–8* (n.p., 1887). It included not only comparative occupational data but also comments on service by domestics, other working women, employment agents, and mistresses. In sharp contrast to the Minnesota study was the elaborate investigation of domestic service done in 1910 by the Maine labor bureau. A thorough study of service from the point of view of housewives, it included fifty pages of quotes from "letters from employing housewives" but not a sentence of prose from a servant: "The Household Servant Problem in Maine," Maine Bureau of Industrial and Labor Statistics, *Annual Report 1910* (Augusta, 1910), pp. 311–393. Other studies of the Maine Bureau included some data on domestics, in *Annual Report 1888* (Augusta, 1889) and *Annual Report 1892* (Augusta, 1893). California Bureau of Labor Statistics, *Biennial Report 1885 and 1886* (Sacramento, 1887) and *Biennial Report 1887–1888* (Sacramento, 1888) provided information on women's wages, including servants. The latter report also included a discussion of the eternal servant problem, "Domestics—Why Girls Will Not Become Servants," pp. 91–94.

A rare survey of rural domestic labor was published in Michigan Bureau of Labor and Industrial Statistics, *Annual Report 1895* (Lansing, 1895). A survey of more than two thousand household workers, it had the largest employee base of any investigation. The Kansas labor bureau provided data on urban and town servants in a rural state. The report on female wage earners in Kansas Bureau of Labor and Industry, *Annual Report 1894* (Topeka, 1895), included data on domestic servants in fifteen Kansas cities. Other reports in 1890 and 1914 included only incidental references to household labor: *Annual Report 1890* (Topeka, 1890) and *Annual Report 1914* (Topeka, 1915). The Kansas bureau's experiences in investigating aspects of women's work typify the difficulty encountered by investigators and underscore the problems historians face in using the data. One major difficulty was that employees were reluctant to reply to a bureau's inquiries. Assistant Labor Commissioner Cougher of the Kansas Bureau of Labor Stiatistics reported to the *Topeka Commonwealth* (May 12, 1888, p. 4, courtesy of Tom Johnson) that he had difficulty in gaining the cooperation of working women when his bureau sought to study their work conditions. He found that many women hesitated because they feared that participation in a bureau study might lead to their being fired. Others did not wish to categorize themselves, according to Cougher, as wage workers, and therefore would not respond. A third group felt that the information requested was personal, not anybody else's business.

Other labor reports that dealt with servants included New York Bureau of Statistics of Labor, *Annual Report 1885* (Albany, 1886), which provided information about the wages of servants and laundresses, and *Annual Report 1896* (Albany, 1897), which included the testimony of servants on the practices of employment agencies. In 1894 the Maryland Bureau of Industrial Statistics surveyed household-labor employment agencies and recorded their practices and fees as reported by the agents. Unfortunately neither servants nor mistresses were interviewed: "Employment Agencies," *Annual Report 1896* (Baltimore, 1897). Missouri shed no new light on the subject: the chief clerk of the labor bureau discussed domestic service in M. V. Carroll, "The Domestic Help Problem," Missouri Bureau of Labor Statistics and Inspection, *Annual Report 1900* (Jefferson City, 1900), pp. 147–151.

GUIDEBOOKS

Household and etiquette guidebooks played an important educational role for women unaccustomed to hiring servants and introduced these women to new ways of organizing their households. Such books also helped spread the gospel of modernization and efficiency in the household, although they cannot be assumed to reflect actual practices of the period.

Author or coauthor of the earliest and most popular household guides, Catherine E. Beecher probably had her greatest impact as an educator. Her writings were consistent with her emphasis on women's education and the elevation of what was considered the women's sphere. See *A Treatise on Domestic Economy for the Use of Young Ladies at Home and at School* (3rd ed., New York, 1845, and rev. ed., New York, 1863); Catherine E. Beecher and Harriet Beecher Stowe, *The American Woman's Home: or Principles of Domestic Science* . . . (New York, 1869); and *Miss Beecher's Housekeeper and Healthkeeper* . . . (New York, 1873). Marion Harland was a rival of Beecher, and her *House and Home: A Complete Housewife's Guide* (Philadelphia, 1889) sold widely. Other household manuals included (Mrs.) Elizabeth F. Holt, *From Attic to Cellar or Housekeeping Made Easy* (Salem, 1892), and Catherine Owen, *Progressive Housekeeping: Keeping House Without Knowing How, and Knowing How to Keep House Well* (Boston and New York, 1896). In their advice on running a home with servants and on dealing with servants, etiquette books were similar to household guides; see for example, Mrs. John Sherwood, *Manners and Social Usages* (New York, 1884).

By the turn of the century, domestic science had become an accepted part of the curriculum of woman's higher education, and the movement had a significant impact on household manuals. One of the first textbooks in the field was Helen Campbell, *Household Economics*, rev. ed. (New York, 1907), based on lectures given at the University of Wisconsin. Similar in its scientific, academic approach was Bertha M. Terrill, *Household Management* (Chicago, 1914); Terrill was professor of home economics at the University of Vermont. While organized around a university curriculum, they were similar to Beecher's *Treatise* and were essentially more sophisticated household guides. Carlotta Norton Smith's *The Homemaker: Her Science. With a Treatise on Home Etiquette* (New York, 1905) represented a more popularized version of the textbook-guides.

Some guidebooks were intended for use by the servant as well as by the mistress. Appropriately, given the ties between blacks and household work, one of the first books by a black American was a guidebook for servants, Robert Roberts, *The House Servant's Directory, or A Monitor for Private Families: Comprising Hints on the Arrangement and Performance of Servant's Work* . . . (Boston, 1827). By the end of the century, American publishers had distributed guidebooks on household service imitative of a genre popular in Great Britain. Not only could they advise housewives as to the proper behavior, dress, and work of servants but they also could be given to the servant for her to follow as well. Generally well illustrated, they often constituted a basic kitchen reference library. Typical of these manuals were Anne Frances Springsteed, *The Expert Waitress: A Manual for the Pantry, Kitchen, and Dining-Room* (New York, 1894), and Janet McKenzie Hill, *The Up-to-Date Waitress* (Boston, 1910). Specifically written for servants was Rev. And. Ambaven, *Suggestions to Girls at Service* (Dodgeville, Wisconsin, 1889). A small pocket book written by a Protestant minister and dedicated to "our Catholic servant girls," it counseled the subservience of employee to mistress.

VICE

The ties between domestic service and vice, specifically prostitution, were a concern of charity workers and reformers at the turn of the century. Frances A. Kellor's *Out of Work* . . . (New York, 1904) documented the connection, as did U.S. Senate, 61st Congress, 2nd Session, Document No. 645, *Report on Condition of Women and Child Wage-Earners in the United States*, vol. XV, *Relation Between Occupation and Criminality of Women* (19 vols.; Washington, D.C., 1911). Turn-of-the-century vice-commission investigations revealed the pattern of black domestics in houses of prostitution: Vice Commission of Chicago, *The Social Evil in Chicago* (Chicago, 1911), and George J. Kneeland, *Commercialized Prostitution in New York City* (New York, 1913). Marian Goldman's "Prostitution and Virtue in Nevada," *Society* X (November/December 1972), 32–38, noted the presence of black servants in houses of prostitution in the late-nineteenth century mining frontier.

DOMESTIC SERVICE—OTHER COUNTRIES

J. Jean Hecht's *The Domestic Servant Class in Eighteenth-Century England* (London, 1956) is the pioneering historical study of domestic servants. He judiciously analyzed the occupation and its role as an instrument in the process of cultural change. He revealed the degree to which the "servant problem" transcended time and culture. The shortage of servants, the recruitment from outside the city, the abuses of intelligence offices, the master/servant relationship, and the high servant turnover were similar in eighteenth-century England and late-nineteenth-century America. Beyond those points, however, it is difficult to use this book to draw a comparison between American and English service because Hecht concentrated on elite service and male servants. More recently, Pamela Horn in her descriptions of nineteenth-century English service in *The Rise and Fall of the Victorian Servant* (Dublin and New York, 1975) underscored the differences between English and American service. The servant tradition and the large household staffs were virtually unknown in the United States. Theresa M. McBride's *The Domestic Revolution: The Modernization of Household Service in England and France 1820–1920* (New York, 1976) is an excellent study focusing on modernization and urbanization. It is, however, less applicable to the American case than McBride assumes, and she too often does not deal with the experiences of servants themselves. See also her "Social Mobility for the Lower Classes: Domestic Servants in France," *Journal of Social History* 8 (Fall 1974), 63–78. Genevieve Leslie's "Domestic Service in Canada, 1880–1920," in Janice Acton et al. (eds.), *Women at Work: Ontario, 1850–1930* (Toronto, 1974), 71–125, is a well-researched and suggestive study focusing on live-in servants. It suggests, as in much of North American history, that research should follow social and cultural patterns regardless of political boundaries. Leslie's findings are similar to patterns of service in the Northeastern United States.

INDEX